Vedic Voices

Vedic Voices

Intimate Narratives of a Living Andhra Tradition

DAVID M. KNIPE

OXFORD
UNIVERSITY PRESS

OXFORD
UNIVERSITY PRESS

Oxford University Press is a department of the University of Oxford. It furthers the University's objective of excellence in research, scholarship, and education by publishing worldwide.

Oxford New York
Auckland Cape Town Dar es Salaam Hong Kong Karachi
Kuala Lumpur Madrid Melbourne Mexico City Nairobi
New Delhi Shanghai Taipei Toronto

With offices in
Argentina Austria Brazil Chile Czech Republic France Greece
Guatemala Hungary Italy Japan Poland Portugal Singapore
South Korea Switzerland Thailand Turkey Ukraine Vietnam

Published in the United States of America by
Oxford University Press
198 Madison Avenue, New York, NY 10016

Cataloging-in-Publication data is on file at the Library of Congress
ISBN 978–0–19–939768–6(hbk.); 978–0–19–939769–3(pbk)

9 8 7 6 5 4 3 2 1
Printed in the United States of America
on acid-free paper

Dedicated to

Baballa [Bhamidipati Yajnesvara Somayaji] and Sundari Somidevamma

Yajulu [Duvvuri Yajnesvara Paundarika Yajulu] and Surya Somidevamma

Cayanulu [Bulusu Vyaghresvara Cayanulu] and Subbalaksmi Somidevamma

Lanka [Lanka Venkatarama Sastri] and Anasuya Somidevamma

Kamesvara [Bulusu Kamesvara] and Satyavati Somidevamma

Laksminayana [Pullela Laksminayana] and Kamesvari Somidevamma

Mitranarayana [Bhamidipati Mitranarayana Sarvatomukha Somayaji] and Anasuya Somidevamma

Samavedam [Samavedam Suryanarayana Avadhani] and Kamala garu

Gullapalli Sitaram Sastri Avadhanulu and Narasamamba garu

Kapilavayi Venkatesvara and Sita Rama Laksmi garu

Kapilavayi Rama Sastri and Maruti garu

and M. V. Krishnayya, Professor Emeritus, Andhra University

Contents

List of Illustrations xi
Preface xv
Acknowledgments xix
Maps xxi

1. The Godavari Delta 5
  1.1. Riverine Lifelines 5
  1.2. A Historical Overview of the Delta 7
  1.3. *Agrahara*, Villages, and Pilgrimage Towns 23
2. *Vedamlo*, "Living in the Veda" 28
  2.1. The Vocabulary of the Veda Pandit 28
  2.2. Choices for Livelihood 38
  2.3. The Vocabulary of an *Ahitagni* 41
  2.4. Bonding with Agni 49
  2.5. The Voices of *Ahitagni* and Other Veda pandits 52
3. A Selection of *Ahitagni* and Other Veda Pandits in *Agrahara*, Villages, and Towns 54
  3.1. The Sriramapuram *Agrahara* 54
  3.2. Kamesvari *Agrahara* Near Nedunuru Village 97
  3.3. Vyaghresvaram Village 106
  3.4. Kakinada Town 110
  3.5. From Kakinada to Vijayawada and Beyond 116
  3.6. Iragavaram Village 132
4. Becoming a Veda 141
  4.1. A Tumult of Veda and the *Brahmacarin* 141
  4.2. The Work of the Text 144

4.3. The *Sama-vartana*: Graduation Day 147
4.4. Advanced Degrees 148
4.5. The *Sabha*: Debating in an Assembly of Veda Pandits 153

5. Becoming a Householder 157
5.1. The Voices of Women 157
5.2. Marriage 162
5.3. Children and Their Life-cycle Rites 170
5.4. Livelihood 176
5.5. Old Age, Retirement, and Thoughts on Renunciation 180
5.6. Death and Beyond 184

6. Becoming Agni 187
6.1. Agni, Private and Extended 188
6.2. The *Adhana*, Setting the Fires for *Srauta Agni-hotra* 190
6.3. The *Agni-hotra*, Sunset and Sunrise Milk Offerings 194
6.4. Offerings to the New Moon, Full Moon, and Constellations 199
6.5. The *Agrayana* Harvest Sacrifice 205
6.6. The *Catur-masya* Seasonal Rituals 206
6.7. The First *Soma* and Animal Sacrifice, *Agni-stoma* 210
6.8. The *Pravargya* 218
6.9. The *Soma*-sacrifice Schedule and Other Rituals 220
6.10. Variations of *Agni-cayana*, Building a Fire Altar 222
6.11. The *Vaja-peya* Drink of Strength 228
6.12. The *Maha-vrata* Great Vow and *Go-sava* Bull Imitation 230
6.13. The *Sautramani* Offering to Indra the Protector 232
6.14. The *Asva-medha*, Sacrifice of the Royal Horse, the *Purusa-medha*, and the *Raja-suya* 234
6.15. Final Absorption into Agni: Funeral Rites 237
6.16. Becoming an Ancestor 243

Epilogue: Becoming "Modern" 247
E.1. A New Cash Economy 248
E.2. Mobility 249
E.3. *Huna-vidya*: A Rival Form of Education 250

E.4. The Powers That Be 251
E.5. "America": Polarities and Dreams 254

Glossary 259

Notes 277

Bibliography 295

Index 323

List of Illustrations

Figures

P.1. Debate among three ahitagni and other Veda pandits, Sriramapuram 1987. From left: Baballa, Bulusu Cayanulu, Duvvuri Yajulu. Photograph by author, unless otherwise indicated xvi

0.1. The Godavari River near Pattisima island 1980 1

0.2. Women transplanting rice near Sriramapuram 1987 1

0.3. Threshing rice paddy near Nedunuru 1987 2

0.4. Bullock carts by the canal in Munganda 1980 3

0.5. Bathing steps on canal ("Kausika River") near Sriramapuram 1980 3

0.6. Sriramapuram *agrahara*, 1987 4

1.1. A sluice gate on Arthur Cotton's 1847 canal system, Mukkamalla Lock 1987 19

2.1. A *brahmacarin* at Surya's door in *madhu-kara*, collecting food house to house like a bee flower to flower, Sriramapuram 1987. The boy is Surya's thirteen-year-old grandson Phani 31

2.2. Some of the twenty-five *brahmacarin* enrolled in the Sarvaratya Veda *patha-sala*, Kapilesvarapuram 1980 32

2.3. Kapilavayi Agnihotra, a *brahmacarin* performing daily *agni-karya* with a fire pot, Annavaram 2005 33

2.4. A blind eighty-five-year-old Duvvuri Yajulu teaching grandson Kirin, Sriramapuram 2000 33

2.5. Another grandfather, Gullapalli Sita Ram Sastri, in *adhyayana* with four *brahmacarin* grandsons at once, Iragavaram 2000 34

2.6. Satyavati, Bulusu Kamesvara, and their hearths, the round *garhapatya* at left, semicircular *daksina-agni* an arm's length away, the *vedi* holding implements in space stretching toward the square *ahavaniya*, Vyaghresvaram 2000 43

2.7. *Agni-manthana*, "churning" of new fire with *arani* as fire-drill to ignite Agni, Sriramapuram 1987. The upper male wood fixed in a spindle is twirled with a rope, its drill point seated in the female block on the ground 51

3.1. Bhamidipati "Baballa" and Sundari, Sriramapuram 1987 57

3.2. Baballa, age eighty-eight, Sriramapuram 1991 57

3.3. Bhamidipati Yajnesvara Prasad, Baballa's grandson, with Laksmi and daughters Rekha, Madhuri, and Kalyani, Sriramapuram 2005 69

3.4. Duvvuri Yajulu and family on his sixtieth birthday, 1975. Seated center right, Surya on Yajulu's left; sons one to five extend from his right hand. Five daughters and four daughters-in-law stand behind, grandchildren sit in front. Courtesy D. Surya Prakasa via D. Girija Sankar 72

3.5. Duvvuri Surya Prakasa Avadhani, Yajulu's third son, and Kanaka Durga, Rajahmundry 2005 81

3.6. The four sons of Surya Prakasa and Kanaka Durga; from left: Phani, S. R. Sastry, Hari Prasad, Girija Sankar, Rajahmundry 1998 81

3.7. Bulusu Cayanulu and Subbalaksmi, Sriramapuram 1987 87

3.8. Bulusu Cayuanulu, Baballa behind, during a ritual, Sriramapuram 1987 88

3.9. Samavedam and Kamala, Sriramapuram 1996 92

3.10. Samavedam, left, with the three *ahitagni* of Sriramapuram, Bulusu Cayanulu, Duvvuri Yajulu, Baballa, 1991 95

3.11. Lanka, Nedunuru 1991, his rice fields and coconut palms in view 98

3.12. Lanka and Anasuya, Lamesvari agrahara, Nedunuru 1987, his books and ritual charts behind 100

3.13. Lanka and author, Nedunuru 1987 101

3.14. Kamesvara and Satyavati, Vyaghresvaram 2005 108

3.15. Mitranarayana, Kakinada 1998 115

3.16. M. V. Krishnayya with Mitranarayana, Kakinada 2005 116

3.17. Kapilavayi Venkatesvara Sastri and Sitarama Laksmi, Simhacalam 1988 122

3.18. Kapilavayi Venkatesvara family, Simhacalam 1999 122

3.19. Kapilavayi Rama Sastri, left, and Maruti (in doorway) flanked by daughters Agnivati Naga Laksmi and Sita Naga Laksmi, Annavaram 2005 126

3.20. Dendukuri Agnihotra Somayaji, right, and son Laksminarasimha Somayajulu, both active *agni-hotrin*, Vijayawada 2005 129

3.21. The side-by-side Dendukuri hearths are in one small room, Vijayawada, 2005. Morning *agni-hotra* have been completed; kindling on the *vedi* awaits offerings at sundown. Courtesy Duvvuri S. R. Sastry 130

3.22. Kapilavayi brothers, Venkatesvara, left, and Rama Sastri, Simhacalam 2014 132

3.23. Four of the five Gullapalli brothers (sons of Sita Ram Sastri and fathers of the boys in Figure 2.5), reciting in alternate pairs in *ghana-patha*, Iragavaram 2005 135

6.1. Ladles used to make offerings into Agni, Sriramapuram 1987 195

Plans

2.1. Floor plan of Duvvuri Yajulu's Sriramapuram house showing his three-fire *agni-hotra* room; the house is typical for an *ahitagni* and *patni* 42

2.2. Ground plan of five temporary fires for the *adhana* ritual setting of hearths 44

6.1. Ground plan of an *agni-ksetra* "field of fire" projection of *agni-hotra* fires outside the house for an extended *srauta* ritual, drawn by Kapilavayi Venkatesvara, Simhacalam 2014, courtesy of M. V. Krishnayya 192

6.2. Ground plan of a *syena-citi*, flying eagle altar for *agni-cayana*, drawn by Dendukuri Agnihotra Somayaji's grandson, Vijayawada 2005 223

Tables

2.1. The four *asrama*, stages of life in classical Hinduism 29

2.2. The Vedic textual tradition 37

2.3. The four major priests (*maha-rtvij*) and their Vedas. Each has three assistants 48

3.1. Eight generations of Bhamidipati genealogy 59

3.2. Four generations of males in the Duvvuri family 78

3.3. Four generations of *ahitagni* and eligible *ahitagni* candidates 139

5.1. *Menarika* marriages of East Godavari Duvvuris (D) and West Godavari Gullapallis (G) 167

Preface

OCTOBER 3, 1980, was the author's initial encounter with the Veda pandits of Sriramapuram. An American professor of South Asian Studies from the University of Wisconsin, accompanied by a professor of Philosophy from Andhra University in Vishakhapatnam, walked unannounced down the single lane of the quiet *agrahara*, a private Brahman hamlet leading off a dusty road a mile from the nearest village. They were met with direct, curious, unsmiling but not unfriendly gazes of several men and boys who were either already sitting on, or gradually emerging onto an *arugu*, a Telugu word for veranda, the platform meant for social exchange in front of each residence. Their white stucco houses marched in two neat rows to flank the dirt path, fourteen houses in all. These were proud, self-possessed, energetic faces. The unexpected visitors identified themselves and were soon seated in the midst of a circle of a dozen old and young men. The American explained that he was seeking conversation with Veda pandits, particularly *ahitagni*, those who had established the three Vedic fires in their homes, and that he had started in the Amalapuram area but found no one still active. Suddenly the senior and recognized spokesman for the *agrahara*, a tall, lanky elder with heavy glasses on a lean face, pointed across the circle and announced "He is an *ahitagni*, he is an *ahitagni*, and I am an *ahitagni*" (see Figure P.1). Debate among three *ahitagini* and other Veda pandits, Sriramaputam 1987. From left: Baballa, Bulusu Cayanulu, Duvvuri Yajulu.) An energetic three-hour discussion of Vedic texts and rituals ensued, leading off three decades of engagement with the residents of this and nearby *agrahara*. When a modest rupee honorarium was extended to the senior *ahitagni* Baballa, following this initial unanticipated meeting, he declined with an elegant, unforgettable phrase: "Your interest in Veda is our *daksina* (ritual payment)!"This book highlights the essential features of contemporary Vedic life by allowing *ahitagni* and other Veda pandits, their wives, and their children to narrate personal experience. This is important because their communities and their individual narrations, all noteworthy and

FIGURE P.1. Debate among three *ahitagni* and other Veda pandits, Sriramapuram 1987. *From left:* Baballa, Bulusu Cayanulu, Duvvuri Yajulu. Photograph by author, unless otherwise indicated

remarkable, are largely unknown to mainstream India. Certainly they are far removed from Western perception. Outside of the subcontinent the general reader of books about India rarely notices the Vedic tradition, and normally considers it a strange and remote period that seems to have ended thousands of years ago. This study explores a valuable living tradition.

The four generations of ten families in this book represent a period of rapid and far-reaching changes. Although they share textual and ritual bases, no two pandits have had the same experience. Despite their relatively uniform training in Veda there is no Vedic template to embrace them all. Any merit in this survey may lie in the revelation of a great variety of personalities, experiences, and attitudes.

The visitors on that October day in 1980 were the author of this book and his younger colleague, M. V. Krishnayya, who shares in its dedication and could truthfully be regarded as mediating Telugu pandit and diplomat, one whose charm, energy, and easy humor in conversation elicited candid and earnest response from men, women, and children of all strata of village and urban coastal Andhra society. Born and raised in East Godavari District, his Telugu dialect and training in Indian philosophy afforded direct access that made this work possible. The pair returned to Sriramapuram and other agrahara, villages, and towns of the delta over the years to record the voices of these exceptional people. In Sriramapuram the pair was sometimes teased, erasing distinctions of color and culture, as "Rama and Krishna paying a visit." The book is about the reciters and sacrificers, their wives and families, their crucial links to a 3,700-year-old tradition that India regards as its foundational culture. It is their voices that should be heard. Although it may appear unusual to skirt their use, first-person pronouns seem intrusive in the distinguished company of these Godavari voices. At times for clarity of context the commonly used Telugu word *dora*, Foreigner or Westerner, is a third-person reference to the author.

Field interviews, well over a hundred in all, frequently lasting for three hours, were recorded, transcribed, edited into field notes, and later entered into computer documents. On some occasions the author was the sole interviewer and at other times Professor Krishnayya, Emeritus Chair of the Philosophy Department of Andhra University in Visakhapatnam, undertook interviews in Rajahmundry, Annavaram, Simhacalam, and Vijayawada when the author was not in India. Lakshmi Narasamamba, PhD, was another invaluable assistant, particularly in her role of entering residential interiors to converse with women. When e-mail came into vogue in the late 1990s it was the youthful Duvvuri Sita Ram Sastry who supplied updated information as well as interview assistance in 2005. A number of other research associates and assistants graciously gave their time and energy, and they are remarked by name in the Acknowledgments.

One of the obstacles for the general reader of articles and books on Vedic studies is the formidable array of technical terms. At the end of the book there is a substantial Glossary of Sanskrit and Telugu words with proper diacritical marks. A few dozen terms, all Sanskrit, could be considered essential for a basic understanding of the flow of Vedic tradition, including the texts and rituals of contemporary Veda pandits in coastal Andhra. These are briefly discussed in Chapter 2, a chapter that might serve as a resource when they recur. All terms in italics are Sanskrit unless noted as Telugu or another language.

Chapter 1 introduces the reader to the Godavari Delta, an area that has received scant attention in studies of the subcontinent, with details on the geographic and historic character of this beautiful, mobile triangle of many rivers and streams, a region much prized for its productivity and therefore a locus—even in the modern era—of constant political contention. Figures 0.1 through 0.6 are scenes in or close to Konasima. Interlined with history are sketched-in references to the mythic, ritual, and symbolic backdrop of a Vedic presence in the delta, leading into Chapter 2 that opens up the meaning of a life lived "in the Veda." This chapter, with presentations of both textual and ritual progression, is essentially an introduction to Vedic tradition as it is expressed in coastal Andhra, one of the two or three dominant Vedic areas of India and the last to perform both soma and animal sacrifices in authentic fashion.

Chapter 3 is a selection of capsule biographies of more than a score of pandits and fire sacrificers in ten families. These families, stretching now over four generations, illustrate the diversity of Vedic careers as well as their remarkable achievements. The next four chapters return to a more detailed examination of the Vedic life in progress outlined in Chapter 2, beginning with Chapter 4 and the young student's learning of the Taittiriya Samhita from his father, grandfather, or older brother. Marriage and eventual residence with a wife lead to the householder stage of life, the subject of Chapter 5. Women's lives, children and life-cycle rituals, the means of livelihood, and an inevitable final passage into retirement, death, and the beyond are further topics here.

Chapter 6 reviews the ritual life introduced in Chapter 2 and sketches in a more nuanced portrait of an *ahitagni* and his wife, routine daily, fortnightly, and annual offerings in their three-fire household, the initiatory *soma* and animal sacrifice, further great sacrifices, and the special funerals required for *soma* sacrificers and their wives. In conclusion, the Epilogue following Chapter 6 sums up the modern experience of *ahitagni* and other Veda pandits and the marked cultural, economic, educational, and other changes from the times of those fathers and grandfathers selected for biographies in Chapter 3.

Acknowledgments

GRATITUDE GOES OUT to numerous people along the way: Wendy Doniger, for her astonishing productivity of books that enrich both mind and spirit; Asko Parpola, for his encyclopedic knowledge of everything Vedic and pre-Vedic plus his limitless generosity of scholarship; my former colleagues of many years at the University of Wisconsin in Madison including Velcheru Narayana Rao for initially directing me to the Godavari Delta not far from where he was born; students in many years of graduate seminars; John Nemec and his seminar students at the University of Virginia in Charlottesville; Griff Chausee, John Cort, Laurie Patton, John Stavellis, Cynthia Talbot, Gautam Vajracharya; my daughters Nicola Knipe, Viveka Öhman, and Jennifer Knipe for their valuable suggestions, and my wife, Susan T. Stevens, who was there in our bungalow by the Godavari River when this project was conceived and has remained an unfailing guide throughout, always lending an archeologist's eye for detail.

In India the list of gracious and willing providers of assistance is enormous and can only be partially acknowledged. It begins with M. V. Krishnayya, Emeritus Professor of Philosophy and Religion at Andhra University in Vishakhapatnam. This book is dedicated to him along with our *ahitagni* and other Veda pandit friends and wives of many years. Thanks go as well to field assistants K. V. S. Laksmi Narasamamba, Duvvuri Sita Ram Sastry, and Duvvuri Girija Sankar.

Gracious interview hours were granted by many not mentioned in the book: Darbha Venkatesvara Avadhanulu, Dhulipala Ramachandra Sastri, Kala Satyanarayana Sarma, Khandavalli Suryanarayana Sastri, Remella Suryaprakasa Sastri, Susarla Venkatarama Sastri, Upadrasta Subrahmanya, and Upadrasta Ganapati Sastri. Longtime friends have taught me the mantras I needed to interiorize, the meanings of a ritual life, and so much else: Satya Narayana Pandey, Laksmana Sastri, Indrakanti Subrahmanya Sastri, Sorapalli Ramakrishna, Chellaboyina Apparao, Narayana Sastry (Bobby), and K. V. S. Kotesvararao.

Gratitude is due also to the Graduate School of the University of Wisconsin-Madison for field research grants, the American Institute for Indian Studies in Delhi for Senior Fellowships supporting research in Andhra, and the Government of India for continual visas. Thanks also to Cynthia Read, David Joseph, Marcela Maxfield, and Charlotte Steinhardt for their efforts to produce this book, and to Chris Cohen at Randolph College for generous assistance with digital maps and photos.

A particular note of gratitude goes to Willem Caland (1859–1932) and Ganesh Thite of the University of Pune for their abilities in making editions and minutiae of Apastamba texts accessible and sensible.

Maps

Andhra Pradesh with its two river deltas

MAP 1. Andhra Pradesh in the subcontinent of India. Map created by Chris Cohen.

MAP 2. The two river deltas of coastal Andhra. Map created by Chris Cohen.

Vedic Voices

FIGURE 0.1. The Godavari River near Pattisima island 1980.

FIGURE 0.2. Women transplanting rice near Sriramapuram 1987.

FIGURE 0.3. Threshing rice paddy near Nedunuru 1987.

FIGURE 0.4. Bullock carts by the canal in Munganda 1980.

FIGURE 0.5. Bathing steps on canal ("Kausika River") near Sriramapuram 1980.

FIGURE 0.6. Sriramapuram *agrahara,* 1987.

I

The Godavari Delta

1.1 *Riverine Lifelines*

Human imagination is drawn into reverie by many natural phenomena, among them fires, cloud patterns, solar and full-lunar appearances and disappearances, the rhythmic pounding of ocean surf on rocks or a broad sand beach. There is also fascination in the seasonal changes of a great river. T. S. Eliot began a poem[1] with such in mind:

> *I do not know much about gods, but I think that the river*
> *is a strong brown god.*

With its source near Nasik only fifty miles from the Arabian Sea, the 900-mile-long Godavari River cuts a diagonal course across the Deccan plateau before it delivers sumptuous brown waters into the Bay of Bengal. At the beginning point of its delta near Rajahmundry it may in full flood be well over two miles wide. To appreciate the true character of the Godavari, however, it should be studied in all of its seasons. In bursting monsoon depths it shakes the surrounding earth like the ferocious goddess it is known to be, great brown folds of water overlapping and tearing away chunks of the levee that are carried scores of miles to end up on the floor of a delta that has broadened this way for hundreds of thousands of years. The roar of rushing water sixty feet deep is as awesome as the sight. Little boys who cannot swim spot great trees or branches hurtling downstream and hurl themselves with more guts than foresight from the levee on "Godavari-horse" palm pontoons. They arm-paddle out wildly, and if they do not drown, intercept and steer potential firewood to a shore many miles down this monstrous water chute. But the seasonal rhythm always turns to its opposite, the dry period when a stream becomes so docile that cows may saunter and cow-paddle from bank to bank where hundreds of new sand islands have appeared. These *lanka* islands, as they are called in Telugu, are settled by fishermen who erect mud-and-thatch dwellings; raise tobacco and vegetable crops; keep chickens, pigs, and goats; and after sundown light oil lamps that appear from distant levees as a newborn Milky Way across the silent river. The washing-all-away season will certainly follow, but for now, Godavari land is free for the taking.

The great river meanders eastward, then southeastward for most of its journey across the Deccan until it emerges from the rumpled Eastern Hills at the Papikondulu, the "Sinful Hills," a curious name for a gorge of breathtaking beauty and star-rich night skies at the southernmost rim of the Northern Circar range. Here the river drops south onto the alluvial plain that separates the Telangana plateau from the sea and in just thirty miles it reaches the apex tip of the delta. Down at the delta's base on the Bay of Bengal coast, the spread of riverine drainage from a tenth of India's land is nearly a hundred miles. Atlas cartographers usually illustrate three or four broad streams between Rajahmundry and the sea. Local perception, however, declares a region of seven rivers, mythically labeled for the seven *rsi*, the famed seers who first intuited the Vedas and whose descendants comprised the seven founding Vedic lineages, namely, Visvamitra, Jamadagni, Bharadvaja, Gotama, Atri, Vasistha, and Kasyapa. Few people can name more than a sage or two, but many tell of encounters with these *rsi* progenitors who still grace—or haunt—the delta with their presence. Sometimes they are glimpsed briefly in the mist that rises from the river before dawn, no more remarkable to locals than Irish folk who claim that a seal now and then emerges from the sea to live among them as a young woman. Several *ahitagni* bathe daily in a stream they call the Kausika, Kusika being another name of the *rsi* Visvamitra. And it is the broad Vasistha that separates two zones featured in this study, East and West Godavari Districts.

Of course, virtually all the great rivers of India are known as goddesses and the Godavari is no exception. Goddess Godavari stands aboard a *makara*, a crocodile-like raft, looking watchfully down from the walled levee at Rajahmundry, as if on guard against her own excesses. Until the 1970s there were indeed crocodiles in this part of the river.[2] She is conflated not only with goddesses Gautami and Ganga (as the south Indian "extension" of the north Indian Ganges) but also Veda Mata, Mother of the Vedas. Either way, seven male sages on one hand, or the feminized collection of their insight on the other, the great river calls attention to the Vedic mystique.

At the heart of the delta, a sort of cockeyed triangle within a triangle, is Konasima, a prize canal-rich zone bracketed by the Vainateya and Gautami branches of the Godavari, blessed with some forty-five inches of annual rainfall. Vengi, a historic name for the fertile stretch of Andhra coast between the Godavari and Krishna deltas, drew the earliest settlements to southeast India, and Konasima became the nucleus of the northerly delta. This is the setting of this book, a lush area, a million irrigated acres of broad wetland rice paddies and coconut palms, the two major crops, as well as sugarcane and betel on irrigated tracts and on dry land cotton, peanuts, pulses, sesame, tobacco, mango, citrus, cashew, jackfruit, areca, and banana groves laced with turmeric, tapioca, betel vines, chili peppers, and other managed plants.

Its reputation is the zone where everything grows plentifully, luxuriously, a cornucopia, and for folks coming from crowded urban lanes it is an *arama*, a pleasure garden. Today the roadways are lined with nursery displays selling flowers, shrubs, trees, and planters to visiting townsfolk, more and more of them in the private cars of the new millennium's affluent middle class. Paddy fields, with two or even three crops a year, are always visible and rice is *anna*, "food." If one has not eaten rice in each meal one has not eaten. Carefully guarded and numbered coconut palms, with a nut-producing life of seventy to eighty years, grow fifty to an acre and every farmer cultivates them for a steady income from meat, milk, oil, and husks beaten into coir or used for fuel. "A coconut tree is more reliable than a son," is a familiar Telugu proverb.

1.2 A Historical Overview of the Delta

1.2.1 Early Centuries

Due to the constant self-landscaping of the two rivers archeologists obtain few results from combing within the Godavari or Krishna deltas. Inland well west of the deltas, great ash mounds of burnt cow dung reveal temporary settlements of Neolithic cattle herders. Also dotted through the interior are numerous megalithic tombs. It is estimated that Telugu developed as a discrete Dravidian spoken language in Andhra early in the first millennium BCE. No historical records have been found, however, earlier than Sanskrit and Prakrit inscriptions of the second century BCE, and inscriptions in Telugu do not occur for another half millennium or more.

The first great empire in India after the Harappan Indus civilization was the Mauryan dynasty in the northern kingdom of Magadha with a capital in Patailaputra, modern Patna in Bihar. In 324 BCE Candragupta Maurya's armies began consolidation of the Gangetic plain. His successor Bindusara penetrated the Deccan and ventured onto parts of the east coast as well. Asoka, third and best known of the Mauryan rulers, added to the empire Kalinga on the Bay of Bengal and for a time may have controlled both the Godavari and

Krishna deltas. During his reign 273–32 BCE Asoka left rock-cut edicts in a Prakrit language carved mostly in Kharosthi and Brahmi scripts, the earliest in India after the Indus script of c. 2600–1900 BCE. Two edicts are north of the deltas on the coast of Kalinga. According to tradition, Candragupta Maurya converted to the Jaina faith and committed *samlekhana*, the fast to death, in Sravana Belgola on the west coast. Asoka, from the tenor of his edicts and late-life practice, evidently had strong Buddhist sympathies.

Both religions were already established in the south, adding Pali as well as Prakrit to the language mix. Sometime after 200 BCE, as in other parts of India, a *stupa*, a great mound embodying relics of the Buddha, was constructed at Amaravati on the Krishna River, upstream from modern Vijayawada. Another was built later at Nagarjuna-konda, where the Dindi River enters the Krishna, with *caitya* halls for assembly and multi-celled monastic quarters (*vihara*). A rock-carved *caitya*, a *stupa*, and some sixty monastic caves at Guntapalli date to the second century BCE. A number of deteriorating Buddhist monuments still exist on the Krishna River at Jaggayyapeta and Bhattiprolu as well as other sites eastward toward the Godavari. Some Saiva temples, in Amaravati and Draksarama, for example, contain Siva *linga* that appear to be salvaged from the ruins of ancient Buddhist marble columns.

A number of Andhra inscriptions commemorate Vedic sacrifices, including two royal ones, the *raja-suya* conscration of a king and the *asva-medha*, a land conquering sacrifice of a successful king's chariot horse. Two caves on opposite sides of south India reveal significant inscriptional details, one at Nanaghat, in the sharply defined gap in the western Ghats of Maharastra, the other in Udayagi, Orissa, both dated as mid-first century BCE. Two contemporary kings emerge into focus here. The first is Satakarni I of the Satavahanas, or the "Andhras" according to some Sanskrit Puranas, an enduring dynasty that emerged from Mauryan roots in the second century BCE. Satavahanas may have originated in the Godavari Delta and expanded upriver to the headwaters on the west coast not far from the Nanaghat cave. Origins are murky and it is more probable that this dominion expanded in the opposite direction, west to east. In any event, Satakarni I, imperial *raja* of the Satavahana capital at Pratisthana (Paithan) on the upper Godavari, claimed to be lord (*pati*) of the south (*daksina-patha*), and performed the great year-long drama of the Vedic *asva-medha*, sacrifice of his intrepid horse that had staked out conquest with the aid of a significant army.

The 900 miles of the Godavari became a conduit for trade all the way from the Arabian Sea to Konasima and the Bay of Bengal, with the Satavahanas in control of most of the Deccan and beyond to the north. Amaravati, for a time the Satavahana capital, became a powerful trade and pilgrimage center where craftsmen were renowned for bronzes of the Buddha and various animals. There is little historical evidence but according to Buddhist tradition the enormously influential Madhyamika philosopher Nagarjuna lived in the Satavahana period, perhaps in the second and third centuries CE, in the place named for him, Nagarjuna-hill. Many kings favored Brahmans with land grants and some took family names as "sons" of Vedic *rsi* such as Gotama and Vasistha. After attaining their peak of power in the late second century CE, Satavahanas were threatened by several tribes of Sakas from north India and it was the Vakataka dynasty that finally replaced them in the third century. There was an interlude of sovereignty by the Iksvaku dynasty with one king celebrating yet another *asva-medha*.

The other powerful southern ruler and contemporary of Satakarni I was Kharavela, one who also claimed *adhi-pati* status as ruler-in-chief over Kalinga (Orissa and parts of modern Andhra). He was a Jaina, like Candragupta Maurya, and was consecrated as king by the Vedic *raja-suya* sacrifice. Inscriptions about him were found in the Jaina cave at Udayagiri.[3]

1.2.2 Contending Dynasties of Regional Kings

The boasts of "southern" supremacy by Satakarni I and Kharavela would no doubt have been ridiculed by kings and chieftains farther south. The Ceras (Keralas) on the west coast, the Colas who gave their name to the east coast (Coromandal, the *mandala* of Colas), and the Pandyas in between, competed for power over the territory during the early centuries CE, a potpourri of kingdoms controlling villages and extracting revenue not only in Tamil Nadu, "land of the Tamils," but also parts of the northern Deccan and up the Kalinga coast. Romila Thapar has aptly dubbed such contention a "see-sawing of dynasties" with relatively equal military strength repeatedly replacing one another in the same region. Hermann Kulke and Dietmar Rothermund extend the image to "triangular contests" since conflicts were often more than one on one.[4]

Saka hegemony was ended with the rise of the Gupta empire. Some six centuries after the accession of Candragupta Maurya, another Candragupta, again at Pataliputra, founded a new imperial dynasty that came to be labeled in the north as India's classical age, a period that produced enduring works in Sanskrit such as the poetry and dramas of Kalidasa and the Kama Sutra of Vatsyayana. The years of Candragupta's rule were 320–35. His son, Samudragupta (r. 350–75), and great-grandson, Kumaragupta (r. 415–55), the fourth successive emperor, extended the dynasty. Samudragupta exercised the *asva-medha* to lay claim to universal sovereignty, presumably after the initial *agni-stoma* rituals with *soma* drinking. His extraordinary rampage down the east coast across Kalinga and on south through Pistapura and Vengi on the Coromandal coast, ended with Kancipuram in Tamil Nadu. That thousand-mile campaign, a show of force against more than a dozen kings and their armies and subjects, must have required more than one stalwart royal mount.

Coastal Andhra, however, like much of the south, remained isolated from that "universe" celebrated in Pataliputra. In the south, the Pallavas attained domination and at least one seventh-century king performed, after his *agni-stoma*, the Vedic *vaja-peya*, the "drink of strength" sacrifice (both detailed later in Chapter 6). He ruled in a dynasty that outlasted most mentioned so far, extending from the sixth through the ninth centuries. Centered in Kancipuram (Samudragupta's momentary trophy), Pallava armies subdued much of the peninsula, including the richly productive coastal zone of "Vengi" from the Krishna Delta up to the Godavari Delta. Cynthia Talbot mined epigraphic records and labeled Vengi as the "core area" of Andhra in this period.[5] Here again land grants to Brahmans were frequent and inscriptions indicate migrations from the north to Andhra. One copper plate records the donation of a village in Guntur District, west of the Krishna River, to one thousand Brahmans from the village of Ahicchatra on the Ganges.[6] In South India, Grantha was a script descended from southern Brahmi in use for writing Vedic and classical Sanskrit texts and one regional variant appeared in Vengi.[7]

New iterations of warring dynasties ushered in new royal names and centers of contending power. The Calukya dynasty founder Pulakesin (c. 503–66) performed a celebratory *asva-medha* in his capital of Vatapi (later named Badami, the site in Karnataka of impressive Saiva, Vaisnava, and Jaina caves). Calukyas and Pallavas alternated control over the eastern Deccan in the sixth and seventh centuries, the Eastern Calukyas at Pithapuram just east of the Godavari Delta again playing a prominent role. Calukyas even fought one another out of Badami and Kalyani in the west as well as Vengi and Pithapuram in the east.

An aggressive entrant into the tournament of warfare was the Rastrakuta dynasty. In north India, Harsa had ruled successfully from Kanauj for the first half of the seventh century, 606–47, until he was opposed by Pulakesin II and his Calukyan armies. After Harsa's death the Rastrakutas commanded the Deccan while the Pratiharas took charge in the north and the Palas in the east c. 750. Every century was scarred by wars either civil or interstate. As Nilakanta Sastri observed, however, almost perpetual warfare did not obstruct cultural growth. He cites the magnificent rock-cut Siva temple in the complex of Hindu, Buddhist, and Jaina caves and temples at Ellora,[8] carved under the 757–78 rule of the Rastrakuta king Krishna I during the period when Vengi on the east coast was repeatedly changing administrations.

It is difficult to separate hagiography from reliable history, but Saiva traditions credit Sankara, the eighth-century founder of the non-dualist Advaita Vedanta school of philosophy, with the establishment of *matha*, religious centers, in the compass points of India's geography. Kancipuram and Srngeri are two in the south and a third, also neighboring Andha, is in Puri (Orissa) to the east. Among Sankara's many works are penetrating commentaries on the Upanisads including the Taittiriya as well as the somewhat older Chandogya and Brhadaranyaka.

The decline of Buddhist influence in the Deccan was roughly parallel to an ascent of Jainism. From their roots in Magadha, Jainas had migrated south into Kalinga in the third century BCE and then further south to Tamil Nadu along merchant trade routes, populating parts of the Andhra coast en route. Stone images of *tirthankara* are still turned up by farmers in the Godavari Delta although today no one remembers Jaina communities. A stronger Jaina migrant route was down the west coast to Maharastra and Karnataka.

In the ninth century, Jaina monks, nuns, and laity were favored by several Rastrakuta kings, including Amoghavarsa who stepped down to become a monk after a remarkable sixty-eight-year reign. Among those he favored were residents of Biccolu, now in East Godavari District. Almost a century later, another Rastrakuta king was Indra IV who underwent the *sallekhana* fast to death in Sravanabelgola in 982.[9] Some Eastern Calukyas were also royal patrons. As a religion of non-violence and self-denial the Jaina faith would appear to be an unlikely choice of warring kings. Kharavela, the permanently warring ruler of Orissa in the first century BCE, was a Jaina. Paul Dundas perceives "images of striving, battle, and conquest" as appealing to the south Indian martial society, the spiritually victorious monk being a model equal to that of the warrior.[10]

Periods of interfaith civility alternated with intense deadly conflicts with other religious communities, militant Saivas in particular. Hindu revivalist devotional movements and the early twelfth-century reforms of Ramanuja effectively limited Jaina influence through the medieval period. Ramanuja's dissatisfaction with Sankara's rigid monism, the equation of *atman* and *brahman*, coupled with his personal experience of Visnu, led him to generate a Vedanta of "qualified non-dualism" (Visistadvaita) and his teachings spread throughout the Deccan via new religious centers like those of Sankara four centuries before him.

1.2.3 The Emergence of Telugu Literature

In the last few centuries BCE Tamil speakers began to compose poetry and prose that foreshadowed Sangam era classics of the first three centuries CE. Gradually Tamil had taken on vocabulary and themes from Sanskrit. By the close of the first millennium CE two more Dravidian languages, Telugu and Kannada, followed suit with literary forms and sizable input from Sanskrit. In the eleventh century Telugu classical poetry received its template from the reworking of the first two and a half books of the Sanskrit Mahabharata by Nannaya, a task continued on palm leaves in the thirteenth century by Tikkana, another formidable and creative poet.[11] Although both Nannaya and Tikkana were Brahmans, Veda pandits or Brahmans as a class did not monopolize the proliferation of Telugu literary works. Also in the thirteenth century, Palkuri Somanatha produced the Basava Purana collection of legends of Virasaiva (Lingayata) saints who rejected Vedic textual authority, class and caste hierarchy, funerary rites, and the whole enterprise of sacrifice. One saint declared that his dog could chant the Vedas better than Brahman pandits and the dog confirmed this.[12] The other great Sanskrit epic also appeared in a Telugu version in the fruitful thirteenth century only a few decades after the Tamil Ramayana, the version composed by the poet Kampan.

"First poet" and first Telugu grammarian Nannaya had enjoyed the patronage of king Rajaraja Narendra in Rajahmundry (medieval Rajamahendri) on the Godavari after the Eastern Calukyas emerged phoenix-like in another dynasty of their off and on again four-hundred-year run until the tenth century and conquest by an energetic Cola king Rajaraja I (r. 985–1015). Rajaraja was succeeded by his son Rajendra I (r. 1012–44). Rastrakuta chiefs as well as other warring communities on the fringes of Vengi made shifts of power nearly continuous.

1.2.4 The Kakatiya Dynasty at Warangal until 1322

Warangal, midway between middle stretches of the Godavari and Krishna rivers, had become the hub of the Kakatiya dynasty from the eleventh to the beginning of the fourteenth centuries as the center of political control moved inland from the coast. The most ambitious of its kings was Ganapati who ruled more than sixty years c.1198–1262, corralling the two deltas (the enlarged meaning of "Vengi") within his kingdom. Subjugation of the coast occurred on Ganapati's way south to reduce Kanci in Tamil Nadu, one of his many victorious battles having been fought at Pithapuram in the Godavari Delta.

The Kakatiyas divided Andhra into *nadu*, regions. Vengi *nadu*, the two great river deltas, could boast 16,000 villages.[13] Portions of regions, or counties, were called *sima* (as in Kona-sima), *kotta*, or *sthala*. Kakatiya rule witnessed the growth of large temple towns, heavily trafficked pilgrim routes, popularity of sacred vows (*vrata*), dedications of Siva *linga*, circumambulations of sacred hilltops, and increased numbers of Telugu inscriptions.

Draksarama temple in the Godavari Delta with eleventh- and twelfth-century inscriptions is the oldest and most famous of the five designated Saiva *arama*, pleasure grove residences of deities. The temple's name is a corruption of Daksa *arama*, the grove where the god Daksa tried but failed to perform his infamous *soma* sacrifice, frequently described in the Puranas. Although married to Sati, Daksa's daughter, Siva was not invited to the great *yajna*. A shamed Sati immolated herself and Siva erupted into his horrendous manifestation as Virabhadra to destroy the sacrifice. A powerful cult of Virabhadra as lord of enraged, deceased children exists in the delta today and no one imagines performing a Vedic sacrifice near Draksarama. The temple there is the residence of Bhima (Rudra), a form of Rudra-Siva, and the universal goddess as Manikyambika, one of India's eighteen Sakti *pitha*.[14] The grove is the site of a poem by the poet Srinatha, famous for his translations of Sanskrit *kavya* into Telugu, and the poet does not fail to mention goddesses Gogalamma, Nokalamma, Mandatalli, and Ghattyambika.

Meditation centers (*matha*) like those attributed to Sankara and Ramanuja also increased in the Kakatiya period, including one so secluded on the tiny island of Pattisam that it is reached only by boat from either the Rajahmundry or Kovvur banks of the Godavari. Despite its inaccessibility it is one of the five great Saiva retreats of India, in the august company of Srisaila, Kalahasti, Kasi (Varanasi), and Kedara.

1.2.5 A New Religion, Culture, and Polity: Islam Enters the Deccan

The grandson of Ganapati was Pratapa Rudra who ruled successfully, by most accounts, from 1289 until the Delhi Sultan Ala-ud-din dispatched armies to subdue the Kakatiya region. Sieges were laid, bargains were struck, but finally the well-fortified city of Warangal and abundant Kakatiya armies were no match for the battle-hardened cavalry tactics and leadership of Ulugh Khan. Warangal fell in 1322 to the fifth successive Sultanate invasion and a captive king Pratapa Rudra was under transport toward Delhi when he died near the Namada River, perhaps by his own hand.[15] It is noteworthy that Marco Polo was traveling in Thanjavur and elsewhere in Tamil Nadu at the close of the thirteenth century after Pratapa Rudra ruled the eastern Deccan.

Consolidation of territory by the armies of the Delhi sultanate expanded Muslim administrations south from the Narmada to the Krishna river and east from the Arabian Sea to the Bay of Bengal, adding to Andhra culture the Persian, Arabic, and to limited extent Urdu languages, the last written in a Persian script. The majority of the population, however, remained Hindu. Minor *raja* and chieftains continued to fight internal revolts and each other, aided by the development of gunpowder artillery and new siege techniques of the fourteenth and fifteenth centuries. The script of the *asva-medha*, in essence land grabbing at the expense of neighbors, was acted out even if no ritual performance was scheduled. One can only imagine the continuing devastation century after century as hungry armies, their mounts, and supply trains trampled the crop fields of the fecund green delta and stole grain stores, coconuts, herds, and perhaps even daughters and young wives before moving on, only to return on the same route a few seasons later.

Islam had represented a cultural tectonic shift for India in the north for centuries before penetration of Muslim armies and civilians into the Deccan. With conquest of the Godavari Delta, mosques began to replace some Hindu temples. Already in 1324 Muhammad Tughluq (Ulugh Khan, who assumed the Tughluq dynastic name after the conquest of Warangal the year before) erected a mosque at Rajahmundry on the ruins of the Hindu temple of Venugopal. His cousin Firoz Shah succeeded him in 1351 and helped to extend the Tughluq dynasty to 1413 in a period of widespread construction of mosques, some created by adding a pulpit after removal of all Hindu *murti*, allowing their stone residences to remain intact.[16] Under Ala-ud-din (d. 1316) Hindus were forced to relinquish half of their harvests; now Brahmans felt for the first time the burden of the *jizya* poll tax on non-Muslims. The Sultanate of Delhi was terminated by Timur's dreadful destruction of the city and its Hindu population in 1398.

1.2.6 Vijayanagara c. 1346–1564

A powerful rival to both the Hindu Kakatiyas of Warangal and the Muslim Bahmani kingdoms arose in Karnataka as Vijayanagara, one of the largest fortifications in Asia with an eventual ten square miles within massive walls. Lasting for almost three centuries, the "city of victory" dominated the center of the southern peninsula from Hampi on the Tungabhadra River, a southern tributary of the Krishna. In 1327, Muhammad Tughluq conquered the Kampili dynasty that had succeeded the Hoysalas in Karnataka and thereby completed a clean sweep of Warangal and other old capitals of Deccan kings. A path was clear for the building of a new Hindu kingdom at Vijayangara in 1336, only twenty miles from the destroyed Kampili headquarters.[17]

The fourteenth-century reign of Harihara II produced the works of two illustrious scholars, Sayana, the gifted commentator on the Vedas, and Madhava, founder of the Dvaita or dualist school of philosophy that directly opposed Advaita Vedanta. Madhava countered Sankara in another respect: he was a devotee of Visnu. Tradition insists the two were brothers although their death dates are seventy years apart. Perhaps the most famous Vijayanagara king was Krishna Deva Raya whose reign, 1509–29, was the centerpiece of the Tuluva dynasty of rulers. Both the Godavari and Krishna deltas were politically embraced under his rule and on the Coromandal coast wealthy ports such as Masulipatam, Motupalli, and Pulicat attracted Dutch and other European merchant settlers shortly after 1600. An effective king who forged alliances with the Bahmani ruler Muhammad Shah, Deva Raya also drove the Gajapatis back north into Orissa, thus ending some two centuries of hostilities with the other great medieval Hindu kingdom in the south. That long contest pitted two neighbors against one another, speakers of different language families, Dravidian Telugu and Indo-Aryan Oriya. The "god-king" Deva Raya traded successfully with the Portuguese in Goa who provided him with modern arts of artillery. His support base for two decades was the solidarity of those he appointed as provincial governors, *nayaka* (Telugu *nayakudu*). An enduring expression of sixteenth-century architecture during Krishna Deva Raya's reign was a unique style of temple construction.[18]

Vijayanagara, "City of Victory," despite its size, wealth, and vaunted million-man army, did not live up to its name when it was destroyed in 1564 during the battle of Talikota by an alliance of the Golconda sultanate and two others of the five Bahmani kingdoms. That alliance did not survive long but the Qutb Shah dynasty of Golconda was able to occupy both deltas and Rajahmundry as well. Hyderabad, future capital of the twentieth-century state of Andhra Pradesh, was established in 1589 a few miles from Golconda fort. The Qutb Shah succession of Shi'a kings lasted from 1512 until Golconda fell to the armies of Aurangzeb and Sunni Mughal rule in 1687.

The empire of the Mughals, founded 1526, had succeeded the Delhi Sultanate in the north but did not expand into the Deccan immediately, not even during large-scale expansion under Akbar who ruled 1556–1605. A seventeenth-century obstacle to Mughal authority in the western Deccan was Sivaji (1627–80), a short but intrepid Maratha general who managed to unite Maratha Brahmans and warrior castes, then contrived an alliance of Telugu Brahmans and Abul Hassan, the Qutb Shah Sultan of the Golconda kingdom.

Sivaji had himself crowned universal emperor in 1674 with 11,000 Brahmans reciting Vedas.[19] While his 60,000-man army camped near Golconda Sivaji took considerable time to worship Bhramarambha, the goddess-consort of his namesake Siva on Sri Saila (Srisala), the remote hilltop above the Krishna River.[20] After the death of Sivaji, Mughal armies conquered the Bijapur Sultanate capital in 1686 and in the following year Golconda fort also fell. Maratha guerilla tactics, however, made it impossible for Mughals to secure territory and they suffered horrendous losses while retreating northward. Aurangzeb, emperor since 1658, having squandered his waning years in vain attempts at pacification, died in 1707, the volatile Deccan having remained "a bridge too far" for the Mughals.

Aside from major and minor territorial wars among Hindu dynasties, from the seventh century on through the medieval period religious conflicts sprouted between Jainas and Vedic Brahmans regarding animal sacrifices.[21] Although some reports may have been exaggerated, inscriptional evidence records that Jainas suffered periodic repressions at the hands of militant Saivas who included cultural heroes such as the poet Tikkana. Jainism, Buddhism, Virasaivism, and Tantric Hinduism had all contested Brahmanical tradition and each ultimately left its mark. Islam in the Deccan, however, produced in the pre-European centuries a different response, not unlike the effect that Christianity, another monotheistic religion with global reach, was to exert in succeeding centuries. And it must be said that Islam and Christianity both took on new guises in their encounters with south Indian culture and religion.

1.2.7 Arrival of the Europeans

Greek and Roman merchant ships in the last centuries BCE and early centuries CE most certainly viewed and perhaps explored the Krishna and Godavari deltas along the Coromandal coast. European colonization of the subcontinent, however, did not begin until well after Vasco da Gama landed four ships at Calicut on the Kerala coast in 1498. The early arriving Portuguese concentrated on India's Arabian Sea coast. A century later the east coast on the Bay of Bengal was the target of Dutch, Danish, and French traders as well as the eventually all-encompassing English.[22] Dutch merchant ships dominated trade in the seventeenth and eighteenth centuries but the English slowly caught up and then surpassed them. In the seventeenth century the English East India Company established from modest origins three seaports, Madras, Bombay, and Calcutta, each to become one of the famous megalopolises of modern India, Chennai, Mumbai, and Kolkata, respectively.

A visit today to the coastal town of Machilipatnam, barely thirty-eight miles from the mouth of the Vasistha-Godavari and close to the northern mouth of the Krishna Delta, reveals little of its fame more than four centuries ago as Masulipatam, the busiest and wealthiest seaport on the eastern seaboard.[23] It was the site of a Dutch weaving center established in 1606 by the VOC, Vereenigde Oost-Indische Comagnie, the United East India Company. English traders were not slow in recognizing the value of the remarkable textiles and organized Weaver-caste families five years later. Danish merchants, having settled farther south on the Coromandal coast at Tranquebar in 1620, became in 1625 the third European nation to focus on Masulipatam.[24]

Many Weaver families in the Godavari Delta contributed their specialty in calicoes with designs penned onto the cloth with vegetable dyes in the technique of *kalam-kari*. A Dutch census in 1680 accounted for eighteen weaving centers near Draksarama alone. Villages with 40 to 900 Weaver families each had an average 418 looms per village,[25] an incredibly energetic homespun industry for Godavari weavers in the seventeenth century. It meant then, as it does today, employment of every able member of the household. English entrepreneurs eventually followed the Dutch deeper into the Godavari Delta to Jagannathapuram. In addition to the main attraction, calicoes, exports included raw silk, yarn, and printed cloth, diamonds, sapphires, and rubies from Golconda and other mines, as well as cotton, sugar, teak, and even slaves. These brought fortunes of staggering size to European merchants, one diamond merchant in London, for example, profiting 100,000 pounds in the year 1676.[26] By 1680, however, Madras had emerged from its sleepy 1639 origins as Fort St. George to rival Masulipatam as the east coast port of choice.[27] Given over to the British by the Dutch in 1825 was another famous Coromandal port, Pulicat, in use as early as the third century BCE by the Cola and Pallava kingdoms.

The French also settled along the Coromandal coast, their equivalent of the East India Companies of the Dutch, English, and Danes being La Compagnie Francaise des Indes Orientales. Their 1674 colony at Pondicherry obtained from the Dutch additional ports at Karikal and Yanam (Yanaon), the latter in the Godavari Delta on the northern branch of the Gautami-Godavari, a deep-water shelter not far from the sea. Yanam, French from 1731 until it was turned over to India in 1954, was something of a back door into the lucrative textile and diamond exports. A visit in the 1980s seeking some lingering expertise in the making of wine and bread disclosed that the old customs border between India and "France" was still evident, but only a walled cemetery, the village toilet, spoke of a former Gallic presence.

By 1736, English East India Company ships eliminated French traders from the Coromandal coast, although Pondicherry, Karikal, and Yanam remained French territory until 1945. The English East India Company had won the day, and from the remainder of the eighteenth century until formation of the Republic of India in 1947 the Godavari Delta was in the Madras Presidency (established in 1653)[28] where it had been situated in 1768. By 1800, all access to roads and property in the Presidency was governed by the Company.[29] After the Sepoy Mutiny of 1857, for which the House of Commons blamed Company mismanagement, 1858 witnessed a transition from Company rule to the British Raj.

1.2.8 Domesticating the Delta

Everywhere on domestic, business, and civic walls, and especially on trees at crossroads and river banks, there are posters and statues of divine beings—Hanuman, Ganesa, all possible *avatara* of Devi, Siva, or Visnu, and the occasional god-man or god-woman stepping back from history into myth—Shirdi Sai Baba or Sarada Devi, for example. Images of two male figures with historical focus are ubiquitous in the delta, as indeed they are in most of India. One is Gandhi, seated cross-legged or in mid-stride, staff in resolute hand, spectacles prominent on a wizened face. The other is the Dalit and neo-Buddhist hero B. R. Ambedkar posed stiffly in white shirt, red tie, and improbable blue suit, his arm pointing out the hope of progress somewhere on the horizon. But in the water-rich deltas of the Godavari and Krishna, as nowhere else in the subcontinent, a third male figure may be seen in landscape statuary, either in standing pose alone in the flat space of a paddy field or in the saddle of a spirited brown stallion.

Remarkably, since most other signs of the Raj have been thoroughly scrubbed away in more than sixty years of independence, this modest black-suited figure is a white man, namely, Sir Arthur Cotton, the nineteenth-century British military officer and civil engineer who tamed the indomitable Godavari River at the end of its rush across the Deccan to the sea. His extraordinary accomplishments began with transformation of the former Rajahmundry District from one of the poorest and most famine-prone to the rice-basket of south India. The delta was accordingly renamed Godavari District and statues of a white man, a saint although a *dora*, a Foreigner, sprouted from this well-watered, now fruitful land.

In 1844, Cotton (1803–99) studied the Godavari flood plain and visualized the building of a 2.25-mile-wide masonry anicut forty-eight-feet thick, a weir or dam known locally as a barrage. He envisioned it across the river at Daulesvaram with a series of sluice gates leading into several hundreds of

FIGURE 1.1. A sluice gate on Arthur Cotton's 1847 canal system, Mukkamalla Lock 1987.

canals that would not only control the flow of water for irrigation but also create safe river traffic of 1,500 miles for both goods and people (see Figure 1.1). Begun in 1847, completed only five years later in 1852, this enormous project changed agricultural life in its rhythms, output, and diversity, and made the delta a prime example of the benefits of large-scale hydraulic engineering. The horrendous rampages of monsoon flooding on the many streams of the delta, an annual rearrangement of every island and shore for scores of miles, became a thing of the past, although serious floods from breeches of levees, locally known as bands, still occur, most recently in 1986 when the river crested at Rajahmundry and left damaged crops and dwellings along much of its course. But the era of large-scale drought-related famines was ending. In 1832–33, after a cyclone killed tens of thousands outright, even more died of famine because of devastated crops.

In 1866 in Orissa, the state on the northern border of Andhra, 1.5 million people starved to death. Cotton poked a finger in the eye of the government that later was to knight him by calculating the exact number of cubic yards of water and the two-thirds of a penny a pound for rice for four months of food that would have saved the Orissans, not forgetting to cite the huge loss in government revenue because nothing was done. "How strange it seems that men cannot understand this," he wrote in 1881. In the newly renamed Godavari

District, after Cotton's efforts and the irrigation of 600,000 acres, the population increased 300 percent from 1843 to 1891.

Cotton went on to tame the Krishna River Delta with another anicut west of Rajahmundry at Vijayawada. He became chief engineer of Madras Presidency, applying his skills in other parts of India as well. A huge waterway system was envisioned, little of which was realized, that also included proposals for a vast east coast set of canals for 380 miles between the Godavari and Madras, the use of wind power to raise water for irrigation, possibilities in Egypt and the Sudan, and even a fanciful vision of linked Indian and Chinese river systems from the Brahmaputra to the Yangtze.[30]

Transformation of the delta came about in many ways. Two years after India's first telegraph line was installed, the first passenger train chugged along rails in 1853, with rapid expansion over the next several decades. Before the close of that century it became essential for the Calcutta-Madras east coast line to cross the Godavari at Rajahmundry, a formidable feat of railway engineering over a wandering river. The first single-track rail line spanned the two miles between Rajahmundry and Kovvur in 1897 on one of the longest bridges in Asia. Through the 1980s the old puffer-billy steam locomotives were still waking people of Rajahmundry before dawn as they performed their explosive morning warm-ups like donkeys greeting the sun. Prior to road, rail, and telegraph links connecting the western and eastern portions of the delta, boat traffic was restricted to the calm seasons of the river. As will be apparent in Chapter 3, deep-seated liaisons between Vaidika families in the delta, particularly those for marital and ritual purposes, were vastly improved by a century of enhanced communication, the latest innovation being a cell phone in every household in each *agrahara* where no landline had previously existed.

The destructive role of water can be far more than the expected annual floods. The delta, wide open to the Bay of Bengal, is highly vulnerable to tropical cyclones (hurricanes, typhoons) and tsunamis roaring inland behind storm surges, walls of ocean water ten to thirty feet high. Kakinada and Masulipatam were destroyed by cyclones in the early nineteenth century and many storms with high fatalities have struck since, most recently, 1969, 1977, 1984, 1990, and 1996. The 1977 cyclone drove eight miles inland, killing nearly 10,000 people. TV and cell-phone evacuation warnings saved tens of thousands in the cyclone of October 2013.

During the period of research for this book, at 5 PM on November 6, 1996, four days before the great autumn harvest festival of Divali, as Venkatesvara, Lord of Andhra, was readied in his Tirupati temple for adornment with diamond-studded gold jewels, a cyclone roared up through Konasima and killed perhaps 2,000 people during a ten-hour rampage. Numbers were imprecise when 1,400 villages were affected, virtually all mud-thatch houses disappeared, and *pakka* houses of brick and cement blew down or became roofless. Newly harvested paddy along with 1.5 million acres of rice fields were destroyed, and the other lifeline, coconut palms, were decapitated with five to eight years required to replace them. Konasima was several years in regaining its cornucopia reputation. Venkatesvara, said many farmers, was angry with us for our sins, while as many others feared it was their neighborhood goddess, who was sure to do it all again. No one spoke of many crores of rupees devoted to sea walls on the east sides of towns that might have mitigated damage. While engineering skills have largely tamed the river, winds and far off earthquakes have remained wild.

A significant aspect of neighborhood goddesses in villages, town, and cities is their ambiguity. They are fierce, violent, blood-demanding creatures, carriers of epidemic diseases, destructive beyond measure. They are also benevolent, merciful, loving, and maternal. Collectively, generically, they are Ammavaru, Mother. Individually, in their temples and shrines, and in the annual festivals in the neighborhoods they patrol from border to border, they are Gangamma, Somalamma, Nukalamma, Paiditalli, and so on. The earlier description exactly describes the delta's great river, a life-giver, a life-taker.

1.2.9 Creating a Modern Telugu Language State

The historian of Andhra, P. Raghunanda Rao, credits English education for intellectual and social reforms leading to the "awakening of Andhra" from medieval stupor.[31] The University of Madras originated in 1857 and by 1873 a government college for the Godavari Delta was established in Rajahmundry. Labeled by the Veda pandits *huna-vidya*, the practice of the Huns (a heavy-handed reference to British colonials), the Brahmans were wary of an educational system that interfered with traditional Vedic culture.[32] The English curriculum and its enlightenment ideology did in fact produce rapid change. A battery of educated and energetic reformers arose and coastal Andhra contributed a fair share. The combination of traditional learning and superior social status of Brahmans was an advantage. According to Kenneth Jones, "between 1876–86 Brahmans accounted for 73% of all successful candidates in Madras University."[33]

Among the Andhra luminaries three nationally influential personalities deserve special mention, all of them born in the mid or late nineteenth century. Kandukuri Virasalingam (1848–1919), born in Rajahmundry, was a lucky survivor of childhood smallpox. Considered by many to be the most significant Andhran of modern times, he was a tireless and aggressive social reformer.

He earned the enmity of traditional authorities, including the Sankaracarya of Kancipuram and many Vaidika Brahmans, by championing female education and widow remarriage with dramatically staged ceremonies for maximum notoriety.

To Virasalingam, his opponents were Lilliputians and he lampooned them in an essay mirroring Jonathan Swift. He published journals and pamphlets, wrote two plays, and lectured widely. Having established the first schools for girls in 1874, as well as others for Untouchable boys, he officiated at the first widow remarriage in Rajahmundry in 1881 and later formed the Widow Remarriage Association for continuing ceremonies. Today a large and thriving women's college in Rajahmundry bears the name of his wife, Rajalaksmi.[34]

Sarvepalli Radhakrishnan (1888–1975) is a well-known name to general readers as well as Indologists because of his highly influential books. He translated from Sanskrit *The Principal Upanishads* and published *Indian Philosophy, the Philosophy of the Upanishads, an Idealist View of Life, Eastern Religions and Western Thought, East and West: Some Reflections*, and *Recovery of Faith*, all between 1923 and 1955. He was the first vice president of India in 1952–62 before serving as president in 1962–67. His distinguished roles included Oxford University professor of eastern religion and ethics (1936–52), chairman of UNESCO (1946–52), vice chancellor of Andhra University and Banaras Hindu University, and chancellor of Delhi University. Born in a traditional Brahman family in Tirupati, he was educated there at the Hermansburg Evangelical Lutheran Mission School where he earned a scholarship to Madras University, thus launching a famous career. His birthday, September 5, is now celebrated as Teachers' Day.[35]

Another Godavari Delta figure of national reputation was Pattabhi Sitaramayya (1888–1959), born in a non-Vaidika Brahman family in Gundugola in the same year as Radhakrishnan. By profession he was first a physician in Machilipatnam but left practice to join the Nationalist Movement. Prominent there from 1920 until independence, he spent eight of those years in British prisons. After release he continued disruptive agitations toward the formation of a separate state for speakers of Telugu.[36] The labors of Sitaramayya and many others had lasting effect: in 1956, Andhra Pradesh became the first of India's "language states," 88 percent of its people being Telugu speakers. In 2013–14, agitation arose in the Telangana interior region regarding formation of a new state divorced from the wealthier and better educated coastal zone of the two deltas. If the central government approves, Telangana's ten districts will comprise the twenty-ninth state of India, Hyderabad to serve as shared capital for the next decade. The two Godavari districts will remain among the thirteen districts of Andhra Pradesh.

Earlier, in 1925, two districts bracketing the Vasistha Godavari were created out of the former Rajahmundry District that in Arthur Cotton's time had been renamed Godavari District. East Godavari District had its headquarters in Kakinada while West Godavari District was governed from Eluru. Similarly, the single polity of Krishna District was split into the adjacent districts of Krishna and Guntur. Just as Rajahmundry is the largest town but not headquarters of East Godavari, so is Vijayawada the largest town in Krishna District while Eluru serves as the seat of governance. Rajahmundry, on the east bank of the Godavari, is forty-two miles from Kakinada, a distance that can be covered by express bus in one hour whereas in 1980 it usually required three to four.

The twentieth century is reflected in the living memories of many of the Brahmans in this narrative. World War I, that shuddered through Europe and the Ottoman Empire and profoundly affected North America, was scarcely remembered by the older pandits and wives; but two decades later, World War II, with Japanese submarines in the Bay of Bengal and some 2 million Indians in the uniform of the British army, left impressions on those born in the first half of the century. Soon after that war ended in 1945, however, January 26, 1947, Independence Day for India, is a date that brought joy to the older folks, all of them remembering Jawaharlal Nehru, "Pandit-ji," who lived until 1964. They also recall the local shake-up in September 1948 when the new Indian army corraled the Nizam and delivered Hyderabad, one of the last two "princely states," to control by the Republic of India.[37] Many events, movements of the freedom fighters and the turbulent period of independence, Gandhi's salt march and *satya-graha,* emergence of the Communist Party of India, unfolded at a far remove from the delta although coastal Andhra contributed numerous leaders, and local newspapers kept people informed.

1.3 Agrahara, *Villages, and Pilgrimage Towns*

When the *dora* (the author of this book) and his wife began residence directly on the left bank of the undivided Godavari in 1980, the state of Andhra Pradesh, an area slightly less than the Italian peninsula, had a population of about 53 million. By 2011 the population had ballooned to nearly 85 million, an increase of 32 million, well over the combined populations of all five Scandinavian countries, and Andhra was adding more than a million per year. Substantial transformations of landscape and culture were quite apparent all the while.

The search for *ahitagni* began in the village of Munganda close to the left bank of the Vasistha Godavari.[38] No Vedic ritualists were to be found, and teaching of the Vedas had long since expired. Authentic Vedic sacrificers, however, were reported to be living in *agrahara* not far away, although at the time, winding, deteriorating roads and footpaths made the distance seem daunting. Directions northeast to a cluster of villages hugging the Billakurru Canal (west of Nedunuru on Map 2) led to a wide neighborhood that included six *ahitagni* and several other pandits vigorously teaching Veda.

An *agrahara*, an entirely Brahman community, is usually an appendage of a village or hamlet, separated, private, yet close enough to obtain necessary supplies and household or field labor from the larger adjoining settlement. Those discussed here are donations of land by wealthy admirers of Vedic tradition who provided plots for house construction and small amounts of rice and coconut acreage for Veda pandits and a few other Brahmans.[39] Such gifts of land have a long history. Cynthia Talbot notes a special tradition in medieval Andhra, *sapta-santana*, "seven offerings," by which donors could perpetuate their names.[40] In addition to having a son, other legacies include provision of a deity image to a temple, constructing a tank for water supply, and donating an *agrahara*. *Agrahara* have secluded lanes, what might be called gated communities in America. Although invisible, the gateway is clearly understood by the far larger non-Brahman population as a threshold into a zone of privilege. Crop fields are sometimes intruded upon, not residential lanes.

Sriramapuram *agrahara*, established in 1940 in land grants to respected Veda pandits by a wealthy merchant, Dokka Rama, originally contained a single straight dirt lane of fourteen houses and a *panca-ayatana* (five-deity) temple housing Isvara, Radha-krsna, Surya, Ambika, and Vighnesvara (Ganesa) (see Figure 0.6). Added to the lane over the years were a small school, playground, post office, and two separate shrines for Subrahmanya and Dattatreya, respectively. Although all Brahman, an *agrahara* such as Sriramapuram is by no means uniform. Vaidika Brahmans live distinct lives and do not marry or dine with *laukika* non-Vaidika Brahmans living next door. Within Vaidikas, the families of *ahitagni* cannot eat food cooked by non-*ahitagni* wives.

Kamesvari *agrahara*, more remote from any main road, has only a few houses on a trio of adjoining short lanes. At the height of Vedic activity in Konasima, four *ahitagni*, sacrificers who maintain three sacred fires in their homes, and several other Veda pandits who taught Vedas to their own sons and often to the sons of others, lived in these two *agrahara* less than three miles apart on opposite sides of the Amalapuram canal. A mile and a half west of Sriramapuram is the village of Vyaghresvaram, at one time *agrahara*-like in size, and the locus of three other *ahitagni*, creating a circle of seven within walking distance of one another.

Another Vedic community that blurs the distinction between *agrahara* and village is Iragavaram, West Godavari District, where a strong presence of Veda pandits in a Brahman hamlet maintains a multigenerational heritage. Iragavaram is across the Godavari River from Konasima in what became West Godavari District after the division of Godavari District into two parts.

Kakinada town, some twenty-five miles northeast of the Sriramapuram-Vyaghresvaram-Nedunuru cluster but only fifteen miles north of the Gautami Godavari, is a seaport on the Bay of Bengal. The next locus for this narrative, it is home to a single *ahitagni*, Bhamidipati Mitranarayana. Formerly known as Cocanada, the town is the seat of government for East Godavari District. On the shore of the Bay of Bengal it is the largest seaport between Vishakhapatnam and Machilipatnam. Strong canals from all directions have provided fresh water for a century and a half. Despite small industries and ship traffic there are still beautiful stretches of sand beaches close to town.

Nomenclature for the region is sometimes confusing although not as drastic as the change in name from Madras to Chennai. As Cocanada became Kakinada and Machilipatnam became the modern name for Masulipatam, so did Daksarama evolve into Draksarama. Vijayawada is still frequently referred to as Bezwada, its medieval name.

Many other towns come into the conversations of the pandits, their wives, and children, particularly the many pilgrimage goals (*tirtha*) in the sacred geography of coastal Andhra. The medieval period produced a number of Hindu temples that achieved fame through their *mahatmya*, Sanskrit or Telugu depictions of their foundation mythologies and subsequent histories. Undoubtedly the primary target today is the Tirupati Vaisnava temple complex of the Lord of the Seven Hills, Venkatesvara, patron deity of Andhra. Until recently the temple took pride for many decades in its reputation as the wealthiest in India. In the town in the valley lives Venkatesvara's sister, the feared goddess Gangamma.[41]

While in this southernmost tip of Andhra many pilgrims broaden sectarian devotion by having *darsana* of the *linga* in the Saiva temple at Kalahasti, only twenty-two miles from Tirupati. The temple dates from the Pallava dynasty, rebuilt in the eleventh century by a Cola king. Kalahasti owns one of the five elemental *linga* of Saivism, the *panca-bhuta linga*, this one of wind, Vayu, the name of a Vedic god with Indo-Iranian roots. It is also the site where Kanappa, a devotee famous in Tamil Saiva hagiography, offered his eyes to restore those of a bleeding *linga*. Kalahasti boasts of being the southern Kasi (Varanasi, Benares).

In addition to Draksarama, described earlier, three more of the sacred *arama* are in the delta. One is Bhimavaram (with another Bhima temple) and a second is Kurma *arama*, Turtle Grove, in a village better known as Kotipalli frequented by the Vedic *rsi* Kasyapa. Siva as Lord of *soma*, the sacred Vedic plant, resides in his temple there. The third is Palakol (Palakollu), also known as Ksiraratna, the Milk Grove, with a *linga* temple now known via sectarian blending as Ksira Rama-lingesvara.

All of these towns with medieval temples attract great crowds of pilgrims, particularly at Maha-Sivaratri, the "great night of Siva" when everyone remains awake in devotion. Fierce gods—Virabhadra, Rudra, Bhima, Bhairava, Narasimha—as well as Bhadrakali and other ferocious goddesses of every stripe seem to dominate the landscape from their thousand-year-old palaces of stone.

Other coastal Andhra pilgrimage goals within reach of bus, train, or boat include two temple towns that employ a pair of prominent Veda pandit brothers featured in this book. One will most likely become an *ahtagni* in 2016. One town is Simhacalam west of Visakhapatnam with its eleventh-century hill temple enclosing a Siva *linga* for an entire year but for the one day in May when sandal paste somehow melts away to reveal an image of the Vaisnava god Narasimha, the true lord of Simhacalam who destroyed the demon king Hiranyakasipu precisely there. The other town is Annavaram in the north of East Godavari District with an equally popular temple, also on a hilltop, Ratnagiri, residence of the god Satyanarayana and goddess Satyavati. Annavaram also demonstrates sectarian rapprochement since the Vaisnava god is flanked by a Siva *linga* as well as the goddess.

Until recent improvement of roads approaching their towns, two renowned temples exacted intimidating journeys from pilgrims. One is Bhadracalam, accessible by boat some one hundred miles up the Godavari from Rajahmundry. Boat people still today are reluctant to go ashore in mid journey. Invariably they "cut" white chickens and break coconuts for the Breech Mother goddess Gandi Posamma at the wide bend of the river south of Devipatnam in hopes of avoiding tigers, crocodiles, and bandits. Only the last have actually been sighted for a generation. She stands guard exactly where treacherous territory begins, with a gleaming five-foot sword in her right hand. Beyond the break in the Northern Circars, Bhadracalam is the site of a temple of Rama built at the place where Sita was kidnapped by Ravana. Temple attendants reveal bedrock that bled when construction began, declaring that the great goddess *is* there, and *was* there, before the Ramayana heroes.

The other remote temple is Srisaila, the only south Indian temple mentioned in the Mahabharata. Millions of pilgrims have worn the road's cobblestones into rounded knobs as smooth as eggs. Located on a wilderness hilltop high above the Krishna River, the temple is the sacred space of Siva as Mallikarjuna and goddess Bhramaramba, a manifestation of Kali. As the *linga* in Kalahasti is one of five elements, this Srisaila *linga* is one of a famous set of twelve *jyotir linga*, forms of divine light.

Pilgrims count other towns on their itineraries as well. They visit Kanaka Durga in her hilltop temple in Vijayawada, Narasimha in yet another of his temples atop the elephant-shaped hill in nearby Mangalagiri, and Markandeya in his temple on the Godavari River in Rajahmundry (Rajahmahendravaram), an eleventh-century fortress town now favored as cultural center for coastal Andhra. Considered the birthplace of the Telugu language, Rajahmundry was the home of the poet Nannaya, author of three books of the Telugu Mahabharata. His benefactor was Rajaraja Narendra, the Calukyan king of Vengi during the first half of the eleventh century. Every twelve years Rajahmundry hosts "Pushkaram" when the Godavari takes its turn among India's greatest rivers for pilgrim bathers. In 2003 some 34 million were claimed by locals to have taken the sacred dip at half a dozen *revu*, the Telugu word for bathing ghats.

Throughout coastal Andhra, in softer focus and without literary recognition but for an occasional paper pamphlet, are numerous diminutive temples and shrines of neighborhood goddesses, many of them renowned for resident possession ritualists who embody them and become their voices in service of supplicants.[42] They are to be located mostly on word-of-mouth maps still in use by the roughly one-third of the population who do not read.

Further remarks on *agrahara* will precede the capsule biographies of Veda pandits at the outset of Chapter 3 and the lives of householders living in these Brahman communities will be the subject of Chapter 5.[43]

2

Vedamlo, "*Living in the Veda*"

2.1 *The Vocabulary of the Veda Pandit*

Essential for an understanding of the structure of Vedic tradition are certain key terms that are common parlance among Vedic Brahmans. These will come into play in the personal biographies in Chapter 3. The Glossary at the end of the book includes these terms along with others appearing less frequently, all of them being Sanskrit unless noted as Telugu. A reader may wish to refer back to pages here at the outset of this chapter for context and details in addition to the brief Glossary definitions. This chapter serves as a primer in living Vedic tradition by introducing first the basic educational system of Vedic pandits (Brahmans in hereditary Vedic families) as practiced today in coastal Andhra, then an outline of choices for maintaining *samsara*, the worldly subsistence of married and certified Veda pandit householders. The third section enters the life of *srauta*, the extended sacrificial tradition of those who establish three fires and become eligible to proceed to *soma* rituals.[1] This requires presentation of a whole new vocabulary and advanced set of procedures. A fourth section follows with attention to the remarkable liaisons between householders, both husband and wife, and their ritual hearth complex, known as *agni-hotra* and as Agni-hotra, the god Agni, Lord of the house and family.

During initial conversations in an *agrahara* it is immediately stressed that certain Brahmans "exist in Veda," *vedamlo unnaru*, a Telugu locative designation setting them apart from—and implicitly above—all others. A hierarchy recognizes the special character of the Vaidika subcaste of Brahmans who have retained "Brahmahood," *brahma-tva*, while others have fallen from their natural heritage and become *laukika*, literally "worldly," secular Brahmans. The latter are always the great majority of the Brahmana *varna* or class. The privilege of being first in the pecking order carries the burden of being responsible for Veda. Having been born into the Taittiriya *sakha*, "branch," of the Vedic textual corpus, the primary division of the Krsna or Black Yajur Veda, a Vaidika boy of seven or eight years may be given over to a guru for hearing and reciting back a lesson (*adhyaya*). It is a process of reciting by heart a portion of the Taittiriya Samhita, the copious initial collection of this Black Yajur Veda. The English translation by A. B. Keith is 637 pages long, but of course the boy is aware not of pages but of oral lessons broken into manageable portions.[2] A "subject" or "course" of study might be a more apt translation since his curriculum extends to eighty-two *panna* over a period of eight to twelve years including text-courses well beyond the Taittiriya Samhita. An American student may cover approximately the same number of "subjects" of study in twelve years of grade school and high school. Memorization, however, is quite another matter and in US schools may be limited to a couple of resentfully learned poems or the Gettysburg Address, all quickly forgotten.[3]

The boy begins his career as a reciter of Veda by undergoing the life-cycle ritual (*samskara*) known as *upanayana*, investiture with a sacred thread over his left shoulder. He hears from his guru his first mantra, the *gayatri* (also known as the *savitri*), Rg Veda 3.62.10, concerning the divine sun, awakener of the mind:

> *tat savitur varenyam / bhargo devasya dhimahi / dhiyo yo nah pracodayat*
>
> May we achieve the divine splendor of Savitr; may he illumine our minds.

He will recite the Gayatri and other mantras every day for the rest of his life in *sandhya-vandana* while sprinkling water offerings at the *samdhya*, "joints" of the day, twilight and dawn, when the sun (Savitr or Surya) sets or rises. This initiation begins *brahmacarya*, the first of four *asrama* or stages of life, that of the celibate student, *brahmacarin*. By becoming a Vedic student and reciting Veda in *sandhya-vandana* he is already discharging one of the three important *rna*, "debts," in the life of every Brahman, the one to the ancient *rsi* who first intuited the Veda (see Table 2.1). The other two he will pay off, respectively, to the gods by sacrificing and to his ancestors by fathering children.

Table 2.1. The four *asrama*, stages of life in classical Hinduism.

brahmacarin, Vedic student, maintaining *brahmacarya*, celibacy;
grhastha, married householder, living in the *grha*, house;
vana prastha, "forest dweller," retiring to the *vana*, forest;
samnyasin, ascetic, one achieving *samnyasa*, renunciation.

The *upanayana* ceremony involves the god Brhaspati, *purohita* (priest) of the gods and also patron of learning. In Telugu he is known as Guru, the deity of Thursday. AGS 4.10-11 with mantras in the second part of the separate Mantrapatha supply a concise program for the seven- or eight-year-old boy, beginning with his bath and the tonsure of his head with a razor. He is instructed to place kindling sticks into the fire and then is directed to place his right foot on a grindstone; put on a new loincloth, a belt of three strands of *munja* grass, and a strip of antelope hide; then receive as staff (*danda*) a slim branch from a *palasa* tree. He sprinkles himself three times with water received into his cupped hands from the guru who places a three-stranded white cotton thread over his right shoulder. After hearing initial mantras he addresses his guru and declares himself ready as a *brahmacarin*.[4]

After this thread-investiture the student lives in the residence of his earthly guru, in modern times most probably his father, grandfather, or older brother. In other words, he continues to live at home. In earlier times, and in some cases still today, the initial guru is an uncle or someone outside the immediate family residence and the student then lives in the guru's home and eats food cooked by his guru's wife, one who serves as interim mother. Proper food for the growing boy is extremely important and serves not only as correct nurturance for mind, body, and spirit but also a means of bonding with the larger community. The *brahmacarin* goes about collecting food by begging from various Vaidika Brahman houses in the *agrahara* or village. Like a honey bee collecting pollen he is a "honey-maker," *madhu-kara*, and cooked food is dropped into a cloth bag slung from his neck that he extends toward the door when a woman answers his call (see Figure 2.1). An alternative "begging" routine, *varalu*, assigns the boy to a different house on each of the seven days of the week, thus the Telugu plural of *vara*, weekday. Either way, he is in the mode of the ascetic, the *samnyasin* or *sadhu* who is dependent on the largesse of ordinary householders while on his spiritual quest. In his case it is the quest for knowledge of Veda. A few boys may be enrolled by their parents in a Veda *patha-sala*, a school for learning Veda such as the one in Kapilesvarapuram shown in Figure 2.2.

Along with his daily meditation prayers the student also becomes conscious of his personal relationship with Agni through daily fire maintenance, *agni-karya*, collecting kindling sticks (*samidh*), removing the ashes of old fires, and tending the household fire of his guru (see Figure 2.3, a *brahmacarin* carrying a fire-pot in the house of his father and guru, a potential *ahitagni*). He is rehearsing for that day when he first establishes a household fire for himself and his wife. This may presage a far more intense, even mystical bond with Agni if he later chooses to enter into *srauta* rituals as a *srautin*, fire-sacrificer,

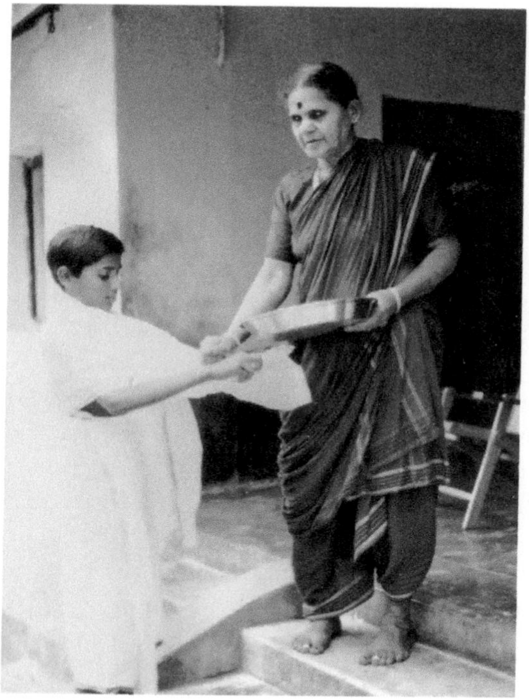

FIGURE 2.1. A *brahmacarin* at Surya's door in *madhu-kara*, collecting food house to house like a bee flower to flower, Sriramapuram 1987. The boy is Surya's thirteen-year-old grandson Phani.

relying on the Srauta Sutras that are themselves based on the Brahmana texts (as distinct from the Grhya Sutras covering domestic rituals).

At some point in his pre-teen or early teen years his parents arrange his marriage to a younger pre-pubescent girl, the five-day ritual *vivaha* creating a union to be consummated years later when he completes his Vedic learning and is ready to advance to the second life-stage and become a householder. This *patni*, wife, selected by his family, is traditionally from another Vaidika family with similar heritage and should be the daughter of a woman who married before puberty in a five-day ritual, thus doubly assuring purity of lineage and ritual sanction. She will be chosen from a family inside the subcaste but outside the *gotra*, clan lineage from one of the ancient sages, the *rsi*. In some families the bride and groom have known each other from early childhood. Often, however, the ceremony becomes "first sight," and when the five festive days are over it may be years before true acquaintance begins. If the bride grew up in a household of Vedic reciters or sacrificers she will be entirely familiar

FIGURE 2.2. Some of the twenty-five *brahmacarin* enrolled in the Sarvaratya Veda *patha-sala*, Kapilesvarapuram 1980.

with the transmission of mantras, performance of rituals, and daily Vaidika routines.[5]

Every day the new student will sit opposite his guru for the daily lesson. (See Figure 2.4, a grandfather teaching a grandson, and Figure 2.5, another grandfather teaching four grandsons at once.) Older pandits in this survey started learning, and then eventually teaching sons, some time between 4 AM and dawn. In recent years public school has intervened for some families and *adhyaya* may not begin until dawn has broken. In any case, if successful at memorizing passages from either the third or fourth section of the Taittiriya Samhita the student will persevere until he has mastered all seven sections before going on to the next three major texts of his tradition, the Taittiriya Brahmana, Taittiriya Aranyaka, and Taittiriya Upanisad. Supplementary lessons will be taught from two ritual manuals preferred in Konasima that may have been composed long ago in the Godavari Delta, one for great sacrifices, the other for domestic rituals, respectively, the Apastamba Srauta Sutra and Apastamba Grhya Sutra.[6]

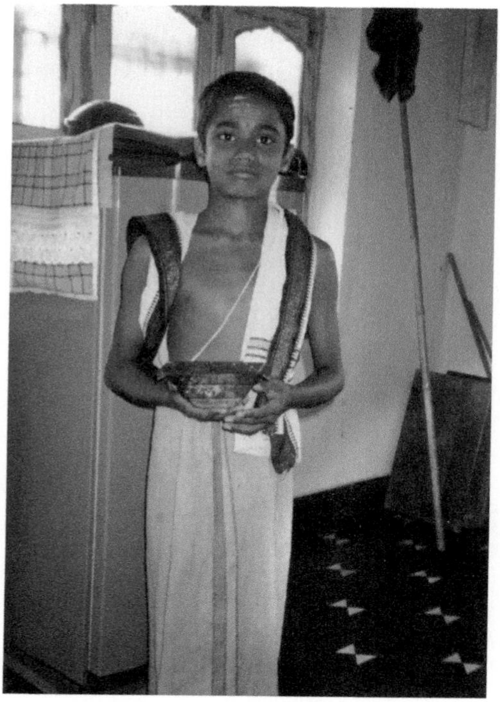

FIGURE 2.3. Kapilavayi Agnihotra, a *brahmacarin* performing daily *agni-karya* with a fire pot, Annavaram 2005.

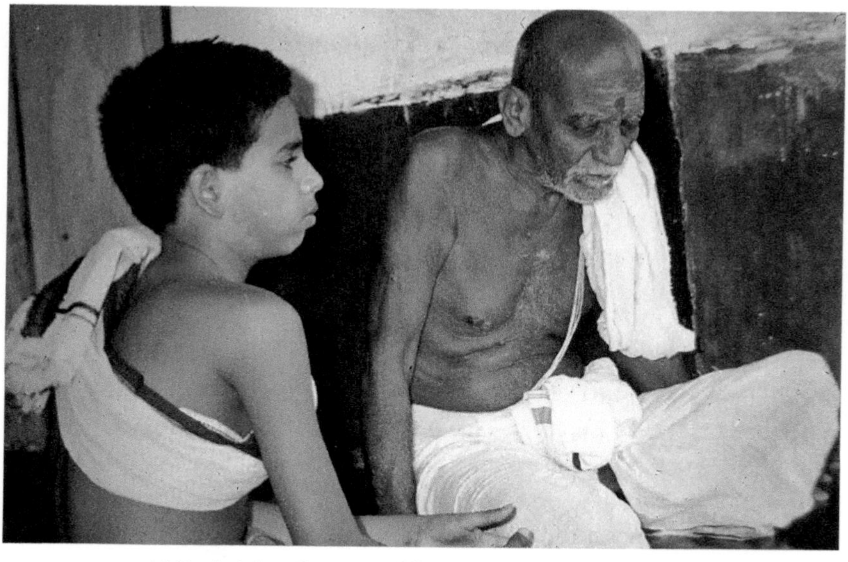

FIGURE 2.4. A blind eighty-five-year-old Duvvuri Yajulu teaching grandson Kirin, Sriramapuram 2000.

FIGURE 2.5. Another grandfather, Gullapalli Sita Ram Sastri, in *adhyayana* with four *brahmacarin* grandsons at once, Iragavaram 2000.

Examinations and certification as a Veda pandit will follow this formal phase of recitation that is significantly marked by a ritual bath, *snana*, heralding his "return," *sama-vartana*, from his guru. The boy will now be a young man in his middle or late teens at liberty to continue textual and ritual traditions of his own choosing or remain under the guidance of his guru. To appreciate the magnitude of this initial recitation achievement, traditionally a basic education lasting eight to twelve years, printed versions in Devanagari or Telugu script, or in English or other translation, could extend to well over 2,000 pages. One feature of this voluminous textual material, particularly true of ritual texts, is an interweaving of essential paradigms; a student frequently encounters passages he has already committed to memory, especially in the transition from Samhita to Brahmana to Aranyaka.

Several critical events await the newly certified Veda pandit. The second *asrama* or stage of his life, *grhastha*, is that of the householder. Although marriage with a traditional five-day ritual had already taken place when he was about nine to sixteen years old, and the younger bride selected for him was perhaps between seven and twelve, the role of householder, including cohabitation and ritual consummation, is not assumed until the bride, still living with her parents, has experienced menarche. The certified Veda pandit and his wife may now establish residence, take embers in a fire pan (*ukha*) from the marriage fire in her parents' home and set a domestic fire for a new "household," either within or outside the joint family in which he has grown up. The couple will now make daily offerings (*homa*) into this single fire, the *aupasana*, also called the household (*grhya*) or domestic (*smarta*) fire. A cooked rice and ghee offering inaugurates their new contract with Agni as lord of their residence and the couple consumes the remains.[7]

The career of the married Veda pandit now follows a trajectory with multiple options. The Taittiriya Samhita is transmitted in several forms known as *vikrti*, modifications of the "original" or model text. The student began with the *samhita*, "continuous," *patha*, "recitation." After completing it he went on with *pada-patha*, the same text over again broken down to separate "words," *pada*, without regard to grammatical rules that alter certain initial and final letters when they coalesce. For a third review he receives the same text in *krama-patha*, a "step-by-step" recitation. Some students do not go beyond the first or second recitation pattern. Most young men, teenagers at this point, stop after *krama-patha* with examination and certification.

If he still has nimble brain cells, however, a student may elect to repeat much of what he has interiorized in a far more difficult recitation, the *ghana-patha*, for example, a compact braided form that is popular among gifted students in coastal Andhra, a few of them relying on careers as *ghana-pathi*, masters of *ghana* who recite professionally at pandit assemblies, weddings, housewarmings, or other auspicious occasions, often in groups of two, four, or more in antiphonal response. The *jata-patha* is another difficult recitation pattern attempted briefly by many but mastered by few. Popular among Nambudiri Brahmans in Kerala is *ratha-patha*, the "chariot" recitation that has not been in style in coastal Andhra.

On the other hand, after the chain of Taittiriya Samhita, Brahmana, Aranyaka, and Upanisad, the gifted student may turn to one of the other Vedas, another *sakha*, and begin learning some portion of the Rg Veda, for example, with the same or a different guru. If his family includes someone with knowledge of the Sama Veda, the Veda of *saman*, melodies in a seven-note scale, an essential text for *soma* sacrifices, the student may elect to learn a segment of that difficult text from him. There is particular pride in learning the "local" Sama Veda since it is considered, rightly or wrongly, to be different not only from the Jaiminiya, Kauthuma, and Ranayaniya recensions (the latter two considered by some Western scholars to be virtually the same), but also different from versions employed by other Taittiriyins.[8]

Now a young man with increasing ability, probably living with his wife and starting a family, he may choose further studies with a pandit elsewhere in the *agrahara*, or in another village or town. His options may also include extra-Vedic texts, Mimamsa, for example, to develop his expertise in Vedartha, inquiry into the meaning of the Veda, or another of the philosophical schools, or Vyakarana, the study of grammar, or domestic rituals in the Smarta curriculum. Another choice might be study of the Apastaba Dharma Sutra, considered to be the earliest of this genre, along with its commentaries. Certification from any further studies will add to his credentials and increase his authority when he attends a local or regional pandit assembly, a *sabha*, for debates and exchanges of information on current Vedic events. If he becomes certified in the Apastamba texts for domestic rituals, often a father-to-son transmission of expertise, he may also become a family *purohita*, priest, for other Brahmans, asked to conduct marriages, housewarmings, thread ceremonies for Brahman boys, or other *smarta* (domestic) rites for small honoraria.

In lineages of *srauta* sacrificers he might be recruited into a role as *rtvij*, one of the staff of four priests necessary for fortnightly offerings known as *isti* on new or full-moon days and annual harvest rites, or even one of the sixteen to eighteen priests in an extended rite such as a fire-altar construction lasting forty days. In other words, after "graduating" from celibate studentship and becoming a householder, the Veda pandit is engaged in post-graduate studies, the lifelong learning that is the mark of *agrahara* residents who never seem to cease their quest for knowledge. And of course "the Veda," with hundreds of primary, acolyte, and commentarial texts, provides unbounded territory for exploration.

Apastamba's Sutras are the preferred manuals, the Grhya Sutra pertaining to domestic rites, various life-cycle rites, for example, and the Srauta Sutra detailing with more elaborate rituals of the three-fire system, including the initiatory *yajna* (sacrifice), the offering and drinking of *soma* in the *agni-stoma*, a ritual in praise of Agni. There are also the Sravana-*pasu* animal sacrifice in July-August; the annual *agrayana* first-fruits sacrifice for new crops, especially rice, usually in October-November; and the building of the fire altar, the *agni-cayana*, with its multiple versions that include a local favorite, the *paundarika*. Both Sutras are like palimpsests, the original texts layered with commentaries, instructions, and interpretive notes that can be followed minutely or modified in innumerable directions. Baudhayana, Hiranyakesin, and other Sutras are used as backups, but usually Apastamba is consulted first.

One who learns some portions of the Rg Veda may also learn its Asvalayana Sutras, and one who receives segments of the Atharva Veda may add some of the Kausika Sutra and the Gopatha Brahmana. Some of the *ahitagni* lineages cherish handwritten books of *srauta* instructions, particularly regarding *soma* sacrifices, and these precious records are in the careful script of great-grandfathers, grandfathers, and fathers. A concomitant result of these familial traditions is that some rituals, both domestic (*grhya*) and extended (*srauta*), may have idiosyncratic versions to which guest priests from other families must be willing to grant accommodation.

Table 2.2 depicts the place of the Taittiriya *sakha* of the Krsna or Black Yajur Veda among the other branches of Veda. It is important to keep in mind the traditional, unchallenged belief in the Veda as unitary and eternal,

Table 2.2. The Vedic textual tradition. Taittiriya texts are highlighted; some collections are fragmentary [fr.]. This table largely follows Staal 1983: 1.36.

Sakha / Samhita	Brahmana	Aranyaka	Upanisad	Srauta Sutra
Rg Veda				
1. Sakala	Aitareya	Aitareya	Aitareya	Asvalayana
2. Vaskala	Kausitaki	Kausitaki	Kausitaki	Sankhayana
Krsna Yajur Veda				
1. Kathaka & Kapisthala	Katha [fr.]	Katha [fr.]	Katha [fr.]	Kathaka [fr.]
2. Maitrayani			Maitri	Manava Varaha
3. Taittiriya	**Taittiriya**	**Taittiriya**	**Taittiriya** Svetasvatara Mahanarayana	**Apastamba** Baudhayana Vadhula Bharadvaja Hiranyakesi Vaikhanasa
Sukla Yajur Veda / Vajasaneyi				
1. Madhyamdina	Satapatha	[Brhad]	Brhadaranyaka	Katyayana
2. Kanva	Satapatha	[Brhad]	Isa	
Sama Veda				
1. Kauthuma / Ranayaniya	Pancavimsa		Chandogya	Latyayana
	Sadvimsa			Drahyayana
2. Jaiminiya	Jaiminiya		Kena	Jaiminiya
Atharva Veda				
1. Saunaka	Gopatha		Prasna	Vaitana [=Kausikasutra]
2. Paippalada	Gopatha		Mundaka Mandukya	

without origin; it is *apauruseya*, without human authorship. There is no literary "chronology" as in modern historical scholarship and therefore a passage in an "early" portion of the Rg Veda that outside scholars might date to the mid-second millennium BCE is part of the same eternal text as an Upanisad dated by text-critical scholars to be well over a thousand years later. Among Veda pandits there is no debating this issue. Contemporary historical scholars have perceived a distinction between a "pre-classical" Vedic period from c. 1200 to c. 800 BCE and the subsequent "classical" era that lasted several centuries after 800. Following a survey of selected families of Veda pandits in Chapter 3, Chapter 4, "Becoming a Veda," provides a more nuanced discussion of textual learning, application of such skills, and opportunities for the study of other Vedic and post-Vedic texts. Similarly, Chapters 5 and 6, "Becoming a Householder," and "Becoming Agni," are, respectively, more rigorous pursuits of the domestic and extended ritual traditions.

2.2 *Choices for Livelihood*

The score of capsule biographies in Chapter 3 illustrates a variety of career options for certified Veda pandits and how the scope of personal choices has broadened over the course of four generations. Some of those who have been recipients of cropland and houses donated by wealthy individuals who favor the Vedic tradition have been freed from financial concerns in order to teach, study, and in some cases perform sacrifices. As noted, some have taken up full- or part-time professions as domestic ritualists, Smarta Brahmans, while others recite as *ghana-pathi* for remuneration. Not available to the oldest of those selected for study here but now undertaken by most Veda pandits is the *parayana* system, usually called the "TTD Scheme," borrowing an English term applied to the Tirumala Tirupati Devasthanam and its program of financial support for Veda pandits in the form of honoraria and pensions.

In most of the homes of Veda pandits in Konasima, a particular framed photo, frequently garlanded, hangs on a prominent wall alongside saints and ancestors. It is a portrait of Uppuluri Ganapati Sastri, credited with establishing the pandits' contractual recitation plan in the delta, a program of public recitation, *parayana*, in temples large and small for two or three hours each day. The TTD is headquartered at Tirupati in the temple complex of Venkatesvara in the Chittor District of southern Andhra, a site now mythically famous for seemingly incalculable wealth. From modest beginnings in 1932 during the Madras Presidency the TTD grew through several Religious and Charitable Endowments Acts (1951, 1969, 1979, 1987, and 2006) and the emergence of

Andhra Pradesh as a state in 1956. Today the trust, in cooperation with the state government, supervises a huge array of institutions, including more than a dozen temples, associated choultries (pilgrim dormitories), hospitals, educational enterprises, libraries, audio-recording projects (including Vedas), and other ventures.

Of numerous "schemes," as they are known, the one that is of immediate impact on the lives of Veda pandits established a schedule of monthly payments to qualified, that is, successfully examined pandits, who are assigned to recite from their own *sakha* in designated temples. They remain unencumbered by routine activities of these temples and are entirely separate from *pujari,* the priests controlling daily worship of the resident deities and distribution of *prasada,* the grace of those gods and goddesses. Rather, in the view of TTD trustees, pandits recruited by the Devasthana promote popular appreciation of the Vedas as visible and audible illustrations of the living texts, even as they serve to legitimate Vedic authority of the temples themselves. An example is the ancient temple of Siva as Mallikarjuna and Kali as Bhramaramba on the mountain top at Srisaila (a site mentioned in Chapter 1) as the locus of eight Veda pandits reciting publicly, two for each Veda.

A majority of the individuals whose lives are to be explored in the following chapters signed on to this *parayana* program and were grateful for the steady family income, particularly in the face of debts accrued from daughters' marriages, divisions of properties for sons, and expenses incurred in a life of routine or elected sacrifices. The security of a pension plan with monthly checks after retirement from recitation duties has strong appeal. After all, reciting in temple service simply involves a "going over" (the literal meaning of *parayana*) of the same passages currently being taught to sons and grandsons. A few, however, including two of the most prominent and regionally famous *ahitagni,* insisted that the scheme was not for them and amounted to "selling" the Veda, *veda-vikriya.* Furthermore, they added, it exposed their impressionable youth to secular life with cash in hand and an inevitable spiral of conspicuous consumption ("a motorcycle when a bicycle should do, and so on," muttered one elder). Both Veda and *srauta* suffer, they insisted, in the environment of temple town life with its wider lens on opportunities outside of Veda, outside of an *agrahara,* the proper constricted venue for Vedic life. The TTD, in response, attempted as far as possible to assign Veda pandits to village temples a short distance from their homes, in one case, for example, a private *agrahara* shrine just a few steps out the door of an aging pandit who had gone blind from glaucoma. A variety of opinions about the positive or negative value of TTD salaries, special honoraria, and pension plans, as well as central government honoraria, is cited as biographies unfold in Chapter 3.

Uppuluri Ganapati Sastri, who is listed first of all in *Veda Pandits in India*, Volume 2, *Veda Pandits in Andhra*, was visited in Kakinada in November 1980 when he was ninety-two years old. His rail-thin frame gave no indication that he could set mantras of great musicality reverberating through the rooms of his modest house. He recited three Taittiriya Samhita passages concerning the fire altar, the rope for the sacrificial animal, and the clay trampled by the horse in the famous *asva-medha* sacrifice, each accompanied by explication of context. His style is bardic, simultaneously story telling, chanting, and sermonizing. Astonishingly, some seventy-four years previous to that visit he had been *adhvaryu*, executive priest, in an *agni-stoma soma* sacrifice in Kakinada in 1906.

The *parayana* program Uppuluri promoted in Konasima expanded over the years. One innovation, for example, pertains to local Brahman societies that wish to meet monthly on or close to *samkramana*, when the sun moves from one *rasi*, sign of the zodiac, to another. The program requires a Veda pandit to recite one of the initial forty-four *panna* in a long series that would take some three years and eight months to complete. Today the rising schedule of honoraria for temple recitations is common knowledge among pandits. In 2005, for example, the salary for reciting *ghana* was Rs. 1,800 per month, about 60 per day, and for those reciting *krama* it was Rs. 1,500 per month, about 50 per day. Retired (*vrddhi*) pensioners, having concluded their temple service, received Rs. 1,000, about 33 per day. At that time early in 2005, the exchange rate was Rs. 43.7 for $1. As evident from the life histories told by the older Veda pandits and their wives, such a plan of reliable income and pension brought an extraordinary change from "the old days" prior to a cash economy. It was an economic shift warmly welcomed by many, although for most it never guaranteed freedom from new monetary worries that unexpectedly seemed to sprout like weeds in a crop field.

Another economic opportunity came from the United Kingdom and the United States after rapid construction of Hindu temples in major urban areas there from the early 1970s to the present. London, San Francisco, New York, Chicago, Houston, Atlanta, and many other cities sought Vaidika Brahman pandits to do *parayana* in new temples, including those constructed according to Silpa Sastras, Sanskrit manuals on architecture, and staffed by *pujari* who spoke the regional language, Telugu for Andhra immigrants. Salaries were enticing and a Telugu-speaking community was assured. At one point an invitation came to Sriramapuram *agrahara* from the Venkatesvara temple in Pittsburgh, Pennsylvania, at the instigation of an Andhra Brahman living there. The elders pulled out this mysterious letter written in English, heard from the *dora* its contents, and flatly rejected the idea. A *parayana* assignment to Srisailem, Hyderabad, or Simhacalam, all in Andhra, was one thing. Accepting a position in America, a land of Christian churches, strange diets, weird customs, infinite temptations, was not for their sons or grandsons.

In an earlier essay (Knipe 1997) that was a precursor to this book there was agreement, regarding Konasima, with Frits Staal's 1983 assessment among the Nambudiri Brahmans of Kerala: Vaidika Brahmans had no interest in coming to America. By the close of the 1990s, however, the situation in Andhra was quite different. Information technology not only had become well established in India but American corporations were now employing adventurous and well-educated South Asians from coast to coast, including sons and sons-in-law of Vaidika Brahmans. When they returned home their reports about life in America did not match long-held opinions of those who had never left the delta. But the conservative elders of Konasima still resisted. No Veda-certified sons or grandsons should leave Andhra, although there was no problem with *laukika* descendants taking employment in the West. Lanka used a Telugu proverb to warn of the perils for a Veda pandit taking employment in America: "From a distance the mountains look soft."

2.3 *The Vocabulary of an* Ahitagni

Veda pandits who have been nurtured within the embrace of *srauta* traditions will be strongly encouraged to continue their heritage and become *ahitagni*, sacrificers who maintain three hearths, not a single sacred fire; perform the twice-daily heated milk offering known as *agni-hotra* that entitles them to be known as rare and privileged *agni-hotrin*; and move on with *soma* sacrifice in mind to perform the ritual known as *yajna*, meaning the *agni-stoma*. Of the total of 626 *ahitagni* listed for India and Nepal by C. G. Kashikar and Asko Parpola, "A catalogue of ahitagnis and srauta traditions in recent times," nearly one-third (200) were residing in Andhra.[9] The *srauta* ritual system, as noted earlier, is an extended one in the sense that a simple domestic routine has been replaced by one far more demanding on the religious energies of the sacrificer and wife. A few may take the life-altering step into extended fires early on, but many wait until mid-life or later. They speak repeatedly about what is *nitya*, obligatory, and invariably distinguish between what is absolutely necessary for the sacrificial life of a Vedic Brahman and what is set aside as either *kamya*, a ritual for a personal desire (long life, for example, or the birth of a son), or *naimittika*, a ritual that is occasional, not calendric (such as rites for a funeral or for rain to end a drought). The last of these three categories, *naimittika*, includes important *prayascitta*, expiatory performances as recompense for failure to do the *nitya* rites in timely fashion.[10]

To begin the life of *srauta* as a *yajamana*, a sacrificer in the more exalted regimen of Vedic rituals, the Veda pandit with his wife as co-sacrificer must augment their single-fire household with its *aupasana* fire by performing *adhana*, the *nitya* or obligatory ritual setting of three fires. This two-day event, usually performed in the spring, establishes on the floor of a special room of the house a round *garha-patya*, cooking fire in the west, a square *ahavaniya*, offering fire to the east, and a *daksina-agni*, southern fire, all in three conjoined hearths of molded clay separated from one another by a *vedi* storage area for the many ritual implements necessary for any particular ritual act, a *kriya* or *karman*. This hearth complex will be the couple's sacred cynosure, unseen by all but the family and ritual collaborators, until the death of one of them, at which time all traces of it will be removed. It is Agni in the most personal sense, a living god established solely for this house, this family, this ritual calendar. Plan 2.1, the floor plan of Duvvuri Yajulu's house, shows this three-fire *agni-hotra* room; the house is typical for an *ahitagni* and *patni*. And see Figure 2.6, the three-hearth complex of Bulusu Kamesvara and his wife Satyavati.

The householder and his wife may have routinely made *homa* offerings into the *aupasana* fire (also known as the *grhya* or *smarta* fire) at sunset and sunrise

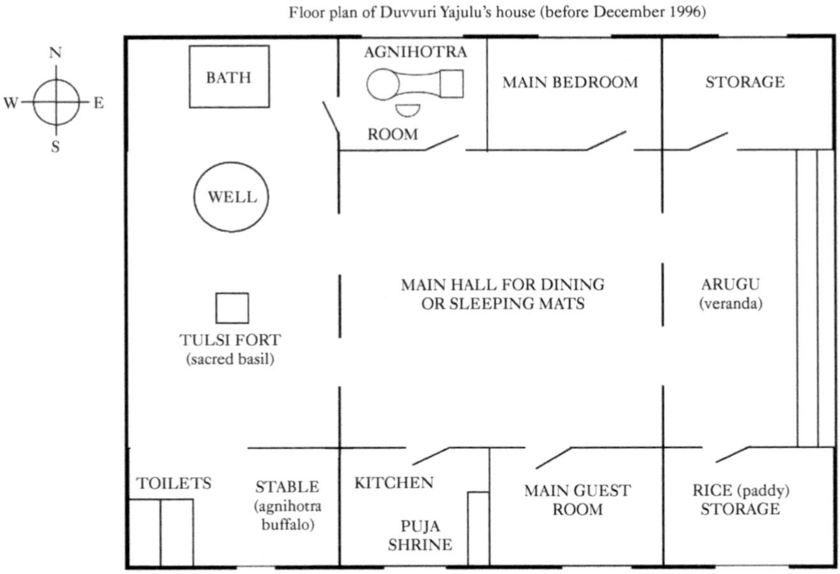

PLAN 2.1. Floor plan of Duvvuri Yajulu's Sriramapuram house showing his three-fire *agni-hotra* room; the house is typical for an *ahitagni* and *patni*.

FIGURE 2.6. Satyavati, Bulusu Kamesvara, and their hearths, the round *garhapatya* at left, semicircular *daksina-agni* an arm's length away, the *vedi* holding implements in space stretching toward the square *ahavaniya*, Vyaghresvaram 2000.

after the *agni-hotra* cow is milked, the remains of the offering serving as the beginning of the evening and morning family meals. Adding kindling sticks to the hearth is itself an offering. This twice-daily pattern mirrors both the *sandhya-vandana* worship that precedes *agni-hotra* and the *vaisva-deva* offerings to various deities, the Visve Devas (All Gods) in particular. Technically, therefore, the marital pair may qualify as *agni-hotrin* with a single *grhya* fire, particularly if a *grhya adhana* is performed. It was the personal choice of Upadhyayula Nagendram of Amalapuram, for example, to perform *agni-hotra* twice daily with a single consecrated fire. The *ahitagni* of this survey, however, understand the *srauta adhana* to be the proper prefix to *agni-hotra* in the *ahavaniya* hearth of *tretagni*, the three-fire complex. Therefore, the evening-morning pattern is retained, but now it is the *garha-patya* fire that heats milk to be offered into the *ahavaniya* fire. The couple "sets fires" by performing *adhana* with five fires (Plan 2.2) that are reduced to three (see Chapter 6 part 2).

This routine that brackets the activities of the day will be done tens of thousands of times in a lifetime, the recipients of the offering and mantras being

Agni and Prajapati in the evening, Surya and Prajapati in the morning. Always it is the deities (*devata*) receiving the libation who are kept in mind. Every two weeks there is a *darsa-purna-masa* new-or-full-moon offering, an *isti* in which *devata* receiving offerings are the dual deities Agni-Soma and Indra-Agni, as well as Agni alone and Prajapati. More elaborate than the simple *agni-hotra*, food for them is pounded rice flour mixed with water into dough that is baked in a loaf (*purodasa*) on terra-cotta rings in the *garha-patya* before presentation to the gods. Although baked and rounded in a small lump it is not unlike the flat steamed rice pancake with which most Andhrans begin their day, an *idli* for breakfast.

First *adhana* and then daily *agni-hotra* and fortnightly *isti* begin a program that may continue with other *nitya* (obligatory) rituals. One year after commencing the three fires the couple is eligible to perform extended *srauta* rites demanding the projection of the indoor three-fire complex out of doors onto a broad "field of fire" (*agni-ksetra*) and a great altar (*maha-vedi*). The initiatory rite for this leap into extended sacrifices is the *agni-stoma*, the first sacrifice of *soma*, the sacred heavenly plant whose ritually pressed juice, provider of wisdom and immortality, is drunk by the sacrificer in the shared company of sixteen *rtvij* priests.[11] (See Plan 6.1. Ground plan of an *agni-ksetra* "field of fire," a

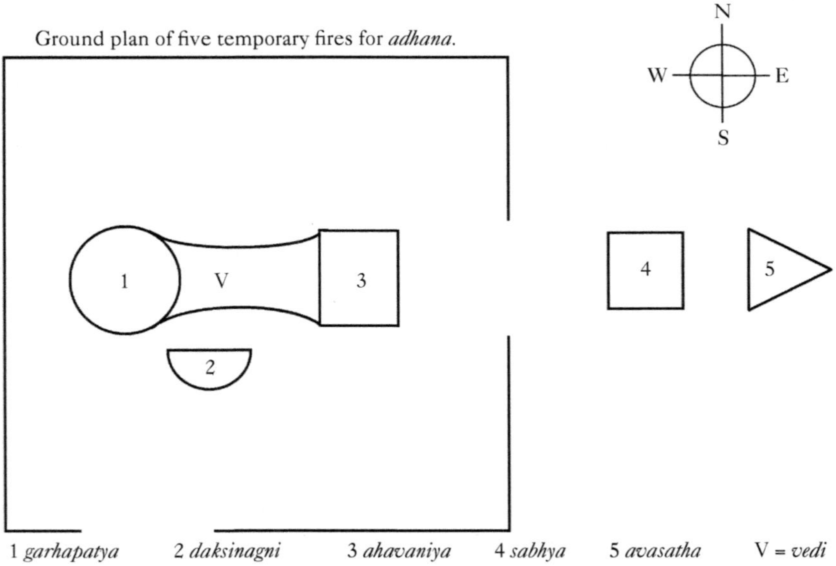

PLAN 2.2. Ground plan of five temporary fires for the *adhana* ritual setting of hearths.

projection of the three *agni-hotra* fires outside the house for an extended *srauta* ritual, drawn by Kapilavayi Venkatesvara, Simhacalam 2014. Construction of the great altar on this field is detailed in Chapter 6, Part 7.)

Soma is immolated and sacrificed in the company of an animal sacrifice, *pasu-bandha*, in modern history, a male goat. The Indo-Iranian antiquity of *soma* is assured by its correspondence to *haoma* in the Avesta. This pathbreaking event, recalled with excitement by every couple for the rest of their lives, is a five-day ritual starting on a new or full-moon day in the spring. The word *yajna* is a generic term for "sacrifice," but so important is the *agni-stoma* that in coastal Andhra the two are synonymous, as in "We performed our *yajna* in the year so and so," with unmistakable reference to the first offering of *soma*.

The couple undergoes an initiatory death-and-rebirth *diksa* consecration, a powerful signal of this transformative moment. Infantile clenched fists and stammering, as if learning anew to speak, are but two of several marks of entrance into new being. Each of the couple is bound by a *munja*-grass belt, a *mekhala* for him, a *yoktra* for her. Stalks of a green leafless, non-hallucinogenic creeper (Telugu *lata*) that substitutes for the original *soma* (perhaps a species of ephedra) are purchased from a seller who is then expelled from the *agrahara*. Brought in a wooden cart to a newly created ritual arena with erected bamboo sheds and fires transferred from the domestic *agni-hotra* room, the *soma* is welcomed as a guest (*atithya*) and a king (*raja*) with rituals befitting a monarch. But Soma is also a god to be killed and ingested, a divine transformer who instills visions of light and immortality in one who drinks its pressed juice. At one point a line of priests creeps stealthily on haunches; they are low-lying hunters sneaking up on an antelope (a metonym for the sacrifice), each holding a shoulder of the one in front. A goat is bound to a pole and sacrificed by suffocation.

On the fifth day there are three pressings (*savana*) of *soma* by the *adhvaryu* and assistants who wield stones on the stalks against an animal hide on a board while the requisite twelve *stotra* of the Sama Veda are chanted and twelve *sastra* of the Rg Veda are recited. The juice is filtered through wool, poured from a tub into a pot and then into wooden cups (*camasa*), each carved with slightly different markings for each priest. After first offering and then drinking *soma*, the priests sacrifice a second goat and conclude the *agni-stoma* with a ritual bath. In keeping with death-rebirth symbolism, the husband and wife are renamed. As a *soma*-sacrificer he is now Somayaji or Soma-yajulu (in Telugu often just Yajulu) and from now on she is never called by her given name but rather Somi-devamma (*somi-deva-amma*), ending in Telugu "mother." When pronounced with normal Telugu rapidity her name is heard as "sodamma."

If the couple chooses to continue with elaborate and expensive *soma* sacrifices beyond *agni-stoma* they may elect to perform one of six others in the set of seven *nitya* rites, the *sapta-samstha*. ApSS 10.1.1 to 13.25.10 covers the *agni-stoma* in great detail in four lengthy sections since it is the model for the others. However, just as recitation patterns (*patha*, discussed earlier) are modifications of the basic *samhita* or connected recitation of the Taittiriya Samhita, so too there are modifications of the paradigmatic *soma* rite, the *agni-stoma*. In shorter compass Apastamba lists the *soma* rituals in 14.1–16 as the *ukthya, sodasin, atiratra,* and *aptoryama*, and continues on with the remaining two of the six modifications, 16.1 to 18.22.22, namely, the *agni-cayana* and the *vaja-peya*.

In coastal Andhra the *agni-stoma* is of course prerequisite, often followed by one of several types of *agni-cayana*, known by a shortened form, *cayana*, each type distinguished by the number of thousands of bricks (*istaka*) laid down. (See Plan 6.2, Ground plan of a *syena-citi*, flying eagle form of *agni-cayana*.) The construction of the fire altar in five layers of bricks is a well-known cosmogonic ritual in which the sacrificer is homologized to Agni as well as the primal sacrifice person, Purusa-Prajapati, and all of time and space are reintegrated and founded anew. Daily, as the bricks are being laid course by course, the sacrificer carries Agni about in a fire-pan (*ukha*). The Satapatha Brahmana in the Sukla or White Yajur Veda tradition devotes more than a third of its chapters to the *agni-cayana* and its mysteries and is best known to Western scholars. Konasima Brahmans, however, know only the Taittiriya version. Perhaps of all Vedic rituals the *agni-cayana* has received the most scholarly attention, inside and outside of the tradition itself. A massive two-volume illustrated study and a widely seen film, *Altar of Fire*, by Frits Staal and Robert Gardner covered a 1975 performance by the Nambudiri Vaidika Brahmans of Kerala.[12] That rite was explained as "the world's oldest surviving ritual" and "perhaps" the very last performance, with no acknowledgment of centuries of an Andhra tradition with routine *agni-cayana* continuing today.

Frequently it is the *vaja-peya*, "drink of strength," that is a next choice in Andhra, a sacrifice peppered with Prajapati's sacred number seventeen. There are seventeen each of the following: *diksa* days, cups of wine (*sura*, brewed from fermented rice, barley, and millet), cups of *soma* pressed on the seventeenth day, "chariots" in a tame facsimile of a race, *stotra* chants and *sastra* recitations, and of black goats sacrificed in the finale. Even the *daksina*, ritual payments, must be seventeen in number although no one in modern times gives away the female slaves, elephants, or chariots recommended by Apastamba.[13] A climactic event has the sacrificer and wife put their feet on the first rung of a ladder braced against the sacrificial post (*yupa*) serving as an axis mundi. They proclaim attainment of immortality.

Beyond the customary *cayana* and the *vaja-peya* are two ambitious *soma* rites, one favorite being the forty-day *paundarika* fire-altar layering, a sacrifice that includes, among other components, the *maha-vrata* with a pretend coupling of a *brahmacarin* and a prostitute. The other grandiose *soma* sacrifice is the *sarvato-mukha* with four altars facing all compass points, requiring four times the number of *rtvij*, an astonishing seventy-two priests in all. As will be observed in the biographies, it also has been performed by a living Godavari delta pandit.

All of these rituals require considerable advance preparation, study of the texts; teaching the wife her mantras and positions on the *maha-vedi*, the field of sacrifice; procuring the priestly helpers, the basic four in particular—*hotr, adhvaryu, udgatr*, and *brahman*; erecting structures on the *maha-vedi*; assigning carpenters and potters to fashion ritual implements; hiring *vanta-Brahman* cooks to feed the staff and expected crowd of observers; raising funds to pay for it all. The four major priests have three assistants each for a normal total of sixteen, augmented for certain rites by a seventeenth, a *sadasya*, sometimes even an eighteenth. All are selected by the *yajamana*, with the aid of an experienced mediator, the *soma-pravaka*, when plans are made for a particular sacrifice. Great care is taken since any error reflects upon the sacrificer. "I would be flung into *papakupa* (Classical Telugu, 'the pit of Hell') by a blunder in mantra," commented one pandit. Until now the *ahitagni* has needed only one helper, an *adhvaryu* for his twice-daily *agni-hotra*, often a son, brother, or other close relative or colleague living in the *agrahara* or village. More commonly there is even provision for assumption of the role himself (*svayam*). For *isti*, twice-monthly offerings at new and full moons, and in the annual harvest ritual, the *agrayana*, he has had to procure an *adhvaryu, hotr, brahman*, and a fourth, the *agnidhra*, an assistant to the *brahman* who actually aids the *adhvaryu*. Again, he has usually relied on his family or other *ahitagni* living nearby, and may have taken any one of the roles himself. Apastamba provides an escape hatch by mentioning the possibility of using only an *adhvaryu* and *hotr*. For the animal sacrifice (*pasu-bandha*) in Sravana (July–August) the *ahitagni* required the largest team, as many as six priestly helpers.

The demands of *soma* rituals, however, exceed those limited staffs and compel him to go outside family and village, perhaps even out of the area to enlist sixteen or more Brahmans he trusts for the challenging roles. Often reciprocity in the history of rituals past may determine these choices. Each of the four major priests selected is linked to one of the four Vedas. Just as the quartet of Vedas reveals a privileged inner trio and a "plus one" formula,[14] namely, the Atharva Veda, so does the priestly foursome break into those responsible for the Rg, Yajur, and Sama Vedas, with a fourth who owns only a contrived relationship to the Atharva Veda. These four and their assistants are listed in Table 2.3. Some of these roles have a deep history going back four millennia to the Indo-Iranian period as Avestan *zaotar* and Vedic *hotr* disclose. Over the centuries Vedic priestly staffs expanded to the ideal number, sixteen, and beyond, and several roles shifted. Sutras record the *agnidhra* as an assistant to the *brahman* supervisor, but as kindler and maintainer of fire, as his name indicates, he is the most important assistant of the *adhvaryu*, the executive priest. ApSS 10.1.9 lists these sixteen as shown in Table 2.3.

In the study of *srauta*, the young Veda pandit perceives connections between text and ritual, between sacred sound and action. He begins to understand the positioning of all the pieces, the *panna*, he has been fed over the years, and realizes that Veda is a sacrificial liturgy. If mantras are the muscles of Veda, then *kriya*, ritual actions, are tendons that unite and press them into service of the dramatic whole, the sacrifice. Recitations from the first Veda, the Rg Veda, are known as *sastra* and are done by the *hotr* and his three assistants. They follow *stotra*, chants from the third Veda, the Sama Veda, sung by the *udgatr* and two of his three assistants, essentially a trio as choir. For example, the *agni-stoma*, first *soma* sacrifice, includes a litany of twelve *sastra*, each preceded by a *stotra* as the *adhvaryu* and his three assistants become workhorses on the sacrificial ground, softly muttering verses from their Yajur Veda correspondent to their ritual tasks. The Brahman, fourth major priest, pronounces a few mantras and performs some actions but remains for the most part a keen-eyed observer, a kind of ombudsman

Table 2.3. The four major priests (*maha-rtvij*) and their Vedas. Each has three assistants.

1. *hotr*, reciter of the Rg Veda, with assistance from the *maitra-varuna, acchavaka,* and *gravastut.*

2. *adhvaryu*, executive priest, reciter of the Yajur Veda, with assistance from the *prati- prasthatr, nestr,* and *unnetr*. The *adhvaryu* and acolytes perform the work (*karman*) of sacrifice.

3. *udgatr*, chanter of *saman* from the Sama Veda, with assistance from the *prastotr, prati-hartr,* and *su-brahmanya.*

4. *brahman*, overseer who knows all priestly roles and mantras, with assistance from the *brahmanac-chamsin, potr,* and *agnidhra*. The Atharva Veda, not used in *soma* rites, is assigned to the *brahman* for taxonomical parity. The *brahman* is a healer (*bhisaj*) who remains silent unless he must act to repair errors that might damage the sacrifice.

who checks every detail, sometimes with a wag of his head, while his three assistants serve in various capacities.

2.4 Bonding with Agni

Chapter 3 illustrates the ways in which these extended rituals and all their supporting intellectual and material preparations ornament the lives of *ahitagni* and *patni* and Chapter 6 enters the ritual life in far more detail. To conclude this chapter, however, it is instructive to review the significance of installing the god Agni as lord of house and family, and what his presence and the obligations of constant ritual attentions mean in the way of creating an alternative reality. Some of this surfaces when we look at the multiple meanings of the word *agni-hotra*. The god and his cult become synonymous when we see that common parlance of *ahitagni* and *patni* employs *agni-hotra* to mean three separate entities: the daily offerings, the fires into which libations are made, and the god Agni himself. So melded are these meanings that one nonagenarian *patni* anxiously shouting "*Agni-hotra! Agni-hotra!*" in her final hours of breath could have been signaling any one of the three. As Christopher Fuller has observed of the standard Hindu worship, "Puja, at its heart, is the worshippers' reception and entertainment of a distinguished and adored guest"[15] and that is precisely the case with the establishment of sacred fire in the household.

The fact that thousands of hours are spent addressing mantras to fires amounts to a lifelong conversation with this elemental form of the sacred. All know that Agni has pride of place in the Vedas: the Rg Veda, and therefore, "Veda," begins with "*Agnim ile purohitam* . . .," praise of him as visible household priest. An entire community of deities, invited by Agni, gathers daily with fires as cynosure and the married co-sacrificers as host and hostess of the ritual assembly. Several *ahitagni* have reported what appear to be mystical experiences, visions stimulated by prolonged engagements with their fires and aspirations for the health and welfare of their families.[16] From the student's task of feeding the fires with kindling-stick offerings, on through a life of *agni-hotra* to the final oblation, one's own body given to *tretagni—ahavaniya, daksinagni,* and *garha-patya,* igniting head, arms, and midsection before burning together as one—devotion to Agni has no parallel in the religious experience of the *ahitagni*. That ultimate manifestation of the deity, the awe-inspiring and beloved god who absorbs, is Agni *kravyad*, flesh-eating Agni.

A potent aspect of the cult of Agni is the seminal notion of purity (*sauca*) and impurity (*asauca*). Maintaining the purity of ritual fires and special areas that are out of bounds for laity is a hallmark of Vedic ritualism. In South Asia, Vedic Brahmans are not alone in this regard. Parsis are the remnant custodians in India of the once-powerful Zoroastrian imperial religion of Achaemenid Persia. Today their priests in Mumbai and elsewhere in India still wear white masks to avoid defiling the sacred fire. Lay Parsis, whose home altars burn incense as a form of domestic ritual fire, may not approach the temple fire. Their Vedic cousins, also descendants of third-millennium-BCE Indo-Iranian cults of fire and the sacred plant **sauma*[17] are equally concerned with protecting sacred fires from impurity. A significant difference, however, is that Zoroastrian tradition long ago turned to their famous Towers of Silence and birds of prey for disposal of the dead in order to avoid defiling fire with the pollution of death, whereas Vedic tradition retained an identification of sacrificer and fire, including final absorption by Agni via cremation.

To take just two examples of fire protection from Vedic practice, consider the necessity of setting fires, *adhana*, and undergoing ritual consecration prior to a *soma* sacrifice, the *diksa*. The reason given by many qualified Veda pandits for not performing *adhana*, or rekindling if there has been a lapse, is the lack of personal space, a house exclusively of one's own. What this means, when pressed for details, is that living in an apartment building or shared house means inability to control the transit of those who may be impure, quite specifically, menstruating women.[18] As for *diksa*, before performing *agni-stoma* or any later *soma* ritual both the sacrificer husband and co-sacrificer wife undergo a ritual equivalent of death and rebirth. This consecration of the couple provides access to the *maha-vedi* arena of sacrifice and renders them impervious to ritual pollutions until the concluding bath, including death pollution in the family or the onset of menses for the wife. If she menstruates, and considering that the *paundarika* is forty days in length she will do so if she has not reached menopause, there is no need for her to leave the sacrificial ground. All participants will be careful not to touch her as she goes on with her duties in a secluded corner, the *patni-sala*, but the ritual theoretically remains undamaged thanks to the protective canopy of *diksa*.

To return to the homology of sacrificers and fires, it is the case that the *agni-hotra* room of the house is an area set apart from profane time and space, just like the *diksa*-shielded home owners during extended rites. In fact, the three fires (*tretagni*) represent a cosmos—earth, midspace, and heaven—in a triadic symbolism as old as the first Veda. In Rg Veda 5.11.2 Agni is established on his "triple seat," the three altars. When a *srauta* ritual is scheduled, this threefold microcosm is projected out of the house to the east to form a macrocosmic world, a great field of fire (*agni-ksetra*). In the case of the several forms of *agni-cayana* this ritual work founds a new world, its east-west and north-south axes and triple representation of Agni entirely a magnification of the *agni-hotra* room. Agni is still there as priest while the deities arrive and depart. Offerings are still transformed by Agni and serve as constant agents of communication and connection.

Another powerful statement of the bond between sacrificers and fires concerns the pair of fire-kindling woods (*arani*) kept safely wrapped together by every *ahitagni* and *patni*. The rectangular lower block is placed firmly on the ground and a small hole in it receives the tip of the upper wood that is twirled rapidly on a connecting spindle until friction causes dry straw and sawdust to ignite. Figure 2.7 illustrates this churning of fire (*agni-manthana*). The act, a procreative one involving an upper male *arani* and lower female *arani*, requires two people, one standing to hold the grooved spindle in place, the other to sit and twirl it by pulling a cord back and forth in the grooves. Unless a guest *rtvij* is involved (as in the photo) the pair is, appropriately enough, husband and wife generating Agni. The *arani* are special wood from an *asvattha* tree, *Ficus religiosa*, found rooted in a crevice of a *sami* tree, *Mimosa suma*, and is prized for its hardness. In the case of transferring fire to another location there are mantras and mystical procedures to draw ghee-activated fire into the two *arani* after they are warmed over the *garha-patya*. A reverse procedure releases fire from

FIGURE 2.7. *agni-manthana*, "churning" of new fire with *arani* as fire-drill to ignite Agni, Sriramapuram 1987. The upper male wood fixed in a spindle is twirled with a rope, its drill point seated in the female block on the ground.

the *arani* onto kindling materials elsewhere. Alternatively, so tight is the Agni-sacrificer connection that fires may be mystically drawn up into the body of the sacrificer for the same ends. Thus in rare instances of traveling away from home, the sacrificer may take fires in three separate terra-cotta pots slung from cords, each carefully labeled *garhaptaya, daksinagni, ahavaniya*, or take only the *arani*, or last, assume them into his body.[19]

Just as Chapter 4, "Becoming a Veda," expands further on textual learning and application, so Chapter 6, "Becoming Agni," delves further into ritual life, both chapters drawing upon illustrations from the lives of Veda pandits presented in Chapter 3. In between, Chapter 5, "Becoming a Householder," addresses, among other concerns, the *samskara*, life-cycle rituals, including the funereal final passage. Chapter 6 provides a more detailed examination of *adhana* in which a symbolic five-fire arena is first established before it is reduced to a standard three.

2.5 *The Voices of* Ahitagni *and Other Veda Pandits*

In the next chapter, ten families are portrayed in capsule biographies of *ahitagni* or other exemplary Veda pandits. Most of these families are now or were for their productive years located in *agrahara* or *agrahara*-like villages in or near Konasima. All families have multigenerational connections to Konasima through marriage and other ritual activities, although one is established across the Vasistha-Godavari in West Godavari District and another is split between two pilgrimage temple towns. Pillars of these ten families include seven *ahitagni* and a smaller number of eligible and aspirant *ahitagni*. All of those discussed here are well known to Veda pandit society of coastal Andhra and some have the distinction of all-India honors in recognition of their achievements.

By the late 1980s the golden age of *srauta* activity in Konasima had passed. In continuing interviews for this book, a crucial research decision was made to remain in Konasima rather than jump to Krishna District more than a hundred miles by road to the west where the Dendukuris, Visnubhatlas, and other families appeared to maintain active *srauta* lives. Guntur and Nellore Districts were other possibilities. This resolution was based on several events. One was an initial attempt in November 1980 to observe a *srauta* ritual in Vijayawada, the major city in Krishna District. The sacrifice was mentioned in Konasima by Lanka Venkatarama Sastri who had a *rtvij* role ongoing for a number of days. After traveling there alone by train, walking to the suburban site, finding that Lanka was not there at the time, and then being asked by the sacrificer to leave, there was nothing to do but conduct an embarrassed retreat. The full and somewhat bizarre story did not emerge until some time later. Three years earlier the young American scholar Harold Arnold (the only one ever known to visit coastal Andhra) went to nearby Jujjuru to witness a *soma* sacrifice. While he sat observing the *paundarika,* the bamboo and straw mat *sadas* caught fire; he was labeled the cause of damage to the ritual and told to leave. Many years later the *ahitagni* Lanka mentioned this catastrophe caused by a *dora* and said mischievously "Was that *you?*"[20]

A second reason for remaining with the known pandits of Konasima resulted from a more fruitful but disconcerting revisit to Vijayawada, this time into the graciously accepting home of the Dendukuri *ahitagni* family. They were forthcoming with some details about their teaching and ritual lives, but mostly the occasion degenerated into a sales pitch and an opportunity to press for money that quickly became distasteful. Perhaps the negative reaction was due to long experience with Baballa, Lanka, Duvvuri Yajulu, Mitranarayana, and other Konasima *ahitagni* shunning of *veda-vikriya,* the selling of Veda, the undermining effect of associating religion and economic gain. And of course an additional reason for adherence to Konasima was a deepening affection for the Veda pandit families there and a conviction that their many robust voices deserved wider recognition. This is the subject of the next chapter.

3

A Selection of Ahitagni *and Other Veda Pandits in* Agrahara, *Villages, and Towns*

3.1 *The Sriramapuram* Agrahara

In an exploration of Veda pandit lives, diverse personalities and family histories become visible, each dense with narratives regarding pursuit of the twin goals: the absorption of Veda and the flowering of a chosen ritual life. The former contains the laborious joy of paying back the debt owed for that privilege by teaching sons, grandsons, younger brothers, and often those outside the immediate family. And each pandit portrays a special ritual past and hopeful future. Within every representation a wife figures creatively as helpmeet, maternal presence, and co-sacrificer. Then it is all the children, with special attention to Veda-trained sons, who enter narratives at every opportunity. Along with all the expected or unanticipated outlines, however, comes a variety of insights into life in India during the rapidly changing decades of the turn of the millennium, the 1980s, 1990s, and beyond the initial 2000 decade. An expanding economy with a cash basis, a burgeoning middle class, affirmative action for the lower classes, changes in transportation, new forms of communication including TV, then color TV and DVDs, cell phones, computers, motor vehicles. At the same time there are carry-overs of the old ways, for example, the delight of successfully arranged marriages and the agony of the dowry system that cripples financial and emotional well-being. This chapter allows the voices of a wide range of Vedic personalities to be heard.

The accomplishments of the pandits selected here are manifold; most are well respected in South India, one being famous in Vaidika circles throughout

India. And yet there is a striking lack of pretension in their statements, a modesty that flies in the face of their extraordinary achievements. Ethnographically speaking, their biographies are precious for they have largely escaped the attention of journalists and scholars alike, living in remote enclaves through the busy changing of the millennia that paid attention to the fading of the British Raj, two great wars followed by successive internecine wars in South Asia, and decades of political struggles within India itself, all widescreen panoramas with little note of a religious tradition that has lasted, by outside historical reckoning, over 3,700 years, and is by inside traditional accounting *anadi*, eternal.

Selected here are *ahitagni* and other Veda pandits, together with some wives and children, to illustrate the activities of Veda and *srauta* in the delta throughout the twentieth and into the current century. In many ways their life histories are extraordinary to non-Vaidika South Asian contemporaries in New Delhi, Nagpur, or Bangalore, not to mention contemporaries in Los Angeles, Paris, or Shanghai, for whom their daily activities are entirely unimaginable. In their own eyes they have led quite ordinary, if secluded and highly disciplined, existences. Their careers should be noted and "attention should be paid," especially to the old generation that is now almost entirely gone. Even for those families who continue a healthy transmission of Veda, if not *srauta*, there is a difference. A Veda pandit and *patni* of the present are not the same Vaidika presence as their grandparents of the early twentieth century, and clarifying this distinction is one of several aims of this study.

Presented in this chapter are glimpses of life in two *agrahara*, Sriramapuram and Nedunuru; two villages, Vyaghresvaram and Iragavaram; a city, Kakinada; and two small temple towns, Annavaram and Simhacalam. Such a broad spectrum allows the unity as well as the surprising diversity of Veda pandit life to shine through the changes of the period under study. The following individuals speak for the most part in their own words collected over a period of three and a half decades. Their lives unfold here not as precise historical biographies but rather as illustrations of one or another aspect of the Vedic tradition, as personifications of the routines, daily dramas, rigors, and aspirations of individuals, families, and small communities *vedam-lo*, "existing in Veda." Their voices will be heard briefly, with many lacunae, some oddities, some in more detail on certain subjects than others, as they provide glimpses of the changing scene of twentieth- and twenty-first century Vedic life.

This chapter provides more of the historical and textual details of Veda and *srauta*, as well as some specific highlights of *agrahara* life. The backdrop for these capsule biographies is intended to give them the brightness of life and authority. Even a small *agrahara* such as Sriramapuram, for example, harbored disparate sets of Brahman families during the course of this study, each governed by special sensitivities to rank, time, space, and ritual proclivities. There was an established hierarchy, with unpublished but careful ranks within the hierarchy: on a short lane with all families living within sight of one another there were *ahitagni*, other Veda pandits with differing degrees of accomplishment, and secular Brahmans. The *ahitagni*, at the top of the pecking order, included *nitya agni-hotrin* with active fires and twice-daily *agni-hotra*, but also those who because of physical incapacity allowed fires to lapse temporarily until the opportunity to rekindle. There were living pairs, invariably in declining years, whose fires permanently expired, and finally, *ahitagni* and *patni* widowers and widows whose hearths were erased after the death of the spouse, their *srauta* ritual lives then concluded (see Figure 0.6, Sriramapuram *agrahara* in 1987).

At the time of the first visit there were three families of *ahitagni* and *patni* living in Sriramapuram. When fires are active, the *ahitagni* and *patni* are bound in space to the threefold hearth and bound in time to performance of two or three baths daily, two *sandhya-vandana* daily, two *agni-hotra* daily, two *isti* monthly, and one *agrayana* annually. They have special relationships to Agni, Candra, *anna*, and Soma for those approaching or beyond *agni-stoma*. Those whose fires have lapsed may do mantra portions of *agni-hotra* without *kriya*, routine baths or "sponge baths" if unable to manage the river or canal, *sandhya-vandana* twice daily, and possible participation in *agrayana*. Widows are bound to the house; widowers are not. Teaching Veda pandits who are *an-ahitagni*, not *ahitagni*, are theoretically bound to the house for specified times of *adhyapana* and scheduled times for *parayana* if employed. For some, the two duties are combined while others may perform elsewhere since they are not bound in space or time to fires other than *smartagni*, the *grhya* fire, and personal programs of household worship. Finally, the majority of the families in the *agrahara* are *laukika* Brahmans with their own schedules of secular activities, including accountants, schoolteachers, and retirees. Except for personal vows and devotions, it is only the widows who have ritual restrictions.

The survey begins with Baballa, senior *ahitagni* during the early years of visits and a Veda-*bhasya* scholar beloved throughout the delta. (See Figure 3.1, Baballa and Sundari, Sriramapuram, 1987, and Figure 3.2, Baballa, age eighty-eight, Sriramapuram 1991.)

3.1.1 Bhamidipati Yajnesvara, "Baballa," 1903–1993

3.1.1.1 An Extraordinary Lineage

Like others in the *agrahara*, this was a household that kept no small pets, no cats, no dogs, only bovines. Therefore, when the *kurma* (tortoise) came to play

FIGURE 3.1. Bhamidipati “Baballa” and Sundari, Sriramapuram 1987.

FIGURE 3.2. Baballa, age eighty-eight, Sriramapuram 1991.

a role in a great *srauta* ritual, and stayed in the house for some days while all the preparations were underway, he—or perhaps she, no one was sure—became the target of everyone's affection. Baballa, sacrificer-to-be, found him irresistible and admired him daily. "For the ritual of placement we dug a hole, lined it with shells, let some honey drip onto his shell and placed him looking at the hole. Face to face with him I recited: 'You are not required here, you are free to go.' The altar bricks for the *aruna-ketuka* were laid in place above him. Next morning he was gone. He found the way out."

Bhamidipati Yajnesvara Somayaji, Srivatsa *gotra*, whose affectionate sobriquet "Baballa" is known all along coastal Andhra, is a good selection to begin this survey of recent and contemporary Veda pandits. Born in 1903, his life stretched across all but ten years of the twentieth century. And it was on the *arugu*, the open-air front steps of his house that most interviews in Sriramapuram were held, even for years after his death a few months short of his ninetieth birthday. His lineage was one of the most *ahitagni*-prolific families in nineteenth- and twentieth-century India. Baballa traced his ancestry back to the eighteenth century and the *mula-purusa*, root ancestor, Bhamidipati Brahmibuta Acarya. Brahmibuta became a *samnyasin*, a renouncer-ascetic, but not before producing a lineage that would become extraordinarily famous by any standard: Virabhadra Somayaji, Acchuta Rama Somayajulu, Yajnesvara Somayajulu, Chinna Subrahmanya Somayajulu, in that order of paternal ancestors, the last being Baballa's father. Baballa's mother was Kamesvara of the Akella Veda pandit family. This fifth-generation union created a sixth generation, six sons who all became *ahitagni*. Five became *soma* sacrificers, including Baballa, and the sixth very nearly joined them but died when his *agni-stoma* was in its planning stages. In the last few centuries, few if any families in India or Nepal have ever had six brothers performing *agni-hotra* at one time.

Baballa's astonishing lineage crashed abruptly when his only son, Subrahmanya Somayaji, with the nickname "Bullebbayi," suffered multiple congenital ailments and could not become an eligible Veda pandit. Neighbors, softly describing his disabilities, including lymphatic filariasis (elephantiasis, a painful disase that also infected his mother, Sundari), called him "somewhat innocent." A further blow was the death of his only daughter at the age of twenty days, a sad event never mentioned by Baballa. Bullebbayi had two sons—one, Somasekhara, given away in adoption to Baballa's younger brother; the other, Yajnesvara Prasad, producing three beautiful daughters but no son. The three girls are today the ninth generation of direct descendants of Brahmibuta, the eighteenth-century *samnyasin*.

Yajnesvara Prasad, a schoolteacher, and his wife Laksmi continue to live in the house at the head of the lane that has always been recognized as principal

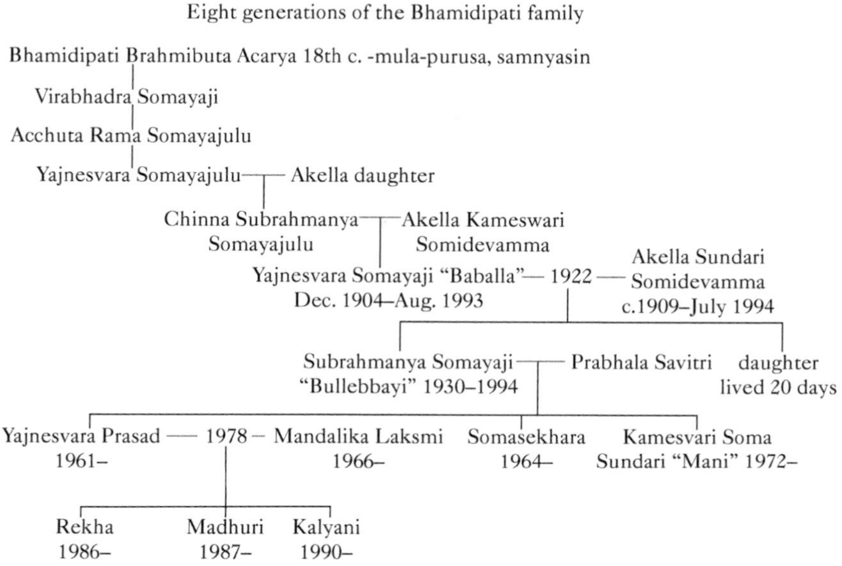
Eight generations of the Bhamidipati family
Bhamidipati Brahmibuta Acarya 18th c. -mula-purusa, samnyasin
Virabhadra Somayaji
Acchuta Rama Somayajulu
Yajnesvara Somayajulu
Akella daughter
Chinna Subrahmanya Somayajulu
Akella Kameswari Somidevamma
Yajnesvara Somayaji "Baballa" Dec. 1904–Aug. 1993
1922
Akella Sundari Somidevamma c.1909–July 1994
Subrahmanya Somayaji "Bullebbayi" 1930–1994
Prabhala Savitri
daughter lived 20 days
Yajnesvara Prasad 1961–
1978
Mandalika Laksmi 1966–
Somasekhara 1964–
Kamesvari Soma Sundari "Mani" 1972–
Rekha 1986–
Madhuri 1987–
Kalyani 1990–

TABLE 3.1. Eight generations of Bhamidipati genealogy

residence of the *agrahara*, the one that welcomes visitors. Table 3.1 is a simplified sketch of the Bhamidipati genealogy. All of these names are here pared down to essentials. For example, the full name of his grandson, born in 1961, that Baballa recited was Yajnesvara Venkata Satya Surya Rama Subrahmanya Somayaji. His was the seventh generation in a row to carry the hopeful honorific Soma-yaji, *soma*-sacrificer, and the second in succession to have that acclimation unrealized. It might be noted here that in marriages to boys who eventually become *soma* sacrificers, girls are known by personal names only until marriage. After that life-changing event no personal or family name is a referent, only the female equivalent of Soma-yaji, Somi-devamma.

Although born in Mukkamala, Baballa was raised in the nearby village of Irusumanda in the home of his maternal uncle, Akella Subha Avadhani, father of Sundari, Baballa's future bride, six years his junior. As youngsters they both attended the school in Irusumanda, Baballa to fourth class, when he could read and write Telugu by the age of nine, and Sundari to third class. When Sundari was twelve and Baballa eighteen, their five-day wedding took place as a *menarika* (cross-cousin) marriage, one that lasted for seventy-one years. They lived first in Mukkamala, then in Sriramapuram.

Baballa's father, famous for teaching many students, was guru not only for Baballa and his five brothers but also for the second Sriramapuram *ahitagni* featured in this survey, Duvvuri Yajulu. At that time there were as many as twenty local students of Veda pandits in Mukkamala, with others arriving from surrounding villages, some by sailboats gliding silently along the river channels, or smaller craft poled through canals, or punt ferries pulled by rope to connect one dirt track with another. Before there were metalled all-weather roads and eventual bus services it was faster to travel by water, usually with no more cost than hitching a ride on a bullock cart or horse tonga. Duvvuri Yajulu, arriving from Kapilesvarapuram, remembered Baballa's father being so deeply lost in reciting the Vedic text of the day that "we students would sneak away on calls of nature and he never noticed we were gone!"

Once he had completed the eighty-two *pannas*, Baballa's energies went into three enterprises: supervision of those crop fields in Gangalakurru he was eventually to inherit, the teaching of Veda to selected students, and continuous browsing into texts beyond the Taittiriya *sakha* he had mastered. His quest for knowledge was a lifelong pursuit, in Veda, *srauta*, Dharma-sastra, Mimamsa, Vedanta, Jyotisa, Vyakarana, and other genres. His hunger for the association of ideas never diminished. After our first unannounced encounter in October 1980, when he had been surprised at noon in the midst of textual studies, he said with genuine excitement and a sparkle in his eyes, "I was looking into *exactly* these subjects you suddenly came to inquire about!" He allowed that initial visit to blossom into an auspiciously destined event. For the second visit the greeting was as warm as for old and dear friends. Even in his latest years, with each visit an almost completely deaf Baballa would be discovered squinting at a book or palm-leaf manuscript held only inches from his glasses. And never did he lose his impish sense of humor.

Baballa thanked his father for providing him a life free from economic worries. "We were very fond of each other. He was a strict disciplinarian, tough on me. But he took care of everything, made sure I could give undivided attention to learning. I enjoyed that luxury and remember a youth as comfortable as swinging in a cradle." As to teaching, Baballa took on fewer students than his father but was known for dedication to those he accepted. At the height of his textual reciting career he had four students living in his house continuously learning Veda. He was the exclusive guru for grandson Prasad who learned all eighty-two *panna* from him during 1971 to 1980. Although he did not appear for his examination by the Parishad, Prasad, who became a schoolteacher in a nearby village in 1986, remembers going to the fields every day in his grandfather's footsteps, accompanied by one or another fellow student—Chirravuri Ramam, Sripada Manikya, Prabhala Krishnamurti, Samavedam Narayana (discussed later), and others who became Veda pandits well known throughout Konasima and other parts of Andhra. They would sit beside the rice paddy or under coconut palms for *adhyaya* and Baballa would take breaks from time to time to check on the field hands. Then they would return to the village for lunch and a review of the morning recitation. Baballa remained a hands-on "gentleman farmer" all his life until finally turning over supervision of the fields to Prasad at the close of the 1990s.

3.1.1.2 Examining Students

Perhaps it was the strict standards required by Baballa that intimidated his grandson-student and made Prasad nervous about appearing before the Parishad examiners. In the 1950s Baballa and his Veda pandit colleagues raised donations and established a trust fund to conduct an examination system for various genres of Vedic and Sanskrit learning, including Veda and *srauta*, first and foremost, but also *smarta*, *apara*, Agamas, Mimamsa, Vyakarana, and other subjects, with assemblies convened in Amalapuram, Rajahmundry, or various East Godavari District villages every year. In Vaisakha month 1987, for example, the village of Vyaghresvaram volunteered to be host and examinations were held for thirty students in Veda, four in *smarta*, and one in Agama, each of them assessed after eight to twelve years of study. Examinations in different texts and recitation patterns took place over a period of two days with the afternoon of the second day spent honoring successful students and established scholars. "For encouragement" each student who passed was given between Rs. 150 and 200 (about $3.75 to $5).

3.1.1.3 Fulfillment in Srauta

Baballa was well into his middle age, after many years' study of *srauta* and reflection on the family heritage with its multiple generations of *ahitagni*, before he seriously considered setting the fires. Nudges came from numerous colleagues and relatives. "As well as one's own commitment," he noted, "one needs confirmation from professional colleagues and the moral support of outsiders. Until I was openly prodded I did not have the courage to do it." He performed *adhana*, a ritual establishment of the three fires for daily *agni-hotra*, in 1959 at the age of fifty-five. Six months later came his *agni-stoma*, first *soma* sacrifice, known throughout Konasima as *yajna*. Lanka Venkatarama Sastri, his friend and highly respected Veda pandit neighbor a half hour's walk away in Nedunuru, was *adhvaryu*, executive priest. Lanka was himself preparing for his own *agni-stoma*.

Baballa's *yajna* initiated an intense period of *srauta* and other rituals that was to last five years, as if the sheer weight of his lineage had suddenly energized him. "I wanted to accomplish without fail all the rituals performed by all my ancestors." After *agni-stoma* came the *sravana pasu* animal sacrifice in the month of Sravana. In Bhadrapada month 1960 he performed *aruna-ketuka*, the construction of a fire altar composed of symbolic "bricks" in the form of water offerings. This sacrifice with his pet tortoise he always described as his favorite and one that both his father and father's older brother had done. For this he did *madhu-kara* for twelve days, a symbolic year of begging for food from house to house as if he had been returned to his youthful *brahmacarin* days. The *catur-masya*, four-monthly sacrifices, were also fulfilled, as was the ritual of the new rice harvest, the *agrayana*, a performance that Baballa and Sundari were to manage in Phalguna month every year through 1990 when he was eighty-seven and she was eighty-one. In 1991, when both were frail and quite deaf, it was regretfully omitted from their ritual schedule for the first time. By then it had been the pattern for some years to allow the *agni-hotra* fires to lapse and then be rekindled for twice-daily offerings and two lunar *isti* bracketing the *agrayana*, a procedure detailed in Chapter 6.

It is not surprising that Baballa also embarked upon lengthy rituals known as *naksatra* or *pavitra* offerings (*isti*). Throughout Andhra, people suffering misfortunes have recourse to temples housing shrines of the *nava-graha*, the nine planets. If Sani (Saturn), for example, appears in a horoscope, his temple in Mandapalli, within walking distance of Sriramapuram, is the place for most people—Hindus, Muslims, and Christians included—to transfer Sani's *dosa*, evil effect, onto a Siva *linga* or onto a special Brahman ritualist who has the temerity to unload it from himself. Baballa did not go to Mandapalli or worship *nava-graha* elsewhere. Vaidika Brahmans have older, and in their eyes more powerful, resources in offerings to twenty-eight *naksatra*, constellations or "star markers." The *naksatra isti*, some forty days in duration, was among other substantial rituals accomplished by Baballa in that energetic period in Mukkamala before and after 1960.

His colorful descriptions of details brought them to life. "The *yajamana* must not touch the bricks of the *cayana* without first undergoing *diksa*. Otherwise he will be burned by Agni like an electrician touching a hot wire without gloves." And with regard to his *agni-stoma*: "Putting *soma* into the fire makes one a *soma-yaji*, and then one travels in a well-grooved path, like a cart moving easily along a track, not like one on an untrodden field."

3.1.1.4 The Move to Sriramapuram

In 1962 Baballa and Sundari were granted a small plot in Sriramapuram across the Billakurru Canal and westward a few hundred yards, almost within hailing distance of the old house. They spent their entire lives within sight of this stream that Baballa, a believer in the Sapta-Godavari mental map, endowed with the name Kausika, that is, the great *rsi* Visvamitra. The donation included money to build a house with an *agni-hotra* room and an acre of cropland with an assured yield of fifteen bags of paddy, unhusked rice. Because of their reputation as open-armed host and hostess for *ahitagni* and other Veda pandits, they were given the roadside plot facing the lane, the better to welcome guests immediately on arrival. Since *ahitagni* may safely take food and drink only from the kitchen of the wife of another *ahitagni*, their house became the natural stopover for those participating in *sabha* (assemblies) in Mukkamala, Sriramapuram, or sometimes Vyaghresvaram.[1]

As mentioned in Chapter 2, the Tirupati-Tirumalai Devasthanam (TTD), the administrative body of the famous temple of Venkatesvara, in cooperation with the Department of Religious Endowments of the state government of Andhra Pradesh, made a major commitment to underwrite Veda teaching, *srauta* ritual, and a heightened public awareness of Vedic tradition. Their projects transformed the lives of Veda pandits in much of South India. With enormous wealth and extensive power in India not unlike that of the Vatican in Rome, the TTD distributes to Veda pandits monthly stipends, pensions, and honoraria and employs them for daily *parayana* (recitation) in temples, not to be heard and repeated by students, but rather to be heard formally by honored resident deities and informally by worshippers passing through. This belongs, of course, to a modern tradition in which public hearing of the sacrosanct Veda became open to the non-twice-born communities.

When invited repeatedly by the TTD to take on a *parayana* position, or at least accept an honorarium, Baballa bellowed his response: "*Not* for *ahitagni*!" To take remuneration of any kind, he argued, would be *veda-vikraya*, the selling of the Veda, an atrocious sin. He was *aparigraha*, not taking honoraria, *dana*, gifts. But the TTD enrolled him in its pension plan anyway and also extended its largesse to his unemployable son. Baballa's fierce independence regarding things monetary extended to the interview situation as well, for which he would never accept an honorarium. If a traditional silk or wool shawl was presented to him he would laugh aloud and say "Oh, this must be for (the god) Dattatreya!" and give it to someone else.

Perhaps more than any other Veda pandit Baballa expressed affection for the local people and an awareness of their beliefs. At one time, out of interest in the fourteenth-century Advaita scholar, Vidyaranya, author of the Pancadasi and other works in the school of Sankara, he thought of establishing a shrine by the bathing platform on the Kausika, just across the road from his house, accessible to all for *japa* but not inside the *agrahara*. Then he became aware that not many knew about Vidyaranya. On the other hand, Dattatreya, son of the great *rsi* Atri, was quite popular. Baballa did not give credence to local folklore that a living incarnation of Dattatreya resided not far away in the Sripada family, but he thought the original god, the amalgamation of Brahma, Visnu, and Siva, deserved a home near the *agrahara*. "All three will be here and people belonging to any of them can worship together." When it was pointed out that Dattatreya is not a Vedic god he broke into his one-tooth grin, "Ah, yes, but Visnu is in the *garhapatya*, Siva in the *daksinagni*, and Brahma in the *ahavaniya*," knowing full well that the local folk knew nothing of these terms and had never seen his *agni-hotra* room. A donor was located and in 1987 the little Dattatreya shrine was founded with mantras and *homa* into a newly rope-churned fire. Baballa also wished to acquire land in order to plant auspicious trees, the *marri, medi, ravi*, and *vepa*, in particular, so that folk in the region could come and worship them and thereby acquire boons.

Baballa was a special person, an independent rustic, witty, good-humored, and earthy. He was always modest, fair-minded, not at all intimidating or threatening yet clearly most senior of the local pandits, even when nearly stone deaf. In America he would be known as a cracker-barrel philosopher, a source of down-home wisdom laced with wisecracks and folklore. A senior colleague described him as a *maha-purusa* (great human) who always replied from knowledge and experience and never hesitated to respond to a query: "Anyone who came to him, young or old, Brahman or Pancama (Scheduled Caste), received his blessing. In my long experience he was always there for others, never self-preoccupied."

Visits to Sriramapuram were occasions for the Veda pandits to gather on Baballa's *arugu*, sometimes even interrupting teaching sessions. They quickly became mini-*sabha* of vigorous debate on every conceivable subject, Baballa acting as moderator-sage, providing balance and well-rounded discussion, pulling others back from confrontational remarks or the occasional wild theory. For example, disparaging comments on Scheduled Caste encroachment or Christian baptisms in the sacred river would be truncated by Baballa as senior scholar: "Hmm, yes, I know about that, but . . ." and the original topic would come back into focus. Baballa was ahead of his time in accomodating cheerfully to the new multiculturalism of Indian society and he had a knack for countering discrimination with softly stated reason and tolerance.

In the eyes of the visitor from abroad Baballa was a precious and invaluable link to an age that has virtually disappeared. It was not only that he spoke from the old chronology ("I was born in the year *krodhi* on the fourth of the bright half of Margasirsa-*masa* and I was married in the year *dundubhi* in the bright half of Jyestha-*masa* . . ."). It was his stubborn resistance to certain changes that allowed him to perpetuate a measure of the nineteenth-century traditionalism of his father and other gurus. Stolidly ensconced in the ritual and dharma of the old school, he was less amenable than others to accommodate to some modern ways. At the same time, his mulishness extended to certain normative *srauta* procedures. For one, he steadfastly refused priestly roles in the *srauta* rituals of others. Only once did he deviate from that vow and that was in reciprocity for his own earlier *yajna* conducted by Lanka. In Lanka's *agni-stoma* he accepted the minor *sadasya* role, the seventeenth priest who assists the *brahman.*

Several justifications were offered regarding his refusals to participate as a ritualist. First, he was guided by his *aparigraha* stance of "non-acceptance" of gratuities for anything connected with Veda. Just as he never accepted *daksina* from a student for *adhyapana* so he could not acquire the cash *daksina* a *rtvij* necessarily receives from the sacrificer in order to complete the ritual. Both would be, as Baballa construed it, Veda for sale. Accepting a donation of land and house was one thing, money for reciting Veda or performing *srauta* quite another.

But also he refused *rtvij* roles because of specific apprehensions, the dreaded negative consequences from performing alongside inadequately trained younger colleagues. Like many senior Veda pandits he was alarmed at lapses in traditional teaching methods, relaxed examination standards, and innovations such as the use of printed books for students to review by reading what had been learned *guru-mukha,* from the mouth of the guru. He feared imprecision in the *kriya* (ritual acts) employing mantras imperfectly interiorized, since the results of those *kriya* could inflict personal as well as cosmic damage. Therefore he was reluctant to join a company of *rtvij* whose training, credentials, and moral integrity were not entirely known to him. On several occasions he spoke about the dangers of *soma-bhaksana,* drinking *soma,* in the company of unfamiliar pandits. Times had changed since his childhood when the accomplished Bhamidipati family alone could supply the eighteen *rtvij* necessary for an *agni-stoma,* if not all seventy-two for a *sarvato-mukha.*

In part, Baballa's disavowal was simple concern over the recent lack of obeisance to patterns of the old school. "What kind of Brahman is he whose *upanayana* was completed in one hour (instead of the traditional four or five days)?" he would inquire of the long shadow of a coconut palm. But perhaps more important was the thought of dark consequences born out of experience and the instruction of elders such as his *ahitagni* guru Bulusu Somayajulu. "Just as a person who does not know precisely how to perform *abhicara* (the use of mantras in spells) can be killed by it, so the consequences can be extremely dangerous from improper sacrifice of animals. Animal sacrifice is not the simple matter its critics and the common people say."

The awe with which he regarded "ritually precarious situations," his phrase for the *pasu-bandha*, was matched on a different track by mystical experiences during *agni-hotra*. Just as he was one of the few to speak casually and without affectation of the hazardous practices of *abhicara*, so was Baballa a rare window into the transformative spiritual side of a ritual life. In choppy, emotionally charged phrases, hands gesturing to animate the inexpressible, he would at times confide details of certain wondrous moments of great impact. "One day while performing *agni-hotra* something very special happened, something luminous, with brilliance (*tejassu*), arose from the *homa* and appeared before my eyes. Then my daughter-in-law conceived and was blessed with a male child." At another time while offering into the *ahavaniya* fire "a four-armed figure (*catur-bujudu*) appeared. Why? I tried to imagine! Well, a second grandson was on the way!"

3.1.1.5 A Funeral to Remember

These emotional revelations out of mystical contexts of Agni, his refusal of *daksina* as guru, *rtvij*, or TTD "employee," his fear of drinking *soma* in the wrong company, all mark Baballa a member of an older stratum of the Vaidika elite that is scarcely present today. "After Baballa," said Samavedam, his next-door neighbor for over three decades, "there is no other." Baballa broke his hip in a fall June 1, 1993, and lay dying on *darbha* grass on a cot, another cot nearby holding his only son dying of cancer. Baballa, fully conscious, longed for his *antyesti*, the "last sacrifice" of his body to be first so that Bullebbayi could perform *sraddha* to advance him into a proper and orderly rebirth after a sojourn with his father and earlier ancestors. He received his wish and died at 10 AM on August 6, less than six months before the death of his sixty-four-year-old son on New Year's Day 1994.

Being an *ahitagni*, the *brahma-medha* funeral was requisite, a special three-hour cremation via the three *agni-hotra* fires along with all ritual implements save those used in re-burning the pulverized bones in another special rite for *soma* sacrificers, the *punar-dahana*. Both of these funeral rites are described at the end of Chapter 6, along with *losta-citi*, a replication of the *agni-cayana* fire altar on the spot of cremeation. For some younger members of Vedic families living in Sriramapuram, Nedunuru, and Vyaghresvaram, this was the first *brahma-medha* they had witnessed, but later in the same decade more were to follow as local *ahitagni* couples were reduced: Duvvuri Yajulu's wife, Surya, and Pullela's wife, Kamesvari, in 1996, Bulusu Cayanulu in 1997, Lanka in 1999.

The day of death and beginning of *asauca*, ritual impurity, are reckoned not from the moment of biological death of an *ahitagni*, but rather from the occurrence of *brahma-medha* and ultimate interiorization of Agni. Baballa requested from his deathbed that nothing be done with his body until the arrival of Ramam, who was at that time teaching in Pune, Maharashtra. After a telegram reached him it took Ramam a day and a half on the train to reach Rajahmundry, with a taxi down to Sriramapuram. For those steamy August days, Baballa's long frail body lay stretched across blocks of ice just outside his *agni-hotra* room, a body, ritually and legally speaking, not yet dead.

Ramam and the others immediately took out Baballa's *arani* kindling sticks and recreated fire in the *garhapatya* and then transferred embers to the *ahavaniya* and *daksinagni* until the final time when fires burned in all three hearths. A final *isti* in the house was completed and *prayascitta*, expiatory rituals as recompense for *agni-hotra, isti*, and an *agrayana* that could not be performed in the last days of Baballa's and Sundari's incapacitation. Embers from each hearth were then dropped into *kunda*, terra-cotta pots slung from cords, each marked "g," "a" or "d" in Telugu letters. A fourth pot was marked for the *aupasana* household fire. These were carried in front of the body out the door and down the path by the terminally ill son, Bullebayi, who required support to walk, as did the quite feeble widow, Sundari. Grandson Prasad was that crutch for both until he had to turn back at the *polimera*, the sacred boundary. His own father, Bullebayi, was still living and he, Prasad, could therefore not participate in Baballa's funeral. Embers from Baballa's three hearths were now transferred a final time onto his body, the *ahavaniya* offering fire beside his head, the *daksinagni* beside his chest, the *garha-patya* cooking fire by his right thigh, each igniting straw that then set wood alight. Within three hours Baballa's body was no more, his *agni-hotra* fires having burned together and conjoined as Agni.

Brahma-medha, punar-dahana, and *lost-aciti* are rarely performed rituals beyond the expertise of local *apara* Brahmans who supervise the last rites of *laukika* Brahmans and non-Brahmans. Even if they knew or had access to the texts, however, it is considered risky to call them into service because of their unclean status. For Baballa, an *apara* Brahman of good reputation, Akondi Suryanarayana, was brought from Amalapuram to conduct the normal rituals from cremation through the twelfth day. On the thirteenth day, however, the bone collection (*asthi-samcayana*), special re-cremation (*punar-dahana*), and layout of a *losta-citi* constructed of blocks of mud bricks (*istaka*) were in the hands of Chirravuri Ramam, Baballa's longtime student and spiritual "son," with Duvvuri Yajulu and Bulusu Cayanulu assisting from the Pitr-medha Sutras. Most of these *kriya* and mantras, being unfamiliar ones, were directed by reading the text, but from time to time well-known mantras would surface and allow the officiating troupe to relax into customary rhythms. Ashes with fragments of bones and teeth had been collected a day after cremation and now a portion was ground on two natural stones found at the cremation ground, mixed with ghee, and reburned in order to obliterate all traces of *soma*.

There was no need to save the remainder of his ashes for the Ganga, said the elders; his beloved flowing Kausika is where they belong. Back at the house the *ayatana* clay fire pits were scraped away two weeks after the *sapindi-karana* ritual that advanced Baballa's *preta* to the status of *pitr*, ancestor. Baballa's necessary monthly rites, *masikas*, were done by Bullebayi only four times, the last on the morning he himself died. It was quite difficult to convince Sundari, Bullebayi's mother, that her son was gone since she was completely deaf and her eyesight too feeble to read signs devised for her. She insisted that he was sleeping. Sundari died in July and daughter-in-law Savitri, in her white widow's garb, became resigned to the sudden absence of two generations from the well-visited house on the corner of the road.[2]

3.1.1.6 The Extended Family

The house at the head of the lane is still a local resource, one sought out by folk in need of *muhurta* and *dharma-sandeha* responses, the former being determination from a *pancanga* astrological manual of the correct "hour" for a particular ceremony, the latter being answers to "doubts about the law." Previously it was Baballa who was the respected authority. Now it is his grandson, Yajnesvara Prasad. From his grandfather Prasad learned all eighty-two *panna* of Taittiriya until age nineteen, at the same time pursuing studies for a bachelor of science degree. A bachelor of education degree followed and he accepted a teaching post close to Sriramapuram. Earlier, in 1978, he had been married to Laksmi Narasakanta from Palakollu when he was seventeen and she was twelve. When Laksmi came of age she was welcomed to Sriramapuram as a lively girl of astonishing beauty, and there was hope of resumed continuity in a Vedic *srauta* heritage. In a few years she gave birth to three successive daughters, Rekha, Madhuri, and Kalyani, whose screams and yelps at play rang down the dusty lane. But there were only daughters, and with the third came a medical report, tragic for any Hindu but devastating for a Vaidika lineage, that she could bear no more children. The Brahmibuta-Baballa legacy was closed.

Yajnesvara Prasad, a gentle, always affable man, and no doubt a compassionate and effective mentor for youngsters, teaches Telugu, math, sciences, and social studies to pupils age six to eleven. Except for Telugu all his subjects are regarded as "English education," *huna-vidya*. Prasad does not speak English but nevertheless advances the curricula of the foreign occupiers of India. On the other hand, more palatable to his elders, he serves as secretary for the Godavari Mandala Veda Parishad in nearby Amalapuram as his contribution to Vaidika society. In his youth he accepted *rtvij* roles, *hotr* in local *agrayana*, for example, but that was years ago. He still recites, but without real authority, in a tentative, almost listless voice. Although he has had encouragement to go further he admits that for him the *srauta* life of his forbears is an unlikely prospect. (See Figure 3.3, Yajnesvara Prasad and Laksmi with daughters Rekha, Madhuri, and Kalyani, Sriramapuram, 2005.)

It was Prasad who described many of the subtler aspects of Baballa's life since it was his *tata-garu*, grandfather, rather than his father who was the true *adhi-kara*, authority, for his upbringing, and Baballa's counsel bore something close to divine imprint in the mind of the youth. Now living in the house constructed by Baballa he is daily reminded of his grandfather's life. Prasad related that Baballa knew every detail of *smarta* rituals but never once performed one. It was Bulusu Cayanulu, another *ahitagni* in the *agrahara*, who served as family *purohita* in a hereditary role going back to Baballa's great-great-grandfather.

FIGURE 3.3. Bhamidipati Yajnesvara Prasad, Baballa's grandson, with Laksmi and daughters Rekha, Madhuri, and Kalyani, Sriramapuram 2005.

Baballa and Sundari understood the needs of *ahitagni* who came to the area for *sabha*, marriages, and other events, so for more than twenty years from the 1970s to 1990s they went to Mukkamalla for forty days in Sravana and Bhadrapada, taking food cooked in Sundari's kitchen for guests who could not eat in non-*ahitagni* houses. And it was Prasad who revealed what Baballa had said of the scholar from America in those early visits in the 1980s: "He is one of us," said Baballa, "and has more interest in Vedic tradition than people here. For some *samsara* reason he was destined to be born elsewhere. But he belongs to our country, our region, our place. To disseminate our tradition he was born in that faraway country."

The extended family might also be said to include Chirravuri Srirama Sarma, "Ramam," Baballa's prize pupil, without whom he said his funeral should not proceed. Ramam assisted his guru for years with routine *isti* and with him studied Veda, Mimamsa, Vyakarana, and Tarka. He was interviewed when he was visiting Baballa in Sriramapuram and also in his own home in Rajahmundry while he was teaching Sanskrit courses in the Government Oriental College. For three years, including the time that Baballa died, he held a teaching position at Pune University but found scholarly life there not to his liking. "People in Pune do research and write books of no practical value to society." The affection between Baballa and Ramam was palpable and in obvious ways the latter was more than the spiritual descendant in the *guru-sisya* relationship; he was the son Baballa did not have. Although Baballa did not remark on it, Ramam's decision to enter a *laukika* career as a Sanskrit rather than a Veda pandit must have been a painful one.

Ramam has his own pragmatic agenda for the significance of the Vedas and will hold forth seated cross-legged on a high square stool for as long as three hours at a stretch. He is convinced that ancient sciences were central in the Vedas and somehow through "a break in the *sampradaya*" this knowledge was lost. "We must recover that wisdom and experiment with it." He shares with some Native American Indians a belief that all the mineral, herbal, and animal resources of the planet are sufficient to solve global problems if only humans recognize and coordinate them. Passionately he wishes to establish a "Center for Research in the Sciences of Ancient India" to mine the Vedas for cures of disease and other misfortunes—leprosy, leukoderma, deafness ("cured with application of seven types of earth, including clay from an ant-hill"), snakebite ("for a cure one needs first to know if it is a Brahman, Ksatriya, Vaisya, or Sudra snake"), fever, heart disease, tuberculosis ("derived from contact with women"), gray hair, wayward satellites in space, and on and on. At the time of the Bhopal Union Carbide disaster he reported that eyesight damaged by poison gases had been restored when Veda pandits recited mantras while pouring ghee into a sacrificial fire. Aside from these views, eccentric even to many within the tradition, Ramam has taught at least one son and thereby provided a measure of continuity from the mouth of guru Baballa into the future.

The loss of Baballa had a profound effect on the four remaining *ahitagni* in the Sriramapuram, Nedunuru, Vyaghresvaram circle as they recognized their own advanced years and the lack of replacements in succeeding generations. Only one of the four had a son who might some day qualify to set the fires. There was much discussion of Baballa's sagacity, quick wit, and remarkable ability to see through ephemera to the reality at hand. Once as he passed by when the *dora* was interviewing Duvvuri Yajulu he remarked affably "What's happening?" "Oh, nothing much," replied Yajulu, "just discussing the texts." In mock horror Baballa immediately retorted, "What do you mean *just* the texts! *You* are the text!"

3.1.2 Duvvuri Yajulu (1915–2005) and His Descendants

When Baballa and Sundari, with son Bullebayi and his wife Savitri and their one-year-old son Prasad, moved to the new *agrahara* known as Sriramapuram, their neighbor across the lane was a younger man who had been offering *agni-hotra* twice daily for some seventeen years, the last seven of them in a newly built Sriramapuram house. This *ahitagni* was Duvvuri Yajnesvara Paundarika Yajulu, born in Kapilesvarapuram in 1915, another Veda pandit with a long and colorful family history of Veda and *srauta*. "Yajulu" is a Telugu personal name, short for *soma-yajulu*, Sanskrit *soma-yajin*, *soma*-sacrificer. Since it occurs as a name in several other families, Duvvuri Yajulu will serve to distinguish him later on, whereas here in this brief sketch he will be simply Yajulu. His *gotra* was Atreya. He possessed a generous spirit and had kind words even for those whom other pandits disparaged.

The author spent more time with Yajulu and his descendants than with members of any other of the ten extended families in this account. Long conversations with him occurred from October 1980 to March 2005, by which date he had almost entirely lost his memory and was to live only four more months until his death at the age of ninety. During the span of interviews, four generations of Duvvuris flourished, including three of certified Veda pandits and the hope of a fourth generation committed to Veda. In 1980, Yajulu's Veda pandit third son was twenty-seven; by 2000 that third son's first son, Phani, was already *ghana-pathi* and had a four-year-old son nearing *upanayana*. The *ahitagni* status of Yajulu and his father and brother, however, is not currently

FIGURE 3.4. Duvvuri Yajulu and family on his sixtieth birthday, 1975. Seated center right, Surya on Yajulu's left; sons one to five extend from his right hand. Five daughters and four daughters-in-law stand behind, grandchildren sit in front. Courtesy D. Surya Prakasa via D. Girija Sankar.

manifest by any Duvvuri. Eligibility for such has been barely maintained and the sons of the *ghana-pathi* grandson taught by Yajulu are no longer candidates for some future attempt at perpetuating the *srauta* lineage. On his sixtieth birthday when the family photo (Figure 3.4) was taken, Yajulu could not have suspected that in 2014, of all the gathered male descendants only one would retain both eligibility and any future desire for *srauta*, an obviously squirming Phani on the lap of Yajulu's third son, Surya Prakasa Avadhani. Surya Prakasa declared in 2014 that he and Kanaka Durga have abandoned plans to set fires and begin *agni-hotra*. Phani's two boys have chosen English education.

3.1.2.1 Veda

To Yajulu, Veda was transmitted first by his father for four years at home, then for another five years in Mukkamala by Baballa's father, Chinna Subrahmanya Somayajulu. After examinations he then went in succession to his older sister's husband in Korumilli, to Vyaghresvaram, and to Tanuku westward across the river, all for *srauta* and other subjects before completing his formal Vedic education at age twenty-four in 1939. By that time he was already married, father of a son and a daughter, and teaching Veda while still a student in *srauta*. "I was illiterate and could not sign my name," he recalls, perhaps with a prideful ounce of exaggeration. "Reading and writing I acquired in the course of time. I never went to school. There was no activity other than Veda." On another occasion Yajulu explained one source of his early commitment: "My grandfather was a *militant* Vaidika!"

One of his prized early accomplishments was correct recitation of "*svasti*," the *svasti-vacana*, Rg Veda 1.89 to the Visvedevas, in *krama*, *ghana*, and *jata*. "One who can recite *svasti* flawlessly is considered to be a *vira*, a hero." Group *svasti* fascinated him. "There is a special spirit generated by performing together. Once we all went from Sriramapuram together with our wives to recite *svasti* for twenty-seven days in Hyderabad. That was a wonderful time!" On another occasion he noted that "because I had to move out of my home village to many other places for the sake of Vedic learning I could not be a farmer and look after our lands. So I could never be like my neighbor Lanka (another *ahitagni*), an active farmer for fifty years."

3.1.2.2 Srauta

Grandson of an *ahitagni*, son of an *ahitagni*, younger brother of an *ahitagni*, disciple of Baballa's *ahitagni* father: it is not surprising, therefore, to hear Yajulu say in his sightless old age "I lived my entire life in the *srauta* tradition. I knew nothing other than this!" Untrue, of course, as his command of Veda was such that even though totally blind and dependent on others to walk a hundred steps to bathe in the river, he was still teaching one grandson at a time at age eighty-six, longer than any Veda pandit in this survey. (See Figure 2.4, a blind Duvvuri Yajulu teaching grandson Kirin, Sriramapuram 2000.)

His devotion to *agni-hotra*, however, did indeed come early. He noted a traditional division of life into three stages: prime, middle age, and old age. "As a rule, *yajna* should be performed when one attains age thirty-three, the beginning of the middle years. By sixty-one, the beginning of the 'immobile' (*sthavara*) years of old age, one's legs and hands may not be in control to maintain ritual procedures." By Yajulu's criteria, therefore, Baballa had barely slipped into *agni-hotra* in time and he himself was ahead of schedule, performing *agni-stoma* at age thirty in 1945, the earliest of the *ahitagni* in this survey with one exception. A decade later, in 1955, Yajulu's nephew Mitranarayana established the fires and accomplished *yajna* at age twenty-two.

The *adhana* and *agni-stoma* for Yajulu were both in Kapilesvarapuram, the village of his birth. He had to prod his older brother to do them first so that he could follow. Four years later, in 1949, he accomplished *agni-cayana* in the cow pasture of Kapilesvarapuram designated for great *srauta* sacrifices. Again he inspired the older brother to go first. During the years between his *cayana* and the forty-day extended form of *agni-cayana* known as *paundarika* in 1969 there were always *rtvij* for his routine *isti* and *agrayana*. As his sons grew into manhood they were recruited into roles at new and full-moon offerings.

At one point Yajulu himself was *rtvij* in a *paundarika* and decided then and there he would like to perform his own. From that moment it remained a fascination in all its details and co-opted any formal interest in *sastra*. Thirty years after that sacrifice he still loved to muse over a feature at a time. For example, in response to a query on the textual requirement of the *maha-vrata* portion of the *paundarika*, sexual intercourse on the *antar-vedi*, the coupling of a *brahma-carin*, a Vedic student under a vow of celibacy, and a hired *pumscali*, prostitute, he circled around this transgressive act meant to arouse mysterious powers of fertility, and found a deft and clever way to excuse it.

On the *arugu* of Baballa's house rather than his own, Yajulu was always affable, welcoming, and a genial conversationalist. Only once did his *arugu* net a visit and that was after Surya died. The view through the open door to the Tulsi fort in the courtyard was memorable: a white *agni-hotra* cow and a black buffalo calf munching hay in the waning sunlight. Guarded, shrewd, even crafty are perhaps also accurate depictions of Yajulu. He did not have Baballa's open personality. Much was offered in long conversations, but some things were withheld, particularly with regard to certain details of *srauta* life. About forthcoming rituals he was even duplicitous, but then so were many others, those cards being held close to the vest, perhaps for fear of saying something in error.

A good illustration of his harbored privacy was revealed by his grandson, Sita Ram Sastry, who had been along on a visit to nearby Vyaghresvaram. The *ahitagni* Bulusu Kamesvara and wife Satyavati (described below in this chapter) were immediately happy to have their *agni-hotra* hearths photographed. Yajulu was shocked to hear this from his grandson. "To show my *agni-hotra* room to others, that would be like lifting my mother's skirts!" That outburst made understandable the fact that during twenty-five years his *arugu* was too intimate a space for interviews, too close to invisible sacred hearths, even when they were finally cold. His personal ritual life was, to use his word, *rahasya*, secret. And his wife, Surya Somidevamma, was not to be seen.

Exaggerated praise is common currency in Telugu conversation and routine wisdom effectively discounts it. There is something defensive in the employment of relentless flattery of an interlocutor. With Yajulu, who identified the *dora* as "a second Maxmuller," or a Mahatma, or "a mine of knowledge," without a hint of sarcasm, it was wise to be wary and remain untrapped. And yet he always maintained a respectful ear to each query. Many years after our first meeting in 1980, the same grandson described how he frequently recounted that occasion when the American, upon hearing that he had done *cayana*, asked "*Which cayana*?" "My God," thought Yajulu to himself, "how many kinds are there! I'd better study them!"

3.1.2.3 Marriage

Marriage was a topic that Yajulu frequently inserted into discussions, sometimes as philosophical reflection, sometimes while marveling at the cultural changes in the passage of four generations. His own marriage of sixty-seven years to Surya (1922–96) was by all indications a fulfilling one, and with ten children as evidence, a creative one at that. His view of the marital union in general was always a lofty, highly positive one. In the context of marriage he spoke of *paramartha*, the highest truth, *sraddha*, faith, and even *brahma-loka*, the heaven of Brahma. And he saw a kind of sacred joy for the entire community in the drama of the ceremony. On one occasion he spoke of husband and wife coming to know one another in truth. "In the *vivaha* the groom looks at the bride, sees her in a profane way, sees whether or not she has fair skin, whether or not clothing covers her body. He may glance at her a hundred times during the five-day ceremony. But that is not *seeing*!" It takes considerable time, he insisted, to arrive at truly *seeing* this partner for life.

Unlike Baballa, who knew his cousin Sundari in childhood, Yajulu had not met his bride before the wedding when she was seven and he was "about thirteen or fourteen." His father and uncle arranged the union with a girl from across the Gautami-Godavari in the isolated village of Nedunuru, well off roads and navigable waterways. She was a distant relative so it was not a cross-cousin marriage. "Those five days were wonderful," recalled Yajulu of the festival more than half a century before. "My wife's father cooked, not her mother! And *mithayi*, special sweets, were served. Those were *pavitra* (sacred, pure) days. I was given a dowry of 116 silver rupees. My brother-in-law carried them in a cloth over his shoulder. In those days a rupee was two and a half *tola* of silver. Also I received a crimson silk *panca* (lower garment) and my sisters each got a gold sovereign worth Rs. 13 each. My father spent Rs. 200 on jewelry for the bride, waistband, necklace, bangles."

It was Yajulu who explained how the husband is guru to a wife, instructing her in the necessary mantras for their ritual life together. "There are special mantras for women, many of them. Only these are to be recited," as he quoted in full the Sutra authority. After sixteen years of marriage, when he had decided upon a date for *yajna*, he taught her the *agni-stoma* mantras. And it was Yajulu who expressed many years later, some four years after she died, that mystery of how she, a *somi-devamma*, obtained *soma* and why her cremated bones had to be reburned in a special ritual. An *ahitagni's* wife, he said, does not drink *soma* but receives the power of this bone-binding sacred plant by eating the food left-overs, the *ucchista*, of her husband.

It was a fruitful marriage, beginning with a son and a daughter before Yajulu had finished his formal education at the age of twenty-four. "My wife delivered fourteen times, always in our house. For four rupees a Yerukala tribal woman came as midwife. Medicines in those days were simple, inexpensive, easy to get." Yajulu never mentioned the four children who did not survive, and Surya was never permitted to appear for an interview although requests were made. Always he spoke with great pride in numbers, five sons, five daughters. "Once when I was visiting in Hyderabad a woman learned that I had ten children and she came in reverance to touch my feet." In an interview in 1996 the tape recorder was drowned out by a tribe of whooping children. "Seems like every pandit in the *agrahara* has twenty grandchildren," ventured the *dora*. "Oh, many more than that!" countered Yajulu, "and I am king of them all with forty so far!"

Settling five daughters' marriages was not difficult, says Yajulu, perhaps the only pandit denying concern over the older dowry system. In the 1940s and 1950s his name and rank were esteemed throughout the delta. By contrast, he complained in the 1990s, the values of society changed so markedly his attempts to facilitate marriage settlements seemed counterproductive. "My son-in-law asked me to arrange the marriage of my granddaughter. She is not a B.A. and cannot go out and earn money, which is what parents want for their sons now. Values have shifted. Family tradition, a Vedic heritage, generations of Veda teaching and *soma* sacrificing, all that falls on deaf ears. My presence will not make any difference in the prospect of her marriage." As patriarch he still decided names for all the newborn, however, right down to the great-grandsons born when he was approaching the age of ninety.

3.1.2.4 A Burgeoning Family

In 1936 Yajulu named his first son Sarvesvara Somayajulu, an obvious hope that he would be the conduit for the long-running *ahitagni* lineage to survive intact. The boy began well, completed Veda entirely with Yajulu at age nineteen, married that year, and went on to complete *ghana* with a Gorti family *ghana-pathi*. But at some point, as Sarvesvara told it, the god Siva intervened and totally captured his attention. His life was turned over to one of studying the Siva Purana, going repeatedly to Kasi to worship Siva in the temple of Visvanatha, bathing in the Ganga "to purify the soul and concentrate on the worship of Isvara to achieve *mukti*," all the while earning a bare subsistence in Konasima from *sambhavana*, honoraria for *ghana* recitations of Veda at weddings or other family rituals. By reciting for Brahmans or other high castes the Satarudriya from the Taittiriya Samhita, Sarvesvara could indulge both his craving to worship Rudra-Siva and his need to earn a Veda pandit livelihood. When asked in February 2000 if he had ever entertained the idea of setting fires he became entirely agitated: "*Yogam*! *Daivam*! Isvara! Isvara! The worship of Isvara! *That* achieves *mukti*!" A remarkable devotion: in twenty-five years Yajulu did not mention Siva by name and his son thinks only of him. Neither of Sarvesvara's two sons learned Veda although one of his two daughters was married to a Veda pandit and has a son who went to Iragavaram for *adhyaya* with great-grandfather Gullapalli Sita Ram Sastri (discussed later).

Lanka, the sage of Nedunuru down the road from Sarvesvara's home in Irusumanda village, noted that Sarvesvara rejected Lanka's offer to teach the ritual Sutras of Apastamba: "He thinks of earning money, has no interest in further learning." By taking cash for reciting Veda he earned the disdain of Lanka, whose view was that a life as Siva *bhakta* (devotee) counts for little against the waste of a highly trained Veda pandit from an *ahitagni* lineage. And further, noted Lanka and many others, he stood in the way of an eligible younger brother, Surya Prakasa Avadhani, who was (at that time) a more probable candidate to set the fires.

The Duvvuri family history provides a good illustration of some of the pitfalls that lie in wait to derail a cherished lineage of *srauta*. *Bhakti* can here be added to the list of tangents alongside inability to complete Veda, failure to marry (and marry properly), sibling blockade when an older brother does not set fires, and incapacity to maintain the ritual purity of fire by living in a separate dwelling. To an observer, Sarvesvara existed in a Vedic/Puranic half-light, a Siva *bhakta*, but not a *pauranika* by profession, an earner of his keep as a Veda pandit *ghana-pathi*, but not one committed wholly to Veda and certainly not to the *srauta* life of his father. Technically not *laukika*, since he was employed by the TTD until he retired on pension as a *vrddha* pandit in 1994, his stance is on the threshold between "Vedism" and Hinduism. All that appeared to change suddenly in 2007 when he declared that he would set the fires and go on to *agni-stoma*. In that same year the younger brother Surya Prakasa Avadhani and Kanaka Durga made that decision. But neither family followed through beyond *vaisva-deva*. Yajulu's second, fourth, and fifth sons entered *laukika* careers outside of Veda. The vocation of third son Surya Prakasa is described later. Four generations of males in the Duvvuri family are presented in Table 3.2.

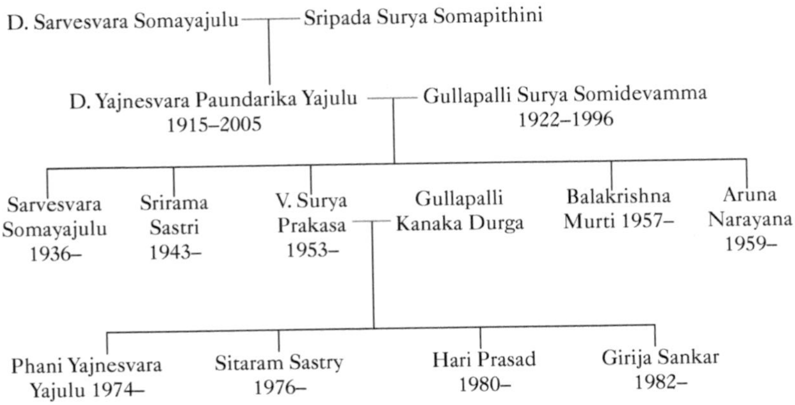

TABLE 3.2. Four generations of males in the Duvvuri family

3.1.2.5 *Last Rites*

Surya spent a long night at a marriage festival across the lane at Samavedam's house. Before resting in the morning she decided to offer special food she had cooked for the goddess Durga for Navaratri. She circled the Tulsi fort of Ammavaru three times, then fell against the compound wall screaming. "I was doing *agni-hotra*," reported Yajulu. "I got up, made my way feeling along the wall until I reached her. With the last breath *karma* mantras have to be recited into a dying person's ears. I could not tell if she was still breathing but I recited those mantras." They were verses from the Taittiriya Upanisad about *brahman* as truth and the breath of life.

After seventy-one years of marriage Baballa died and received Agni in the form of the three fires that he and Sundari Somidevamma had maintained as co-sacrificers. Sundari lived less than eleven months without him before her ordinary pyre was ignited by *arani*, the only ritual implements to survive his *antyesti*. With the death of Surya in December 1996 the other side of such co-sacrificial termination is visible. No *prayascitta* expiations were required for Surya; both had taken pains to perform *agrayana* together as always at Dipavali in the autumn of 1996. The *musi-vayanam* for the auspicious wife who dies first was performed by the side of the canal.[3] For her funeral it was now the *patni* who received *brahma-medha*. Yajulu, sightless, stood by and listened to the crackling fire consume all their ritual implements from fifty-one years of *isti* and *soma* sacrifices. "She took the fires with her! Now I will have to go with kitchen matches!" said Yajulu with a macabre sense of humor. But up in the rafters of the house they had shared for the last half-century of their sixty-seven-year marriage he knew that *arani* lay wrapped in gunny cloth awaiting a final task, the kindling of his own cremation fire at the burning ground where Surya's ashes had now been gathered for reburning.

Only after her death did Yajulu reveal to his family an almost folkloric account of a wise man's prophecy. His third son provided his words: "After my *agni-stoma* I went to a *sabha* in West Godavari District in Sravana *masa*. An old man faced me directly, 'Are you the one who performed *yajna*?' I answered him 'yes' and then he said 'Took a lot of trouble to do it but you will have no benefit.' I was in shock. What is he talking about? I just completed it three months ago and now I am hearing this inauspicious comment. Seeing my dismay, the old man said 'Have no fear. After you have crossed the line of eighty years all these *agni-hotra* will be taken away by your wife.' And it is a pattern in the family: my grandmother died first, her mother-in-law, my father's older brother's wife."

As a widower Yajulu could eat no rice for the evening meal, only *phalahara* snacks, with rice, essential "food," at noon only. One day in his last years he reminisced and recalled his mother at the age of eighty-six. "She suddenly asked me a strange question: 'Boy, has God (*devudu*) forgotten to call me? Somebody please tell him!' I understand her feelings now." He died July 30, 2005, only four months after an annual *sabha* was founded in his name in Sriramapuram. He was burned on the same spot as Surya almost a decade before.

3.1.2.6 Third Son Venkata Surya Prakasa Avadhani

The year 1953 brought disastrous floods in the region with the river breaching levees and cresting at the old Havelock railway bridge at Rajahmundry at sixty-five feet. The Kapilesvarapuram area was devastated. But that year brought good fortune in the form of a third son for Yajulu and Surya, some seventeen years, almost a generation, after Sarvesvara. Venkata Surya Prakasa, born in Kapilesvarapuram, had his *upanayana* eight years later, and learned Veda from his father only, completing the course in eight years. Up at 5 AM for *snana* and *sandhya-vandana* while his father did *agni-hotra*, it was then Veda until noon when it was time to accompany his father for midday *snana* and *sandhya-vandana*. At age twenty he was examined in Veda and *srauta* by the Godavari Mandala Parisad when it was in Vyaghresvaram in 1973. Avadhani could then be added to his name.[4] Marriage to Kanaka Durga, a cousin Gullapalli daughter, had already occurred in Iragavaram in 1970 when he was seventeen and she was twelve. He had no formal schooling until age sixteen and like his father felt unsure of the Telugu alphabet, *aksara-bhasya*, until he began to walk from Sriramapuram to a school in Mukkamala.

After examinations he was on track to follow in his father's footsteps but decided instead to prepare for a career as a Telugu/Sanskrit pandit and completed studies to that end in a college in nearby Moddekurru, finishing in 1976. Traveling by train he also took a five-month course in Warangal. A surplus of qualified pandits made employment difficult to find and he took up the study of *kavya* in Sriramapuram under Ravi Cayanulu, living on loans until he could repay them with honoraria from reciting at *sabha*. He appeared at several examination centers, Vyaghresvaram, Rajahmundry, Guntur, and two in Vijayawada.

In 1982, almost age thirty, Surya Prakasa moved from the Sriramapuram *agrahara* for the first time for five years of Mimamsa studies, five hours every day, with Remella Surya Prakasa Sastri in Rajahmundry, the town where the first of almost twenty interviews for this survey took place. Long train trips to Hyderabad, Srisaila, and other distant places brought *sambhavana* honoraria for joining in recitations and there were also local life-cycle rites to conduct. The full range of procedures for *samskara* he had learned from Yajulu, who seldom if ever exercised the craft. Once in Hyderabad for a marriage in a traditional Brahman family he was stunned to find no *agni-hotrin* wife cooking food, his first such encounter, and he had to survive on snacks. All these years he served as *adhvaryu* for his father's routine *isti*, and those of another *ahitagni*, and recited daily in TTD service in a temple in Mukkamala first, then the Satyanarayana temple in Rajamundry (see Figure 3.5, Surya Prakash Avadhani and Kanaka Durga).

By January 1988 he and Kanaka Durga, now with a full complement of four sons (Figure 3.6), with no daughters or irksome dowries, were celebrating the marriage of their first son, Phani Yajnesvara Yajulu, a student in Veda with grandfather Yajulu in Sriramapuram *agrahara*. Again for a new generation, the Duvvuri-Gullapalli cross-cousin marital scheme was operative and Phani was married to Laksmi (Nagalaksmi) in her home village of Iragavaram, West Godavari District. Embarking on the four sons and no daughters pattern, soon there were two sons and no daughters.

Surya Prakasa, a soft-spoken, serious, and thoughtful man who speaks slowly and in full detail after he gives every question long consideration, made a remarkably candid observation regarding his relationship with his father Yajulu: "It was only when I had sons of my own that I was able to sit down with my father for anything other than learning Veda." In 1987 Surya Prakasa confided his plans to return to Sriramapuram *agrahara*, continue in TTD temple recitation for livelihood, and then eventually set fires and do *agni-stoma*. It

FIGURE 3.5. Duvvuri Surya Prakasa Avadhani, Yajulu's third son, and Kanaka Durga, Rajahmundry 2005.

FIGURE 3.6. The four sons of Surya Prakasa and Kanaka Durga: from left: Phani, S. R. Sastry, Hari Prasad, Girija Sankar, Rajahmundry 1998.

appeared to be a conscious effort to replicate his father's career. All the same he was well aware of the distance between his father's generation and his own. "Since I cannot live like my father," he offered, "the best path open to me is to try to minimize my needs and interaction with others. To the extent that it is possible I will try to emulate the ideals of Vedic life. But I am conscious of the society in which I live."

A decade later, however, he was still in Rajahmundry. Circumstances changed in an interesting way when a small enclave in the thriving town became a makeshift *agrahara*, an opportune replacement for Sriramapuram. A wealthy member of the Duvvuri clan donated a house and its beautiful walled-off compound to Srngeri Pitha with the intention of founding a school. No teacher was available and Surya Prakasa was given the house and its stunning enclosed orchard as a *guru-kula* where he could live rent-free as long as he taught Veda to his own and his brothers' sons.

3.1.2.7 Duvvuri Phani Yajnesvara Yajulu

Surya Prakasa's first son is a good illustration of a betwixt-and-between educational pattern, flip-flopping between Veda and *huna-vidya*, a Vaidika or a *laukika* career. Phani, born in 1974, received Veda in Sriramapuram *agrahara* from grandfather Yajulu in the old man's waning, completely blind years, but also went to school and did an intermediate degree in English studies. He is the first and, to date, the only certified Veda pandit in this entire survey to speak any English. His plan to follow a bachelor of commerce with a master of business arts degree and find employment in the Karnataka State Bank changed when he turned back to Veda and followed his *krama* examination with one in *ghana*, having learned first from Samavedam Venkata Ramana in Sriramapuram, then from a well-known *ghana-pathi* in Vijayawada, Visnubhatla Laksminarayana. Phani took the train and spent three days a week with the latter, who served more as monitor of his progress than as traditional guru. Immediately after his 1999 certification in *ghana* at the age of twenty-five he plunged into Mimamsa, as his father had done, and advanced in *srauta* studies.

Phani, a solid man with a sturdy body, huskier than his father or grandfather, has a strong round face and pleasant disposition. He was married at fourteen to ten-year-old Laksmi (Nagalaksmi), daughter of his mother's brother, Gullapalli Venkata Rama Suryanarayana. Two sons were born to them, Surya Prakasa Pavankumar Sarma, named for his paternal grandfather, in 1996, and Syama Sundara Srirama Sarma, two years later. When brought out for viewing, the latter was described, in deference to family planning, as "the final one." At the age of eight the older boy began Taittiriya texts with his father in February 2005. Not surprisingly, given his father's abilities in English, he also studied in an English-medium school, with roughly equal time, five to five-and-a-half hours each day for Veda and English. He is the first Veda pandit descendant in this study to attend elementary school classes in English.

Like other young pandits in Konasima, Phani received offers from Hindu temples to do *parayana* in America and once received an invitation to be a *rtvij* in a ritual in New Jersey. When asked if he might take up such invitations he replied in 2005 that grandfather Yajulu forbade such an assignment, "and that means not now or ever." Earlier, in February 2000, the *grhya-pravesa* house consecration was performed for a newly constructed five-room flat in another part of Rajahmundry and the young four-member family moved in, leaving the Srngeri-*pitha* house to his parents and three remaining younger brothers. In 2009 Phani accepted a teaching position in Sri Venkatesvara University in Tirupati where his facility in English as well as Veda allowed him to advance rapidly to assistant professor in the department of Krishna Yajurveda studies. He is the first Veda pandit in the region to become a professor in a university. The Kanci Pitha honored him with the title of Veda-*bhasya* Ratna.

"It was the turning point in my life," said Phani in 1998, "when my grandfather Yajulu said to me '*You* are the one to continue!' I no longer vacillated between Veda and *laukika* careers." Now, sixteen years later, the Duvvuri legacy in Veda is assured, with additional merit awarded to a university professor. But the Duvvuri *srauta* heritage now hangs by a slender thread. There may have been a point at which Phani said commandingly to son Surya Prakasa or his younger brother, "*You* are the one to continue!" If so, the admonition was not heeded, and the necessary certification in Veda did not occur. Early in 2014, health problems in the form of diabetes increased for both Surya Prakasa and Kanaka Durga. The 2007 plans to follow *vaisva-deva* with *adhana* and *agni-stoma* were set aside.

3.1.2.8 Duvvuri Sita Ram Sastry and "Saving the Dynasty"

Like Phani, the second son of the elder Surya Prakasa began *adhyaya* with grandfather Yajulu. Sita Ram Sastry (his chosen spelling of Sastri, his full name being that of his maternal Gullapalli grandfather) sat down with Yajulu first, then his older brother Phani. But neither effort at learning a portion of the Taittiriya Samhita was successful. Stress brought on problems with his throat, that indispensable organ for recitation, and he could not continue. Thus his redemption, in his own words, was to become "savior of the dynasty" in a Veda pandit family by obtaining degrees in information technology, securing an appointment in the United States in order to send dollars home to support his Veda-reciting father, brother Phani, and Phani's sons, all of them at that time representing the direct hope of Yajulu's continuity in *srauta* as well as Veda. A Veda pandit manqué, he could thus turn his ambition in going to America into rupees for the home effort. And so he became one of an estimated 65,000 immigrants from India who entered the United States that year. He flew to Hartford, Connecticut, his first time out of Andhra Pradesh, assigned by Satyam Computers to the Cigna Insurance Company. Eventually his wife, Girija Syamala, along with son Karttikeya and daughter Pranati joined him.

Outsourcing in reverse, that is, the luring of trained Indian computer experts to the United States, attracted another of Yajulu's grandsons who arrived within three months of Sastry early in 2007. Sastry's cousin Yajnesvara Yajulu, first son of Yajulu's first son Sarvesvara and therefore bearing Yajulu's exact name, flew to Milwaukee, Wisconsin. Yet a third grandson of Yajulu, Girija Sankar, employed in 2013 by Value Labs in Hyderabad, awaits assignment abroad. Remarkable is the coincidence of American demands for staffing urban Hindu temples for expatriate Indian communities on one hand, and the needs of high-tech corporations on the other, both finding an Indian solution. The older Veda pandits of Konasima who disdained temple requests now have a growing number of descendants crossing the waters to fulfill the technological requirements of corporate America.

Surya Prakasa continues to be a valuable source of fine points of Vedic life and thought. He leans down, elbows on knees as he searches the floor for the clearest way to reply to queries and then, his voice deepening and softening, spins out details. His four sons, grandsons of Yajulu, all took Gullapalli brides and now have sons of their own. One became *ghana-pathi* and a university professor. One has been employed in the United States for five years and may soon be joined by another, a far-off land he has no intention of visiting. The final segment of this chapter concerns the Gullapallis, and part of Chapter 5 continues discussion of the paradigmatic Duvvuri-Gullapalli cross-cousin marriage pattern. A portion of the Epilogue returns to the question of America, "polarities and dreams."

Strong memories of Sriramapuram linger for the *dora*: Yajulu's powerful voice belting out long mantras in response to a query on *srauta*. A courageous Yajulu pacing back and forth beside the petite Pancayatana temple reciting Atharva Veda mantras against the fading powers of his glaucoma-arrested eyes and, years later, the sightless widower insisting on finding his way alone across the dusty track to visit another house. And there was that leave-taking one scorching afternoon while starting the trudge out the shadeless tar-streaked road toward the bus stop in Mukkamala Lock, catching blind Yajulu's self-ironic shout, "When you get to America, tell them I am looking for employment!"

3.1.3 Bulusu Cayanulu (1915–1997)

The fifty-year-old house next-to-last at the far end of the *agrahara* lane stood boarded up and empty for a year to allow ghosts and demons time to clear out. If one had to walk that way it was done quickly with averted gaze. Rituals were done against "wind," *gali,* and dust, a common Telugu expression for ghosts and other dangerous malevolent forces. Inside the house a few cracked, dried fragments of clay fireplaces scotched the floor. They should have been cleared away to assure safe journey onward for the deceased house owner, but he had died suddenly under an inauspicious constellation. After funerary procedures the house was hastily abandoned.

The deceased was Bulusu Vyaghresvara Cayanulu (1915–97), the third *ahitagni* on the fourteen-house lane of Sriramapuram *agrahara*. Subbalaksmi, her widow's white sari draped over her cropped white hair, returned to the house in which she had lived as a *somi-devamma* for more than three decades, but stayed only a short time before moving to the spreading town of Rajahmundry to live with a daughter and family.

Curiously, although not unique within communities of pandits who bear names of popular deities, ancient villages, and accomplished or wished for rituals, there were two identically named Vaidika Brahmans of the same *gotra* (Gautama), born in the same tiny hamlet (Vyaghresvaram) only a few years apart. Both became Veda pandits and then *ahitagni*. One remained in his natal village all his life and became Bulusu Vyaghresvara Soma-yaji while the other moved into Sriramapuram *agrahara*, performed *agni-cayana*, and therefore acquired the full name of Bulusu Vyaghresvara Cayanulu. Hereafter, this second Vyaghresvara will be Bulusu Cayanulu to distinguish him from other Bulusus and other Cayanulus (such as Ravi Cayanulu, a *smarta* Brahman neighbor in Sriramapuram but neither an *ahitagni* nor performer of *agni-cayana*).

Everyone in the *agrahara* knows the story of the ancestor of Bulusu Cayanulu who worshipped Ganesa all his days. In his old age, one day he was surprised by the elephant-headed god's sudden appearance before him. A boon was granted as reward for lifelong determined devotion: for three successive *purusa*, generations, his descendants would be distinguished Veda pandits. Bulusu Cayanulu represented, in this fortuitous but sharply bordered prediction, the third and final generation. When he died in 1997 he left no visible direct descendant in Veda.

One of three brothers, he was the only one who became a Veda pandit. Along with a boy of the same age, Renducintala Venkatacalu, he became a *brahmacarin* student of Venkatacalu's father. This providential association had long-term consequences. Venkatacalu became Renducintala Yajulu, the most famous sacrificer and promoter of *srauta* rituals in twentieth-century India, one whose name is a string of thirty-some sacrifices, a veritable litany recited with awe and admiration by most Veda pandits of Andhra. The chanting of his name always has the ring of an ideal mantra!

Renducintala was born in the delta. Unlike Bulusu Cayanulu, who remained in Konasima within a few miles of his birthplace, Renducintala Yajulu spent most of his life in Kasi (Varanasi) where he died in 1987. Frequent visits to Andhra, mostly to a second house in Vijayawada on the Krishna River, but also to the Godavari River Delta, kept him informed of the state of Veda and *srauta* in the territory of his birth. He and his wife, Laksmikanta, performed their first *yajna*, the *agni-stoma*, in 1936, their last one in Kasi in 1980, and managed more than half a century of *agni-hotra* over all.

To return to Vyaghresvara (who was to become Bulusu Cayanulu), after he and Venkatacalu completed the eighty-two *panna* the paths of the two former classmates—now established Veda pandits, both married with families started—intersected again when Vyaghresvara's twenty-four-year-old wife, Rama Suryakanta from Prakkilanka, suddenly died of typhoid fever in 1945. The *musi-vayanam* ritual for a wife who dies first was performed on the tenth day by a *brahma-muttaiduva*, a special Brahman woman ritualist who made the lengthy journey to Vyaghresvaram village from Rajahmundry. The young couple's son, Ramana Murti, was six years old. Venkatacalu, now known as Renducintala Yajulu, wanted to recruit Vyaghresvara as *rtvij* in a *paundarika* for his increasingly ambitious schedule of sacrifices. But a *rtvij* cannot be *apatnika*, without a wife. He must have married a pre-pubescent girl in an authentic five-day *vivaha*. Therefore Renducintala Yajulu took on the project of legitimizing his boyhood friend and colleague. In Gangalakurru village he located a Brahman family willing to give fourteen-year-old daughter Subbalaksmi to a promising young pandit, although a thirty-year-old widower. They were married eight months after the unfortunate death of Rama Suryakanta, and Vyaghresvara became eligible for *srauta* roles.[5]

Subbalaksmi subsequently gave birth to three daughters, then a son, and then a fourth daughter. (See Figure 3.7, Bulusu Cayanulu and Subbalaksmi, Sriramapuram 1987.) Ramana Murti, the son from Vyaghresvara's first marriage, was raised by his grandmother in Vyaghresvaram and remained there when the new family was invited to live in Sriramapuram, only a twenty-minute walk through the fields. The lives of Renducintala Yajulu and Vyaghresvara

FIGURE 3.7. Bulusu Cayanulu and Subbalaksmi, Sriramapuram 1987.

connected yet a third time when they struck a marriage alliance. Yajulu's son Satyanarayana would marry Vyaghresvara's third daughter with no demands for dowry. In lieu of cash or land, Vyaghresvara agreed to teach this prospective son-in-law and became Satyanarayana's principal guru. When the boy and girl reached respective ages of fifteen and ten, they were married in Vijayawada.

Meanwhile, Vyaghresvara had pursued multiple career paths. In accord with a hereditary relationship, he prepared a more rigorous program in *smarta* than the normal Veda pandit curriculum. This began at age fifteen and concluded with exams three years later. Baballa's Bhamidipati ancestors had depended for generations upon Vyaghresvara's Bulusu ancestors for services as *brahma (purohita)* for *samskara* and other domestic rites. Absent from such services would be *apara*, funerary rituals that called for a special Brahman. Until his declining years prevented further service and the Bhamidipati family was forced to go outside the hereditary link, Bulusu Cayanulu remained as *brahma* for Baballa's descendants. To a greater degree than any other Veda pandit covered here, Bulusu Cayanulu, with a lifetime of experience in both *srauta* and *smarta*, was able to articulate what he clearly understood to be a close relationship between the two ritual traditions and the Grhya and Srauta Sutras of Apastamba that support them. It is sometimes said by scholars that Smarta Brahmans are sharply delineated from those who perform *srauta*, but Bulusu Cayanulu was living proof otherwise.

In addition to this dual profession he taught for fourteen years in a *veda-patha-sala* in Billakurru, north of Vyaghresvaram on the other side of the canal. He became an examiner in the Veda-certification process. And he was invited regularly as *rtvij* in the rituals of Renducintala Yajulu and others in Vyaghresvaram village. He estimated his participation in approximately fifty or sixty rituals including six *paundarika*, often as *udgatr.* The *srauta* ethos of Konasima in the 1960s was infectious and in Magha 1965, at age fifty, he performed *adhana* with *agni-stoma* on the following day by the side of the little temple in Sriramapuram. And four years later, this time choosing his natal village of Vyaghresvaram as site, he managed the *sarva-prstha agni-cayana* that endowed him with the name Cayanulu. This was in 1969, the same year in which his neighbor Duvvuri Yajulu added Paundarika to his full name. (See Figure 3.8, Cayanulu, with Baballa behind, and others in a ritual, Sriramapuram 1987.)

Having founded the Sriramapuram *agrahara* on the right bank of the Billakurru Canal, known more affectionately as the Kausika, the Dokka family invited Vyaghresvara and Subbalaksmi to live there. A house plot plus an

FIGURE 3.8. Bulusu Cayuanulu, Baballa behind, during a ritual, Sriramauram 1987.

acre of cropland were the donation. His ancestral lands had been sold off, and then his donated agricultural acre had to be sold to pay for his daughters' dowries (with the exception of the daughter given to Renducintala in exchange for teaching). Eventually, when the TTD *parayana* system kicked in, he took up service at age sixty-one in a temple in his natal village of Vyaghresvaram, with additional recitations in nearby Pulletikurru. His retirement came at age seventy-eight as a *vrddha* pandit pensioner with seventeen years of service. Financial worries pursued him, however, and he continued to attend *sabha* that brought in small honoraria. The central government in Delhi provided honoraria for *agni-stomin* for some years before he learned about it, giving him opportunity to grouse: "The other *ahitagni* kept this secret from me."

Several "felicitations" honored him, one being in Hyderabad where he was surprised to be greeted by the prime minister of India, P. V. Narasimha Rao, a fellow Andhra native. No one had informed him of this distinction. To be there, the eighty-year-old man had to bounce along alone for some twenty hours on overnight buses. The honorarium for that event was rupees amounting then to $35.13. But he was delighted by the honor. Another tribute came from the Andhra Pradesh Chief Minister, the former film star N. T. Rama Rao, a distinction in itself, having the familiar silver-screen idol Rama or Krishna make the presentation.

In family album photos Bulusu Cayanulu appears in his prime as a strikingly handsome man. He was an impulsive, naturally affectionate man, the only *ahitagni* ever to reach out and grasp the *dora*'s hands in both of his (once only). He was a dependable, trustworthy individual, faithful to his professional and familial duties, sincerely devoted to his own ritual life and to the ongoing *samskara* and *isti* of others who depended on him as expert *brahma* or *rtvij*. *Srauta* rituals fascinated him, the form of *agni-cayana* that he had accomplished in particular. In his later years he was preoccupied with performing the *catur-masya* rites, which Baballa and Lanka had done and he had planned but never followed through. Left undone, this complex ritual weighed heavily on his mind as a significant unfulfilled duty. The *agrayana*, however, he and Subbalaksmi did as usual in February 1996 in his eighty-first year, rekindling fires with *prayascitta* for failing to do it as he had intended in one of the three autumnal months of 1995, and then following up with *isti* for the subsequent fortnight.

Bulusu Cayanulu was not the philosopher of the adjacent *agrahara*. Baballa and Lanka were sought first as authorities, then Duvvuri Yajulu. He stated his opinions forcefully, categorically, but often they were the odd ones out in deliberations of the group and he was dismissed as eccentric. For example, the aim of *srauta*, he would insist, is the cessation of births. But before he could elaborate he would be cut off, overridden with contrary views. And his statements were sometimes whimsical and extravagant. "In a Telangana village called Manthini," he once pronounced grandly, "there are 800 Brahman families, all *ahitagni*, all *ghana-pathi*, and there they perform *vaja-peya*." He possessed a charming naivete. When visits to Sriramapuram occurred a week or so apart he assumed a commute back to America had intervened. When presented with a 1975 book by the *dora*, inscribed to all in the *agrahara* and meant to be shared, he assumed with worried demeanor that it was about him. It was never seen again. Cayanulu inadvertently added a capricious tenor to conversations. In early years there was no admission to the interior of his house, and when asked, while sitting on his *arugu*, about the exact location of his *agni-hotra*, room he could find no way to describe it. A careful map of the *agrahara* was drawn for him, including the path separating the two rows of houses and a large empty square for his house. No amount of prodding gave results. Finally, in desperation to locate his *agni-hotras* for the inquisitive *dora* he shouted "Here!" and stabbed the map with the point of a pen in the middle of the path.

Without lingering outside his door as he had done with Baballa, Mrtyu, Lord of Death, rushed swiftly into Bulusu Cayanulu's house and felled him without warning. The heart attack came after he cycled home from the village to unload groceries in anticipation of a visit from a daughter and her husband. The older folk in the *agrahara*, prone to ruminate on the suffering that precedes death, admired this as a proper, painless way to go. His funeral just outside the *agrahara* included not only *brahma-medha* and *punar-dahana*, but also the *losta-citi* ritual of piling mud bricks in commemmoration of his *agni-cayana* twenty-eight years before.

Subbalaksmi, a shy, pretty woman with an affectionate smile, was always in the shadow of her much older husband's wishes, fulfilling all chores and then tending the *agni-hotra* during the thirty-two years she spent as a *somi-devamma*. "From the time I was fourteen I was very reticent. I had so much *bhaya* (fear) in the early days of our marriage." Then, as one of several white-clad widows in the *agrahara*, and later in her neighborhood of Rajahmundry, having long since completed her constant program of *nomu*, ritual vows that are largely for the protection of husband and sons, she spent her time reading about the *dasavatara*, the ten incarnations of Visnu, and reading aloud to herself the *sahasra-nama*, litanies of the thousand names of Visnu, the goddess Lalita, and other deities. This she enjoys immensely. Subbalaksmi claims not to have had knowledge of *aksara* (letters) until a few years after her husband's passing. He had always opposed, she says flatly, her desire to learn to read and write. Unlike the other *somi-devamma* with daughters living only a few villages away, Subbalaksmi's daughters are spread out far beyond Konasima, perhaps due to liaisons made long since through the more cosmopolitan center of Vijayawada and the auspices of Renducintala Yajulu. Daughters have gone to Bangalore, Tirupati, and Hyderabad, although remaining in Rajahmundry are one daughter as well as her only son. With far better bus service on vastly improved roads, Rajahmundry can now be reached on a good day in less than two hours instead of the five or more of former days.

Bulusu Cayanulu's legacy of Veda ended in the male *vamsa* (lineage) but may possibly feed into another male line through a daughter, as in the case of Lanka, Bulusu Kamesvara, and other *ahitagni*. His third daughter, married to Renducintala's fourth son, has a son with a college degree who also learned Veda at home. Bulusu Cayanulu's first son, Ramana Murti, who was raised by his grandmother after the death of his mother in 1945, has a son doing *smarta*, and thus another dimension of Bulusu Cayanulu's career may also continue.

Subbalaksmi has a photo album on her lap spread open to reveal the handsome young man in white, Bulusu before he became Cayanulu, Bulusu before she was born. When she reflects about her life, Subbalaksmi has said on more than one occasion: "Way back when he was born in Vyaghresvaram village, 'Cayanulu' was written by the god Brahma on his forehead. And marriage to him was what was written on mine."

Cayanulu was the second of Sriramapuram's trio of *ahitagni* to go, leaving only Yajulu. By 1997 the lane had not changed much in seventeen years. Off to the south through the trees some houses had become visible in an expanding non-Brahman hamlet. The school at the lane's end boasted a new play area. On a steamy March day half a dozen nearly naked workers split and husked coconuts for coir while others loaded mammoth lorries destined for Gujarat, Maharashtra, Madhya Pradesh. On that morning no sounds of Veda competed with the new enterprise.

3.1.4 Samavedam (1932–2008) and Sons

A fourth habitually visible figure in the *agrahara*, well known and respected throughout coastal Andhra, was Samavedam Suryanarayana Avadhani, Harita *gotra*, resident of Sriramapuram for well over half a century. His grandfather was an *ahitagni* in Mukkamala but neither his Telugu pandit father nor Samavedam himself chose the life of *agni-hotra* and *srauta*, preferring instead to concentrate on steering sons into Vedic education. "I teach and recite Veda," said Samavedam, "and this is all my life." In fact, both father and son accomplished the same feat, each carefully preparing two out of four sons for careers as Veda pandits and seeking as far as possible to marry daughters to Veda pandits.

Samavedam had the clear-eyed gaze of a fox on the hunt and the restless, spare build of that focused prowler. There seemed to be no apparent limit to his entrepreneurial energy. He was born on the next to last day of 1932, fourth of the four brothers of his generation. After *upanayana* at age ten he spent ten years learning Veda, initially with his oldest brother at home in Mukkamala, then with Bulusu Vyaghresvara in Billakurru. This was long before this Bulusu (Cayanulu above) became his guru and subsequently a neighbor in the actual hamlet of Vyaghresvaram close to Sriramapuram. Yet another mentor was Rani Hayagriva in Indupalli. Samavedam did *varalu* and *madhu-kara* in each village of his three successive gurus and appeared successfully for his exam in *krama* in Vijayawada in 1955.[6] By that time he had married Kamala, younger sister of Baballa's daughter-in-law, of the Prabhala family in Velcheru, and they had a boy and a girl of their eventual six children (see Figure 3.9, Samavedam and Kamala, Sriramapuram 1996).

The new *krama-pathi* was granted in that same year of 1955 a plot in Sriramapuram along with Rs. 1,000 to construct a house, plus an acre of land with an assured yield of fifteen bags of paddy. It was barely more than a ten-minute walk from the busy village of Mukkamala, but Samavedam's mother objected to the move on the grounds that they would be lonely "way out there." Samavedam, however, youngest of the sons, with little hope of inheriting the

FIGURE 3.9. Samavedam and Kamala, Sriramapuram 1996.

house of a burgeoning extended family, wanted his own home, even if there were only five other families in the outlying *agrahara*. By the first decade of the new millennium, buses, huge trucks, cars, and motor scooters all zoomed constantly with excessive blasts of air-horns to force bicycles, pedestrians, and animals off the road; electric and telephone wires bounced in the wind above asphalt paving; and only those of Samavedam's generation recalled that peaceful but remote 1950s era. "If we tried to walk the dirt path back to Mukkamala it was difficult. In the dark it was dreadful, terrifying. Will someone jump out and seize me? It was a long way between settlements."

Samavedam's acre of paddy was tilled by a tenant farmer for some years until problems arose with Scheduled Caste encroachments. "They built huts to live in, stole the coconuts, started chicken farms, so I sold that acre at a low price and bought a half-acre elsewhere." But he came out even when the new land yielded two rice harvests per year instead of one. Eventually he sold that half-acre as well, upon discovery that he could gain a steady income as a Veda pandit. Samavedam was never shy about soliciting money. "I went to a lot of people asking for money to build up a career." Always on his mind was the tension between going out to seek funds by reciting, or staying home to teach sons on a daily basis. "If I don't earn money I cannot maintain this *samsara*. If I do go out and earn money, teaching suffers. The two are incompatible." His compromise was to start Veda with all four sons, then select the most mentally agile pair for continued *adhyaya* while steering the other two into *laukika* careers, hopefully something in Sastra as pandits like their grandfather. By the time the fourth son reached the minimum age for *upanayana*, the oldest was twenty-four and the middle sons—those who were to complete the eighty-two *panna*—were twenty-two and twelve.

When Samavedam went out of the *agrahara* it was mostly to do *asir-vacana*, a blessing via mantras recited at a wedding, housewarming ritual, or other auspicious event. Or it could be to recite in a *sabha* assembly, or at a large festival such as Mahasivaratri to do *svasti-vacana* at the Virabhadra temple in Pattisima, or a Varuna *puja* in Tirupati, or to observe a *srauta* ritual to which he had been invited. Of the last he said without a hint of apology, "I go only to receive money and then leave." He never observed a complete *srauta* ritual. He became a Vedic voice for hire and to his last day would go anywhere, anytime, as long as a fee was assured. Without recourse to notebooks he was an astonishing font of information, expatiating on all recent and forthcoming Vedic events, with places, dates, names of all the sponsors and, most important, all amounts of remuneration. The territory routinely canvassed included the whole of the two Godavari districts, but long-range forays into Guntur, Krishna, and Vishakapatnam districts were not infrequent, and he often narrated his visits to "a very rich Telugu Brahman in Madras" among others.

Occasional windfalls arrived closer together in his later years and each was remembered with pleasure. For example, in October 1994 a Vaisnava "*yaga*" (pseudo-Vedic sacrifice) required 150 Veda pandits to do *parayana* from 7 AM to noon for twelve successive days while a thousand *homas* were addressed to Laksmi-Narayana. Samavedam and both sons were there. The trio was then again involved in a group of sixty pandits reciting Veda seven days in August 1995 for a sixtieth-birthday celebration in Kanci. Each received Rs. 1,116 plus a sovereign of gold, fourteen *tola* of silver plate (approximately Rs.1,000), new clothes, and silk saris for the three wives. Only three months later they went to Puttaparthi to honor Sathya Sai Baba's seventieth birthday as three of the invited seventy pandits. Again Samavedam produced a rapid recital of rewards: "Each Rs. 5,000, an 'automatic' watch, new clothes, and for each wife, silk saris, two solid gold bangles, a pressure cooker, free food and lodging for a week, Rs.1,000 for travel."

All of this shows that Samavedam was a professional reciter and expected, even demanded, to be paid well for professional service. He was direct, straightforward, totally honest about his career of reciting for remuneration. He was also quite content with his life, something that cannot be said of every Veda pandit. "There is work and there is enjoyment from work," he allowed. They were a familiar traveling trio, a spry, bouncy, effervescent Samavedam, always preserving yon Cassius' lean and hungry look, and the softer, more phlegmatic sons, products of a different diet, more passive ethos, and always the comfort of an established home in a stable hamlet.

In his mind Samavedam had a clear distinction between *satkara*, honoraria for blessings or other felicitations at marriages and such, and *dana*, ritualized gifts or donations. The former are earned and are always acceptable. The latter require examination. The 1955 donation of land and construction costs was proper. His degree qualifications and his homelessness rendered him deserving and the gift was "clean" from the point of view of Dharmasastra. On the other hand, recalling that 1995 sixtieth-birthday celebration in Kanci, he found the presentation of a cow (*go-dana*) along with free fodder for six months ("a Rs.3,000 value in itself," he remarked) quite unacceptable. A cow falls in the category of *ugra-dana*, a dangerous gift that could have life-threatening consequences for the recipient. "Only Brahmans of low status will accept a cow, even though it is quite valuable. In Krishna and Guntur districts Brahmans take all kinds of *dana*. For them it is all right. But we Konasima Brahmans are strict. We are known as those who purify fire with water. If *dana* are accepted, a lot of *santi* has to be performed, *japa*, Gayatri mantra, etc. Hopefully, the *dana* will not then eat away the recipient. *But one cannot be sure.*" (See Figure 3.10, Samavedam with the three *ahitagni* of Sriramapuram, 1991.)

FIGURE 3.10. Samavedam, left, with the three *ahitagni* of Sriramapuram, Bulusu Cayanulu, Duvvuri Yajulu, Baballa, 1991.

When not out on the *sat-kara* circuit Samavedam was usually found at home teaching on the *arugu* of his house. His second son, Venkatarama, was a quick learner and was pulled out of school at third class in exclusive devotion to Veda. After nine years on the eighty-two *panna* he went on for three more years to excel in *ghana,* stood first in his exam, and added Ghanapathi to his name. Venkatarama was married to Kumari and after she joined the household in Sriramapuram, two sons and two daughters were added to the extended family. Both boys entered a *veda-pathasala* in Hyderabad, the older one after a year of learning under grandfather Samavedam. One of the two girls was married at fourteen to a *ghana-pathi* in Iragavaram, West Godavari District, in yet another liaison between that village and the Sriramapuram *agrahara.* Samavedam's third son, Bhaskara, had his *upanayana* several years later than Venkatarama, remained in school until eighth class, but nevertheless completed *krama* and then *ghana,* and was married at twenty-two to Sundari, age thirteen, in 1986. This second couple added a boy and a girl to the growing list of Samavedam's grandchildren and brought the number living in the house to twelve.

Of Samavedam and Kamala's two daughters, the older, Laksmi, was married to a Veda pandit, her mother's brother, Prabhala Krishnamurti. This couple produced a son for their extended family in Velcheru as well as a daughter. Venkatarama, who bears the same family name as Laksmi's brother, was taught

Veda from the age of eleven by grandfather Samavedam for ten years until December 1995, his successful examination occurring the following March. The second daughter of Samavedam and Kamala, Visalaksi, was married in 1982 to a *laukika* husband, a salesman, at age sixteen after a fruitless search for a second Veda pandit son-in-law. Unlike the *ahitagni* lineages with their fixation on pre-pubescent marriages, there was no concern over a post-menarche ceremony. The dowry and expenses for Visalaksi were Rs. 23,000 and Samavedam well remembers being in debt for five years. "When I buy in the vegetable market it's the same price for me as for anyone, no discount for being a pandit. It's true also in the son-in-law market. If I say I'm a Veda pandit the dowry stays the same." Decrying the change in cultural standards he said: "Parents today do not want their sons in an *agrahara*. They want them to go to an office and sit under a fan."

The remaining two of Samavedam and Kamala's six children, born first and last, with sixteen years between them, Suryanarayana Murti and Mallesvarudu, respectively, learned some Veda but gravitated toward *laukika* careers. The firstborn married a granddaughter of Duvvuri Yajulu. By the year 2000, Samavedam and Kamala had thirteen grandchildren. One granddaughter was married away to the older of the two sons of Chirravuri Ramam, Baballa's favorite student, in Rajahmundry.

In sum, this is a remarkable family record. Before he died suddenly in 2008 Samavedam had taught two sons and one grandson the complete Taittiriya corpus, taught the other two sons and another grandson in part, and married a daughter and a granddaughter to Veda pandits. *Adhyaya* occurred entirely within the family, so there were no *daksina*. It would appear that Samavedam and Kamala were exactly the kind of pair for whom the *agrahara* was established in the mid-twentieth century.

When asked if he ever accepted a student from outside the family, Samavedam replied in the negative. "That invites problems," he volunteered. "You have to set him up in your house, find families in the village to feed him. In some of those houses there will be days of impurity. Other families may think I am imposing on them. So I don't accept outsiders." Ritual purity was a lasting concern as Samavedam only taught when in *madi*. If a visit to Sriramapuram interrupted *adhyaya*, he came and sat near but then shrank from any possible touch by children running through, and he asked that any photo prints from the previous visit be dropped on a nearby bench so that he could look at them later when out of *madi*.

At times Samavedam could not wait for another visitation and would come to Rajahmundry, sons in tow in all their glowing red silk-shawl finery, clean-shaven, top-knotted, and gold-earringed, to provide a lusty *asir-vacana* blessing in three-part *ghana* and receive an overly generous Rs. 500 each plus

200 travel money. For them it was a merry holiday on buses out of the *agrahara* to the big "city," and for the astonished staff of a sleepy, drab hotel their arrivals and departures in bicycle rickshaws were always awe-inspiring conversation pieces. It was never possible to explain to the staff how these people live, and what it is they do, to quote Lewis Carroll's "Red Knight's Song."

Given the perpetual urge to seek monetary compensation for recitation, it is remarkable to note the refusal of invitations to go to the several Hindu temples in America seeking Veda pandits. At one point the two sons were among eighteen Konasima pandits who received requests from Pittsburgh. "None of us has any *asakti* (interest)." said Bhaskara. "The *vrata* (vow) of a sacred life would be broken with no fruit to show for it. My elders never ate in the same line with a man who had gone to America and returned. Such a man was shunned, excommunicated. One man went to America. His father died and the son was not there for him. Of what use is that son? Religious obligations are expected. Those who go to America only want money." These scruples in the face of potentially high income are noteworthy since there was no mention of any paternal caveat similar to the line that Duvvuri Yajulu drew for his descendants.

Several aspects of Samavedam's life distinguished him from some of the Veda pandits surveyed thus far. Beyond his successful dedication to teaching Veda to carefully selected sons and grandsons there was his total disinterest in *srauta*, even as an observer; his energetic, uninhibited acceptance of the new cash economy; and his openness to revealing the ritual schedules of others. In the matter of perpetuating Veda by oral instruction within the family, Samavedam would be Exhibit A for the TTD promotion of stipends and honoraria. His life is instructive in any attempt to understand the dynamics of the wider Vedic community. After Samavedam's death, third son Bhaskara Avadhani and Sundari took over the house in the Sriramapuram *agrahara*. Second son Venkatarama Ghanapathi and Kumari are currently living in Hyderabad.

3.2 *Kamesvari Agrahara Near Nedunuru Village*

3.2.1 Lanka (1912–1999)

At 2:30 on a sunny February afternoon, three men are already waiting on the verandah steps. After some time, Lanka, on the arm of a granddaughter, appears unsteadily with badly swollen knees, eyes squinched against the brightness. He is deposited slowly, carefully into the dimple between stacks of books and papers, his work-nest. Heavy gold earrings tug his earlobes down, wide gold rings cover four fingers of the right hand, a gold armband rides as a torque on a pale forearm, and a crystal-bead necklace hangs over a bare torso that reveals his white cotton thread between sharply pointed breasts. His eyes strain for a glimpse, the toothless white-bearded face crumples with the pain of being unwell at eighty-four, and his voice emerges almost inaudibly but cheerily, welcoming all.

Two of the men respectfully request his judgment regarding the timing of a marriage. Lanka consults a Pancanga, eyebrows nearly touching the pamphlet, gives his verdict, but so softly that one man asks him kindly to repeat. The other man tries to leave a five-rupee note but is waved away. The third man, quite young, holds up two sticks about eight and ten inches long. They are the heights, he explains, of two *murtis*, images of deities that have been in his household for generations but are no longer worshipped. "How should I go about donating them to a temple?"

Three more men approach, identify themselves loudly and briskly by surnames so Lanka knows them to be Brahmans and can gesture them past the *arugu* and over his feet where they can sit inside the more privileged threshold to the main hall. They are from Ambajipeta, just passing through on no real mission; they simply want to pay respects. In other words, they seek *darsan*, auspicious sight, of the great man of the region. Touching Lanka's feet and their own foreheads three times each they back away, as from a deity or a Maharaja, relinquishing the *arugu* to the *dora* and the Andhra University professor for a two-hour discussion of Veda and *srauta*. The view from his bucolic study is stunning as always, a half dozen shades of green glowing from soaking paddy fields, coconut fronds, tapioca leaves, and distant foliage. (See Figure 3.11, Lanka, his rice fields and coconut palms in view, Nedunuru, 1991.)

FIGURE 3.11. Lanka, Nedunuru 1991, his rice fields and coconut palms in view.

The elevation of Lanka Venkatarama Sastri as the Andhra Veda pandit most learned in *srauta* since the demise of Renducintala Yajulu and Kapilavayi Yajnesvara Agnihotra Sastri is not immediately perceptible. He delayed setting fires until relatively late, put off *agni-stoma* beyond normal requirements, performed for himself no further *srauta* after *yajna*, and allowed his fires to lapse some thirteen years before his death. The reputation of this universally respected man who garnered status normally granted only to renunciants, was built on two remarkable achievements in knowledge: appropriately, Veda and *srauta*. Lanka was sometimes called *abhinava*, the "new" Apastamba, in recognition of his prowess in the indispensable ritual sutras. He had diverse knowledge of Veda beyond the Taittiriya corpus, including considerable Rg Veda, selected portions of Athar Vaveda, and acquaintance with the inner workings of Sama Veda. He served as examiner for Veda, *srauta*, Dharmasastra, and was consulted on *jyotisa*. As *brahman* he was required to know all the *rtvij* roles for mantra as well as *kriya*. Lanka wrote and published in Sanskrit as well as Telugu. Second, although *yajamana* only for his own *adhana* and *agni-stoma*, he had such command of the Brahmana texts and ritual sutras that he was able to supervise every detail of major *srauta* performances. By the time he performed *agni-stoma* himself he may well have been the most experienced *adhvaryu* in India.

Beyond his sharpness of mind, however, was a manifest dispassion of soul that earned widespread admiration. In *sabhas* he always demonstrated equanimity and spoke in soft, measured tones only after careful reflection on the subject at hand. When the TTD requested Baballa to fill a salaried position, Baballa shouted "Not for *ahitagni!*" Lanka simply ignored them. When a *tuphan* (typhoon, cyclone) roared up the delta from the Bay of Bengal on November 5, 1995, tore the roofs off houses, destroyed coconut palms, cropfields, and livestock, the whole region was in shock. Lanka, located where trees, cows, goats, and homes disappeared and heavy roof-tiles clattered down like leaves, commented like a stolid Daoist philosopher: "Cyclones come, cyclones go." His deep knowledge and unflappable demeanor combined to make him a local legend.

Lanka's early years are as instructive regarding traditional Vedic education as those of Baballa. Born and raised in Nedunuru village, he became a student of Baballa's father in Mukkamala. It was an arduous, disciplined routine for a small boy. He rose at 3 AM for a two-mile walk in the dark on a dirt path to the Bhamidipati house. After a full morning of *adhyaya*, lunch was served by Kamesvari, his guru's wife, followed by the long afternoon review of morning lessons. After *sandhya-vandana* at dusk was the walk home, again in the dark, for supper from his mother and bed at 8 PM. "My father always taught me two *sloka* before I could lie down to sleep." All his life Lanka kept to this routine so well established in his *brahmacarin* period, "except," he commented in his declining days, "in recent years I don't need as much sleep, so I wake at 2:00, stay in bed till 3:00 while others sleep, and I listen to the day begin." After six years in the Bhamidipati house, Lanka proceeded with three years of *ghana* from a second guru, the father of his future son-in-law, still in Mukkamala. Along with a half dozen other boys he did *varalu* then, taking his lunch in seriatim with different village households for a week at a time.

Marriage for Lanka, as with education, was still within the powerful Bhamidipati fold. He married Baballa's cousin Anasuya, age seven, when he was ten. Lanka's bride's father, grandfather, and great-grandfather were all *ahitagni* and she was entirely familiar with a *patni's* life and responsibilities. After flowering at fourteen she began her new life with him in Nedunuru village, where she was to bear a girl, also named Anasuya, and then deliver eight successive boys, one dying in infancy. (See Figure 3.12, Lanka and Anasuya, and Figure 3.13, Lanka and the author, both Nedunuru 1987.)

As a child Lanka learned agriculture from his father on land that he would one day inherit. Among the many shared features in the lives of Baballa and Lanka was hands-on supervision of crop fields as "gentleman farmers,"

FIGURE 3.12. Lanka and Anasuya, Lamesvari *agrahara*, Nedunuru 1987, his books and ritual charts behind.

FIGURE 3.13. Lanka and author, Nedunuru 1987.

managers of *kuli* labor crews who did the plowing, harrowing, seeding, transplanting, harvesting, winnowing, bagging, and constant regulation of flowing water for paddy fields. And both taught their students in shaded spaces among the coconut palms and small crops interspersed among them, "offices" in the fields where villagers could also come for *muhurta* and *dharma-sandeha*. Field supervision of the hired crews, whose numbers were expanded by migrant labor at times of rice and coconut harvests, was "in the old days," a dawn-to-dusk task. In recent years field hands have been unwilling to work such long hours and foremen have been designated to take over some of the supervision. Echoing Samavedam's comment about the insoluble tension between teaching at home and reciting on the road for money, Lanka recites a sloka to the effect that *krsi* (cultivation) impedes Veda, and Veda impedes *krsi*. "One who wants to farm cannot be a pandit as well. But in my case," he adds, "I was fortunate because most of my learning and study was completed before I was in charge of agricultural duties."

His father died in 1947 at age seventy-two when Lanka was thirty-five. He and Anasuya, along with his mother and others, took the long train journey to

Kasi to perform *sraddha*. The property had been divided between Lanka and his brothers and Lanka received acreage with the high yield of twenty bags of paddy minimum. Still there were debts, mostly for children's education. "My life has never been free of debts," he remarked matter-of-factly. Rs. 400 *katnam* (dowry) had been paid long since for the marriage of young Anasuya to Bhamidipati Mitranarayana of Korumilli, son of an *ahitagni* and destined to become the youngest *ahitagni* in Andhra, perhaps in India. Ironically, then, it was only this first child, left unmentioned by Lanka when enumerating his offspring, who directly extended his Vedic heritage into another generation.

Teaching Veda to the first two sons had been a failure. Anasuya's terse comment on child-rearing in a Veda pandit's house in an *agrahara* designated for Veda pandits was caustic: "I brought up our daughter with the ideal of living as an *agni-hotrin*'s wife. That worked. He (Lanka) tried to teach Veda to two sons. That didn't work." Baballa's seemingly iron-clad lineage of *soma*-sacrificers, expanding laterally with almost six *ahitagni* in his own generation, proved too fragile in his own lifetime, broken by an ill-starred son and then the sonless wife to his only remaining grandson. And simultaneously the promise of Lanka's continuing Veda legacy, so bright with the production of seven sons out of eight children, also faded in Lanka's middle years as he witnessed all seven enter *laukika* careers.

"I had cherished a wonderful dream," Lanka recounted in our initial 1980 meeting; "four of my sons would know the four Vedas, and the other three would learn Sastras. But it all came to naught." In a subsequent interview he elaborated: "I taught Veda to the first two sons, but both complained, expressed unwillingness because they would not have salaried careers. So I said to them 'Why not be cultivators *and* Veda pandits?' But there was pressure from relatives who asked me 'Why do you keep them captive? Release them! Let them study what they want, they are good students.' It was not an easy decision for me. I made up my mind, sent the first son to a good Brahman family in Kakinada, a family with ritual purity and traditions maintained. My mother cooked for him. There he finished high school, went on to Hyderabad to complete his bachelor's degree. Grandsons, even more than sons, are further away, alienated from our tradition. But all sons and grandsons came here to stay with me for *upanayana* and to learn to interiorize *sandhya-vandana* and," Lanka added with his special forgiving grace, acknowledging a degree of pride in his sons'achievements in their non-traditional lives, "to learn to do things independently." His last son eventually became the leading comedic actor in Telugu films.

A godsend in those early days was the donation of a house and a half-acre of cropland in a new *agrahara* founded by Nedunuri Srirama Murti on March

4, 1960. It was established not far from Nedunuru village, and he named it Kamesvari *agrahara* after his mother. There were only four other houses in this quiet, isolated enclave in the midst of orchards and paddy fields, none of them in Veda, although the Chirravuri family did produce Baballa's favorite student, Ramam, and later the Sripada family settled in with one son, Manikya, in Veda. It was the perfect location for Lanka to teach, supervise agriculture on his seven acres (including those inherited from his father), and write privately published books and pamphlets on Veda and *srauta*. Occasionally he would attend local *sabha* or take a bus to Rajahmundry and then an east coast train south to Kanci or Sringeri to participate in discussions of *vedartha*, the deep meanings of the Veda.

Although he seldom commented on it, the percentage of Brahmans in nearby Nedunuru village steadily shrank over his years of residence in the *agrahara* to about 2 or 3 percent, with Scheduled Castes (SCs) and BCs (the so-called Backward Castes, Settibalijas dominating, followed by Kamsalis, Devangas, Kummaris, Mangalis, Cakalis, and others) making up a solid majority of the populace. He was acquainted with virtually all the service castes and the SCs provided his agricultural labor crews. And all recognized him as their most famous resident. Nedunuru still celebrates two *sabha* every year, one in Lanka's name, the other in the name of Siva, patron deity of the village.

Before deteriorization of his health, Lanka could talk with endless energy about the details of any sacrifice or the metastructures of *srauta* in general. Of his own ritual life, however, he was extremely reticent. By reconstructing fragments from many conversations with others, it appears that he hired a carpenter in Nedunuru village to fashion ritual implements and set fires there in 1957. He intended to do *adhana* only, an odd stance since later in life he insisted that *agni-stoma* was "incumbent upon every Brahman to remove the stain of *dur-brahmana* (being a bad Brahman)." It was Anasuya who later credited herself as the motivating force. "She wanted to perform *yajna*, so she did," said daughter-in-law Surya proudly. Allied with Anasuya was their son-in-law Mitranarayana who actually taunted his elder by caricaturing *adhana* as insignificant and useless without the follow-up *soma*-sacrifice. After a three-year gap, Lanka went back to the carpenter, prepared himself, and performed *agni-stoma* in 1960 in the crop fields of Kamesvari *agrahara*. At that point, Mitranarayana had gone on to perform *sarvato-mukha*.

The narrative of Lanka the unflappable has many contributors. In addition to his laconic comment after 160-mile-per-hour winds ravaged his house and destroyed his son's house only fifteen feet from his workspace, there was a time years ago when everyone came to commiserate after unusually heavy rains washed out much of his cropland. "Oh it's fine!" said Lanka, "No problem." "He was born with detachment," commented Duvvuri Yajulu; "he just doesn't get involved." Once during Lanka's declining years the *dora* attempted to express sympathy for his three-month stay in a hospital for surgical removal of a toe following complications from diabetes. It was met with "Oh, really? *I* didn't know about the toe! How did *you* know?" And when the supernumerary Sankaracarya of Kancipuram, venerated in South India as if he were a maha-raja if not a deity, suddenly appeared one day in the tiny *agrahara* just to see Lanka, not in a *palki* (palanquin) in the style of his customary travels with an entourage, but in a car, like a businessman, everyone pressed him for details on this extraordinary visitation:

DUVVURI YAJULU (EXCITED): "What did he say?"
LANKA: "What *would* he say?"
D.Y. (AWED BY THE THOUGHT): "Did he come in here, right into this very house?"
LANKA: "Yes."
DORA: "What did he say?"
LANKA: "What *would* he say?"
D.Y.: "Did he ask about your health?"
LANKA: "Ahh" (meaning yes).
A THIRD VISITOR: "Did you speak in Sanskrit?"
LANKA: "No, Telugu."
D.Y. (TRYING ONE LAST TIME): "Was there any message from him?"
LANKA: "No.

And when at another time the *dora* complained that he was constantly receiving contradictory and misleading information about *srauta* performances, Lanka's acerbic wit had the perfect solution. "Just write," he counciled drily: "sometimes they do rituals, sometimes they don't."

Lanka was much like Baballa in his outspoken distaste for anything that might smack of *veda-vikraya*, the selling of the Veda. A year after his death, Anasuya was asked if she had encouraged Lanka to perform more rituals after their *agni-stoma*. Her reply was revealing: "We had our own house and there was no lack of *rtvij* for sacrifices," she said, stating the two most common excuses for non-performance. "Qualified people were available in Nedunuru and Sriramapuram, including my younger brothers, Duvvuri Yajulu, even mature pandits here to study with him. The problem was *dabbu* (money). Not enough. It's all centered on *dabbu*, soliciting *dabbu*, collecting *dabbu*. India somehow became a *dabbu* culture. We were content with just doing *agni-hotra* every day." And so the pandit most informed about *srauta* in the entire region was content to be a supervisor and lender of wisdom rather than a sacrificer garnering additional titles. And as a director, his reputation and awards increased as though he had been an actor. When he received the Padma Bhushan from the president of India on May 7, 1994, he shrugged and said, "It's all just propaganda."

One of the most appealing aspects of Lanka's personality was his insatiable curiosity. He would turn the tables on the *dora* in the midst of detailed explanations of *soma* pounding, for example, and suddenly engage in a long discussion of karma or God (*bhagavantudu* or *devudu* in Telugu), evil, and freedom in human action. Frequently, observing evangelicals among the Scheduled Caste hamlets, he asked about Christianity. Once he presented a startling query without a hint of mischief: "How are George and Victoria?" Did he think that Queen Victoria (died 1901) and King George VI (emperor of India until 1947, king of Great Britain until his death in 1952) had retired to watch history from the bleachers? Quite possibly he meant to imply that nothing of significance happened in the twentieth century.

When his swollen legs failed him in 1991 and he could do only the mantras for *agni-hotra*, no longer able to get up for *kriya*, he joked: "Quite a trio of *ahitagni* we are: Baballa has no ears, Yajulu no eyes, I have no legs." Assisted by a son, however, in 1994 he became the only Konasima *ahitagni* to fly in an airplane, off to Delhi to accept the presidential citation. Two things convinced Lanka that he would die in his seventy-second year: his astrological *mrtyu-cakra* (astrological death chart) with a heavy burden of the planet Rahu on his back, and the deep impression made by his father's death at that age in 1947. Rahu struck him, he said, with "a fatal illness," but he was successful in countering Death with mantras and *japa*.

Lanka's health was not the same again, however, and two years later he ceased *agni-hotra* after a thirty-year career. It is called *jirnadu*, he explained, being consumed and "digested" by Old Age, by Kala, Time. Like all Veda pandits he had memorized the haunting refrain that concludes Taittiriya Upanisad, *aham annam aham annam*, "I am food, I am food." But he was not yet fully digested. There are provisions, he added, reciting the appropriate texts, when an *ahitagni* or *patni* can no longer maintain requisite strength. A new *mrtyu-cakra* prepared in 1988 gave him until age eighty, but this one was no more accurate than earlier ones and was off by seven years. At his *sahasra-candra darsana*, the eightieth birthday celebration for having lived to see a thousand full moons, he was on the mend from foot surgery and feeling chipper. At age eighty-three he was teaching Vyakarana to a new graduate student. "Death is inevitable," he observed, "but the will to live is strong." He did not suddenly drop dead like Cayanulu, or go gentle into that good night like Baballa and Duvvuri Yajulu, but endured through considerable suffering, including the loss of his memory, for his final two years. He died at 1:03 PM on Sunday June 20, 1999, age eighty-seven.

The 1995 cyclone severely damaged the house in Kamesvari *agrahara* where Lanka and Anasuya raised their eight children. Immediately opposite on the narrow lane, a similar house was occupied by their fourth son, the one to whom Lanka had turned over crop cultivation in 1988 and one who had previously been president of the agricultural co-op of Nedunuru and two adjacent villages. After the cyclone, that frame house was rebuilt on a new concrete slab and there Anasuya lived out her days. The old house of the greater part of seventy years of married life was boarded up in 1999, opened only for *masika*, the monthly *sraddha* for Lanka. Not until his anniversary *sraddha* could the house once again be considered for another's habitation. In 2000 it was too soon said Anasuya with a clear, bright face: "Too many memories."

As with Lanka, her final years were difficult, and when visited in March 2005 she was unable to rise from her blanket on the floor or recognize anyone, not even the son and daughter-in-law who cared for her. She seemed then to be playing Lady Macbeth, mumbling worriedly, endlessly tugging something, imaginary rings perhaps, from the fingers of one hand, then reversing to wring out the five fingers of the other hand. Finally, she would rise from her blanket with sudden energy and shout "Agni-hotra! Agni-hotra!" She breathed her last on the final day of the year, December 31, 2005, at 2:30 in the afternoon, having lived to the age of ninety, longer than anyone known to her lineage.

3.3 Vyaghresvaram Village

3.3.1 Bulusu Kamesvara (1926–2010)

In addition to Bulusu Cayanulu's family in Sriramapuram there was another Bulusu lineage a short distance away in the village of Vyaghresvaram. Tucked away among palm groves off the main road from Mukkamala Lock to Amalapuram is a small village named for Siva as Lord of Vyaghra, the tiger. The soft rumble of wooden bullock-cart wheels on dirt tracks is still a pleasing sound there today. Only a ten-minute bicycle ride from Sriramapuram, it seems as quiet and undisturbed now as Nedunuru was in 1980, far from motor traffic noise and bustle, as remote as any village could possibly be in twenty-first century-India. Long ago, the visitor is told, a Brahman was treed here by a roving tiger. The tree he escaped into happened to be a Bilva, sacred to Siva. The Brahman prayed and did a treetop *puja* to "Vyaghresvara-*maha*!" When he finished his worship the tiger had changed into a Siva *linga*, and the name of the place became Vyaghresvara-puram, later shortened to Vyaghresvaram.

Here this second Bulusu family raised two brothers, the elder named Vyaghresvara after the village and the younger named Kamesvara. Close by, the Pullela family raised their son, Laksminarayana. All three were destined to become *ahitagni* in this quiet *agrahara*-like neighborhood. The father of the Bulusu boys, a schoolteacher in Munganda, did not set the fires, but his father and father's brother had both been *ahitagni*. The latter, Antana, went on to perform *cayana*, so the young boys had two older models in *srauta*, their grandfather and uncle. In addition, strong influence came from two itinerant promoters of *srauta*, as energetic as they were charismatic, Renducintala Yajulu, who had once been a student in Vyaghresvaram village, and Kapilavayi Yajnesvara Agnihotra, who was born in Konasima. In April 1967 the Bulusu brothers established fires and performed *yajna* together on consecutive days, sharing *rtvij*: Vyaghresvara's *adhana* first, Kamesvara's *adhana* second, Vyaghresvara's *agni-stoma* beginning immediately, followed by Kamesvara's *agni-stoma*. At this point the older brother became Bulusu Vyaghresvara Soma-yaji, the younger one Bulusu Kamesvara Soma-yajulu, and both wives added Somi-devamma to their given names.

Vyaghresvara, as older son, inherited their *ahitagni* grandfather's ancestral home in the center of the village and Kamesvara established a separate residence for his family nearby. Kamesvara encouraged his older brother to go on and perform *cayana* as their uncle had done. But Vyaghresvara was reluctant and said "No, no, you do it!" and eventually this older brother was instrumental in making preparations for *agni-cayana* to be performed by Kamesvara. Suddenly, however, Vyaghresvara died. A dispirited Kamesvara and his wife Satyavati abandoned their plans for additional sacrifices beyond the *nitya* rituals of *agni-hotrin* and *patni*. At this point the once vigorous *srauta* life of Vyaghresvaram village remained with Kamesvara and Satyavati.

Bulusu Vyaghresvara's untimely death occurred long before he could be interviewed. The experiences and reflections of Kamesvara and Satyavati must be representative. Kamesvara, born in 1926, received his sacred thread at age seven and then spent thirteen years about six miles away in Indupalli learning Veda from his guru, Rani Hayagriva Avadhani, the same Rani who was Samavedam's third guru. The Apastamba Sutras he received from his older brother Vyaghresvara. He was married to Satyavati (named for the goddess of the famous temple of Satyanarayana and Satyavati on the hillltop of Annavaram in the north of the district) before completing Veda at age twenty. Together they raised ten children—six sons and four daughters. Neither of the Bulusu brothers succeeded in teaching Veda to sons. But like Lanka and Anasuya, Kamesvara and Satyavati did marry one daughter to a Veda pandit, Sripada Manikya Avadhani Ghanapati of the Kamesvari *agrahara* outside of Nedunuru, and he is still eligible to set the fires if so inclined.

Soft-spoken Kamesvara's gaze was open and direct, augmented by an easy smile. Satyavati is forthright, good-humored, affable, another ready smile bracketed by high cheekbones and twinkling eyes. And always she was completely focused on the conversation. Of all the *ahitagni-patni* couples interviewed for this survey during more than three decades, this pair was the most congenial and forthcoming regarding intimate details of their life of *srauta*. Upon first inquiry regarding their *agni-hotra* hearths, these were immediately shown with all ritual implements exhibited and explained in detail. There was no hesitation about purity. It was, of course, a period when the fires had lapsed for contingencies and before they were to be rekindled with appropriate *prayascittas* for the interruption. With both there was not the slightest reluctance to share personal relationships with Agni, nor any dissimulation regarding their *srauta* schedules. Satyavati, as knowledgeable as Kamesvara, adds a wealth of information about their thirty-five years of *agni-hotra* together, commenting on ritual terms while drinking tea or coconut juice and sitting alongside. Along with Maruti, wife of Kapilavayi Rama Sastri in Annavaram, she was one of only two *patni* to be so well informed, articulate, comfortable with male guests, and eager to contribute from her considerable knowledge and experience. Many of her observations are cited below in Chapter 4. (See Figure 3.14, Kamesvara and Satyavati, Vyaghresvaram 2005, and Figure 2.6 earlier, the couple beside their hearths, Vyaghresvaram, 2000.)

FIGURE 3.14. Kamesvara and Satyavati, Vyaghresvaram 2005.

Over the years Kamesvara estimated that he had been invited to some twenty-five to thirty *srauta* rituals, including *vaja-peya, paundarika*, and other *cayana*. For some of these he was *rtvij*, including the role of *adhvaryu*. None of the three or four students who began Veda with him completed the Taittiriya *sakha*. He was, however, more successful in teaching *smarta* to almost thirty students, continuing to teach well beyond his eightieth year; most of these students are now employed as *smarta* pandits in Hyderabad or other parts of the state. Kamesvara's Vedic continuity is assured, if not in sons, certainly in the excellence of mantras recited in rituals over much of Andhra. Kamesvara died in 2010 at the age of eighty-four, last of the *ahitagni* in the Sriramapuram-Vyaghresvaram-Nedunuru circle, leaving only Mitranarayana in the broader area.

3.3.2 Pullela Laksminarayana (1920–1999)

The third *ahitagni* who established fires in Vyaghresvaram village in the 1960s was Pullela Laksminarayana, Kaundinya *gotra*, born in 1920 in Narendrapuram on the Gannavaram Canal beside the Vasistha Godavari River. As a new *agni-stomin* about 1970 at the age of fifty, his full name became Pullela Laksminarayana Soma-yajulu and his wife became Kamesvari Somi-devamma. He was the only son of an *ahitagni*. Sripada Laksmi Narasimha Soma-yaji, a maternal uncle in Tondavaram, was another strong motivator for Laksminarayana's *srauta* career.

Kamesvari (1926–96), from the Vemparala family, was the granddaughter of an *ahitagni* in the same village of Tondavaram, south of Gangalakurru. She was married to Laksminarayana there on the left bank of the great horseshoe curve of the Vainateya Godavari River in 1936 when she was ten and he was sixteen. They raised eight children, four boys and four girls. None of the girls married Veda pandits and as was the case with the two Bulusu brothers of Vyaghresvaram, none of the sons learned Veda. The sons of Laksminarayana and Kamesvari, now beyond their middle years, blame economic hardship for this but also, perhaps defensively, mention a certain shyness in their father with regard to authoritative teaching. Following his *ahitagni* father, Laksminarayana had wished to set the fires but delayed until a private house could be obtained. About 1962 he and his family moved east a few miles to Vyaghresvaram in search of a better livelihood, aided by the provision of a house from Kamesvari's older sister. Vyaghresvaram in the 1960s, like the adjacent villages of Mukkamala, Nedunuru, and the Sriramapuram *agrahara*, was a lively scene of *srauta* activities, with the *yajna* of Lanka and three Bulusus, Duvvuri Yajulu's *paundarika*, Baballa's *aruna-ketuka*, and others. Laksminarayana and Kamsvari set the fires and began *agni-hotra* twice daily, routine *isti* for new and full moon, and the annual *agrayana*. Like Lanka, however, he waited several years before his first *soma* ritual, finally performing *agni-stoma* in 1970 with Lanka as *adhvaryu*, Mitranarayana as *brahman*, Kamesvara and other Konasima pandits among the eighteen *rtvij*.

Laksminarayana was known for fidelity to his fires and *isti*. He and his sons were frequently seen collecting dead wood for kindling, making noises in the scrub trees to scare off snakes. He was faithful in *agrayana* on *amavasya* or *purnima* of a harvest month, usually favoring the time of Dipavali. The *sravana pasu* he performed once only, immediately after his *agni-stoma*. No other *srauta karma* were projected.

Smarta employment was not a career choice and the family's economic situation was consistently shaky. It was only about 1986 at age sixty-six that Laksminarayana entered the TTD lists, and then as a non-reciting pensioner, a *vrddha* pandit. He and the family were relieved to have an assured monthly income at last. In later years the lack of *rtvij* was worrisome and at times his Telugu pandit son, Laksmi Narasimha Murti, a schoolteacher, would stand in as one.

Kamesvari Somi-devamma died in 1996 and took the three fires with her in the *brahma-medha* supervised by Duvvuri Yajulu and Bulusu Cayanulu of Sriramapuram, with Bulusu Kamesvara of Vyaghresvaram also present. Due to the couple's advanced age, fires had lapsed some three or four years earlier. The *laukika arani* and "the other," a euphemism for the female kindling block, were saved as the final pair of ritual implements necessary to churn fire for the cremation of Laksminarayana only two years later. There were no legatees of the Pullela lineage continuing "*vedam-lo*."

3.4 *Kakinada Town*

3.4.1 Mitranarayana

Like his departed elders Baballa and Lanka, Bhamidipati Mitranarayana Sarvatomukha Somayaji (hereafter, Mitranarayana), Sandilya *gotra*, is the son of a well-known *ahitagni*, *ghana-pathi*, and Veda-*bhasya* scholar. The father, Bhamidipati Sesadri Somayaji (c.1909–89), performed his *agni-stoma* in 1935 when he was in his mid-twenties. Mitranarayana was there for that *yajna* as a five-year-old, too young an observer for recollection. Sesadri received certificates of distinction in Veda and *srauta*, both an *urlam patta* and a Bezwada (Vijayawada) *patta*, something like receiving PhDs from both Harvard and Oxford. He and his wife, Surya Somidevamma, whose grandfather, father, and brothers all performed *agni-stoma*, had ten children, three of them sons, and Sesadri taught two sons to completion with certification as Veda pandits and succeeded in marrying one of the seven daughters to a Veda pandit as well. Lanka, only three years younger than this elder Bhamidipati, was one of his many other students. When Lanka eventually set his fires, Mitranarayana—married to Lanka's only daughter, Anasuya—became son-in-law as well as son of an *ahitagni*.

Mitranarayana, the first male child of Seshadri and Surya's ten children, was born in 1930. He completed Veda entirely with his father in the village of Korumilli by age sixteen. Korumilli is near Kapilesvarapuram, the home village of Duvvuri Yajulu, due north of Nedunuru on the left bank of the eastward-flowing Gautami-Godavari River. At age fifteen Anasuya crossed this broad stream to begin her life with Mitranarayana in Korumilli. After the birth of the first of their seven children, *adhana* and *agni-stoma* were performed in 1955 to initiate a brief but intense *srauta* career. Strongly motivated toward *yajna* by his inlaws as well as his natal family, Mitranarayana became an *ahitagni* himself at the youthful age of twenty-two, four years earlier than his father. His *agni-stoma* occurred before all others reported here—Baballa, Bulusu Cayanulu, Lanka, Laksminarayana, Bulusu Vyaghresvara, and Bulusu Kamesvara—with the sole exception of Duvvuri Yajulu. With such an early start in *agni-hotra* he was intrigued into further *srauta karma* and before 1970 had accomplished a *cayana* and a *sarvato-mukha* in Nedunuru, the *sarvato-mukha* demanding seventy-two *rtvij* to work at fire altars facing in all four directions. It was the first in the delta since Renducintala Yajulu had performed one some fifty years previously. The youthful sacrificer now bore the title Mahagni Catur Sarvatomukha Yajulu.

Duvvuri Yajulu, a close relative, was a major source of inspiration, and the two were mutually supportive even when one or the other was across the river in Konasima for Vedic learning or *srauta* service. Throughout the 1950s and 1960s there was no lack of *rtvij* support system for routine *isti, agrayana,* and *sravana-pasu.* In a span of only seven years Mitranarayana managed to perform four significant *srauta* rituals on top of *nityagnihotrin* duties. On the teaching side of his career, however, Mitranarayana was no more successful than his father-in-law Lanka in transmitting Veda to any of his four sons. Just as with Lanka, continuity in Veda was assured only by teaching the sons of others, and this continued into his late seventies.

Mitranarayana credits Uppuluri Ganapati Sastri, one of the founders of the TTD *parayana* program for Veda pandits, for the furtherance of his career in several ways. Uppuluri, born in Dangeru in 1888 on the Bank Canal directly east of Korumilli, lived for most of his nearly one hundred years in the District headquarters town of Kakinada. Uppuluri brought Mitranarayana to a donated house in Kakinada in 1977, facilitating his appointment as a Veda pandit in the Venkatesvara temple only a few miles south in the village of Jagannaikapuram. The rent-free house enabled him to support a family of nine. For many years his routine was to bathe, do *sandhya-vandana* and *agni-hotra*, eat breakfast, recite in the temple 8 to 10 AM, return home by bus for lunch at 11, teach a student in the afternoon, *sandhya-vandana* and *agni-hotra* again, dinner, and sleep. By 1992 his TTD salary for *parayana* was Rs. 1,000 and by 1998 Rs. 1,800 per month.

The four-altar fire stretched out his enthusiasm for performing further *srauta* rituals as *yajamana*. "By the end of the *sarvato-mukha* I had *vairagya* (indifference, even aversion toward) *srauta*." But for many years he was and still is sought as supervisor and *rtvij* for major and minor sacrifices of others. For example, by 1998 he had supervised eight *paundarika* and two *vaja-peya* as *brahman* or *adhvaryu* and served as *udgatr* or *hotr* in numerous other rituals including *naksatra isti* and *panca-ratna yaga* in places such as Machilipatnam. Finally, he exhausted himself serving as *brahman* in a *paundarika* in Vijayawada that began in late January 2005 and seventy-five-year-old Mitranarayana had to return to Kakinada to recover.

As to his own ritual life, after some seven years of continuous *agni-hotra* in Kakinada he allowed the fires to lapse, rekindling them only for *agrayana* and *sravana-pasu*, with *prayascitta* and subsequent *darsa-* or *purnimasa isti*, as he had moved to a rented house rather than keep his own house. But after construction of a new private house in an attractive suburban area of Kakinada he still did not rekindle for continuous *agni-hotra*. There were various explanations over the years: the *agni-hotra* room in the new house was not finished, his wife's health was not good, there were not enough *rtvij* available for *isti*.

And it was true that Kakinada had grown increasingly more isolated from the *agrahara* of Konasima, and both students and qualified Veda pandits had dwindled away in numbers. When Uppuluri died in 1988, almost a centenarian, Vedic life in Kakinada was more or less defined by Mitranarayana alone. By the spring of 1992 he was reduced to teaching only a retired engineer, two years his junior, eight hours every day, working on the fourth *kanda* of the Taittiriya Samhita in *krama patha,* the sixty-year-old "student" reading aloud from a book as Mitranarayana recited with eyes closed, his mind absorbed in the text he himself had learned in his father's voice more than half a century before. It was a moving scene for the *dora*, one displaying the complex history of a "text," the unchanging oral Veda in a changing era of print. Later in Kakindada there was something of a revival with the establishment of a Veda *patha-sala* in a hamlet outside of town. The school lacked *srauta* expertise, and

Mitranarayana, after a request for aid, received five students, ten to twelve years old, to learn Taittiriya segments on *adhana, agni-stoma,* and *agni-cayana.*

In his middle years, Mitranarayana was a good-looking man, tall like his father and father-in-law Lanka. He is likable, with a strong face, his gold earrings bouncing as he gestures rapidly with hands, arms, head, fingers waggling with rapid wrist movements to affirm or negate a statement. In April 1992 a "felicitation" was held in Kakinada to honor him, with Remella Surya Prakasa Avadhani, the stodgy Veda-*bhasya* scholar from Rajahmundry, as chief speaker. Mitranarayana was disappointed that father-in-law Lanka was not hearty enough to travel from Nedunuru for this. Other felicitations and *patta* certificates occurred in Chennai, Kanci, Tirupati, Rajahmundry, and Delhi. But he is wary of such honors. "All sorts of temptations get in the way of Vedic life. 'We will honor you . . .' 'We will photograph you . . .' 'We will set up a statue of you . . .' That kind of attention can wipe out all sense of devotion and security and interfere with self-knowledge."

By the close of the century Mitranarayana, rail-thin and feeling the weight of his years, announced abruptly that he had only a few years of active life remaining. Complete baldness exaggerated a long face bracketed by heavy gold rings tugging at his earlobes. But well over a decade into the new century he remains active and highly respected by colleagues young and old. "He is an excellent scholar in *srauta,* very much self-sufficient, independent, one who speaks with authority and erudition" was Duvvuri Yajulu's observation years ago. And now Duvvuri Phani ranks him even higher than his own father, referring to Mitranarayana as a *tri-kanda* scholar, one with universal knowledge of the essential three subjects: ritual, worship, and knowledge—*karma, upasana,* and *jnana,* respectively.

He retains both his instinctive sense of humor and withering sarcasm. Setting high standards in his own performance, Mitranarayana is also known for his unusually stringent, at times scathing critiques of others, including both students with "empty learning" and clueless contemporary colleagues. When he goes to the Virabhadra temple on Pattisima Island in the Godavari River he joins a great throng of one to two hundred Veda pandits to recite for much of Maha-siva-ratri night. He notes that "only five or six" others actually know correctly the *svasti-vacana* they have been summoned and paid to recite. And recently, replacing Duvvuri Yajulu as one of the board of examiners of newly minted reciters of Veda, he deplored their lack of skill: "I was asked to rank first, second, third class. *What* class? About a hundred students came from different areas. I did not approve of a single one! They did not deserve to pass! So I tried to remain a spectator and let the other examiners decide." Regarding Vedic Sanskrit he often sounds like an American college professor grumbling about current students who can neither speak nor write with coherence in their own language. Mitranarayana sees himself as an outlier, one who is both the last of the old guard keepers of tradition and a critic of all that has gone wrong in modern life.

Of today's youth who attempt to maintain English education alongside Veda he is contemptuous. *Huna-vidya* he sees as the main cause of the decline in Veda and *srauta*. "Vaidika life has disappeared, the spirit has gone, it is a period of *huna-vidya*. . . . The generation of accomplished elders is over. . . . There are no *rtvij*-priests, there is no eligibility (*adhikara*) remaining for someone to become a sacrificer." Those *srauta* rituals still going on are "tasteless," he concludes, while admitting that he travels south to participate, even supervise. "If motives are not pure the performer of rites receives no intended results. He gets only the pressed stalks, not the sweet juice of the cane." Here he expresses special contempt for sacrificers in Krishna District who spend most of their time demanding money.

And vehement vituperation Mitranarayana reserves for his aging colleagues who, unlike himself, "fear death." When his famous father died in 1989 and required the *brahma-medha* funeral deserved by *ahitagni*, it was difficult to find experts willing to participate, including a longtime friend and colleague he now castigates without mercy. "By attending they think they too will die. So I took the book, read it, did it myself," he said proudly. "Otherwise, without *brahma-medha*, my father's funeral would have been that of a dog." It is possible that the solicited Veda pandit used Dharmasastra cautions to beg off from fulfilling the request despite the urgency of a rarely performed ritual.[7]

In 1988 Baballa predicted that *srauta karma* in the delta would last only another ten years. He was close to the mark. By the century's end Bulusu Kamesvara and Mitranarayana were both discussing rekindling. All other fires were extinguished and no one was convincingly projecting *adhana*. And the two remaining *ahitagni* of Konasima lacked the passion so evident in the Dendukuri families of Vijayawada in Krishna District or in the Kapilavayi brothers discussed later.

Although the son-in-law of Lanka, seemingly a generation younger, Mitranarayana is still of the "old school" like Lanka and Duvvuri Yajulu. He adheres to the old calendar, referring to the named years Nandana, Durmukha, Sarvari, respectively, for his performance of *adhana/agni-stoma, agni-cayana*, and then *sarvato-mukha*. And like Duvvuri Yajulu, he speaks easily of *srauta* life as a family *vidya*, practice. Always reliable for candid remarks, Mitranarayana seems to enjoy receiving occasional visits from the *dora* and Krishnayya, the Andhra University professor. Kakinada is a town drained of Vedic life over the decades and now busy with its political function as district headquarters. Discussion of Vedic teaching and especially *srauta* details brightens his day and energizes him. Today he gesticulates in the front room of a pleasant and comfortable house with sunlight and breezes filtering through coconut palms. (See Figure 3.15, Mitranarayana 1998 and Figure 3.16, M. V. Krishnayya in Mitranarayana's house in Kakinada, 2005.)

Anasuya, inside with domestic chores, always remains within earshot. A beautiful daughter, Lanka's granddaughter seen so often in Nedunuru or here in Kakinada, serves tea. Mitranarayana and Anasuya now have thirteen grandchildren. Behind Mitranarayana are shelves loaded with brittle *tala-patra* palm-leaf manuscripts, some well over two hundred years old, many written in his Veda pandit grandfather's hand, all carefully handed down from his

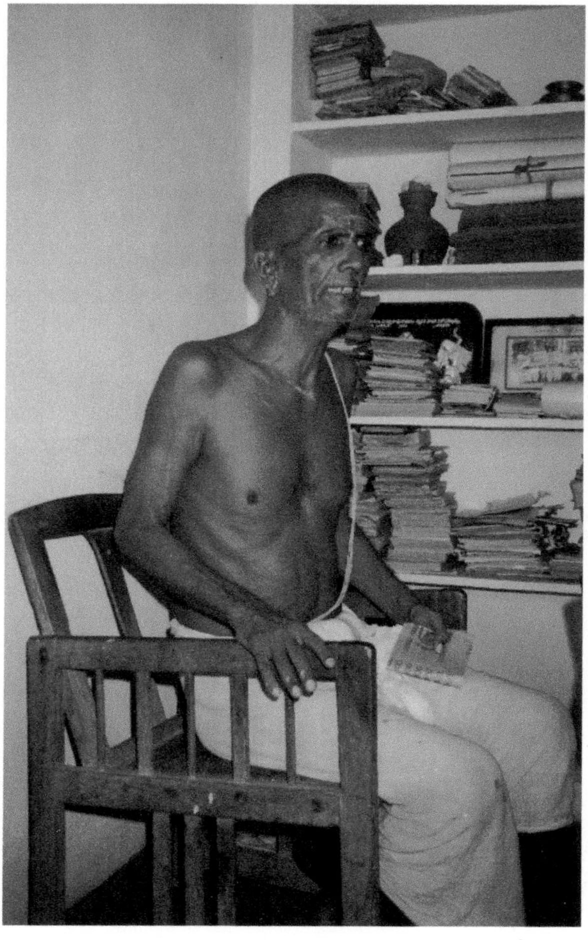

FIGURE 3.15. Mitranarayana, Kakinada 1998.

FIGURE 3.16. M. V. Krishnayya with Mitranarayana, Kakinada 2005.

ahitagni father. "Recently," reports Mitranarayana, "a man came from America and asked for books. So I told him to take all these, and he will come for them." On the same wall are class photos from Andhra University in Visakhapatnam that include two sons, with years of *huna-vidya* behind them, now well placed in secular jobs. Bank managers have little use for *tala-patra* in an unlearned language. "Once," says Mitranarayana, resigned to his role as sole survivor of Vedic *srauta* tradition in his part of India, "I received a telephone call asking me to recite Veda over the phone. I was reluctant but my colleagues made me yield. I asked about results at the other end and they told me it recorded very well and everyone was pleased. An honorarium of Rs. 1,116 came. What a great profession this is! All I need is one phone call per day and I don't have to do anything else!"[8]

3.5 *From Kakinada to Vijayawada and Beyond*

3.5.1 The Kapilavayi Family

The white Andhra University van was surrounded by excited townsfolk pressing close to peer through its windows. Something nefarious must be under way, particularly since a Foreign woman was inside with three men. The sound of chanting was unsettling. After the recording session was completed, the crowd was told that the *dora* from America, his wife, and a professor from Andhra University were scholars seeking to learn about the Vedas from the young pandit assigned to *parayana* in the nearby temple here in Simhacalam, and that the van afforded the only quiet place for recording. The recitant so generous with his time and expertise on that December evening in 1980 was Kapilavayi (Kapilavai) Venkatesvara Sastri.

Most of the narratives thus far have disclosed the unfortunate termination of lineages of *ahitagnis* and other Veda pandits. The recent family histories of Baballa, Bulusu Cayanulu, Lanka, Bulusu Kamesvara, Laksminarayana, and Mitranarayana all highlight an extraordinary and seemingly irreversible attrition in Konasima at the close of the twentieth century. At that point only the lineages of Duvvuri Yajulu and Samavedam, among all those families selected here for review, gave promise of continuity in Veda. As for *srauta*, one by one the *agni-hotra* fires went cold like the lamps of a village abandoned to sleep. Konasima darkened in the six-year period 1993 to 1999 with successive losses of Baballa, Duvvuri Yajulu's wife Surya, Laksminarayana's wife Kamesvari, Bulusu Cayanulu, and Lanka, leaving at the close of the century only the hearths of Bulusu Kamesvara and Mitranarayana, both at that time with fires in abeyance. With the loss of Bulusu Kamesvara in 2010, only Mitranarayana remained. It is revealing therefore to turn to a final pair of families extended out from Konasima to the west and to the north, both of them illustrating strong lineages of Veda, and one suggesting eventual vitality in *srauta* as well.

The first of these two families to be considered is the Kapilavayis and the second will be the Gullapallis in Iragavaram, West Godavari District. Two active Kapilavayi Veda pandit brothers, ages sixty-one and fifty-seven in 2014, are employed in *parayana* positions in regionally famous Andhra pilgrimage temples and both maintained strong aspirations toward *ahitagni* life upon retirement. Each projected hopeful and elaborate plans for increasingly complex *srauta* sacrifices for years beyond *adhana* and *agni-stoma*, these life-changing rituals to take place after completion of temple duties. These two might be charged with boastful daydreams were it not for their remarkable pedigree. They are Kapilavayi Venkatesvara Sastri and Kapilavayi Rama Sastri, the two sons of Kapilavayi Yajnesvara Agnihotra Sastri of Kakinada, a colleague of Renducintala Yajulu. Together, these two elder statesmen were assiduous promoters of Veda and *srauta* throughout Andhra for all of their twentieth-century careers.

3.5.2 Yajnesvara Agnihotra Sastri (1909–1983)

The brothers' narrative begins with an astonishing family history that reads like the plot of a Salman Rushdie novel. A nineteenth-century *ahitagni* named Kapilavayi Venkata Somayajulu and his wife Subbalaksmi Somidevamma raised five sons and three daughters in Kakinada, the town where Mitranarayana is now the sole remaining *ahitagni*. Their first son, Pedda Rama Sastri (1889–1987) lived for ninety-eight years. He was an extraordinarily dynamic Veda pandit but remained a lifelong bachelor and was therefore ineligible for a single consecrated fire let alone aspirations to *tretagni*. A second son born to Venkata and Subbalaksmi was also a renowned Veda pandit, did marry and maintain the *grhya* (*smarta agni*), but never set three fires as his father had done. He was Chinna Rama Sastri (1904–85), a contemporary of Baballa. Chinna (Little or Younger) Rama followed Pedda (Big or Elder) Rama in birth order. A third son was born and then twenty-one years after Pedda a fourth son arrived.

Named Yajnesvara, this youngest was taught Veda by his oldest brother Pedda, whose age made him equivalent to biological as well as spiritual father. He too excelled and went on to become Yajnesvara Agnihotra Sastri (1910–83), Kasyapa *gotra*, famous throughout South India for his sponsorship of Veda and *srauta*. Sponsorship, supervision, promotion, boosterism are all the right words. Although fully qualified through precocious acquisition of Veda in the best of places in India he, like his older brother Chinna Rama Sastri, he did not accomplish *adhana* and therefore not *agni-stoma*, not from lack of desire but rather from sibling blockade. He could not set fires because his two older brothers had not done so. As compensation he became an expert *srotriya* and the most impressive promoter of *srauta* in the modern history of India.

It is a narrative of filial devotion and stubborn guru loyalty combined, one that makes sense only to those *vedam-lo*, in Veda. A younger brother may not set fires if his older brother has not already done so. There are, however, Dharmasastra provisions for *parista*, supercession, in which the older brother's permission may be sought. Why was this not a manageable solution, particularly in the unusual situation of a brother who chose, for personal reasons, never to marry and become a householder qualified for Agni? The answer was that Yajnesvara found it inconceivable to "one-up" his elders, in particular, Pedda, his own guru. Becoming an *agni-stomin*, a *soma* sacrificer, confers privileged rank. He would have surpassed both older brothers, becoming *karmadhikara*, the official person in rituals for the family. Even sitting in the same row to eat would be unacceptable. Furthermore, there was always the danger, in ritual theory at least, that the second brother, Chinna, might change his mind and perform *agni-stoma* after all, even in advanced age, thereby negating the fruits of the younger brother's sacrifice. And so, in this "always a bridesmaid, never a bride" situation, never having been *yajamana* in a *yajna* he, Yajnesvara, literally "Lord of Sacrifice," became promoter of *yajna* par excellence, eventually to the point of being lauded with the title "Agni-hotra," the name of that elusive rite whose *srauta* version he would never perform.

Yajnesvara's *upanayana* was at the early age of six when he began to learn the Taittiriya corpus from his brother Pedda. According to the family he was something of a Wunderkind. On January 25, 1984, two months after Yajnesvara's death, M. Chandrasekhar published a hagiographical piece for *The Indian Express* accompanied by a photo of Yajnesvara displaying a certificate in front of his chest like a sculpted Roman senator with tablet. The article included these lines (orthography retained):

> The elders in the family and neighbours were wonderstruck to find Yagneswara Sastry at 12 mellowing into a scholar with Vedavedangas, Vidhyaranya Bhashya, Shatsastras, and sroutas on his fingertips. . . . At 16 he conducted [i.e., supervised] the first yagna independently. . . . [H]e went to the guru-kula asram of Kanchi Pitham at Kumbakonam and dug out three tala-patras [palm leaf manuscripts] which the native pandits failed to comprehend. He laboriously worked on the scriptures till he unraveled the hidden meanings.

However overblown this praise, Yajnesvara became the epitome of an itinerant seeker of Vedic knowledge. He was on a lifetime quest for teachers and texts. Sometimes in the company of brothers Pedda or Chinna or both, sometimes followed by his wife and children, he took trains and buses from point to point. Or much of the time he and his companions walked long distances, *sadhu*-like, carrying peanuts and cashew nuts for sustenance, in search of Veda pandits who might be harboring little or unknown textual recensions or ritual *paddhati*. At times he joined the entourage of one or another *pithadhipati*. Often he collaborated with his good friend Renducintala Yajulu, the other great widely traveled Veda pandit with constant connections to the Godavari Delta. It was a remarkable age. Today, mendicants of all stripes still walk the roads but Veda pandits celebrate their recent affluence by riding in trains, buses, or even taxis.

Yajnesvara's personal acquisition of Vedas extended beyond his middle years. At the age of fifty, for example, he learned the Sukla Yajurveda (Vajasaneyi Samhita) in Kasi, up before dawn for *adhyaya*, retiring for rest only at 8 PM. His special text was the Apastamba Srauta Sutra, simply labeled "Srautam," and his favored ritual was the *paundarika*, a type of *agni-cayana* he studied in a dozen forms and endorsed all over Andhra. Yajnesvara was a supervisor of sacrifices over the territory of the great rivers, the Godavari, Krishna, Kaveri, and well beyond, Ramesvaram, Sringeri, Kanci, Trichi in the South to Bhadrinath, Delhi, and Kasi in the North.

The Taittiriya corpus was of course the Urtext, but the Sama Veda became a special preoccupation for Yajnesvara. Early in his career he had studied the Ranayaniya recension in Vijayanagaram, and then the Kauthuma recension in Kanci. The Jaiminiya recension apparently was unknown to him or too remote to be of personal interest. As noted in Chapter 2, contemporary scholarship on the Sama Veda is divided, some scholars seeing little or no difference between Ranayaniya and Kauthuma, others suggesting some distinctions.[9] Nevertheless, according to his sons, Yajnesvara was able to identify the Sama *gana* in use in the Godavari Delta as a variant distinct from any Ranayaniya or Kauthama version known elsewhere. The difference was sufficient enough to cause a serious rift between *srauta* families in the late twentieth century.

As for the Atharva Veda, there has been more than one line of transmission in the delta. Tangirala Balagangadhara Sastri, Lanka's source, has been mentioned earlier. He also taught Yajnesvara in Kapilesvarapuram, and Yajnesvara responded by teaching the Rg Veda, a case of Veda pandit reciprocity in Vedas outside the Taittiriya corpus. Tangirala had learned the Atharva Veda in Kasi in a special manner, mornings only, with an Agni vow (*vrata*), bearing an earthen pot with burning coals on his head, a wet cloth cushioning the pot. And "student" Yajnesvara did the same.

Yajnesvara and Sita Mahalaksmi built a house in Vijayawada in Krishna Lanka in 1975, relocating in Andhra after many years of peregrinations. Like Lanka in his late years he continued to serve as supervisor for rituals, a Vajapeya in Nedunuru, for example, in which Lanka and Yajnesvara together were in charge.

3.5.3 Venkatesvara Sastri and Family

Both contemporary Kapilavayi brothers inherited their father's passion for the life of *srauta* and benefited from a childhood spent not only learning Vedas but being on the move with their father, uncles, and others, observing sacrifices ordinary and extraordinary. From seven to twelve years of age Venkatesvara, born in 1953, learned the Taittiriya Samhita with Apastamba and from thirteen to fifteen he undertook the three *khandas—adhvaryava, hotriya,* and *audgatriya*—with the aid of a well-worn palm-leaf bundle about twenty inches thick, "the Srautam" in Sanskrit Telugu script of his grandfather. His next task was the Rg Veda, Sakala *sakha*, with Asvalayana. After that came the Atharva Veda, Saunaka *sakha*, which he completed in 1979 at age twenty-seven with much inspiration from Lanka. The Sama Veda was not omitted and he learned portions of what he claims, in accord with his father, to be three different *sakha* or variants thereof. It was these that he recited in the van in 1980 recounted at the beginning of this segment.

His paternal uncle Chinna Rama Sastri retired from service at the Simhacalam temple and recommended Venkatesvara for the post. Still today Venkatesvara recites daily as Rg Veda pandit, one who, like his father, claims the status of *catur-vedin*. The temple is a famous shape-shifting site in the history of Hinduism and an important pilgrimage goal. Normally the central image is one of the Vaisnava god Narasimha, the fierce Man-lion who, according to the temple *sthala-purana*, rescued his devotee Prahlada from burial at sea by the demon Hiranyakasipu. But on one day of every year the seemingly solid sandalpaste *murti* miraculously melts down to something resembling a *linga* and, according to many devotees, reveals the true deity to be Siva!

At the age of nineteen Venkatesvara married Annadanam Sita Rama Laksmi, daughter of a Veda pandit in the Aryapathi *agrahara* near Tenali, Guntur District, and together in Simhacalam they raised three daughters and two sons. Venkatesvara was an aggressive, demanding teacher of the sons, enterprising in method and attempting to succeed where so many had failed. In April 1992, for example, he was taking his sons along when he had temple duty. At ages thirteen and eight, both boys had been removed from school. "Did they like this idea?" was the query for Venkatesvara. "Who cares? I decided for them." Rising at 5 AM every day they tackled the third *khanda*, second *panna*, a five-hour lesson for the boys and the father's *parayana* simultaneously. Rama Yajna Varaha Narasimha Murti, his *upanayana* well behind him, was repeating on schedule and Agni Rama Kumar, his *upanayana* still weeks ahead, was hearing this for the first time. "He joins his brother as an 'outside observer,'" confided Venkatesvara, "so when it is his actual time to 'study' he will have experience." Eventually, however, both returned to school and six years later Rama achieved Intermediate status and prepared for a career in the navy while his younger brother was in tenth class with his first Veda nearly completed. (See Figure 3.17, Kapilavayi Venkatesvara and Sita Rama Laksmi, Simhacalam, 1988, and Figure 3.18, the family in 1999.)

By May 1998, daughters Sitaram Laksmi, Sita Mahalaksmi, and Sridevi were all married and soon all produced grandchildren for their parents, the eldest daughter with a matched pair of twins after delivering two girls. Twins are regarded with circumspection in Vedic history and require special protection. Venkatesvara and Sita Rama Laksmi discussed, as they

FIGURE 3.17. Kapilavayi Venkatesvara Sastri and Sitarama Laksmi, Simhacalam 1988.

FIGURE 3.18. Kapilavayi Venkatesvara family, Simhacalam 1999.

did for three decades, the decision to set the fires and assume the honors and burdens of *agni-hotra*. It had been a comfortable life for the family, living only a few miles west of the sprawling seaport of Visakhapatnam, population over 2 million, with distractions so foreign to *agrahara* life. Venkatesvara, with a good income from Rg Veda recitations, was the first Veda pandit to own a motorcycle, the first to have a television set, and later a cell phone. Middle-class comfort and amenities became second nature and they knew the roles of *agni-hotrin* and *patni* would mean a considerable change in life style.

Sadly, that step was not to be when Sita Rama Laksmi contracted cancer and died at the young age of forty-nine in 2010. Her death was devastating to the wider family as well as to Venkatesvara, the children, and grandchildren. Without remarriage, not only was he blocked from setting fires just as he reached the age of retirement from TTD service, but so also was younger brother Rama Sastri. Family history repeated itself. Rama Sastri found himself in the same bind as his uncle Kapilavayi Chinna Rama Sastri and father Yajnesvara nearly a century ago. They could not set fires because elder bother Pedda Rama Sastri never married in the course of his ninety-eight years.

There is a devastating antiphonal irony here regarding fire. In coastal Andhra, when a youthful man dies, his widow and her friends and relatives all gather to lament mournfully "*gunda, gunda*!" the Telugu word for a pyre or pit of burning embers meant for fire-walking. In modern India it is no longer the case that a widow enters her husband's funeral fire, but so irreversibly altered is her life that in this stressful moment committing *sati* appears as preferable option. On the other side is the death of the youthful wife of an aspirant *ahitagni* where the setting of fires is prohibited and a sacrificing career is ruthlessly denied. Venkatesvara confided that his astrological chart indicates that he will remarry. He wishes to defy that planetary prediction, however, as remarriage, for the sake of a pure lineage, requires a pre-pubescent bride. That would not be right, he said in 2014, when he was sixty-one and his older son already thirty-five.

In the meantime, fortunes were reversed for the two sons of Venkatesvara and Sita Rama Laksmi after both achieved certification as Veda pandits and gained employment by the Andhra Pradesh Department of Temple Endowments. Rama Yajna does *parayana* in Kancipakanam, Chittoor District. He and his wife have a son, Rama Yajnesvara, who lives with his guru, none other than grandfather Venkatesvara in Simnacalam, and anticipates his *upanayana* in 2014. Younger brother Rama Kumar is a Rg Veda pandit in Visakhapatman and does *parayana* in an Anjaneya (Hamuman) temple.

3.5.4 Rama Sastri and Family

The second son of Yajnesvara Agnihotra grew up with the free-spirited demeanor of a self-confident younger brother. He is a completely open and guileless man. Although he frequently participates in rituals with his brother, four years older, the distance between Annavaram and Simhacalam assures him freedom to live his own quite similar life in another popular pilgrimage town, serving *parayana* as an Athar Veda pandit in the temple of Satyanarayana. Perhaps in a form of obeisance to Venkatesvara, whose business cards read "*Catur-vedin*," Rama Sastri, with virtually identical training, although weighted somewhat more in the direction of the Atharva Veda, including its Brahmana, claims only "*Tri-vedin*," master of three and not all four Vedas.

Annavaram is north of Kakinada, still in East Godavari District but outside of Konasima and somewhat less involved in the Vedic life of the *agrahara* surveyed earlier. The Satyanarayana temple perches brightly on the hilltop Ratnagiri above a lake and the town of Annavaram, attracting the eye of pilgrims on trains between Rajahmundry and Tuni. Tens of thousands of women come for the Satyavati *vrata*, a vow to the famous goddess of the temple who stands on one side of Satyanarayana while a *linga* occupies the niche on the other side of this Vaisnava god. By 1998 the temple had acquired eleven pandits reciting daily, one for the Rg Veda, six for Taittiriya, and two each for the Atharva and Sama Vedas. Three of them are *ghana-pathi*.

With such a vigorous representation of daily Vedic recitals it is not surprising that this Vaisnava temple frequently softens the borders of "Hinduism." In March 1998 a " "yajna" inside the compound featured ten offering altars, two sets of five separated by a great cloth screen into two *sala* with wicker mat roofs, scores of pandits working at each, all hosted by Rama Sastri as *adhvaryu*. Venkatesvara and many other famous Andhra pandits were among those offering ghee onto the burning slabs of wood. During a break in the daylong sacrifice the brothers described the event, their speech a seamless flow of mantras, as if a single voice, reminding the listener that they share the same paternal guru.

The newer government-assisted Veda pandit economy has been as rewarding for Rama Sastri as it has for his brother. His house on Kapilavayi Street is an impressive reinforced concrete structure of five stories, all but completed by 2005 when two daughters, long since married, were still living at home along with Agnihotra Sarma, the only son. The fifth floor is a splendid library of more than 150 *tala-patra* stored in steel trunks to ward off insects, with many other younger books and manuscripts on neat shelves. By 2014 the house was as electronically up-to-date as any American household.

Rama Sastri had his *upanayana* in Kasi at age eleven when the whole family was in peregrination mode, his father again serving as guru to a son. As Venkatesvara was directed to the Rg Veda after completion of the Taittiriya corpus, rather than going on to the *ghana* recitation pattern, so was Rama Sastri steered by his father into a second Veda, this time the Atharva Veda, as if to program his future appointment.

Like his older brother, Rama Sastri has an open, generous, and unrestrained personality, perhaps somewhat more relaxed than Venkatesvara who has taken on the more imposing demeanor of his father and uncle. Rama Sastri happily unrolled a canvas bedroll containing his collection of ritual implements, *aranis, juhu, upabhrt, camasa,* and other cherished items and handed them out for inspection. On more than one occasion he interrupted discussion to offer rice for lunch, the only pandit to open this sacred gate to commensality, solo coffee or tea being the normal limit for a non-Brahman guest. And twice he offered overnight stays.

His wife, Bonapalli Maruti, a truly remarkable woman, is equally outgoing, bold, eager to display her wide knowledge of Veda and *srauta,* adroitly and without affectation inserting a relevant point into a circle of male discussants. Daughter of a Veda pandit with wide *srauta* knowledge, granddaughter of an *ahitagni,* she grew up in an *agrahara* in Repalle, Guntur District, not far from the *agrahara* birthplace of Venkatesvara's wife but closer to the mouth of the Krishna River. Both Kapilavayi brothers were students of her grandfather, living in the house six months of the year, and it was Rama Sastri to whom she was given in marriage. When she joined her husband to live in Kasi at age sixteen she had already witnessed and understood many major *srauta* rituals. For the first seven years of residence with her Kapilavayi family she ate *prasada* from various sacrifices, *yajna payasam,* rice pudding thought to aid in conception of a son. Of all the *patnis* over years of interviews it was the energetic, ever youthful Maruti who provided the most nuanced observations of Vedic life, frequently clarifying important points that had been overlooked.[10]

On one afternoon in 2005 she rocked a three-month-old grandson, first side to side in a wooden cradle, then head to toe in a green hammock suspended from the ceiling of the spacious and immaculate new house. The baby had just started making fists as a new motor skill and therefore was visited by relatives who brought fist-sized balls of rice flour in his honor. As Maruti performed the age-old rocking task she elaborated on the stringent Sutra rules for the *patni* in safe-guarding the household fires. (See Figure 3.19, Kapilavayi Rama Sastri, left, and Maruti (in doorway) flanked by daughters Agnivati Naga Laksmi and Sita Naga Laksmi, Annavaram, 2005.)

FIGURE 3.19. Kapilavayi Rama Sastri, left, and Maruti (in doorway) flanked by daughters Agnivati Naga Laksmi and Sita Naga Laksmi, Annavaram 2005.

Rama Sastri is dedicated to an extreme. He agreed to be *udgatr* for a *paundarika* in Tirupati in 2005. He had seen *paundarika* in his childhood and youth but had not observed one for twenty years and was anxious about his competence. He commented:

> My long-deceased father appeared in a dream and assured me that I would be all right. In my dream I was arranging the charts [he brings them out as he narrates] and suddenly a breeze came and scattered them, pages all flying about. I shouted "Please find them!" and a voice said "Let them go, don't worry!" I asked my father "How can you say

that? Tomorrow I have to perform *paundarika*!" He replied: "Don't be afraid. I am with you." When I woke up I was chilled by this.

Similarities between the careers of the brothers are evident. As with Venkatesvara, all three daughters were married on schedule. Sita Nagalaksmi, having achieved a bachelor of commerce degree in computer sciences and employment as an English teacher, married a Veda pandit in Bapatla village, Guntur District. She is an exceptionally beautiful young woman with a mellifluous voice for singing devotional hymns. Agnivati Nagalaksmi, three years younger, married a Veda pandit from Draksarama and now lives in Vijayawada. Svaha Devi, youngest daughter and the only one to remain in East Godavari District, was married at age eleven in 1998 to a Smarta Brahman, a former student of her father from Elesvaram. The momentous news in 2005 was the decision announced by Sita Nagalaksmi that she and her husband, Pavan Kumar Sarma, a Veda pandit in the Bhavanarayana temple in Bapatla, Guntur District, were ready to set the fires for *adhana*. A decade later they are still waiting for Rama Sastri himself to set fires, now planned for his retirement date in 2016.

Agnihotra Sarma, after his *upanayana* in May 1998, did *agni-karya* at home (see Figure 2.3, Kapilavayi Agnihotra Sarma doing *agni-karya* with a fire pot, Annavaram, 2005). Also in the image of his father, he began to assume *rtvij* roles at a young age. At fourteen, while in ninth class in school and moving up to *padam* in the Taittiriya corpus he served as *prastatr* in the Tirupati *paundarika* in which his father was *udgatr* and his uncle Venkatesvara was *hotr*. Earlier he had been *subrahmanya* for an *agni-stoma* with his acquisition of ritual roles well under way. By 2014 he achieved two titles, Sama Veda teacher in the Bapatla Sankara Vidyalayam and Yajur Veda pandit doing *parayana* there. The hopeful *srauta* lineage continues with his son, Rama Sastri and Maruti's grandson, Maruti Rama Yajnesvara.

3.5.5 *Srauta-kaksa*, Ritual Rivalry

Over several decades both contemporary Kapilavayi brothers have narrated without hesitation the ritual rivalry in which their father was engaged. What is termed *srauta-kaksa*, rivalry in both performance and knowledge of *srauta*, is as old as the rituals.[11] The expectation of a great many texts, the new or full-moon sacrifice every fortnight, for example, is that the sacrificer has enemies, one adversary in particular who is to be brought to mind. For the Kapilavayi family it is the Dendukuris of Vijayawada, Krishna District, who serve this age-old function, particularly after Yajnesvara built his house there in 1975. Evidence of this divisive relationship comes mainly from debates in assemblies that occurred long ago.

Only the Kapilavayi side of these verbal combats is known and mentioned here; no doubt the Dendukuri case would be weighted quite in another direction.

Several matters have been fissiparous. Kapilavayis claim that Dendukuris failed to invite anyone from Konasima to a particular sacrifice and were therefore shunned when Dendukuri requests were made for *rtvij*. Forced to turn to Daksina (southern, i.e., Tamil Nadu) pandits, they eventually introduced a southern *gana* of the Sama Veda to replace the traditional one that Yajnesvara taught to his sons and recommended generally as the "Andhra" *gana*. "How could we use someone else's *gana*?" the Kapilavayis demand.

Another bone of contention had to do with multiple sacrifices, whether or not two can be performed in the same area simultaneously. Yajnesvara said yes with qualifications: the sacrificers may not be related or friends, the two venues must be separated by a river or hill and beyond earshot of one another. Some topics were presented to the Swami at Kanci *pitha* and, according to the Kapilavayi account, he accepted the textual evidence supplied by Yajnesvara.

Here the narrative turns deadly. It is claimed that *abhi-cara* was employed against both Yajnesvara and Lanka, the latter having sided with Yajnesvara in the dispute. Lanka became seriously ill according to the Kapilavayis, employed countermeasures, probably mantras from the Atharva Veda, and survived. Yajnesvara also fell ill but despite last-minute awareness of the source of his affliction, *abhi-cara*, he was defenseless and died at the age of seventy-four in November 1983. Animosity lives on a generation later in this Andhra version of Hatfields versus McCoys.

Over the years other issues have been mentioned and these are of interest in the history of Vedic practice. From the Kapilavayi side is the charge that some Dendukuri *rtvij* are ineligible for performance because they did not marry pre-pubertal brides. A broader charge is that the Dendukuris have created a "business" (inserting the English word) out of *srauta*, spending their time soliciting money for sacrifices without considering their transcendent value and performing abbreviated rites in less than half the time required in order to pad their resumes. The Dendukuris could no doubt reply that the very thin *srauta* record of Konasima in recent years has produced resentment, essentially sour grapes. But once a multigenerational rivalry is in motion consequences radiate outward in the form of alliances, rejections, and manifold marital liaisons.

For example, the Dendukuris contributed to the financing of Duvvuri Yajulu's *paundarika*, thus co-opting him as ally but further alienating others in Sriramapuram and Nedunuru. Yajulu was strategically "bought," declared one elder pandit who is neither a Kapilavayi nor a Dendukuri. He described *srauta-kaksa* as "all politics." Of course, marriage is also understood by some as "all politics," and complicated multigeneration marital alliances have further added to the dynamics of rival factions. Both the Duvvuris and the Dendukuris have multiple marriage arrangements with the Gullapallis, the West Godavari family surveyed next in this account. As an old Arab proverb has it, "the enemy of my enemy is my friend," and friends are always in short supply.

In March 2005 the *dora* paid a visit to the Dendukuris in Vijayawada along with Duvvuri Yajulu's grandson, Sita Ram Sastry, who was warmly greeted amid high praise of his "fifteen-generation" Vedic ancestry (Dendukuris claiming only ten generations on their resumés). It was a remarkable occasion, entering the little house smack up against a cinema hall on a crowded lane of an expansive, noisy city and finding not one but two *tretagni* hearths in action, one of Dendukuri Agnihotra Somayaji, the other of his second son, Laksminarasimha Somayajulu. (See Figure 3.20,

FIGURE 3.20. Dendukuri Agnihotra Somayaji, right, and son Laksminarasimha Somayajulu, both active *agni-hotrin*, Vijayawada 2005.

FIGURE 3.21. The side-by-side Dendukuri hearths are in one small room, Vijayawada, 2005. Morning *agni-hotra* have been completed; kindling on the *vedi* awaits offerings at sundown. Courtesy Duvvuri S. R. Sastry.

Dendukuri Agnihotra Somayaji and son Laksminarasimha Somayajulu, both *agnihotrin*, and Figure 3.21, their two hearths in one small room, Vijayawada, 2005.) Immediately, Sanskrit and Telugu books and palm-leaf manuscripts emerged from great plastic bags, professionally xeroxed color copies of impressive resumés were distributed, expensive albums of hundreds of color photos of sacrifices were passed, and, as anticipated, requests were made for substantial rupee or dollar funds to continue regular *isti* and upcoming major *srauta* sacrifices.

These requests were renewed not once but over and over. It was not the *aparigraha* ambiance surrounding Sita Ram Sastri or Baballa, Lanka, Yajulu, Mitranarayana, and others in Konasima. The subject of *srauta-kaksa* with the Kapilavayis never surfaced through all the blatant demands for money. In an attempt to enter the Dendukuri mind a perspective is recognizable: World-maintaining sacrifices must be perpetuated and to that end solicitation of funds, an age-old requisite, is not for personal gain but for *yajna*. For the *dora*, being seen and pressured only as an ATM machine was an uncomfortable situation.

Nevertheless, it was readily apparent that a research focus on Vijayawada rather than Konasima would have resulted in quite a different account. The critical *srauta* period for the latter was drawing to a close in the 1980s whereas it was still building in Vijayawada, 180 miles to the west. By late 2005 Dendukuri Senior reported that there were twenty *ahitagni* in Krishna District, twelve of them in Vijayawada, including the two *nitya-agnihotrin* Dendukuris and members of the Renducintala, Visnubhatla, Kappagantulu, Madduri, and other families. After his 1965 *agni-stoma* in Vijayawada, Dendukuri Agnihotra's aggressive pursuit of *srauta* surged in the 1990s and earned him the title "Bahu-yaji." A *vaja-peya, sarvato-mukha, aruna-ketuka*, three *paundarika*, and other rituals shine from his resume pages. He taught all three sons, married both daughters to Veda pandits, founded a *sabha*, and is clearly a pivotal mainstay of Krishna Delta Vedic life.

Although he counts him as adversary, Kapilavayi Venkatesvara nevertheless grants Dendukuri Senior full credit for "competence in all eighteen *rtvij* roles, like Lanka." A small, nervous man, Dendukuri Agnihotra, constantly leaving the crowded room to talk on his cell phone while leaning over the adjacent *agni-hotra* hearths, appears driven to excel in a competitive family environment. His grandfather, father, and older brother Paundarika Yajulu all became *ahitagni*. His father decided to trade their quiet village Nallapadu in Guntur District for the boisterous hub of Vijayawada. Agnihotra, despite diabetes and joint pains, is determined to surpass all of their records, not to mention the hallmarks of twentieth-century greats such as Kapilavayi Yajnesvara and Renducintala Yajulu.

To return to the Godavari Delta once again, it would appear that any revival of *srauta* traditions there will depend on the intentions of the Annavaram Kapilavayi and Duvvuri Phani lineages. Kapilavayi Venkatesvara, now without a wife, has given permission to younger brother Rama Sastri to go ahead of him with fire setting and then *agni-stoma*, which are planned for the same day. Rama Sastri and Maruti hope to proceed in 2016 when he turns sixty and retires from

FIGURE 3.22. Kapilavayi brothers, Venkatesvara, left, and Rama Sastri, Simhacalam 2014.

Annavaram temple service. When Rama Sastri and Maruti establish fires, then daughter Sita Nagalaksmi and husband Pavan Kumar Sarma in Guntur District will proceed to do the same. In Annavaram, in addition to son Agnihotra, a reliable network of pandits for assistance remains in the temple area. Venkatesvara once compared routine *isti* to a cricket match, assembling the right players and getting them onto the field in time. While awaiting his own ritual entry to *srauta* routines Rama Sastri continues to aid others. In February–March 2014 his temple authorities sent him to Madirajugoduru village in Nellore District to advise in proceedings for another *vyudha paundarika*, this time with Renducintala Krishna Cayanulu as *yajamana*. (See Figure 3.22, the Kapilavayi brothers, Simhacalam, 2014.) It now remains to survey one more family, the Gullapallis of West Godavari District, a lineage with strong ties to Konasima.

3.6 *Iragavaram Village*

3.6.1 The Gullapalli Family

Well west of the Konasima *agrahara* is a space of riverine indecision where the great current again hesitates in a floodplain before proceeding on two wide courses. Toward the center of the delta, the Godavari-Vasistha's eastern neighbor is the winding Godavari-Vainateya, named for Vainateya or Garuda, son of Vinata. Until modern bridges spanned these two channels of the Godavari this water was impossible to cross except by sturdy ferries in calm seasons. Modern political geography has a label for the region off the right bank of the Vasistha, West Godavari District, with headquarters in Eluru.

To the eye of the traveler who proceeds westward, however, this river-and-canal-laced land of rice grids, coconut palms, sugarcane, turmeric, chili peppers, and tapioca looks exactly the same as East Godavari District. The birds are here as well, white crane sentinels spaced across the flooded paddy fields and astonishing blue flashes of the *pallapitta.* To ancient and medieval settlers who cultivated the soil, sought pastures for livestock, harvested the trees, and alternately fled or fought maverick streams, it was the delta, a vast unruly triangle that somehow redesigned itself with monstrously swollen waters every June, July, and August. It was terrain exactly like the powerful goddesses who hovered about, those who could nurture and protect like gentle mothers, or strike fiercely like wrathful hags and destroy everyone. Sudden super-abundances of water, as well as periodic drought, epidemic disease, or cyclone, were among the manifold faces of devastation. The dreadful tsunami that drowned more than 232,000 people on one day, December 26, 2004, was a shock when it hit the subcontinent well south of the delta, but similar attacks by cyclones have always—*always*—shadowed living memory.

Closest to Konasima is Tanuku Taluk, centered on the town of Tanuku, almost within sight of the Vasistha-Godavari. More than a dozen prolific Veda pandit families live today in the town and surrounding villages such as Iragavaram, Juttiga, Nidadavolu, Khandavalli, Siddhantam, Kanuru *agrahara*, and Mukkamala (a name identical to the East Godavari District village between Sriramapuram and Nedunuru). Several families have generated *ahitagni* in the twentieth century. For his *agni-stoma* in 1991 Pisapati Venkata Siddhanti asked Duvvuri Yajulu of Sriramapuram to serve as *soma-pravaka*, the one who invites all *rtvij*. But the area is more famous now for dedication to the training of expert Veda pandits, including numerous *ghana-pathi.* Iragavaram, six miles from Tanuku town, regards itself as Veda pandit capital of India, the single village most richly endowed with Veda pandits in the subcontinent, with certified *krama-pati* numbering more than thirty and about half that number in various stages of preparation, many of them in the Sankara Veda Pathasala opened in 2007. No one to the east across the rivers would contest that claim today. Iragavaram in fact has the look, sound, and fervor that made Konasima's Mukkamala famous a century ago.

Iragavaram's pride in a Vedic heritage is well deserved. The website www.iragavaram.com displays copious albums of color photos and videos of the annual *sabha* (for example, the twelfth one in 2008) that honor outstanding pandits with speeches, garlands, shawls, and fruits, seating them one by one on a red plush golden peacock throne. One among several eminent lineages in Iragavaram today is the Gullapalli family, already mentioned with regard to Konasima marriage alliances with the Duvvuri family as well as the Dendukuris. In order to examine more closely the dynamics of one line of Gullapallis, a three-generational cluster is selected for details: Sitaram Sastri and his wife Narasamamba, their five sons, two daughters, and several grandsons. Four of the five sons were first encountered in Tirupati in October 1980 when they were among the sixteen Andhra Veda pandits invited to the great temple of Venkatesvara to do a Varuna *puja*, thereby bringing rain to the drought-stricken Seven Hills. The Gullapalli line illustrates a remarkably total commitment to Veda in a close-knit extended family that now, in affluent times with assured careers in Veda, lives in separate modern houses in a spacious Brahman neighborhood functioning much like a well-heeled *agrahara*. This family's continuity is instructive in several other ways. It reveals changes in *adhyaya* over the generations, it highlights the benefits of assured employment that ease the period of textual learning and eliminate anxieties about the future, and it displays a range of opportunities for post-graduate studies, with two of the five sons attaining *ghana-pathi* rank. Last but not least interesting, a striking sequential marriage network with a Konasima Veda pandit family, the Duvvuris, emerges from tracking the two most recent Gullapalli generations.

Sitaram Sastri Avadhanulu, Lohitasa *gotra*, is now as focused on completing his grandsons' educations in Veda as he was a generation ago with their fathers. Born in Iragavaram in 1925, with *upanayana* at age ten, he studied with three successive gurus, Kambhampati Laksmana Avadhani in Poddagatlapalli, across the Vasistha on an island-like spit of Konasima, Tangirala Subba Avadhanulu in the Undi *agrahara*, and Visvanatha Jagannatha Ghanapati in Rajahmundry. His education was, therefore, largely within or on the fringe of Konasima. Reversing the normal pattern, he studied *sastra* first and then Veda, followed by *vedartha*. Exams were passed in Vijayawada, Rajahmundry, and Sallepalle. Sitaram Sastri chose not to pursue *srauta* for self-fulfillment, but nevertheless was well educated in both *srauta* and *smarta karma*, and on frequent occasions others sought his expertise. The Tangirala family of Iragavaram (apart from Tangiralas in Konasima and Krishna District) produced several *ahitagni*, and Sitaram Sastri was chosen to serve as *adhvaryu* for the *agni-stoma* of Tangirala Rama Somayajulu early in the 1970s.

Vivaha was at age sixteen for Sitaram, when Narasamamba, born in 1924, was fourteen. After their *aupasana* fire was established, seven children were born in the 1950s and 1960s. Of these, both daughters were married to Veda pandits and all five sons, taught by their father to completion, chose careers in Veda and married Veda pandit family girls before the brides attained puberty. One son wavered, thought briefly of a path other than Veda, but then returned to the fold and made Sitaram Sastri's report card an unbeatable seven for seven. (See Figure 2.5, Gullapalli Sita Ram Sastri in *adhyayana* with four *brahmacarin* grandsons, Iragavaram 2000. The boys are sons of Sita Ram Sastri's sons reciting *ghana* in Figure 3.23.) "I thought at first I would be wearing slacks and shirt," says the hesitant son, "but in coming to my senses I decided it was better to go for Veda!"

With all five sons in *parayana* employment, the supremely amiable and grandfatherly Sitaram Sastri rounded out his career by teaching all grandsons after *upanayana*. "Every grandson stopped English education at fifth class," he said with great pride, "so there is no one still in school. All are in Veda only." He owns an illuminative smile set in a face of pure kindness, but his teaching is rigorous and demanding. While Konasima has a rule against teaching more than two *brahmacarin* the same text, Sitaram has no such stricture. For example, early in 1998 he gathered a group of five grandsons aged ten to twelve,

FIGURE 3.23. Four of the five Gullapalli brothers (sons of Sita Ram Sastri and fathers of the boys in Figure 2.5), reciting in alternate pairs in *ghana-patha*, Iragavaram 2005.

with *upanayana* mostly at age eight, and began them all together on the fourth *kanda* of the Taittiriya Samhita. Leading then through *kanda* one to three, then five, six, and four, they finished the seventh in March 2000 and were ready, save for four months of review, for their *samhita* exam on forty-four *panna* in Sravana *masa* (August). Then it was back to that initial fourth *kanda* to do the text all over again, this time in *pada*.

Remarkably, considering the speed at which they handled the *samhita* recitation, the schedule of these five cousins seems relaxed by comparison with that of Baballa or Lanka some eighty to ninety years before. They need not get up at 3 AM as Lanka did to walk to the home of his guru and start at 4 AM. Their grandfather lives and teaches in the road-level front room of the modest old house in which he has lived almost his entire life, only two minutes away for startup at 7:30 or 8:00 and *adhyaya* until 11:00. This is, of course after they have finished *snana*, *sandhya-vandana*, and *agni-karya* at home. Only once did these boys do a symbolic *madhu-kara* since their meals are taken from their mothers' kitchens.

Published texts of the *samhita* (known as *pustakalu* or "bookulu" in Telugu) are sometimes used by the students for afternoon review sessions or on rare mornings for review when their grandfather is not available. But it is insisted that each boy first hears the text *guru-mukha*, from the mouth of the guru. A student may never read ahead of the guru. The use of any book for review purposes is regarded by the old pandits with considerable disdain as a concession to modern times and the intrusion of an English curriculum into what should have been years devoted only to Veda study. If a printed text is consulted, they say, the *brahmacarin* may grow to be dependent on it. Some would go so far as to say that learning to read at all—whether Telugu or, in recent years, English—irrevocably impairs early retention of the oral text.[12] These five boys, added to their five fathers and others in between, bring the total number of students of Sitaram's teaching career to at least thirty. Despite reservations about the use of "bookulu," those pandits teaching Veda in Iragavaram today have great respect for their students and nothing of the acidulous tongue of Mitranarayana with regard to declining intellectual standards and study habits. They are, it goes without saying, inordinately proud of their descendants.

Like Baballa and Lanka in Konasima, Sitaram Sastri is *aparigraha*, one who accepts no gifts, graciously deferring honoraria that go instead to his student *brahmacarin*. That non-worldly stance seems in danger of passing as the new generation of students has become accustomed to cash rewards for recitations that sometimes resemble theatrical perfomances. The *dora* was astonished, prior to their recitations, to spend considerable time making rupee change to assure that all received the correct cash reward. The *dabbu* culture deplored by Anasuya in her final years would appear to be a strong tide indeed.

Certainly there is every sign of affluence in the neighborhood, a far cry from the minimalism of Sriramapuram in the 1950s. With the exception of Sitaram Sastri's old-style cottage, the Gullapalli houses are substantial two-level constructions marching along spacious lanes with colorful stucco exteriors, stately columns, flowering shrubs around the forecourt wells, and sumptuous, attractively decorated interiors, all of them sparkling, airy, and conspicuously modern. One has a large fully occupied sparrow nest suspended from the ceiling of the "living room" with birds free to fly out the open windows. All have walls of prominent shelves holding numerous large color photo albums documenting family events, five-day marriages, *upanayana, sabha*, and award ceremonies. When the *dora* first entered the nearly completed house of Venkata Naga Srirama Avadhani, the thirty-four-year-old forcefully shook his hand, a laid-back overture that had never happened in the previous twenty years of greeting Konasima Veda pandits. It was one of several markers in the distance between generations. A very large two-floor Brahman *sabha* hall named Ghanapati Bhavan is available to all Veda pandit families for marriages as well as community meetings.

Not surprisingly, the five brothers look remarkably alike. In order of seniority they are Gullapalli Ramakrishna, Venkata Surya Subrahmanya Avadhani, Venkata Rama Suryanarayana Ghanapati, Venkata Naga Srirama Avadhani, and Chinna Anjaneya Ghanapati. Commonplace are intricate networks of gurus and *sisya* on one hand, or of pre-pubescent daughters and newly certified sons in arranged marriages on the other. In one case the two types of alliances melded, as illustrated previously with Renducintala's dowry-free son promised in a marital liaison with Bulusu Cayanulu's daughter, exchanged for Cayanulu's teaching of that son prior to the marriage in 1946. For a systematic, well-designed inter-familial series of marriages, however, the one established between the Gullapallis of Iragavaram and Duvvuris of Sriramapuram-Rajahmundry is most informative. As noted, Sitaram Sastri was successful in marrying both daughters to Veda pandits. One of them, Kanaka Durga, was married in 1971 to Duvvuri Yajulu's third son, Venkata Surya Prakasa Avadhani. At that time the young man was eighteen, having just completed the eighty-two *panna* under his father in Sriramapuram, and she was twelve, having grown up in Iragavaram. Over the next eleven years four sons were born to this Duvvuri couple, no daughters. The five brothers of their mother, that is to say their Gullapalli uncles, are the five sons of Sitaram Sastri. In the traditional *menarika* cross-cousin marriage pattern, a boy marries his mother's brother's daughter. Therefore, Duvvuri Surya Prakasa's four sons, Phani Yajulu, Sitaram Sastri (named for his grandfather in Iragavaram), Hari Prasad, and Girija Sankar were married to their Gullapalli cousins, respectively, Nagalaksmi, Girija Syamala, Kamesvari, and Pallavi. These four girls are daughters of four of Sitaram Sastri's sons, respectively, sons three, two, one, and four. This sequential alliance therefore founded four new Duvvuri families by receiving daughters from four out of Sitaram Sastri's five sons, the fifth son having provided a daughter to a Dendukuri family.

As noted earlier in the capsule biography of Duvvuri Yajulu, Phani Yajulu, the first son of Surya Prakasa, was the only one of the four sons to complete Veda. In fact, he went on to become *ghana-patni*. Therefore, of these four granddaughters of Sitaram Sastri, only Laksmi (Nagalaksmi) was given to a Veda pandit groom. The other three went to young men who had as background some Veda but are all at present in *laukika* careers. Laksmi, eldest of the four Iragavaram brides, has two sons. With a *ghana-pathi* father, the sole grandson of Duvvuri Yajulu completely educated in Veda, it appeared likely that one or both of this third generation of descent from Duvvuri Yajulu would perpetuate the textual side of his career. But that did not happwn when both boys chose English education. On the Gullapalli side, Sitaram Sastri's practice of multiple grandsons committed at an early age to Veda, appears to cover his legacy more thoroughly.

By 2000, only the first son of Duvvuri Surya Prakasa, that is, Phani Yajulu, had established a "household," sharing with his parents the rooms of a newly built house in Rajahmundry, for which the housewarming ritual, *grhya-pravesa*, was celebrated in March of that year. The other three sons were married in their teens with full five-day ceremonies, but their wives remained in Iragavaram in their Gullapalli parents' homes until the young men became established and self-sufficient, thereby eligible to consummate their unions with *sambhoga* and begin their own families. The respective age of each son at the time of *vivaha* rose incrementally from fourteen (Phani Yajulu), to sixteen (Sitaram Sastri), to seventeen (Hari Prasad), to eighteen (Girija Sankar), while on the other hand the pre-pubescent Gullapalli daughters' age at marriage was retained, usually about age ten. This reflects on the male side the longer time of preparation required for college degrees, possible graduate degrees, and acquisition of *laukika* employment, and on the female side a traditional safeguarding of the lineage for eligibility of offspring to become Veda pandits and potential sacrificers. It is an intriguing gender asymmetry.

Sadly, Sitaram Sastri's wife Narasamamba died at the age of fifty-nine in 1983 and he ended his *grhya karma*, allowing his single *aupasana* fire to expire. His situation discloses the Veda pandit's affiliation with household Agni, just as in the more formal and complex association of an *ahitagni* with his triple fire. Whether there be one or three fires, the ritual relationship inheres to the married couple in the home. His two daughters given away to other villages, his twilight years devoted to the teaching of grandsons, content with his small ground-level home, he is surrounded now by his energetic and industrious sons, all in modern multileveled residences, houses filled with vibrant Vedic voices.

Table 3.3. Four generations of *ahitagni* and eligible *ahitagni* candidates

O L D born 1903–1933:

Bhamidipati Yajnesvara Somayaji ("Baballa") * 1903–93
Kapilavayi Yajnesvara Agnihotra Sastri 1909–83
Lanka Venkatarama Sastri * 1912–99
Duvvuri Yajulu * 1915–2005
Bulusu Cayanulu * 1915–97
Pullela Laksminarayana * 1920–99
Gullapalli Sitaram Sastri 1925–
Bulusu Kamesvara Somayaji * 1926–2010
Bhamidipati Mitranarayana Sarvatomukha Somayaji * 1930–
Samavedam Suryanarayana Avadhanulu 1932–2008

M I D D L E born 1934–1964:

Duvvuri Sarvesvara, 1st son < Duvvuri Yajulu 1936–
Gullapalli Ramakrishna Avadhani, 1st son <Gullapalli Sitaram Sastri 1950–
Gullapalli V. Surya Subrahmanya Avadhani, 2nd son < Gullapalli S. S. 1952–
Duvvuri V. Surya Prakasa, 3d son < Duvvuri Yajulu # 1953–
Kapilavayi Venkatesvara Sastri, 1st son < Kapilavayi Y.A.S. # 1953–
Kapilavayi Rama Sastri, 2d son < Kapilavayi.Y.A.S. # 1957–
Samavedam Venkatarama Ghanapathi, 1st son < Samavedam S. 1954–
Bhamidipati Yajnesvara Prasad, grandson < Baballa 1961–
Samavedam Bhaskara Ghanapathi, 2nd son < Samavedam S. 1964–
Gullapalli V. R. S. Ghanapathi, 3d son < Gullapalli S. S. 1964–
Gullapalli V. Naga Srirama Avadhani, 4th son < Gullapalli S. S. 1964–

Y O U N G born 1965–1995:

Gullapalli Chinna Anjaneya Ghanapathi, 5th son < Gullapalli S. S. 1966–
Duvvuri Phani, grandson < D.Yajulu via D. Surya Prakasa #1974–
Kapilavayi Rama Yajna, 1st son < Kapilavayi Venkatesvara #1979–
Samavedam Sivarama, grandson < S. via S.Venkatesvara 1983–
Kapilavayi Rana Kumar, 2d son < Kapilavayi Venkatesvara #1984–
Samavedam Ramu, grandson < S. via S. Venkatarama 1988–
Kapilavayi Agnihotra Sarma, only son < Kapilavayi Rama Sastri #1991–
Samavedam Aditya, grandson < Samavedam S. via S. Bhaskara 1994–

R E C E N T born 1996–

Duvvuri Surya Prakasa, great-grandson <D.Yajulu via D.Phani #1996–
Duvvuri Syama Sundara, great-grandson <D.Yajulu via D.Phani #1998–
Duvvuri Kattikeya, great-grandson of D. Yajulu via D. Sita Ram Sastry 2004–
Kapilavayi Rama Yajnesvara, grandson <Kapilavayi Venkatesvara #2000–
Kapilavayi Maruti Rama Yajnesvara, grandson <Kapilavayi Rama Sastri #2000–

Note: * indicates *ahitagni*; # indicates eligible *ahitagni* candidates.

Table 3.3 is a summary of this survey listing four generations in thirty-year stretches, 1903–33 for "Old," 1934–64 for "Middle," 1965–95 for "Young," and 1996 following for a "Recent" generation including those whose *upanayana* thread ceremonies occurred a few years after the turn of the millennia. In the Epilogue at the close of this study, the first three generations are labeled, respectively, Traditionalists, Selecters, and Opportunists. The list reveals the continued health of Veda certification on one hand but a sharply reduced number of and eligible *ahitagni* candidates on the other, the only likely Veda pandit in the near future being Kapilavayi Rama Sastri in Annavaram.

4

Becoming a Veda

4.1 A Tumult of Veda and the Brahmacarin

Senior Konasima Veda pandits and others who were youngsters in the 1960s recall the days when there was "a tumult of Veda" heard before dawn as freshly bathed gurus and *brahmacarin* faced one another to immerse minds and voices in ever-continuing lessons. Chapter 2 provided a brief overview of the transmission of Veda from an older to a younger generation and the progression of the student from his initial portion of the Taittiriya Samhita to his examination and certification as a Veda pandit. Chapter 3 gave numerous examples of individual development. There is more to be said of this evolution and the larger meaning of interiorizing Veda within the topography of Vedic pandit.[1]

The first question an outsider asks is, "What *is* 'Veda' for these *agrahara*-based Vaidika Brahmans?" Their replies portray Veda as at once symbol and symbol system. Veda appears to represent an alternate reality, Gaston Bachelard's *univers imaginaire* in the sense that it exists as the *real* world, a whole world, as opposed to the illusory fragmentations of *laukika*, mundane, existence.[2] For the Veda pandit this is an accessible world and, once entered, a usable world, for it is the *mantra* and *kriya* that make up reality and daily negotiate its perpetuation. The dedicated Veda pandit speaks, as noted earlier, of "existing *in* Veda." At the same time, Veda is not in the least demystified through such proximity and accessibility. Always it retains its properties of mystery (*guhya, rahasya*). It abides in the realm of the numinous because it is eternal, *apauruseya*, without human origin, a hierophany in simultaneity inside and outside of time and space. No human can ever appropriate all of it, not even the self-proclaimed *catur-vedin* who has become all four Vedas. All of this speaks to the density of the text that has enabled the two-syllabled word Veda to command priority of attention across several millennia of Vedic-Hindu civilization.

A second question an outsider might ask is, How does one "learn" Veda? In the West, there is a particular educational model regarding knowledge: a teacher who is a "knower" facilitates a student who does not know in a process of turning the latter into the former. Perhaps, however, the term "education" might be exchanged for "transmission." What is the process of transmitting this beginning-less oral phenomenon Veda to a living Vaidika Brahman? The epistemological question follows: What does it mean to "know" Veda when the word *veda* itself is "knowledge."

Brahmanical tradition includes a prized phrase, *ya evam veda*, "who knows thus," who knows the correspondences, equivalences, connections to unseen realities. The boy already understands that the fire he tends corresponds to, *is* divine Agni, and in his morning and evening prayers he discerns an equivalence of human breath with cosmic *prana*. He is beginning to "know" as his dive into the Taittiriya Samhita deepens with constant cross-fertilizing associations regarding *soma*, the moon, altar bricks, enthronement of the fire pan, and so forth. By the time he gets to the Taittiriya Upanisad and its famous correspondence of self and cuisine in the great chain of being, *aham annam*, "I am food," he will have absorbed basic mysteries of correspondence and equivalence (*nidana, sampad*, or *bandhu*). It is esoteric knowledge, *gnosis*, in the sense that a precious few legatees of the ancient *rsi* carry these sacred mantras and their entourage of text. If he grows up in or near an *ahitagni* family he will observe the application of these mantras in daily ritual life. Mantras, in the apt definition of Frits Staal, are those "bits and pieces of the Vedas put to ritual use,"[3] and the boy will find daily illustrations all about him.

The blueprint for the *brahmacarin* is straightforward. Transmission begins on an auspicious day in the spring with the *upanayana* when a frail boy of seven or eight years has his head shaved before his bath. Then he is invested with a sacred three-stranded cord (*upavita*, or *yajnopavita*, sacrificial thread) and hears from his guru his first mantra, the *savitri*, in the *gayatri* meter. So significant is this moment that it constitutes a second birth, the guru being his father, the Savitri (also known as Gayatri) mantra being his mother, as he himself is born again, *dvi-jati*. In addition to the thread worn for a lifetime (and occasionally renewed in a special ceremony) he receives a staff (*danda*) of *palasa* wood, a symbolic piece of the skin of a black antelope (*krsnajina*), and a waistband (*mekhala*) of three strands of *munja* grass (later replaced by a three-strand cotton cord like the *upavita*). Rg Veda 3.8.4 is a mantra recited by the guru as he knots the belt. Elderly pandits or their sons or grandsons will present for admiration today the staffs and skin fragments carefully kept for eighty or more years. Sons who are quick learners are given special privileges and are sometimes exempt from secular chores taken up by their siblings. Baballa, for one, credited his father with providing him a secure learning environment and a youth that he recalled with great affection some seventy years later.

Konasima Brahmans who wish to preserve the integrity of their lineages insist on a full five days for both *upanayana* and marriage ceremonies. After investiture, the second and third days of the former are devoted to instructions of the boy in *agni-karya* since he now takes on responsibility for collecting firewood and maintaining the ritual fire, or fires if the guru is a *nitya* or continual *agni-hotrin*. Here is the youngster's first step on the path to becoming Agni, the detailed subject of Chapter 6. His duties now may also include milking the *agni-hotra* cow if he has not already assumed that task. The guru instructs him in proper procedures for two essential rituals that will endure through life: first, making *homa* offerings into the fire, and second, worshipping the sun, Savitr or Surya. The latter, known as *sandhya* or *sandhya-vandana*, occurs at the two "joints" of the day when direct sunlight begins or ends, standing for the former, sitting for the latter. This involves several short exercises that quickly become habitual, beginning with recitations of the newly learned Gayatri mantra and followed by offerings to the sun of water (*arghya*) into his mouth over the heel of his hand and then scattered across his body three times. Involving his body again in *sandhya* he performs *prana-yama*, yogic breath control, and the strategic touching and purifying of his body in *nyasa*. Scores of interviews for this book were curtailed due to the evening *sandhya*. In something of an apology for having not one of his seven sons learn Veda, Lanka several times would say, "Well, at least I taught them correctly in the Gayatri and *sandhya*." Women of the household may also be simultaneously worshipping the sun in Surya *namaskara*, although without the Gayatri.

On the fourth day of *upanayana medha-janana* is the ritual instillation of wisdom (*medha*) and the necessary memory for Veda, actually a reinforcement of an early *samskara*, rite of passage, his initial birth, known as *jata-karma*, performed by his parents and the family purohita. The fifth day is a concluding ritual when the boy does *bhiksa*, begging for food as an ascetic from house to house, like the honey bee described in Chapter 2, first circling back to call at his own front door where he is certain to receive food from his mother. As the community of householders is bound to sustain world renouncers, those beyond the first three life stages, so the same community supports the *brahmacarin* at the outset of his Vedic career. The two modes of existence, both celibate, bracket the passionate world of *samsara*.[4]

With his new thread over his left shoulder and under his right arm the seven- or eight-year-old touches the feet of his *guru*, usually his father but possibly his grandfather, older brother, uncle, or more distant relative, and in the technique of *adhyaya* sits down before him to hear and then recite back a phrase at a time. They begin sometime after the dawn *samdhya* and continue daily through the dark and bright halves of the lunar month with the exception of eight specified break days of *an-adhyaya*, days without new recitations when review of past lessons, or study of Mimamsa, Dharma Sastras, or other acolyte texts take the place of a fresh Taittiriya recitation. Each new- or full-moon day, as well as the day succeeding, is considered a day off. Lanka noted that trying to learn Veda on *amavasya*, new-moon day, is like fetching water in a sieve. Rolling thunder and lightning strikes, sometimes dangerous near tall palm trees, may also be grounds for cessation. Calendars of astrological reckoning (*pancanga*) are routinely consulted to discover exactly when lunar days, *tithis*, begin and end.

After eight to twelve years of this routine the young man who survives the rigors of *brahmacarya is* Veda, or at least his hereditary portion—in this case, the Taittiriya tradition with Apastamba as a set of Sutras. Upon successful final examinations he is certified as a Veda pandit and his "commencement" activates a Vaidika career.

4.2 *The Work of the Text*

The process of retaining successive phrases of text, however, is familiar to outsiders only in part. The small boy with impressionable brain cells has a calling and faces a syllabus unbelievably daunting in its totality. True, he is adding but one line at a time. Nevertheless, pressure from the cumulative weight of successive days is enormous, the task being so formidable that the dropout rate is high. The survivor of early learning is enrolled in something close to a degree program broken into eighty-two "questions," the classical Telugu *panna*, from Sanskrit *prasna*. This might be compared with a sequence of eighty-two "courses," all of them charged to memory. As noted in Chapter 2 the Konasima syllabus for the Vedic student, anticipating the examination system, begins with the third or fourth *kanda* of the Taittiriya Samhita, those two sections considered to be softest for starters. The seven *kanda* are memorized in five portions, making up forty-four *panna*, or slightly more than half of the syllabus. The "dependent" (Telugu *parayatta*) portion of thirty-eight *panna* is the second half of the *brahmacarin*'s course work, that is, the Taittiriya Brahmana of twenty-eight *panna* followed by the ten *panna* of the Taittiriya Aranyaka and Taittiriya Upanisad. Thus they make up the eighty-two *panna* in what might be construed as the common Vaidika high school diploma plus undergraduate degree. Tacked on are the aphorisms of two ritual manuals, Apastamba Srauta and Grhya Sutras, further explored in Chapter 6 on the ritual life.

It was stressed in Chapter 2 that the traditional belief in the Veda as *apauruseya*, without human authorship, without origin, being unitary and eternal, goes unchallenged among Vedic Brahmans. There can be no admission of a literary chronology, or even the suggestion that writing intruded upon the Vedic oral heritage as it did in the disastrous case of the Avesta in ancient Iran.[5] Outside readers, however, require some buoys in this great sea of material and perhaps here is the place to launch some quite rough estimates to date the four Samhitas and ensuing texts, all dated BCE. Clearly the Rg Veda is the original one, its early portions compiled in the middle of the second millennium with hymns that may have been composed as early as 1700 and a fuller set of ten collections extant perhaps two centuries later. The other three Samhitas, Yajur Veda, Sama Veda, and Atharva Veda, depend upon the Rg Veda and are presumed to have been compiled between 1500 and 1000. The Brahmana-texts, including the Taittiriya, were probably assembled during the centuries from 1000 to 800 and the Aranyakas, again including the Taittiriya, perhaps well before 600. The two early Upanisads, Brhadaranyaka and Chandogya, are dated to the seventh or sixth centuries, with a probable period of composition for the Taittiriya, Aitareya, and Kausitaki in the sixth or fifth centuries and the remaining Upanisads in the late centuries BCE. The Srauta Sutras were perhaps composed in the sixth or fifth century, Baudhayana and Apastamba counting among the oldest, with Hiranyakesin slightly later, these three Taittiriya Sutras being most frequently followed in Konasima. The dependent Grhya Sutras for domestic rituals followed within another two centuries. Many of these round-figured dates are contested among scholars although there is far more of a consensus today than half a century ago.[6] It is remarkable to think of the millennium of time during the composition of the Taittiriya corpus that is transmitted in Andhra although, again, no one who receives it and passes it on to another is ever permitted to imagine such a chronology.

To return to tradition and the youngster in the predawn twilight striving to control the nineteenth of the forty-four *panna* of the Taittiriya Samhita, it is understandable that he has no more distancing from the massive text of Veda, no more appreciation of immense and variegated genres still in front of him, than an American fifth-grade student has of the place of civics or trigonometry in the great scheme of things. Transmission of the approved Western academic curriculum is just something that happens, and keeps on happening, until some light dawns and connections regarding "knowledge" are obtained. Something, however, is said to occur in the *brahmacarin* who survives the early dropout stage of *adhyaya* and aspires to become one among these rare repositories of Veda.

Two key terms are applied to those who are receptive to transmission: *vyasana*, passion, and *asakti*, curiosity. The word *vyasana* that Telugu inherited from Sanskrit connotes not only passion but also obsession, excessive attachment, even addiction. Vaidika Brahmans use the term in a positive sense, redolent of prideful censure for overdoing it, with reference to those addicted to a lifetime of learning through Veda and beyond. The younger two generations describe the old men—their fathers and grandfathers—with unmitigated awe. *Their* kind of passion, their addiction, the young men say, is gone, and may not be seen again. The old men agree, and speak with nostalgia of bygone times in the *agrahara* when that tumult of *mantra* could be heard at all hours of the day, except, they add, "perhaps between midnight and 3:00 AM." But the old men also invoke the Telugu word *asakti*, curiosity, inquisitiveness. A stretching of the imagination about Veda should occur before passion is aroused. In a child such curiosity can be identified as easily as passion, and no one today says that it has disappeared entirely.

What must be added to an understanding of Veda *adhyaya*, however, is the mythic dimension adhering to the space of transmission, namely, the *agrahara* itself. It is impossible to overestimate. The surrounding terrain is *punya ksetra*, a sacred site, a place of merit and power, and therefore a place where *adhyaya* is possible. It begins with the fact that the *rsi*, said to live "for 300 or 600 years," are still here and can occasionally be glimpsed in predawn mists on the Kausika stream, the Godavari channel named for Kusika, the *maharsi* Visvamitra. Also here are the ancestors (*pitr*), including senior *ahitagni* who died in recent years, who "watch everything we do." The certified Vedic Brahman identifies with both, the fabled *rsi* of the Great Time in which Veda was first overheard, and the ancestors who have transmitted Veda into the present day. Some *ahitagni* provide names of both maternal and paternal lineages for eight to ten generations in their Veda pandit heritage. Other holy beings who emerge in this *punya ksetra* include powerful *sadhu* who validate the terrain as a place of power and possibility. Surely, reflects the intrepid *brahmacarin* who hears his elders' tales in the early darkness of the evening meal, prodigious feats of learning may continue in a place such as this.

Transmission involves, in a remarkable reciprocity, what might be considered sound mysticism. The student, day by day, year after year, is bonded to his guru by mantric sound (*sabda*). He hears, and replicates, the guru's voice as text. He will *always* hear the guru's voice as text because he has appropriated Veda in that voice as his own. The Vedic Brahman enlivens a remark of Bachelard's: "By certain of its traits, childhood lasts all through life."[7] These infinite strands of sacred sound accumulated over the years of childhood are a single resident voice, simultaneously the voice of the *rsi*, of the guru, of the carefully constructed textual self. This remains true long after the death of this latter-day *rsi* who has given spiritual birth to him. And when he participates in group recitations he inserts his own voice, his guru's voice, to blend into the community text. As the text has entered his mind so has he interiorized and immortalized his father and grandfather. After years of emulation, syllable by syllable, accent by accent, the guru endures as aural seed, until each recitation is a re-presentation of the guru. In *bhakti*-like reverence, the Veda pandit may frequently say of a guru who was not his biological father, "First I remember *him*, and then I remember my father." And it was noted of the forty-four-year-old son of Duvvuri Yajulu (who did serve as guru) that when he began to teach Veda to his own sons he could finally approach his father to say something although he still could not "sit down with him" because that was the exclusive posture of *adhyaya*. The Vedic student carries for life the mnemonics of place—the *agrahara* resounding with *mantras*—and the mnemonics of time—*brahmacarya* as a rite of passage. In later life every recitation has the capacity to evoke the guru's voice, the guru's house, the *agrahara*, the auspicious territory.

In his studies of the Greek New Testament Paul Ricoeur discussed what he perceived as parallelism between the Gospels as encompassing narrative and parables embedded within them, a "mirror relation" between large and small texts and the ways in which something passes from one to another. He was also intrigued by what he called "the work of the text," a "reverberation of the narrative-parable on the person who tells it."[8] This perspective may shed light on dimensions of the Vaidika career, both textual and ritual. The Vedic student appropriates a given embedded micro-text in an entirely personal scale, being held responsible for it whenever he is ready, two months, six months, eight months, a year. There is no enforced schedule, and variations in overall student readiness, as noted previously, may be measured in years. The *brahmacarin* "makes haste slowly" at his task as all the while he encounters the encompassing macro-text, Veda, in various guises. Further, he will discover on a daily basis familiar mantras embedded in his newly heard lessons, powerful, familiar sound bytes he has overheard in various contexts, and these enable him to link together alien elaborations on unfamiliar passages. It is the text working, reverberating on the reciter, although here it is not visual but aural senses that are conduits for solidification and intensification.

4.3 The Sama-vartana*: Graduation Day*

When Lanka was judged by his guru, Baballa's father, to have completed the Taittiriya curriculum he could then go home, put behind him those long daily walks in darkness between Mukkamala and Nedunuru, eat his own mother's evening meals, and await his examination by a Veda pandit review board.But first there was a marker for this momentous occasion, *sama-vartana*, the "return" from the guru's house. The focus was a ritual bath, *snana*, when he received the title *snataka*, one who has undergone the well-earned bath. It was a graduation ceremony with a tonsure, shaving of head and facial hair by the barber, bathing, applying sandal paste and perfumes to his body and kol to his eyes, putting on two new garments and earrings, first the right, then the left, new chappals for his feet, and a garland that he placed on his own neck. At hand were an umbrella and his staff. Finally, he took a mirror and checked out his appearance, makeup and all. The *brahmacarin* vow of celibacy was over and he was now free to marry. The entire day was spent indoors behind the pen for the *agni-hotra* cow, shielded from the sun, and he could move about only after sundown and *sandhya-vandana*.

Lanka was of course part of the "old school." Today most Vedic students indulge only symbolically in "return" since Veda learning with their fathers occurs at home. The ritual bath, however, prevails and still follows AGS 12.1–1.4, including the feasting of the boy in the company of a number of neighborhood Brahmans. He hears himself described as one with "divine splendor." The daily chores he has done all these years are behind him and may now go to a younger brother. Inattention to personal appearance, part of the rigorous celibate vow, ends abruptly. Well after the age when testosterone kicked in, the new graduate may now entertain without shame thoughts of sleeping with his bride. They were small children when they married but, if he got lucky, from time to time at social or ritual gatherings he may have caught precious glimpses of her from another room or another house and noticed her gradual flowering into a young woman. Those not so fortunate never see their wives between marriage and the day, many years later, of ritual consummation and establishment of a new household fire.[9]

4.4 Advanced Degrees

The career of the long-married Veda pandit, soon to be united with his wife, now follows a trajectory with multiple options. The Taittiriya Samhita is transmitted in several forms, *vikrti*, "modifications" of the "original" or model text. The student began with the continuous (*samhita*) recitation (*patha*). After completing *samhita-patha* he then proceeded to *pada-patha*, the same text over again broken down to separate words, *pada*, without regard to grammatical rules that alter certain initial and final letters when they are adjoining. Then he could continue for a third time with the same text in *krama-patha*, a step-by-step recitation. The first and second recitation patterns are normative; most teenage students opt for a *krama-patha* examination and certification.

The best and brightest students, however, may take a plunge into the more difficult recitations of the Taittiriya Samhita, the *ghana-patha,* for example, a compact braided form that was mastered by Duvvuri Phani, Yajulu's grandson, and by the sons of Gullapalli Sitaram Sastri and now his grandsons. Some may generate a career out of such recitations as *ghana-pathi,* masters of *ghana* who recite professionally at pandit assemblies or other auspicious occasions, sometimes in pairs or quartets for antiphonal response.[10] They become alchemists working the sounds, transforming the mantras, and transporting their hearers and quite frequently themselves, with their rich and powerful symphonic performances. They do this in an entirely different mode from that of the specialists in the Sama Veda during a *soma* sacrifice. The *jata-patha* is another difficult recitation pattern attempted briefly by many but managed by few. Popular among Nambudiri Brahmans in Kerala is *ratha-patha,* the "chariot" recitation that has never been in fashion in Konasima.

On the other hand, rather than pursue other textual modifications of his hereditary Veda, after the sequence of Taittiriya Samhita, Brahmana, Aranyaka, and Upanisad, the skillful student may turn to one of the other Vedas, another *sakha,* one of the several other schools or "branches" of Veda that emerged in India during the centuries of composition of the Upanisads.[11] For "grad school" there are choices. Family tradition may direct the student into a second Veda such as the Rg Veda, followed perhaps by portions of the Sama Veda, and later the Atharva Veda. These students will "collect" portions of Vedas from other gurus, often in other places. Lanka, for example, learned the basics from Baballa's father, then *ghana* and a great deal of *srauta* knowledge from the *ahitagni* father of Mitranarayana, his future son-in-law, and later in life acquired much of the Atharva Veda from yet another mentor. In his early years Duvvuri Yajulu learned first from his father for four years before spending five years more, like Lanka, with Baballa's father, Chinna Subrahmanya Somayajulu, in Mukkamala, followed by years with gurus in Korumilli, Vyaghresvaram, and Tanuku learning *srauta,* Sama Veda, and additional texts. The pandit Samavedam learned from three successive gurus in three different villages but stayed within the Taittiriya corpus and did not study *srauta.*

If the "returned" Taittiriya student begins *adhyaya* in some portion of the Rg Veda, for example, with the same or a different guru, he faces a Samhita with 1,028 hymns (*sukta*), comprised of *rk,* metrical verses, and collected in ten *mandala.* His childhood went into learning the Taittiriya texts and within them were numerous Rg Veda mantras and *brahmana* discussions of them. Lanka, who learned about three-fourths of the Rg Veda Samhita, his lessons coming from a division of the text into *astaka,* eight sections, was also drawn to the Asvalayana Srauta Sutra, the ritual manual for the Rg Veda. In one remarkable pedagogical swap Kapilavayi Yajnesvara Agnihotra Sastri and Tangirala Balagangadhara Sastri exchanged guru and student (*sisya*) roles in Kapilesvarapuram in reciprocal teaching of the Rg Veda and Atharva Veda Samhitas. So dominant is the Taittiriya Samhita, however, that only a few hereditary families of Rg Vedins may be found today in the Godavari Delta.[11]

If a family member has gained knowledge of part or all of the Sama Veda the student may aspire to learn from him some of that astonishing seven note score. The *udgatr* priest chanting alone, or becoming a choir with two of his three acolytes, employs the *saman*, chants in a musical scale, to extend, repeat, and draw out every possible ounce of meaningful sound from the basic Rg Vedic mantra it highlights. Most *saman* make use of mantras found in hymns from the ninth or eighth *mandala* of the Rg Veda. The *udgatr* hymnal is a *gana*, a collection of melodies essential for the most sacred of sacrifices, the *soma*. The *gana* generated from each *saman*-mantra can number in the thousands and no one claims mastery of all. Mitranarayana in Kakinada, a member of the Pisapati family in West Godavari, and the Kapilavayi brothers are among the last of the old guard with a longtime *srauta* heritage still capable of using a Sama-*gana prayoga* compilation that has been handed down through generations.

As noted in Chapter 2 (n. 8) the few remaining *soma*-sacrificing families highlight the significance of retaining coastal Andhra's Sama-*gana* tradition and insist on its unique character and style, unlike recensions employed by Taittiriyins elsewhere in India. The Jaiminiya recension of Kerala is never mentioned. At stake are Kauthuma and Ranayaniya, versions considered by some Western scholars to be essentially the same. If they were identical, however, there would not persist an enormously contentious matter in Konasima, the bitter charge that the Daksina (Southern) or Madras Sama-*gana*, derived from the Kauthuma, was incorrectly imported to Andhra by the Dendukuri family, thus "contaminating" the age-old *srauta* tradition. Perhaps it is a composite of Ranayaniya *gana* in the "local" style. Lanka insisted that diluting Ranayaniya with Kauthuma elements was a dangerous mixing of traditions. Now that the elder Konasima *ahitagni* have passed on and a tradition of routinely held great sacrifices has moved west from Konasima to Krishna District it will be far more difficult to sustain that charge regarding the Sama-*gana* role in *yajna*.[12]

Kapilavayi Yajnesvara Agnihotra Sastri, the itinerant collector of Vedas, went to live in Kasi (Varanasi) in order to learn all forty *adhyaya* of the Sukla (White) Yajur Veda, a Veda known also as the Vajasaneyi Samhita, concluding with the Isa Upanisad. Hereditary Vajasaneyins are as few in East Godavari today as Rg Vedins.[13] Separation of pandits by *sakha* is not as severe as once was the case. Middle generation Vaidika Brahmans remember a time when interdining, sitting in the same line for food, was not possible between Taittiriyins and Vajasaneyins. Now, however, they may eat in the same hall. Honoraria for recitations were also unequal in the past, Vajasaneyins receiving only half as much, even when reciting the same text, as their syllabus was considered to be less demanding. And it is true that the Vajasaneya Samhita is perhaps half the length of the Taittiriya Samhita. Unlike the Krsna Yajur Veda that contains *vidhi* or *brahmana* portions, injunctions and commentaries, mixed in with mantras and *yajus* formulas, these explicative passages are reserved in the White Yajur Veda corpus for the quite lengthy Brahmana, the Satapatha, the Brahmana "of a hundred paths." An interesting if extremely derogatory Telugu epithet is used by Taittiriyins with regard to such *sakha* distinctions. Vajasaneyins of the Madhyandina recension of the Sukla Yajur Veda (not the Kanva branch) are known locally as *madhyanna* Malas, meaning they are Untouchable Malas until midday (Telugu *madhyanna*) when they suddenly become Brahmans. Such verbal antagonism may reflect an ancient dispute between the *sakha* in this region of South India.[14]

The Atharva Veda Samhita has two mostly similar recensions, Saunaka and Paippilada, of which the former is known in the delta. Like the Taittiriya Samhita, the text is arranged in *kanda*, collections, of *sukta*, hymns, 730 hymns assembled in twenty cycles, mostly metrical but containing some prose. There are no Atharva Veda hereditary families although more than a dozen individuals have received all or substantial portions of the Saunakiya recension of that fourth Veda, primarily for personal, not community-wide rituals. Pandits surveyed in Chapter 3 include Lanka who learned much of the Atharva Veda, his guru being Tangirila in Kapilesvarapuram. Duvvuri Yajulu also learned numerous portions, one reason being his need for mantras in a vain attempt to stave off increasing blindness from glaucoma. Neither of them learned hymn by hymn in a fashion that might be expected by an outside scholar, however, but rather by selection of *anuvaka*, portions of *kanda*, for specific ends. Lanka claimed the benefits of *santi*, peacefulness, *pusti*, prosperity, and *abhicara*, by which he meant counter-sorcery or defensive charms that he recited to ward off an enemy's malign intent. At one critical juncture he believed that Atharva Veda mantras saved his life. The Kapilavayi brothers also learned the Atharva Veda, Rama Sastri in order to serve in *parayana* in the Annavaram temple as an Atharva pandit, Venkatesvara in order to qualify as a *catur-vedin* and emulate his father's record as knower of all four Vedas.

In addition to pursuing other *vikrti* of the Taittiriya Samhita or turning to Vedas in other *sakha* the young man with increasing abilities and an expanded resumé, thinking ahead to living with his wife and starting a family, may choose further studies with a pandit elsewhere in the *agrahara* or in another village or town, with a focus on one of the Vedangas, "limbs of Veda." These texts, some as old as the fifth century BCE, aphoristic in style, are designed as sciences to further transmission and understanding of the Vedas. Already mentioned are the Sutras of Apastamba, his Srauta, Grhya, and Dharma Sutras, respectively, manuals for sacrificial, domestic, and legal or traditional rituals. In the delta these are part of the standard curriculum. Popular options beyond Apastamba include Vyakarana, grammar, obviously significant for textual learning, particularly important in the transition from Vedic to Classical Sanskrit, and Jyotisa, astronomical and astrological reckoning to determine and interpret calendric time.

Less frequently studied are phonetics, prosody or metrics, and etymology, respectively, Siksa, Chandas, and Nirukta. Loosely counted as another limb is Mimamsa, inquiry into the meaning of the Veda, *vedartha*, going beyond mantras and precepts to contextualization. Duvvuri Surya Prakasa, as noted in Chapter 3, invested several years in post-graduate studies of the *vidhi*, injunctions that lie beneath ritual acts according to ritual theory in Mimamsa.[15] He also studied Dharma Sastras, evolved from the earlier Dharma Sutras, reserving considerable attention for Manava Dharma Sastra, the Laws of Manu.

Certification from further studies in any of these branches of learning adds to credentials and increases authority when attending a local or regional pandit assembly, a *sabha*, for debates and exchanges of information on current Vedic events. If he becomes certified in the Apastamba texts for domestic rituals, often a father-to-son transmission of expertise for hereditary clientele, he may also become a family *purohita* for other Brahmans, asked to conduct marriages, housewarmings, thread ceremonies, or other auspicious *smarta* (domestic) rites for small honoraria. This was a role that Bulusu Cayanulu fulfilled in Sriramapuram and one that Duvvuri Surya Prakasa still holds.

In lineages of *srauta* sacrificers a young pandit might be recruited into a role as *rtvij*, one of the staff of four priests necessary for fortnightly offerings known as *isti* on new- or full-moon days and annual harvest rites, or even one of the sixteen to eighteen priests in an extended rite such as a fire-altar construction lasting forty days. Kapilavayi Agnihotra Sarma served as *rtvij* in such a *paundarika* at the age of fourteen. Even after graduating from celibate studentship and becoming a householder the Veda pandit is engaged in post-graduate studies, the lifelong learning that is the mark of *agrahara* residents who never seem to cease their quest for knowledge. And of course "the Veda," with scores of primary, acolyte, and commentarial texts, provides unbounded territory for exploration.

4.5 *The* Sabha: *Debating in an Assembly of Veda Pandits*

A *sabha* is an assembly of Veda pandits that meets in a particular venue on scheduled occasions, often annually. At the turn of the millennium it seemed that all the Vedic communities were either instituting a new *sabha* or reviving a moribund one. The word, in use since the Rg Veda with the general meaning of assembly or congregation, is in common parlance, as in the two houses of parliament of modern India, the upper or Rajya Sabha and lower or Lok Sabha, respectively, the assemblies of the states and the people. A new Vedic *sabha* was founded in the name of Duvvuri Yajulu March 28, 2005, when some seventy Veda pandits gathered in the Sriramapuram *agrahara* to observe his ninetieth birthday. Already ninety-four on the Telugu calendar, the blind and memory-less Yajulu was enduring the final days before his death a few months later. His family and colleagues wished to found this new *sabha* in his name to honor him while he still could participate, even without his faculties.

Across the wide Vasistha Godavari, Iragavaram Veda pandits such as the Gullapalli family vigorously promote their annual *sabha* and post colorful, lively video clips on their website each time. The Dendukuri family is among the Vijayawada *soma-yaji* who send out their curricula vitae along with regular flyers about their *sabha*. All are aggressively seeking funds either to establish new *sabha* or keep existing ones afloat. Local and regional coherence of Vedic tradition is much to the point. One wealthy Telugu Brahman who lives in Chennai is an active supporter of Veda and sponsors an annual *sabha* during Navaratri in Vijayawada. Clearly *sabha* have blossomed in number, size, and wealth over the past generation.

What does a *sabha* mean to Veda pandits? It is a gathering to debate a particular subject, often an unrealistically expansive one such as *srauta, sakha*, or *patha* that will draw a crowd and intimidate no one, young or old. Much like an American college faculty meeting with an announced agenda, that subject will be broached, addressed in prepared speeches or offhand remarks by some, circumvented by others, dismissed by a few, and perhaps tabled for the next meeting. Blowhards will dominate. The wise will remain silent unless their opinions are directly solicited. Personal scores will be settled, often with clever repartee and innuendo. Expected individuals will insist on "the rules." Private conversations in the back row will determine participants in a forthcoming ritual, examination, or marriage arrangement. A few will leave with satisfaction and a sense that the subject has been adequately settled.

There are substantial differences, however, between a Vedic *sabha* and an American faculty meeting. One is that the *sabha* is open to the public, an audience that for the most part understands nothing of the Sanskrit and little of the esoteric Telugu, but arrives anyway to bask in the esteemed company of Brahmans of consequence. Second, attendees at the college meeting, particularly junior faculty, are more or less forced to be there and are not paid, whereas Veda pandits have come voluntarily and receive honoraria. The honorarium (*sambhavana*) is the reason they are there.

One *ahitagni* of sound pedigree had a low opinion: "The Godavari *sabha*," he commented, "intends to promote the learning of Veda, but the President is a rich man, the Secretary a lawyer, both busy with their own affairs. They come on the day of felicitation neatly dressed to show off and beat a drum to say they are strongly behind Veda study, hand out a few thousand rupees to pandits, and have absolutely no other interaction with them." Others, however, consider them worth attending to hear different opinions on Vedic subjects and catch up on area news. There is, of course, considerable at-home practice for *sabha* in the continual debates on the *arugu* of *agrahara*. The *sabha* is an expanded version of such in-house deliberations.

Lanka noted that three things are essential for a successful Veda *sabha: upanyasa*, by which he meant precise statements on Vedic subjects, supported by references to the texts; *satkara*, hospitality, including respect for the Brahmans, good food, and honoraria; and third, *svasti*, group recitation of the *svasti-vacana*, Rg Veda 1.89, addressed to the Visve-devas, "All the gods," a moment of great pleasure for those reciting as well as hearing, *patha* succeeding one another in increasing order of expertise.

In its heyday, Sriramapuram, with its wealth of *ahitagni* and other well-educated pandits, had routine discussions of Veda, *srauta*, Dharmasastra, Mimamsa, Vyakarana, Jyotisa, and other subjects, interspersed with illustrations from epic and Puranic mythology. As seniority gradually slipped from Baballa to Duvvuri Yajulu, with occasional visits from Lanka, the recognized authority on every matter of *srauta*, the dynamics of these discussions gradually shifted. Seniority in the *agrahara* cluster has been observed over the years and *sabha*, whether all-district or statewide, carry out the same protocol. Usually everyone knows or has heard of the principals who address the larger gatherings or challenge the finer points of discussion.

Some routine meetings, open to the general public, are also called *sabha* even when the subjects are more frequently post-Vedic. Every day, for example, from 4 to 6 PM. there is a pandit *sabha* on the generous concrete floor of the Markandeya Swami Temple in Rajahmundry. Various *mela*, mass gatherings at pilgrimage centers, also harbor Veda *sabha* amid all the festivities of a religious fair. Oldest and most famous is the Kumbha Mela at Prayag, near Allahabad, at the confluence of the Ganges, the Jumna (Yamuna), and mythical

Sarasvati rivers, held every twelve years. Both the Godavari and Krishna rivers eventually became hosts in the twelve-year cycle. Known as Pushkara (from the pilgrimage center Pushkara in Rajasthan) these *mela* bring Veda pandits from across India, Nepal, and now the United Kingdom and the United States. The Krishna Pushkara precedes Godavari Pushkara by one year and most local pandits attend *sabha* during both, centering on Vijayawada for the former, Rajahmundry for the latter. Recent Godavari Pushkaras occurred in 1969, 1981, 1993, and 2005. Several million bathers appeared in Rajahmundry in 2005 with probably a record Veda pandit turnout, although the pandit choice for a river dip was often not the mobbed public *revu* (Telugu for bathing ghats). Siva-*ratri*, the night of Siva, is another occasion for a great throng each year, one popular venue being the rocky island of Pattisima (Pattesam) in the Godavari, upriver from Rajahmundry about halfway to Polavaram. A *sabha* there draws as many as 200 pandits to chant the *svasti-vacana* and other texts.

On the other hand, even the smallest of villages may hold a *sabha*. To cite an example, on the first two days of November 1980 a Brahman householder sponsored an assembly in his house in Munganda, a village with a population of 3,000 close by the divide between the Vasistha and Vainateya branches of the Godavari. A great red carpet was spread on one side of the pit in the atrium typical of sumptuous village houses. Intentionally left visible to the audience of adults and some twenty children was the open granary with its huge yellow mound of husked paddy. A dozen pandits invited from this and nearby villages wore the *tri-pundra* forehead mark. Exposition of Veda, Veda-*pravacana*, provided the introit, followed by recitations and a chance to show off prowess in *pada, krama, jata*, and *ghana patha* of selected portions of the Taittiriya Samhita. As usual, *ghana* was the *piece de resistance*, with four pandits facing four others in team antiphony. Then discussions began, some in Sanskrit, most in Telugu, with Vedic texts and traditions leading to a focus on local *antyesti* and *sraddha* practices concerning funerals and ancestor worship, respectively. The session lasted five and a half hours. Every Sravana month, dark or bright lunar half, this village, like many others, provides such a *sabha*. Sometimes it is linked to the beginning of a local student's Vedic instruction in which case it occurs on a full-moon day after his *upanayana*.

Nedunuru, also a small village, has two *sabha* every year, one since 1980 to honor the village god, Chennamalaisvara (Siva), the other, begun in 1986, named for the resident *ahitagni* Lanka. Another considerably larger *sabha* occurred in the town of Palakollu on the first of January 1988 on Mukkoti Ekadasi, "three crores (of gods) eleventh," also known as Visnu's Eleventh. About a hundred pandits and a dozen *brahmacarin* students attended from 3 to 7 PM with brief excuses for *sandhya-vandana* outside the hall at sundown.

They came from East and West Godavari, Krishna, and Guntur Districts and were seated and honored in a hierarchy of specialties: *srauta, veda, smarta, puranika, brahmacarin*. Honoraria came as money in envelopes from cloth bags and fruit from baskets. At one point an elderly woman circulated among the students and presented each with coins.

Frequently, the congregation of pandits for a *sabha* is the occasion for examinations of students in Veda. The Rajahmundry Parishad, for example, draws together pandit examiners from Gangalakurru, Annavaram, Kottapeta, Machilipatnam, and of course the villages containing *agrahara*. Sriramapuram, Vyaghresvaram, Mukkamala, Iragavaram, Kakinada, Samalakota, and Amalapuram have all been selected for joint East and West Godavari District *sabha*-examination meetings usually lasting two or three days, including business meetings for the selection of secretaries, treasurers, and other Parishad officers.

As the number of Veda *sabha* continues to increase so does the range of opportunity for honoraria, and many pandits track the schedules for increasing their livelihood. Samavedam, for example, knew the venues for all upcoming *sabha* within a hundred miles or more and took both sons along. Before there was a *parayana* scheme, honoraria from *sabha* and recitations at marriage ceremonies or new house openings were the elder Samavedam's principal source of income. For the diligent student Duvvuri Phani in the late 1990s, not yet employed in *parayana*, with one child and another on the way, *sambhavana* became a series of stipends upon which his survival depended. At that time a standard honorarium was Rs. 400 to 500, about $10 to $12.50. Elderly pandits attend as long as their health permits travel by train and bus.

Ahitagni have been of two minds regarding honoraria. Baballa flatly refused any and all, disdaining them as *veda-vikraya*, the selling of the Veda, and therefore did not attend *sabha*. His *an-ahitagni* grandson Prasad still refuses invitations today out of respect for Baballa. Lanka relied on *sambhavana* for much of his career in order to keep from sinking under debts, but later dismissed all except for travel and maintenance funding, understanding correctly that his knowledge and experience were often crucial to debates on *srauta*. Frequently he went south to Sringeri, occasionally to Kanci, for larger *sabha*. Mitranarayana, for his part, remarks today regarding *sabha* and *yajna*: "In the past we did not stir out of our villages. But now the activity of Veda is diversified, so we constantly receive invitations to go to other places. I enjoyed the opportunities to go to Hyderabad, Delhi, Ujjaini, and other cities." Young, newly certified Veda pandits entering[16] the *grhastha* stage of life and looking forward to opportunities in *parayana* and a steady income in a lively cash economy, heartily agree with him. The householder's way of life is the focus of Chapter 5.

5

Becoming a Householder

5.1 *The Voices of Women*

The bridge over the Billakurru canal is packed tight with all imaginable colors flowing in brilliant sun, a kaleidoscope of scintillating saris and glistening bangles on girls and women thronging the road toward Jaganathota. It is the long-awaited Tadithota festival, an assembly of gods from fourteen villages in a spacious palm orchard some three miles from Sriramapuram. Shouting troupes of men lug giant *prabha*, garlanded bamboo and papier-mâché floats for every village god and goddess, each grand enough to carry several riders along. Formerly they were thirty feet tall with masts strapped on bullock carts but the new god of electric wires reduced their vertical scale. As if to compensate, each village increased its amplified drum-and-bugle legion in competitive cacophony. Men are always out and about but today in this local Mardi Gras it is the joyous release of girls from school and auspicious wives from the confines of house and lane. Their best cotton frocks or silk saris and lustrous oiled and jasmined braids command almost as much attention as their broadly smiling faces.

Girls and women—wives, mothers, daughters, daughters-in-law—have appeared only briefly in Chapter 4 on textual studies since the *upanayana* and access to Veda learning has been exclusively male for many centuries and the social system is patrilocal. In this chapter on the life of householders, however, women are center stage and their oral histories are particularly noteworthy, providing a counter-narrative to claims of patriarchal supremacy. In Chapter 6 on the ritual life, wives are further recognized in co-sacrificial roles. Some brief details about the lives of fifteen *patni* were featured in the overviews of families in Chapter 3. In the order of that village-by-village survey, wives of *ahitagni* included Sundari, Surya, and Subbalaksmi in Sriramapuram, Anasuya in Nedunuru, Satyavati and Kamesvari in Vyaghresvaram, and Anasuya in Kakinada. Discussed also were the wives of other Veda pandits, some of them potential *ahitagni*: Laksmi, Savitri, and Kamala in Sriramapuram, Narasamamba in Iragavaram, Sita Rama Laksmi in Simhacalam and Maruti and Sita Nagalaksmi in Annavaram. Finally, Laksmikanta, widow of the Konasima-born *srauta* champion Renducintala Yajulu, graciously contributed her reflections on a half-century of *agni-hotra*.

As sources of information about women "living in Veda" they varied considerably, as did the circumstances of interviews. Some were present on numerous occasions, often in the company of their husbands for long, multifaceted conversations about Veda, *srauta*, and life as *patni* in general. Only one was not permitted by her husband to be consulted; some were in poor health or in seclusion at the time of visits. A few contributed strongly only after they became widows and enjoyed the uninhibited opportunity to speak about their lives. Among the most informative of all were the youthful and energetic Maruti, wife of Kapilavayi Rama Sastri in Annavaram, and their married daughter Sita Nagalaksmi when she was still living at home; a reflective Anasuya in Nedunuru, particularly after she became the widow of Lanka Venkatarama Sastri; Satyavati, wife of Bulusu Kamesvara in Vyaghresvaram; Subbalaksmi in Sriramapuram after she was Bulusu Cayanulu's widow; and Laksmikanta, the strong-willed, assertive widow of the senior Renducintala in Vijayawada.

Narasamamba Laksmi, a skilled folklore field worker teaching high school in Rajahmundry, with the additional cachet of stemming from a Vaidika Brahman family, was freely able to enter the interiors of the more traditional houses where male outsiders were not welcome. She provided valuable recorded interviews with Anasuya, wife of Lanka, their daughter-in-law Savitri, wife of Baballa's son Bullebbayi, Subbalaksmi, second wife of Bulusu Cayanulu (whose first wife, Rama Suryakanta, died at age twenty-four, c. 1945), and others. It should be noted that familiar use of first names of *patni*, quite untraditional, is apologetically adopted here to aid the reader in following the narratives of scores of individuals. As mentioned before, all wives of *soma* sacrificers are known as Somi-devamma, an honorific that replaces given names (and is contracted to "Sodemma" in colloquial Telugu). This title is the equivalent of Soma-yaji or Yajulu that may be affixed to the name of the *yajamana* after first offering *soma*. Wives of *an-ahitagni* (non- *ahitagni*) pandits usually have the traditional *-amma*, "Mother," suffixes: Kamala, for example, is known as Kamalamma. Since girls are named for goddesses at birth, and unlike boys lose their family names when married, there is a certain amount of name duplication. In the following remarks Anasuya, wife and later the widow of

Lanka, is quoted, not her daughter Anasuya, wife of Mitranarayana, who was not interviewed.

Women speak their minds on many topics from the drudgery of kitchen duties to joyous recollection of ritual roles. Conversations tend to focus, however, on several themes: the utmost importance given to *madi*, ritual purity, the numerous tasks assigned in ritual life, failure of the new generations to maintain traditional standards of their elders, the bearing and raising of children, the loss of an older husband and trauma of widowhood, and the fragility of health in old age. A constant topic is first in this list, the significance of remaining pure in self, kitchen, food, ritual rooms, and the household in general, particularly when serving as hostess for visiting Veda pandits. To be pure is to be auspicious; conversely, impurity carries the onus of being inauspicious.

Sundari and Baballa, occupying for many years the house on the corner of Sriramapuram's single lane and Mukkamalla road, served as gatekeepers for the *agrahara*. No one could pass without notice. They became hosts for *agrahara* events large and small. Since a visiting *ahitagni* must rely on food cooked only by a Veda *patni* this meant considerable labor for Sundari and then later her sole daughter-in-law Savitri. Added to that burden was the loss of a child only twenty days after her birth and care-giving for needy son Bullebbayi. Her neighbor across the lane, Surya, wife of another *ahitagni* and also a frequent hostess, bore fourteen children, of whom ten survived. What the historical novelist Russell Banks captured in nineteenth-century America as "the dark fatigue of women and the death of infants"[1] must certainly be acknowledged as a fact of twentieth-century life as well. The recounting of life-experience by *patni* themselves, however, varies from matter-of-fact or upbeat acceptance to the rare lamentation over the dark side.

It was Laksmikanta, performer of *agni-hotra* for half a century alongside her husband, Renducintala Yajulu, who expressed with animation the hardship as well as the joys of the *patni*: "It is not easy to play the role of cook as wife of a *srauta* ritualist. Guests come without prior notice and the wife should be ready at all times to change into *madi* (Telugu ritual purity, Sanskrit *sauca*) and prepare food. Chores in the kitchen are untold suffering for the wife of a performer of *srauta*." In the same conversation she also gave voice to a commonly held opinion regarding the softness and ill-preparedness of the next generation: "My daughters-in-law are modern and have no faith in ritual life. My sons help them in domestic chores and that is not right for men!"

Satyavati, then in declining years, was amazed in recollection that she managed to accomplish *adhana* and continuing *agni-hotra* alongside husband Kamesvara: "I had a baby on the hip, a baby on my lap, a baby in the stomach (Telugu *kolupu*), all these babies! But people in the village said 'Don't be scared! If you perform *agrayana* once a year you'll be fine as *agni-hotrin*." By the time of *agni-stoma* there were eight of an eventual ten children underfoot and Satyavati was quite reluctant to advance into *soma* rites: "Children require so much attention, my elderly mother-in-law needed care, and the thought of cooking and serving so many people for five ritual days plus an additional one was overwhelming." Kamesvara prevailed, however, both of them offered *soma*, added *soma*-sacrificer to their respective names, and decades later Satyavati was proud to be Somi-devamma.

For a *patni*, maintenance of an *agni-hotra* room and a *puja* area in the kitchen in constant states of ritual purity is not the sole concern. As the moon has its monthly phases she has monthly (*masika*) cycles[2] but unlike the moon her body may pose a threat. As noted in Chapter 2 the culture at large maintains deep-seated apprehensions about menstruation. The impurity (Telugu *maila*, Sanskrit *asauca*) of a woman in her period, like death pollution, is particularly damaging in ritual situations. ApSS measures *an-alambhuka*, her period, as three days. As the moon is invisible for three days per month, so is a woman in her prime "invisible."[3] "Untouchable" is a heavily loaded, now a constitutionally proscribed and outmoded appellation in the caste hierarchy, but the Sanskrit term for a woman in menses means exactly that: she is neither to be touched nor to touch any person or item connected with food. She turns her drinking cup upside down as a signal and withdraws into privacy. In addition to the *diksa* that covers the impurity of death and menstrual blood for a *soma* ritual there is another measure that can protect daily *agni-hotra*. The belt of *munja* grass that encircled the *patni* for initial moon rites may take her place near the offering fire for those three days while her husband performs alone.[4]

It has been an indological custom to treat the *yajamana* as sole sacrificer. Here, however, as in previous publications,[5] the *patni* is termed co-sacrificer. It must be acknowledged that patriarchal subjugation prevails, as in most aspects of life in the subcontinent. Vedic texts subordinate the *patni*, her mantras and *kriya* are far fewer and she receives instructions in both domestic and extended rituals from the *yajamana*, *adhvaryu*, and other males. Marriage is sometimes described as her *upanayana*, the husband being her guru. At the same time it should be recognized first that every Veda pandit stresses the essential role of the *patni*. Baballa expressed it in January 1988: "Without a wife neither domestic ritual nor great sacrifices can be performed. One obtains the authority of a ritual life, *karma-adhikara, only* if she is present." Lanka was quick to point to ApDhS for that authority, noting that no distinction can be made between husband and wife since rituals are performed jointly.[6] Examples of the wife's participation are legion. To take but one example, after offering the omentum of an animal (today always a goat) the wife must accompany the *yajamana* and priests to the kitchenette outside the arena for the necessary self-cleansing because she too has sacrificed (ApSS 7.21.6).

A second substantiation for applying the term co-sacrificer is self-referential: *patni* have referred to themselves as *agni-hotrin* and have cited other women as performers of extended sacrifices, as for example, Anasuya addressing Duvvuri Sastry, "When your grandmother *performed paundarika* . . ." A third reason concerns Agni: if an *ahitagni* needs to be away from home for a fortnight or a month he may perform, respectively, *paksa homa* or *masa homa*, fortnight or monthly offerings, and let the wife cover *agni-hotra*. If she too must leave the home the fires become *laukika*, no longer sacred. In other words, Agni cannot remain in a house without one or both. There should be no hesitation in perceiving a joint role in the household either on the *grhya* or *srauta* level of sacrifice. "I know," said Laksmikanta proudly, "that rituals cannot be done without me." Maruti expressed it more bluntly: "One who has no wife is useless, practically a corpse." And more than one pandit confessed that after his initial hesitation it was his wife who was impetus for advancing to extended sacrifices beyond *agni-stoma*.

Some wives of *ahitagni* and potential *ahitagni* take enormous pleasure in recollecting the details of sacrifices or planning to undertake them. Maruti is a fine role model for three daughters. She is as tough as she is alert, totally in control, adroitly inserting her knowledge and experience into discussions of *srauta*, carefully explaining the difference between *yajna* and *yaga*, correcting mistakes in the observations of males in the room. Having grown up with her *ahitagni* grandfather performing *agni-hotra* and *isti* on a regular basis she was thoroughly acquainted with extended ritual life before marriage, then gained far more as she married into a *srauta* family and traveled with the Kapilavayis from sacrifice to sacrifice. "My husband routinely being a *rtvij*, I am now experiencing the same *srauta* life I knew as a girl. A *rtvij* may bring his family if he wishes, a matter of choice, and we stay in the same *yajna-sala* (temporary sacrifice hall of bamboo and fronds) as other *patni*, sleep, eat, spend our time there." Kapilavayi Yajnesvara trained his two sons well in both text and ritual and they are now reciting in famous temples, one in Simhacalam, the other, Maruti's husband, in Annavaram. But he and his wife also educated their three daughters, in particular the firstborn of the five children, one who now lives with her husband in Tenali and has knowledge of the Sama Veda as well as the Taittiriya Samhita

Satyavati, already mother of eight, including a baby of three months, when she underwent the *diksa* consecration for *agni-stoma*, happily recalled all details in a conversation many decades later. But a tinge of sadness entered her voice as she commented: "My husband and I were so tied up with ritual actions we had no opportunity to observe the great number of people feasting. We only heard from others about the beauty of the whole scene. Feeding everyone in the area at noon and again at 7:00 PM is so important. All who come should eat, without exception. It is *prasada*, grace. Feasting at a *yajna* is special, full of merit for it is *anna*-feeding, rice-feeding! Vyaghresvaram was famous for that, but those days are gone." And here Kamesvara added a bit of folklore heard in other *agrahara* as well: "One day more people came than expected. There weren't supplies enough. Hired Brahman cooks (*vanta-brahman*) were extremely busy. One merchant in town gave a full bag of *tavudu* (the outer cover of a rice grain after the husk is removed, usually given to livestock) and the cooks spiced up a special dish! It disappeared quickly and people remembered our *yajna* for this special food!"

5.2 *Marriage*

A marriage (*vivaha*) is a splendid spectacle, everyone liberated from routines, moving about with the electricity of a holiday outing, brilliant costumes, some outrageous colors, an aroma of spices loading the air as Cooking Brahmans labor to prepare vast quantities of food. And yet a marriage also means solemn rituals with long midnight hours of mantras, fire offerings, seemingly endless recitations of pedigrees. "Marriage is performed out of *paramartha*, the highest truth, and it must be continued always with *sraddha*, faith. Achieving *brahma-loka*, the heaven of Brahma, is the whole import of marriage. In a marriage ceremony happiness is not only for the bride, groom, and relatives. It is a matter of joy for the entire community." This earnest declaration by Duvvuri Yajulu was seconded by others of both genders. Marriage enables the girl to develop into the coveted role of a *su-mangali*, an auspicious married woman, one who has, in T. N. Madan's apt phrase, "a beneficent influence on the lives of other people."[7]

Always popular in any gathering is a discussion of marriage, affording opportunities to explain two important features that only those in Veda require. First, in order to guarantee the purity of a continuing Vaidika lineage the choice of a bride for a Veda pandit must be *rajasvala-purva*, a pre-pubescent girl who is the daughter of a woman who was married before puberty. This is double insurance that no non-Vaidika, or worse, non-Brahman male might have crept in from the shadows. Second, unlike most Brahmans, Vaidikas insist on a full five-day ceremony, no skimping of ritual details or requisite mantras. If sleepiness overcomes many, including bride and groom, no matter, the correct mantras have been sounded. Highlighted are liaisons with other Veda lineages guaranteed to be reputable, some of them declaring multigenerational allegiance to particular families and villages. And in common with virtually the entire population of India past and present there is enthusiasm for sharing the precise monetary cost of a wedding, dowry being for many the heavy burden of unloading a daughter and consequently going into debt, thus providing a credible explanation for insufficient funds today.

It should be noted, however, that animated pleasure structures most conversations on marriage, an emotion valorizing positive qualities of relationships that in many cases, given the youthful ages of brides and grooms, have lasted seven or more decades. Lanka and Anasuya were married for seventy-seven years, Baballa and Sundari for seventy-one years, Duvvuri Yajulu and Surya for sixty-seven years, and Kamesvara and Satyavati for sixty-six years. Pandits and *patni* alike have great delight in detailing their own marriages and those of children and grandchildren. The tradition of a man having a "co-wife" (second wife), sometimes discreetly acknowledged in the wider culture and openly known among Vedic Brahman Namputiri (Nambudiri) in Kerala (M. Parpola 2000: 209-12) is not mentioned.

The guru in charge of a student's learning has a say in marriage arrangements only if he is a senior male within the family, matrimonial decisions being the province of parents and grandparents. So important is Veda pandit lineage preservation that marital prospects are often lined up before the birth of a child. In the case of unions not so pre-arranged, rigorous investigations into family backgrounds precede betrothal. Birth horoscopes are consulted and there must be assurance not only of ancestry but also of correct and timely performance of all *samskara*, life-cycle rituals, prior to marriage. Both purity and character development are said to be cumulative concomitants of the sequence of rites of passage that begin with conception and continue from birth to the age of sixteen. There is hesitation about going too far afield to secure a bride or groom. Background checks prove more difficult at a distance, local villages being safer.

In addition to Vedic branch (*sakha*), parentage, age, ritual refinement, education, and compatible horoscope, two other qualifications concern *gotra*, clan, and *pravara*, ancestral lineage. The term *gotra* has descended from Indo-Iranian **gautra*, cattle place or pen, indicating a close relationship between cattle-herding communities and their herds. In India centuries later, Vedic meanings held social and religious import—tribe, family, clan.[8] One must marry inside the subcaste, Vaidika Brahman, and one should marry inside the *sakha*, Taittiriya, but conversely the choice must be outside both *gotra* and *pravara*. Every clan claims descent from a patronymic ancestor and each Veda pandit provides the name of his *gotra* as identification, for example, Duvvuri Yajulu, Atri (Atreya) and Bulusu Kamesvara, Gautama, to name two of the seven or eight ancient Vedic seers. Samavedam's *gotra* was Harita and Baballa's was Srivatsa, two other ancestral lines of import but not among the famous *rsi*. With regard to this exogamy, "marriage outside," a bride should not be united with a groom with the same *pravara*, the litany of ancient *rsi* considered to be ancestors. Both *gotra* and *pravara* (the latter a rapid declaration of three names) are recited twice daily in *sandhya-vandana*, along with one's *sakha* (Taittiriya) and Sutra (Apastamba), and at stated moments in sacrifices. Paternal ancestry is always kept firmly in mind, as is the constant connection with those worthies of ancient days who first intuited the Veda. As Apastamba states in his chapters on *pravara* (ApSS 24.5.1–10.18) the gods recognize a person when he names his *rsi* ancestors.

Ideally, the groom should follow the approved sequence of *upanayana, brahmacarya* and Veda study, successful examination, and then marriage. Apastamba prescribed no precise age, but as the period of *adhyaya* is approximately twelve years beginning at age seven or eight, the average age of the groom should be about nineteen, the age of Kapilavayi Venkatesvara, for example. But many boys achieve certification at a younger age. Laksminarayana and Gullapalli Sita Ram Sastri were both married at age sixteen. Some boys who married prior to certification, however, included Lanka at ten and Duvvuri Yajulu at "thirteen or fourteen" he recalled. Recent attendance in modern English-curriculum schools has lengthened education in a direction parallel to Veda study and the age of Veda completion has been extended but not necessarily the age of marriage. For example, Duvvuri Surya Prakasa was seventeen when married in 1971 to Kanaka Durga, six years younger, and their four sons, all with longer English curricular (not language) public schooling never experienced by their father or grandfather, were married at ages fourteen, sixteen, seventeen, and eighteen, respectively in birth order. What did increase in that generational shift was the age of consummation and cohabitation of bride and groom, that is to say, the departure of the bride from her parents' home to residence with the groom.

The age of the pre-pubescent bride has remained relatively fixed, usually within a range of three to eight years younger than the groom. When Lanka was ten his bride was seven. When Kapilavayi Venkatesvara was nineteen, Sita Rama Laksmi was eleven. And when Laksminarayana and Gullapalli Sita Ram Sastri were both sixteen-year-old grooms, their brides, Kamesvari and Narasamamba, respectively, were ten and thirteen. *Balya-vivaha*, child-marriage, proscribed by the 1955 Marriage Act, is proudly affirmed by

Veda pandits. As one announced: "This is our tradition and we do it openly," the safeguarding of a lineage being the primary consideration.

Consummation, the sexual act that completes a marriage, awaits the arrival of "blossoming" and puberty rituals for the child bride who continues to grow up in the home of her parents. After first menses, seclusion in a darkened room or screened off corner is concluded with a ceremonial bath three days later. The *rajasvala* girl receives a coconut as symbol of fecundity and a sari as adoptive grown-up attire. Puberty rites, not covered in the Sutras, have no mantras or *kriya* and are transmitted in women's oral traditions.[9] She continues her schooling but otherwise remains in the house, expecting eventual release to her husband for the merit-filled and auspicious act (*punya-* and *subha-karya*), proper terms for consummation of the marriage. In ApGS 3.8.7-11 the culmination (and definition) of *vivaha* is "leading" the bride to the home of the groom. Three nights of chastity sleeping on the ground with a clothed staff between them (a third "person" on guard instead of a sword between the medieval knight and his chaste damsel) are followed by first sexual intercourse, a highly ritualized event late in the fourth night after many hours of delayed gratification. But Apastamba's schedule was no longer possible when pre-pubescence became the overriding desideratum for a bride's qualifications. Thus a gap of years occurs, sometimes many years, between the marriage ritual and "the auspicious act," requiring an expiation, *prayascitta*, to be pronounced during the nuptials. Elder Anasuya, for example, married at seven, was fourteen when she left the home of her parents to live with Lanka and a generation later their daughter Anasuya was fifteen when she joined Mitranarayana in Korumilli.

In the most recent two generations a groom might require time to become "established," financially secure, which may mean employment in another town until his bride joins him. For example, Duvvuri Sita Ram Sastry married (Gullapalli) Syamala in 1991 when he was sixteen and she was ten. In February 2000 during a visit to her home in Iragavaram where he had arranged research meetings for this book with his maternal grandfather and five uncles (one being his father-in-law), he was twenty-five and she was nineteen. Highly embarrassed and furtive, they found a moment to speak to each other for the first time. Previously he had had only distant glimpses of her during brief visits to Iragavaram. When he finally completed his computer degree program in Hyderabad she could join him there a dozen years after their marriage and today they have a son and a daughter, all of them living in Hartford, Connecticut. Although he is *laukika* and not "*vedam-lo*," at least the marriage rules of the Veda pandits have been upheld and this will no doubt be of significance in marriage arrangements for their children. His life goal is no less than to earn enough in the United States to re-establish Sriramapuram as a true Vedic *agrahara*.

A prominent feature of South India is cross-cousin marriage such as the one just mentioned. In *menarika* (Telugu) a boy marries his mother's brother's daughter; a girl marries her father's sister's son. Long-term genetic effects of consanguinity is a subject that elicits no interest, this being a tradition with deep roots in some cultures of Dravidian languages but one proscribed by Manu (11.172–73) and some other legal authorities outside the South. A striking case of serial *menarika* is the pattern of Duvvuri–Gullapalli marriages uniting families across the Godavari River over several generations. Among the children of Gullapalli Butchiram Avadhani and his wife Subbalaksmi were a daughter, Surya, who married Duvvuri Yajulu, and a son, Sita Ram Sastri, who married Narasamamba. Both of these couples were featured in Chapter 3. The first pair had five sons and five daughters and the second pair had five sons and two daughters. These new generation sister and brother families with seventeen children between them afforded opportunities to continue Duvvuri–Gullapalli marital connections. Turning to the following generation (Gullapalli) Surya and Duvvuri Yajulu's third son, Surya Prakasa Avadhani had four sons, grandsons of Duvvuri Yajulu, growing up in Rajahmundry. Each was married to one of the granddaughters of Gullapalli Sita Ram Sastri, these brides being the respective daughters of the first four sons of Gullapalli Sastri. Bride and groom share the same grandfather, FaFa in the bride's case, MoFa for the groom. Since a male child is often named after his grandfather, in more than a vague sense in Telugu culture reincarnating the old in the young, it is as if a girl has been given to her grandfather. In the example given above, Duvvuri Yajulu's grandson Duvvuri Sita Ram Sastry (the computer programmer now living in Hartford, Connecticut) is named for his mother's father (his grandfather), Gullapalli Sita Ram Sastri. In 1991, as just mentioned, he was married to his mother's brother's daughter, Syamala, *also* the grand-child of Gullapalli Sita Ram Sastri. (See Table 5.1 for a chart of marriages between East Godovari Duvvuris and West Godavari Gullapallis.)

Marriages with tight-knit pools of eligible grooms and brides often mean that people are related in multiple and complex ways. Interconnections of the several Veda pandit families surveyed here are legion: one of Duvvuri Yajulu's sons was married to one of Lanka's granddaughters and his second daughter married a Bhamidipati relative of Baballa. Even without cross-cousin marriage, proximity often produces liaisons, as for example, guru and student. Lanka's guru was an uncle of Anasuya so they grew up together as children in the same household before they were married at ages ten and seven, respectively, this union being non-*menarika*. Maruti, granddaughter of an *ahitagni*,

Menarika marriages of East Godavari Duvvuris (D) and West Godavari Gullapallis (G.)

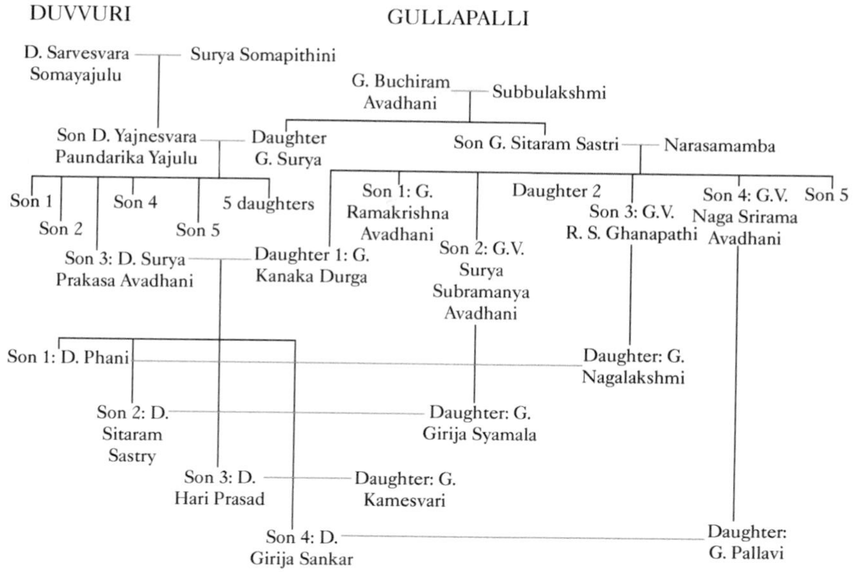

TABLE 5.1. *Menarika* marriages of East Godavari Duvvuris (D) and West Godavari Gullapallis (G)

remembers that the two Kapilavayi brothers, Venkatesvara Sastri and Rama Sastri, came to stay in the house for half the year to study with her grandfather. "They spent so much time with my grandfather they felt obliged to take a granddaughter, so I was acquired by the Kapilavayi family as a special request." She was married to the younger brother.

It was noted in Chapter 2 that Bulusu Cayanulu gave a daughter to Renducintala's son in direct exchange for teaching that son in his house over a period of years. But Cayanulu had three other daughters and in order to pay dowry for one he had to sell land, including part of the acreage he received in the Sriramapuram grant. Lanka paid Rs. 400 dowry to Mitranarayana for him to marry the younger Anasuya, no land, cash only, and it was a considerable debt for him. Costs on the other side for the hosting family of the bride are also extensive as relatives might stay in the *agrahara* or village as long as two weeks.

Many of the pandits in this survey have been involved in marriage ceremonies either within their own community or for local folk of the higher castes. Bulusu Cayanulu routinely officiated, as does Duvvuri Surya Prakasa Avadhani in the present. Baballa's grandson Prasad does *muhurta* timings by consulting birth horoscopes to determine the most auspicious months, days, and hours, a service regularly performed by Baballa and Lanka in decades past. Samavedam picked up honoraria by reciting blessings at marriages, "never less than Rs. 500" being his reward.

The program for the five nights of a Veda pandit marriage, although longer, shares most standard procedures of ceremonies performed throughout India today. ApGS 1.2.12–3.9.11 provides details for Taittiriyins. After some preliminary remarks betrothal and marriage are the Sutra's first topics, with mantras from RV and AV marriage hymns cited in a separate text, the Mantrapatha. Early on, Apastamba observes that it is women who must be consulted for local customs, an admission that it is the *oral tradition* of the distaff side that keeps track of certain important details laced into the proceedings. He displays knowledge of the ways of men when he recommends a girl who is eye-catching to the groom but not one who has an attractive younger sister.

The groom is welcomed by the bride's parents into their house with *madhu-parka,* a dish of honey in curds traditionally offered to a guest. The bride and groom look intently at one another. In some ceremonies he pours water over her as she stands under a sturdy wooden bullock yoke with a piece of gold near the hole. When she has dressed he wraps a *darbha*-grass cord around her waist and leads her west of the fire to sit down for offerings and mantras. By her right hand he leads her north away from the fire for seven steps, they walk around the fire keeping it on the right, and then together make offerings into Agni during a steady stream of mantras from both sets of family priests, his and hers. Then in another key moment the groom directs the bride to place her right foot on a working grindstone north of the fire with the admonition that she should be as firm and steady as rock (he will remember doing exactly this himself during his *upanayana*). She clasps cupped hands together and waits for him to sprinkle ghee onto roasted grains that are dramatically poured from his upraised hands into hers at waist level.

Repeated circumambulations of the fire and her foot placed on the stone alternate with offerings, all with continuing mantras. Highlights on agricultural symbols—the yoke, grindstone, ghee, and grains—are backdrop to sonorous mantras emphasizing the promise of fertility from this new union. These are deep-seated traditions and the symbolism of the hole in the yoke, to take one example, has a long chronicle from Rg Veda 8.80.7 to the marriage hymn of Atharva Veda 14.1.41 down to Apastamba and commentaries a thousand years later. And everywhere in the marriage hymns, of singular import to past, present, and future *soma*-sacrificers, are celebrations not only of Agni but also of the god Soma as lord of procreation and long-lived lineages.

When nuptials are completed the bride remains in her parents' home while the groom returns to his village and his guru. She will live through years of schooling until menarche when the couple's departure from her parental home is as dramatic as the escape of newlyweds from a Western wedding. This "leading away" of the bride, the *vivaha*, is augmented by the carrying of live coals from her parents' fire in a pot slung from cords, embers that will transfer Agni for the pair in their new residence. Once established on dry kindling, offerings into that fire take priority. At night the groom points north for the bride to identify first the north pole star, Dhruva, its fixed position in the night sky being a model of unwavering attachment, and then the star Arundhati, Alcor, a dim but traceable star among the seven *rsi* that make the constellation *saptarsi* (known in the West as *Ursa major*, the great bear, or the plow, or the big dipper). Arundhati is the wife celebrated for fidelity to the great *rsi* Vasistha. The new bride husks rice, he cooks it with ghee in a pot, and together they make this cooked rice offering in the ritual simply called *sthali-pakana* (described in Chapter 2), first to Agni, then to his alloform, Agni Svista-krt. For many couples this becomes daily observance morning and evening prior to eating breakfast and supper, sometimes with the first offering going to Surya.

To those who have witnessed Hindu weddings in India, North America, or Europe many of these procedures are quite familiar. Most have been in place in Grhya Sutras for well over two millennia and some mantras accompanying specific acts derive from Rg and Atharva Veda hymns composed another millennium earlier. For example, *kanya-dana* is the gift of a girl from father to groom. Apastamba alludes to this moment without making it the highlighted ritual act it later became. Although he states that she will not return to her natal home (like most *dana*, ritual gifts, it is permanent) she will in fact visit from time to time, particularly during periods of childbearing. Other Sanskrit terms in use throughout India include the joining of right hands, *pani-grahana*, taking seven steps, *sapta-padi*, circumambulating the fire clockwise, Agni *pradaksina*, placing the bride's right foot on a stone, *asma-rohana*, pouring puffed rice from groom to bride to fire, *laja-homa*. Even the "driving," *udvaha*, from the bride's home and village toward the groom's residence has remained true to ancient practice although the get-away vehicle today is a brand-new rented car rather than a chariot (*ratha*) drawn by two beasts of burden, and today all five nights are captured on tape by professional videographers. The tying of the *mangala-sutra*, an auspicious thread on the bride's neck, so important today, and the addition of toe rings to the bride, are both addenda well after the Sutra period.[10]

In the matter of remarriage, a strict double standard prevails. It is acceptable for the widower but unthinkable for a widow to remarry and ApDhS 2.6.13, a discussion of inheritance and paternity, rules widow remarriage sinful. Bulusu Cayanulu married again only eight months after the death of his typhoid-stricken young wife. Fourteen-year-old pre-pubescent Subbalaksmi, purchased in Gangalakurru, became his ritual partner for Renducintala's *paundarika*. Of the eight different forms of marriage listed in Asvalayana Grhya Sutra 1.6.1-8, ApDhS 2.5.11-12 mentions six, the one known as *daiva* marriage pertaining to a girl who becomes *daksina*, ritual payment by the sacrificer to a priest who is serving in his ritual. In Cayanulu's case, however, the payment was oblique since the *yajamana*, Renducintala, was not the father of the girl.

5.3 *Children and Their Life-cycle Rites*

In the center of the main room of the spacious and immaculate new house a three-month-old baby is constantly rocked side-to-side in a wooden cradle by his grandmother, Maruti, then swung vigorously head-to-toe in a green hammock suspended from the ceiling. He sends out no cry for Dramamine. Maruti has just performed a minor rite, something like an extra *samskara*, life-cycle rite. The baby started making fists with his hands, as if squeezing imaginary balls, so relatives came to be fed with fist-sized lumps (Telugu *mudda*) of cooked rice. Here, as in every household, babies steal center stage from older children running about. In Chapter 6 the *diksa* consecration is detailed, a *srauta* ritual in which both sacrificer and wife are reborn, stammering and making fists like babies.

"In the old days there was no ban on having children. In fact, the goal of marriage is to obtain children." Having said this, the correct ritual life always uppermost in his mind, Lanka was quick to point out the three-debt obligation, the *rna* mentioned in Chapter 2, as he effortlessly recited Taittiriya Samhita 6.3.10.5: "At birth a Brahman is born with three debts, studentship to the *rsi*, sacrifice to the gods, and children to the ancestors." Here Lanka recalled our previous discussions of *avadana*, cuttings, portions of the dismembered goat in *pasu-bandha*, animal sacrifice. Paying off these debts, he said, is accomplished in the fashion of offering pieces of the goat one at a time: learning and reciting Veda as a student, performing sacrifices, and having a son to perpetuate the lineage are the three debt payments.[11] Lanka, like the other pandits, was solicitous of the *dora* who has three daughters, no sons, and no continuing lineage in his name.

Lanka and Anasuya had eight children. Duvvuri Yajulu and Surya raised ten children and so did Kamesvara and Satyavati. Such large families are striking in contemporary America and Europe but not so unusual in earlier times. Lyman Beecher, the renowned nineteenth-century American evangelist, had twelve children, one of whom was the equally eminent Henry Ward Beecher, father of ten children. The Abolitionist, John Brown, hanged in 1859, had twenty children, seven from his first wife, thirteen from his second. Until family planning was introduced and encouraged in mid-twentieth-century India, a sizable number of offspring, especially sons, was the norm. Lanka and Anasuya, with seven sons in a row, were considered in their day a peerless model. The showcasing of sons is evident in Duvvuri Yajulu's family photo. (Figure 3.4 shows Duvvuri Yajulu and family on his sixtieth birthday, 1975. Seated center right, Surya on Yajulu's left; sons one to five extend prominently from his right hand; five daughters are mixed with sons' wives in the fading background.)

Details about marriage rituals, laws, celebrations, dowry and other costs, and sons were readily forthcoming from all Veda pandits but information about daughters and grandchildren had to be gleaned from women, not always immediately approachable until after several visits. In Baballa's family a daughter who lived only twenty days was mentioned only by a younger female member of the family, not by Baballa himself. Lanka, when asked about children, would always report on the seven sons. A daughter, the firstborn and, as it turned out, his sole line of continuity in Veda, was an afterthought. A review of the Veda pandit families outlined in Chapter 3 shows a range from one to ten in the number of children actually brought up in the household: Duvvuri Yajulu and Surya, ten; Kamesvara and Satyavati, ten; Lanka and Anasuya, eight; Laksminarayana and Kamesvari, eight; Mitranarayana and Anasuya, seven; Sita Ram Sastri and Narasamamba, seven; Samavedam and Kamala, six; Bulusu Cayanulu and Subbalaksmi, five (with Cayanulu and his first wife Rama Suryakanta one, for a total of six); Baballa and Sundari, one. Of these nine senior pandits, identified here as the "old" generation as opposed to their sons and colleagues in the "middle" generation, and their grandsons in the "young" generation, the average number of children is seven. The number of children who died in infancy, an understandably sensitive and largely undisclosed topic, again reminiscent of nineteenth- and early twentieth-century Europe and America, was rarely disclosed (one in one family, four in another).

With the "middle" and "young" generations there is a sharp decrease in the number of children, sons and grandsons with their spouses adhering closer in each generation to the national slogan "We are two, we have two," in an India where half the population is under twenty-five years of age. With the exception of Baballa, no pandit of the senior generation had fewer than six children. In the "middle" generation few families are that large, and in the "young" generation, those now still in their childbearing years, it appears that once a son or two is born, family planning locks in. Conception is celebrated as an enormously significant milestone for newlyweds. Maruti moved to Annavaram at age sixteen to begin a new household with Kapilavayi Rama Sastri. "For seven years I did not conceive. I tasted *yajna-payasam* (rice pudding made on the sacrificial ground, believed to promote conception) from different sacrifices. I was present at many *yajna* as I accompanied my husband and father-in-law from sacrifice to sacrifice." There was proof in the pudding: Maruti delivered three girls and then finally, the obligatory boy to close her childbearing years with four. Duvvuri Phani declared in 1998 after becoming father of two children, both sons, that the second was the "final" child. Family planning, essentially vasectomies, tube-tying, and contraceptives, denigrated by Lanka and blamed for what he weighed as softness and a lack of stamina in the younger generation, has been welcomed in a new age. In the case of Baballa's grandson Prasad and wife Laksmi, three daughters were followed by Laksmi's inability to bear more children. Sonless, with three girls requiring dowry, surrounded by women who bore mostly or all sons, Laksmi's vast, luminous eyes rapidly dimmed with deep sorrow.

Much has been said about the *upanayana* and Vedic study of boys from the age of seven or eight. In Veda pandit lineages, girls, although ineligible for the initiatory ritual and *adhyaya*, are not neglected when it comes to a Vedic future. Married as early as seven or eight, the same age as boys hearing their first mantra from a guru, girls hear the mantras for five nights in the *vivaha* ritual. If their families have a tradition of *srauta* practice, they will have grown up observing *sandhya-vandana*, twice daily milk offerings, new- and full-moon rites, harvest rituals, and many other ceremonies, and become entirely familiar with the rules of *madi*. As a boy progresses through his portions of Veda, largely unknown to his bride in another village or *agrahara*, her parents will be conscious year by year of her suitability as *patni*, possibly in a sacrificial career.

Turning now to the *samskara*, rites of passage, some have already been noted, including the *upanayana* thread investiture for a boy that marks entrance into the first life stage (*asrama*), that of the celibate student; the *sama-vartana* that signals completion of initial Veda instruction; and the *vivaha* marriage ceremony that observes passage into the second life stage, the householder. Also noted was the rite of impregnation (*garbha-dhana*), placement of an embryo in the womb of the bride, originally on the fourth night of marriage but today occurring after the bride attains puberty and leaves the home of her parents to live with her husband of several years. As the *upanayana* is the most significant life-cycle transition for a young boy, so is puberty the crucial life change for a girl since it indicates readiness for marriage and entrance into womanhood. And yet the event of menarche is not a *samskara* and goes without remark in the male-oriented Sutras. The concern for proper paternity of offspring has pushed back the timing of marriage to a safe distance prior to puberty and allowed the bride's biological change to take place in the parental home with due family, but not priestly, recognition. Nothing, however, has altered the central emphasis on procreative powers of females as the key to continuing existence. The principal image of the bride is a fertile field where seed will be sown and a living child emerges in verification of fecundity.

The total number of life-cycle rites is not fixed and there is no tradition of performance required of everyone. Most families, however, adhere to the same pattern and follow Apastamba's Grhya Sutra coverage of what are sometimes taken to be a set of sixteen, a number perhaps derived from the ancient *soma* tradition. Like several other Grhya Sutra authors, Apastamba begins with betrothal, marriage, and a desired conception of a new being. As noted, fire from the bride's parents' home (venue for the five-day marriage) is taken to establish the new domestic hearth, and that fire will be the cynosure of all subsequent rites of passage. Just as rice, coconuts, and other agricultural products are central to marriage rituals, so too will they recur in many *samskara*, ripening being a key metaphor for the steady progress of an individual life-body.

In the sixth chapter of Apastamba two prenatal rituals are addressed, the *pumsavana* with its desire that the embryo be a male child, performed usually in the third month when pregnancy becomes visible, and *simantonnayana*, the upward parting of the wife's hair by the husband, usually in the fourth month of the first pregnancy only, a graphic expression for safe delivery from the womb. Although the general belief is that the mother's contribution to an embryo is uterine blood and the "soft" internal parts, while the father's contribution is semen and the "hard" parts, with the stronger one determining gender, the astonishing fact that a ritual such as *pumsavana* can alter gender a dozen weeks into embryonic development testifies to the power of mantra and performance. If the result is a male child, confirmation is readily announced. If no one mentions *pumsavana* again, a female child was born.

Both prenatal rites employ special items, the one for a male child a green shoot from a banyan tree bearing two figs resembling testicles. The mother-to-be lies on her back near the fire while her husband presses into her right nostril a small bit of the ground shoot from that tree famous for its aggressive spread. Mantras express hope for an easy delivery. For *simantonnayana* she sits by the fire while her husband stands behind and combs her hair three times, first with a porcupine quill with three white spots, then three blades of *darbha* grass, finally with a twig from a different fig tree, the *udumbara*. New barley sprouts are fixed to her hair and she touches a calf.

The delivery itself becomes a ritual, *jata-karman*, birth-rite, performed if possible even before the umbilical cord is cut. The "production of wisdom" is the initial act when the father uses a gold spoon or ring dipped in honey, curds, and ghee to touch the infant's mouth while whispering into the right ear the name of Vak, sacred speech. Mantras about *ayus*, long life, are followed by the endowment of a secret name, known only to the parents, and the infant is given to the mother's right breast. The next ten days are the period of confinement of mother and child in the birth room, a place of impurity where a special prophylactic fire or lamp, *sutika-agni*, is burning. Emergence of mother and child on the tenth day is auspicious and calls for *nama-karana*, the rite of name giving, when the secret name is augmented by a public name for lifelong use until honorific titles are earned in replacement, Yajulu, Cayanulu, Somidevamma, Somayaji, for example.

The number ten is significant. For ten lunar cycles (nine solar months) the embryo developed in the womb, undergoing personal construction through *samskara* from *garbha-dhana* to *jata-karman*. At the other end of this existence, this rebirth, there will be a similar period of ten days after death and cremation for ritual construction by means of mantras, rice, sesame, and water of a temporary cover for the naked, vulnerable spirit (*preta* or *jiva*). Those ten days after cremation will simultaneously eliminate the pollution of death and create, body part by body part, a transitional shelter that allows the enduring spirit to become a *pitr*, ancestor, and receive a new body to continue in another birth. Thus mother and newborn child are freed from the impurity of birth pollution in the confinement room, as the baby exited the mother after gestation, as the spirit emerged before and will emerge again from its previous and future temporary bodies, all on a scale of ten.[12]

The next important ritual after name-giving is the first feeding of the infant with solid food, most significantly, rice, in the *anna-prasana*. The baby's lips were touched at birth with honey and two products of the cow, curds and ghee. Now, after about six months of mother's milk, it is sacred homegrown rice (*anna*, the same word meaning "food") that is featured in another ritual, cooked rice being mixed with the trio of honey, curds, and ghee. Apastamba makes no mention of *nis-kramana*, literally stepping out, the first occasion for the baby to go out of doors in the arms of a parent to see the sun and moon, usually in the fourth month. It is, however, observed by some pandit families as it is in the wider Hindu culture.

Apastamba finds a place in the child's third year for the *caula* ritual, also known as *cuda-karana*, the first tonsure. This mirrors something of the *simontannayana* for the mother-to-be in the use of a porcupine quill, *darbha* grass, and fig-tree twigs to comb the hair of a male child before it is shaved away, leaving only the *cuda*, tufts at the back of the head as daily reminder of ancestors when they are named during *sandhya-vandana*. The placement of a wire ring, right ear first for boys, left ear first for girls, is the earlobe piercing, *karna-vedha*. Apastamba and Hiranyakesin tuck this rite in at the end of the *upanayana* when the boy ornaments his body in the ritual attempt to make him presentable for marriage. Here Hiranyakesin, who invokes the two Vedic meters known as Viraj and Svaraj, supplies mantras and details including an encomium on the formative powers of gold. Current Veda pandit families perform this on babies of three or four months. Later in life the *ahitagni* acquire heavy gold earrings to mark the completion of *soma* sacrifices, their earlobes strikingly drawn down to reveal large rectangular gaps.

At the age of sixteen the first shaving of facial hair on a boy is accompanied by another shaving of the head, this time including the tufts at the back left growing during *cuda-karana* some thirteen years before. It is remarked by Apastamba as *go-dana*, the gift of a cow, ostensibly to the guru. It is also known as *kesanta*, reserved for later beard growth well after completion of the majority of *samskara*. In addition to the *sama-vartana* "return" from Veda studies and consummation of the marriage this rite marks the passage from childhood to adulthood, the monstrous Scylla and Charybdis of childhood diseases and child-snatching demons having been successfully navigated. Again, the number sixteen, as in the ideal number of *samskara* recalls the importance of the *soma* tradition in this gradual perfecting of a given life-body. It is apparent that most life-cycle rites are concerned with the vulnerable period from conception to that more secure teen age since the only one remaining is the final rite of passage, *antyesti*, cremation after death, the "last sacrifice" being that of a used body. In the tradition of the endless sacrifice, that final *samskara* is also the *first* one for a new body, residence of a new embryo.

Hiranyakesin, Baudhayana, and other Grhya Sutras supply additional details and the *patni* are always forthcoming with regard to local customs, but it is Apastamba who covers almost the full spectrum of traditional rites of passage. Birthdays, not considered *samskara*, are also celebrated. Karttikeya, great-grandson of Duvvuri Yajulu, was feted in 2005 in the home of his grandfather, Surya Prakasa Avadhani, by his father, Sita Ram Sastry, and mother, Syamala, in a gathering of some forty Veda pandits and family members including Gullapalli relatives from Iragavaram. Blessings were recited in *ghana*, and a birthday cake with pink frosting honored his first birthday.

In sum, *samskara*, each requiring the domestic fire, sprinklings of water, a declaration of intent (*samkalpa*), and an auspicious constellation (*naksatra*) for proper timing, are believed to construct gradually a true and worthy person, one refined, perfected, and purified by the full sequence of rituals. Duvvuri Yajulu noted that "it is not possible to expect an integrated character from those who neglect proper performance of *samskara*" and he lamented the modern reduction of rites of passage in both number and duration.[13]

5.4 *Livelihood*

Long walks on rain-drenched roads from Nedunuru to Vyaghresvaram allow the traveler to see the ways the local folk make their living. Coffee-colored mud trying with every step to suck chappals from feet, bursts of showers sending rivulets into shoulder ponds, jade leaves of tapioca gleaming in sporadic sunlight, scenes heightened every few hundred meters by vistas of a score of women bent over rice transplants, their brilliant red, yellow, and blue saris shouting over the passionate green of the fields. Well ahead is the harvest season when lines of men will move at a steady trot, balancing loads of this paddy on their heads, aiming for a far corner of the field where bullock carts wait for the next load. Never a tractor in any of these expanses. This tropical hike in part follows the same track as Lanka half a century ago trudging to and from his Veda lesson of the day. The village of Mukkamalla bustles. A woman at the well filling her brass *lota* douses all her neighbors within a hundred meters with salty invectives. A boy of perhaps nine years swings a massive hammer onto the glowing ruby iron on his father's anvil. He will do this every day for another fifty years, performing his duty, in the parlance of the Gita, even as another nine-year-old acts according to his *dharma* by reciting back the fourth *kanda* of the Taittiriya Samhita.

A great yellow Tata truck fills the Sriramapuram lane beside an immense mound of coconuts from surrounding orchards, reminding an observer that the learning of Veda and performing of offerings are not the only activities here in the *agrahara*. Sweating brown men in skimpy loincloths punch the heavy nuts onto sharp spears standing upright in the ground as others collect milk and meat or strip husks to load the truck for sale in Hyderabad. Coir will soon be turned into doormats for American, European, and other markets. As mentioned before, a tongue-in-cheek Telugu proverb ranks a coconut tree as more reliable than a son. The coconut haul, like the great stacks of paddy in burlap bags at the time of the two rice harvests, affirms the *agrahara* as a productive segment of one of India's choicest agricultural zones.

Economic aspects of Vedic life are not favorite topics of discussion for pandits although many will point to financial insecurity when attempting to explain the disappearance of *agni-hotrin* and extended sacrifices from Konasima. Most give credit to the TTD *parayana* scheme and affirm the honoraria, pension plans, and other subsidies that enable pandits to teach their sons and others, maintaining the Taittiriya texts despite a declining ritual tradition. The transition to a cash economy in the late twentieth century was overwhelming to a number of families. Samavedam, as noted in Chapter 3, was a good illustration of the dilemma, attempting to teach sons and grandsons while feeding and clothing an extended family, trying to reconcile two demands, *adhyapana* at home and paid recitations away from the *agrahara*.

The founding of two Brahman *agrahara*, Sriramapuram in 1955 by the Dokka family and Kamesvari in 1960 by Nedunuri Srirama Murti, occurred with the generous notion of providing subsistence to qualified pandits, many of them entirely devoted to Veda and *srauta*. The *dana* for each pandit selected, eventually fourteen in Sriramapuram and five in Kamesvari, included a half or full acre of agricultural land with a respectable yield, a house site, and Rs. 1,000 for construction of a new house. The disposition of land, a valuable possession in an agricultural region, had different histories over the generations as each family grew, divided, traded, sold, and experimented with crops. All the pandits either rented out their acreage for others to work for a portion of the yield or became "gentlemen farmers" who supervised *kuli* laborers from the abundant supply of low-caste families in the area. According to *varnasrama-dharma*, the laws of class and stage of life, a Brahman may not directly cultivate the land.

Some pandits have been more intensely engaged in agriculture than others. Lanka and Baballa were both true hands-on farmers who monitored every crop through its seasonal changes. Lanka inherited six and a half acres from his father and could see all of it from his study, expecting the fine yield of twenty bags of paddy per acre each harvest as well as robust production from coconut palms. As a boy he watched his father manage the local S.C. (Scheduled Caste) labor crews from dawn to dusk regulating irrigation ditches, then plowing and harrowing with bullocks tugging carved wooden plows, then seeding and transplanting by teams of women, then harvesting, winnowing, and bagging with additional migrant labor. When he took charge he imitated Baballa by turning crop fields into office space where he could teach students, consult with colleagues, counsel folk who came unannounced to the local sage for advice, watch over the laborers and negotiate prices with merchants. The half-acre of land that came with the original donation he turned over to a tenant farmer who paid with either paddy or cash. Intercropping of cocoa plants, tapioca, or gherkin cucumbers between coconut palms was one experimental technique, as were additional crops such as green grams, mangoes, sugarcane, and tobacco. Fear of drought, so prevalent inland in Telangana, is seldom in mind for those in water-rich Konasima. In fact, local Veda pandits are sometimes recruited to cure drought-stricken areas. A visit to Tirupati on November 17, 1980, revealed among the sixteen pandits praising the gods in a Varuna-*puja* several pandits included in this study.

Veda pandits in general have strong attachment to and concern for the land and its produce. Duvvuri Yajulu spoke of *ksema*, the peace, security, and welfare of the land (*desa*), and Lanka had intense respect for the traditions of landholding, refusing to turn to the new hybrid seeds that were claiming responsibility for India's green revolution. "That seed is not native but foreign," he objected. He used bovine manure only and cited Dharma Sastras that confirmed his view that synthetic pesticides and chemical fertilizers damage the soil and produce unhealthy food. A buffalo or cow gave milk for *agni-hotra* and the family, any excess not to be sold but to be given to others.

If one follows agricultural reports on production in Konasima, Lanka's organic farming principles may have cost him considerable rupees. Despite his farm income and the minor earnings in honoraria for *rtvij* service and examiner's fees he stated with equanimity that he had been in debt his entire life. Not long after his death Anasuya complained about the oppressive *dabbu* (money) culture of modern India and the distasteful necessity of soliciting rupees for sacrifices. That, she explained, is the reason we did not perform them ourselves after *agni-stoma.*

After years of working his land Baballa sold it when he was crowded out by squatters. Samavedam, perhaps the shrewdest Veda pandit when it came to finances, also sold his plot in order to buy a smaller one with a better yield from a tenant farmer. He reported that he had to pay Rs. 43,000 for the marriages of his first and second daughters and had to scour much of the east coast picking up honoraria for recitations, a practice his sons continue today. Bulusu Cayanulu first sold his inherited lands and then the *agrahara* donation to pay the marriage expenses of a daughter, after that struggling to remain within the budget of a TTD salary and occasional *sabha* honoraria. Duvvuri Yajulu was the last of the Sriramapuram Veda pandits to keep his original acre. His third son, Surya Prakasa Avadhani, has been fortunate in living in a splendid *agrahara*-like compound in the town of Rajahmundry, rent-free as long as he teaches Veda. He and other middle-aged pandits such as the two Kapilavayi brothers and the five Gullapalli brothers, each of these seven living in a substantial modern house, have ever known the penury of their elders. The Kapilavayi brothers entered TTD salaried employment early in their careers and can look forward to pensions when they retire from temple service. Fulfillment of *ahitagni* and *patni* aspirations appears to be imminent for Rama Sastri and Maruti.

The *agrayana* harvest sacrifice, to be considered more carefully in Chapter 6, is the most important obligatory ritual for *ahitagni* beyond *agni-hotra* and lunar *isti*. Until recent years it was also an annual domestic ritual for many Brahmans with only a single fire. So significant is *agrayana* that many struggling with the incapacities of old age make special efforts to complete it every year either on new- or full-moon days of Asviyuja or Karttika in the autumn, or Phalguna in the spring, rekindling lapsed fires just for this. Baballa and Sundari, for example, continued until he was eighty-seven, in a special *sala* constructed in front of the house. Blind Duvvuri Yajulu, the effervescent granddaughters of Baballa-- Rekha, Madhuri, and Kalyani-- giggling furiously around him, declared that 80 percent of the benefits go to the community and insisted on performance of *agrayana* to the end. No one may eat the new rice until it is offered in a rite that takes two or three hours, and of course no one may eat rice at any time without being in a state of ritual purity. The connections between the land, the people, and food are always palpable.

As noted in the second section of Chapter 2 the entry into pandits' lives and fortunes of the Tirupati-Tirumalai Devasthanam (TTD) and the Andhra Pradesh Charitable and Hindu Religious Institutions and Endowments Acts made all the difference for the recent generations. The officers of the temple famous for its wealth channeled funds for decades into promoting "Vedic culture" through salaries, pensions, and honoraria to Veda pandits for special or daily recitations (*parayana*) or, more recently, for their publications and other accomplishments. As noted earlier, opinions of the overall impact of these programs has been mixed. Some see a waning Vedic tradition saved by temple and government largesse, and point to historic support for Veda pandits mentioned in *sthala-purana* and inscriptions such as the Simhacalam temple appropriation from its treasury for Veda *adhyaya* dated 1383.[14] Many Andhra pandits signed on to the recitation schedule. Samavedam, for example, the most eager participant, started at age thirty and remained until he died. Duvvuri Yajulu, Cayanulu, and Mitranarayana received the higher *ahitagni* salaries and served until incapacities became restrictive and they accepted pensions. For them it was a worthwhile program. And without doubt the TTD also succeeded at inserting Vedic tradition into popular culture. Cassette recorded recitations are heard on local bathing ghats and every important temple in Andhra dramatizes one to four different Vedas being recited live.

On the other hand, the TTD is blamed by some for interfering with traditions regarded as reclusive, virtually secretive, away from public scrutiny and institutional control. Baballa and Lanka were among those who rejected offers to become, as they saw it, "employees" of the TTD who descend into "selling" the Veda in exchange for a steady income. They also worried about invitations to young pandits from Hindu temples in New York, Chicago, Pittsburgh, Atlanta, Houston, and other American cities. "Only in the isolation of an *agrahara*," elders said, "away from worldly distractions, can an *ahitagni* survive. Our young men will go there and not return and that will mean the destruction of *srauta* as well as the teaching of Veda here."

5.5 *Old Age, Retirement, and Thoughts on Renunciation*

In his green-canopied house under beckoning palms in Nedunuru Lanka was asked how he was feeling. "Jirna!" he replied, summoning the Telugu and Sanskrit word for digestion. Never a complainer, he was not indicating stomach or bowel problems but a larger, insoluble one. "I am being digested by Time" was his message. When he used the familiar metaphor of food for the untreatable process of aging he might have been reflecting the Taittiriya Upanisad refrain he learned about the age of ten: *aham annam, aham annam*, "I am food, I am food!"[15] As noted in Chapter 3, Lanka announced that he would die at age seventy-two because that was his father's age at death in 1947. Also, a *mrtyu-cakra*, death chart, prepared for him by an astrologer, indicated severe negative effects from the planet Rahu. But what seemed like Rahu's fatal illness was countermanded by Atharva Veda mantras that he knew by heart. Medicine prescribed for his diabetic condition might have had something to do with a return to health. Two years later he and Anasuya discontinued *agni-hotra*, a cessation permitted by Apastamba after thirty years of daily performance. In 1988 a kinder death chart predicted that he would live to be eighty and indeed he celebrated *sahasra-candana darsana*, his sight of a thousand full moons. At eighty-three he enjoyed taking on a new student and commented: "Death is inevitable but the will to live is strong." The satisfaction of living on was replaced by suffering at eighty-six, however, with paralysis, inability to walk or feed himself, slurred speech, and dimming eyesight. "There is no more necessity for existence. There are some remaining days, that's all we have," and he died at age eighty-seven in June 1999, fifteen years beyond the first astrological predictive reading.

Anasuya, married to Lanka for seventy-seven years and with eight surviving children, died on the last day of 2005. Her age of ninety was unmatched by anyone in her lineage. A woman of advanced age owns increased prestige in the *agrahara* or village and Anasuya fit the description by Duvvury (n. 9) of the *fully* auspicious married female, the "ultimate goal of every woman."

Duvvuri Yajulu and Baballa, next-door neighbors in Sriramapuram, also became nonagenarians like Anasuya. They were ninety-four on the Indian calendar by which they reckoned. As indicated in the capsule biographies of Chapter 3 the Konasima pandits and wives have an enviable longevity record. Laksminarayana, the youngest *ahitagni* to die, did not quite reach his eightieth birthday. Kamesvara and Mitranarayana, both in their eighties, ceased *agni-hotra* but continued to teach, Smarta manuals for the former, Taittiriya Samhita for ten- to twelve-year-old students for Mitranarayana, who followed the tradition of his father before him, teaching Veda fifty years or more after *agni-stoma*. In sum, the average age at death for *ahitagni* in this survey of the close-knit complex of Vyaghresvaram village and the *agrahara* of Sriramapuram and Nedunuru was eighty-six and a half years.[16]

"Retirement" is therefore a qualified term for Veda pandits who may leave TTD *parayana* service but continue to teach Veda and other subjects as long as they have voice and stamina. Becoming a wilderness wanderer in *vana-prastha*, the third *asrama* between householder and world renouncer, is sometimes the traditional recommendation when a man finds gray in his hair and his sons have sons.[17] But such withdrawal from *agrahara* or village is seldom a choice for pandits who live on and die in their homes, not the forest. And retirement now has an entirely new face since the advent of TTD, state, and central government honoraria and pension funds for Veda pandits, with special considerations for *ahitagni*. The Veda pandit family suddenly became like the families of those employed by the State Bank of India or the Indian Railways, free from financial distress or dependence on largesse from children and grandchildren, with a check arriving on schedule monthly. The security derived from a reliable pension is inestimable.

The Vedic ritual life, on the other hand, is subject to retirement and may be abbreviated or curtailed when senescence begins to limit mobility. ApSS 3.14.12 suggests thirty years as a possible minimum for the performance of *agni-hotra*, an honest recognition of what is generally called "body weakness," afflictions magnified by age. Joints are distressed from constant rising, sitting cross-legged, rising again, not to mention smoke-filled eyes and, worst of all, failing memories of mantras and *kriya*. Remaining "*madi*-tied" to rules of purity and pollution when reciting or offering also may exact a toll, the necessity of bathing, for example, particularly in the chill of December and January waters, loading fevers and colds on the aged. Extended sacrifices are fatiguing and older pandits accept fewer guest-priest roles when offered. In a forty-day *paundarika*, for example, there is no beverage or cooked food, nothing until late-afternoon *phala-hara* snacks of fruits, nuts, and cold leftovers. During a sacrifice a *rtvij* is permitted a rice-and-curds meal cooked on either the *garha-patya* or *daksinagni* fires but often this is declined in the busy-ness of the event and the general desire to prevail in traditional pandit *opika*, endurance. Read machismo here.

When it came time to diminish their daily routine, blind Duvvuri Yajulu, with an increasingly frail wife Surya, explained that *agni-hotra* can be performed in two ways, one with *kriya*, the other with mantra, and it was the former, the actions, they were compelled to abandon. "We now perform with mantra recitations, allowed for those in old age with physical handicaps." *Parayana* in the small *agrahara* temple only a few steps from his house was done for two decades until he retired at age seventy in 1985. Samavedam was only thirty when he signed on for TTD recitation in 1963 and served for the rest of his days, Cayanulu participated until pensioned in 1993, and Mitranarayana, who enrolled at age forty-nine in 1979, remained active until he was almost eighty. The *ahitagni* recited in local temples with a higher salary than other Vedic Brahmans.

In a marriage ceremony the boy (never the girl) is ritually presented with a mendicant's staff and offered a choice: Kasi-*yatra*, running away to Varanasi to become a renouncer, or proceeding to tie the knot with his parent-chosen bride. Invariably, the life of *samnyasa* being as remote to a twelve-year-old as the dark side of the moon, he goes on with the ceremony at hand as the lesser evil. The ideal of the renouncer's mode and its power, however, remains vivid in the Vedic community of elders. Ascetics, in the eyes of Veda pandits, are supernumeraries, perhaps because Apastamba, particularly in the Dharma Sutra, pays close attention to them.[18] In the general population an ambivalent evaluation of *sadhus* and other ascetics prevails.[19] On one hand they are suspect, thought to be fakers, not fakirs, sluggards who have copped out of real-world effort. On the other hand, they are marvel workers worthy of attention. Balayogi of Mummidivaram, east of Nedunuru on the Gautami branch of the Godavari, was an ascetic who was believed to eat only one day a year, on Siva-*ratri*, the all-night worship of Siva. After he died in 1985 his foster brother, "Little" Balayogi, acquired similar fame. Even a decade after his death in 1992 crowds were so immense that special buses, police patrols, and water supplies still came to Mummidivaram in the heart of Veda pandit land.

These pandits claim to be unimpressed by the Balayogi pair and similar pop yogis but they all have their own ascetic narratives to tell. Floating in a high echelon above all other Brahmans, the Veda pandits seem suddenly to size themselves down in the company of renouncers who have exchanged worldly life for a lifetime of wandering village to village, sleeping wherever possible, eating whatever food is offered, serving as illustrations of a life-stage beyond householder. A few may have bizarre outfits, such as one who came for alms from the *dora* wearing around his neck a bright yellow plastic Donald Duck. But *vairagya*, disgust with worldly desires, is treated with utmost seriousness as a vow, in the words of the Kapilavayi brothers, "requiring courage, extremely difficult to uphold." Baballa pointed with pride to his *mula-purusa*, root ancestor, Bhamidipati Brahmibuta Acarya, who became a *samnyasin* after producing sons to initiate five generations of *soma* sacrificers.

Sathya Sai Baba, who died at eighty-four in April 2011, served up a good case for a renouncing figure of widespread appeal. A Sudra, a lowly rank to the high-born Vaidikas and presumably one not to be touched, he was nevertheless widely accepted as "guru" for his charitable works and his famed "presence."

Beyond that, he was a target of devotion as a deity become human. His seventieth birthday celebration on November 23, 1995, was much the topic of conversation in Konasima that autumn and Duvvuri Sarvesvara, Bulusu Cayanulu, Samavedam, and others provided effusive descriptions of their invited week in Puttaparti in southern Andhra, not forgetting emoluments for lending Veda to the party. "I had not seen him before," said a beaming Cayanulu. "For seven days I recited Veda in his presence. That was wonderful! I was given new clothes, Rs. 5,000, Rs. 1,000 for travel, and my wife (Subbalaksmi) received a new sari, gold bangles, a pressure cooker. Until I went to see him I was feeling weakness but I recited with great ease. My daughters pointed out that all this was due to his blessings, because I had *darsan* of him." Lanka's son, Annapurna Sastri, knowing that Sathya Sai Baba had dramatically cured himself in 1963 of a disease described by devotees as either tubercular meningitis or stroke, went to his free hospital for heart bypass surgery. At his death the Sathya Sai Baba Trust was reported to be worth at least $8.9 billion.

Mitranarayana also talks about Puttaparti but without obsequious tones. "Sathya Sai Baba offered me Rs. 40,000 to sponsor a *yajna*. I asked about the animal sacrifice that is dictated by Veda and Baba accepted on the grounds of those Vedic sanctions. But I thought what if we are in the midst of the sacrifice and he dismisses us with full fee. We would be committing the sin of an incomplete sacrifice. How many other *yajna* would I have to perform as compensation?" Mitranarayana did not trust the famous saint to keep his word and therefore excused himself.

Equally unimpressed was Lanka, who had absolutely nothing to report about the sudden visit of the entourage of the senior Acarya of the Kamakoti Pitha, Jayendra Sarasvati Swami, to his tiny, remote house beyond Nedunuru. It was a manifestation that struck Duvvuri Yajulu with wonder, as if the swami were the Maharaja or a new incarnation of Siva. Lanka did, however, wonder if he should offer food to this Jagadguru Sankaracarya who, contra Balayogi, probably ate on most days of the year.

In the final analysis, Konasima pandits appear to follow Manu in understanding *moksa* as "a synonym of renunciation,"[20] virtually the Niebuhrian relevance of an impossible ideal with no immediate reward. Renunciation and liberation are there as supposition for the next time around, a future rebirth. As for *ista-purta*, which Kane tidily defines as "the cumulative spiritual result of merit due to . . . performance of sacrificial and charitable acts,"[21] Duvvuri Yajulu summed it up: "Merely for doing sacrifices, *janma-rahita*, absence of rebirths, will not occur. Performing a karma does not bring freedom from rebirth. Those *samnyasin* who renounce everything . . . they alone are eligible for *janma-rahita*."

Another elder in Konasima found a metaphor to describe *svarga loka*, the heaven promised to the performer of a rite such as the *vaja-peya* in which the sacrificer climbs a ladder placed against the sacrificial post and proclaims on behalf of his wife and himself together: "We have reached heaven, we have become immortal." What does this mean? "It is like a summer resort," he offered. "A tourist can have a good time as long as his purse is full but when the money is gone he has to return home." Brian Smith also noted this temporary character of *svarga loka*: "The ritual journey to heaven taken by human sacrificers . . . must be a round trip."[22] The contradictions of an exalted status as lifelong sacrificers, yet householders short of renunciation render the co-sacrificers model enigmas, those who, in Jan Heesterman's words, "should encompass the world and at the same time keep out of it."[23]

5.6 *Death and Beyond*

The subject of death and dying has its own folklore in India, and here the Veda pandits are not immune. To begin, the vocabulary of thanatos, like that of eros, is circumvented to every extent possible. Terms for the burning ground (*smasana*), cremation (*antyesti*), ancestor rituals (*sraddha*), and funeral priest (*apara-vetta*) all require pronominal circumlocutions ("there," "then," "those," "that one," respectively). The word for widow (*vedhava*) is unspeakable. Unlike the easy discussion of Vedas and Sutras, pandits are uncomfortable talking about current funerals with procedures found in texts separated from auspicious rites of passage. When a certain temporal distancing has intervened, a few terms regain normal use, such as words for annual and monthly observances for the deceased (*abdika* and *masika*, respectively). At times these sensitivities create tensions. As noted earlier, Mitranarayana expressed surprising displeasure with his own guru over refusal to administer last rites for Mitranarayana's *ahitagni* father.

One folkloric theme has to do with time, sequential deaths in a particular family, for example. Among the Bhamidipatis, Baballa died, then his son, then his wife, all within eleven months. Shortly after Cayanulu's death his son-in-law became victim of a fatal scooter accident. Duvvuri Yajulu's eldest daughter died only months after his wife and Surya Prakasa Avadhani noted that Duvvuris not only had a pattern of the auspicious wife dying first but many die in Dhanur-*masa*, the month of Dhanus or Sagittarius. There is widespread belief that fates are determined and the arrival of Mrtyu, Death, is no happenstance. Protective measures such as wearing selected gemstone rings for either defense or supplication concern specific *nava-graha*, nine planets, Sani

(Saturn), Kuja (Mars), and the lunar eclipse nodes Rahu and Ketu being those most feared in one's horoscope.

Another folkloric aspect concerns space. When a house has been visited by Mrtyu it must be vacated for a time. Bulusu Cayanulu's house was boarded up for a year and his widow, Subbalaksmi, found it necessary to live in Rajahmundry after his sudden demise in the house, apparently under an inauspicious constellation. Lanka's house, also closed, was opened only once a month for *masika* rites at the place of his death. Laksmikanta and her fifth son, Renducintala Yajulu Narayana, recall the death in Kasi (Varanasi) of husband and father when authorities demanded that the special funeral known as *losta-cayana* be done on the opposite bank of the Ganges, not the Kasi side, quite contrary to his desire. Rites were permitted only when it became known that he was a highly honored *ahitagni* who had performed more *soma* sacrifices than anyone in India.

A widow in the *agrahara* is conspicuous by her absence. She is no longer the auspicious married woman (*su-mangali*) but an inauspicious (*a-mangali*) person who must wear white with head cover, no flowers, perfume, eye make-up, or *pasupu-kunkum*, the auspicious turmeric and vermilion cosmetic. She remains away from auspicious events. Her *mangala-sutra* marriage necklace was broken on the day of her husband's cremation. As T. S. Madan phrased it, she "has lost her own blessedness as well as the power to bless."[24] In contemporary India her existence is not as bleak as in former times and the practice of *sati*, self-immolation on her husband's pyre, is considered ancient, foreign, and barbaric in coastal Andhra. Today she may no longer be required to sleep on the ground, regularly shave her head, or restrict herself to a single meal a day, although some do choose the last as appropriate. The Tadithota festival that opened this chapter would not be a choice for her as she is an inauspicious sight to others and remains at home. Although she eats food with no spices and regularly fasts she may still travel to visit children and grandchildren and enjoy pilgrimages to local or far off sacred sites. As Subbalaksmi noted in Chapter 3 she experienced a kind of rebirth in learning to read and recite praises of deities and she was happy to return to her old neighbors in Sriramapuram after a year's absence.[25]

A tradition apparently not practiced in full outside of Andhra is the special funeral for an auspicious wife who dies "out of order," that is, before her older spouse. Never becoming a widow, she remains auspicious and her last rites are positive ones. Known as *musi-vayanam* in Telugu, it is remarkable for its female-directed procedures, including a *brahma-muttaiduva*, a special Brahman priestess who ritually embodies the *preta*, the spirit of the deceased released from the cremated body, reverses time until she is a bride again, transforms her into the goddess Gauri and (in direct conflict with brahmanical *sraddha* programs of absorption into either her husband's lineage of ancestors or her own maternal lineage) dispatches her to Gauri-*loka*, the heaven of the great goddess spouse of Siva.

This is a dramatic, sometimes boisterous ritual, essentially a possession (*avesa*) of the Brahman priestess by the deceased who may act out objections to her premature demise. Two cases of *musi-vayanam* were mentioned in Chapter 3, Rama Suryakanta, Bulusu Cayanulu's first wife, who died of typhoid at the youthful age of twenty-four after bearing a single child. Duvvuri Yajulu's wife Surya, who died after a full life and delivery of fourteen children, also received *musi-vayanam* in 1996. The husband does not participate although he sometimes watches from a distance two crowds of all-women mourners, those from her natal side and those from his side, converge. They present in winnowing fans separate offerings at the feet of the deceased-as-priestess and then take away as *prasada*, grace, the consecrated leavings of the goddess—bananas, turmeric, saffron, incense, little mirrors, combs, and bangles—each woman receiving these in a winnow. Since it is auspicious for the wife to die first, she having succeeded in protecting her husband from the grim reaper, it is the sole providential funeral, and mourners, all with flowers in their hair, may shed no tears or express any sorrow, only admiration for one who escaped the dreadful fate of widowhood.[26]

That which lies beyond death for the householder Veda pandit and *patni* is the subject of numerous *agrahara* or *sabha* discussions and is closely related to the matter of renunciation reviewed earlier. Deliberations, to the ear of an outsider, are firmly constricted by a universal belief in the unitary nature of Veda, the inadmissibility of any change in worldview between the Samhitas and the Upanisads, for example, thus ruling out acceptance of innovative doctrines of karma and rebirth in the latter. Karma, *samsara*, and *moksa* are simply read back into "the Veda" as a whole and no historic or linguistic shift may be considered. Discussion of these subjects, however, certainly provokes queries: Does a lifetime of *agni-hotra* or *yajna* lead to *any* afterlife rewards? Baballa thought his performance of *aruna-ketuka* would allow him to enter the world of Brahma, *brahma-loka*, and communicate with the absolute lord without hindrance. Does drinking *soma* produce results beyond the here and now? When funeral texts state that the deceased join their ancestors in heaven, *which* heaven is this? Is it the same one reached by a ladder in the *vaja-peya*? Many are the queries, but replies do not always form a consensus. The last part of Chapter 6 reviews the final *samskara*, death rites, including special funerals designed only for *ahitagni* and their *patni*.

6

Becoming Agni

A LONG LINE of virtually naked men march the sand shore hauling a half-sunken barge upstream, pulling sluggishly but relentlessly with an over-the-shoulder rope fixed to the top of the mast. Within sight further upriver are more day laborers, blue-black skin glistening in the heavy sunlight. They are also skeletal in structure but immensely strong, struggling to carry a water-soaked tamarind trunk slung on vine-ropes up the steep levee toward a lumberyard. Washer folk stand thigh deep at the river's edge endlessly slapping folds of cloth against flat stones. Altogether they provide rich tone poems to the music of the wide Godavari in scenes that an observer today notes would have been the same 3,000 years ago.

This chapter collects portraits of contemporary Vedic ritual life that, astonishingly, are also some 3,000 years in age. When stalks of a green creeper are enthroned and worshipped as a king whose fate is to be pressed into *soma* juice and drunk by a sacrificer who then claims immortality, there is resonance in early Vedas of a thousand years before the Common Era. When sixteen priests line up in crouching postures to snake-crawl their way through the ritual ground, the hand of each on the shoulder in front, stealthy deer hunters stalking the very sacrifice they are conducting, there is witness to a mystery predating any historical text, perhaps even the Rg Veda. The same open-air altar is being constructed today as in ancient India; invitations go out to the same gods of earth, midspace, and heaven to join in the drinking of *soma* and feasting on roasted animals; and the same chorus of mantras floats on the air as in antiquity.

In order to appreciate these grand rituals, however, there must first be a review of the ritual life introduced in Chapter 2 and a more careful definition of the single-fire household and then extension of Agni into a three-fire system and potential *soma* and animal sacrificial dramas. This chapter considers the crucial steps taken when Agni, lord of the household, becomes threefold, fivefold, a receptor of *soma*, and eventually the medium of transcendence and cosmic incorporation in the funeral ceremonies.

Mentioned in Chapter 2 was an important distinction between "pre-classical" and "classical" periods of Vedic texts and rituals. If one were to employ an "archeology" of Vedic tradition it would be the Vedic Sanskrit Brahmana texts and ritual Sutras that represent the "classical" rituals this chapter is about to explore. In the case of coastal Andhra this means primarily the Taittiriya Brahmana, its appended Aranyaka, and the Srauta Sutras of Apastamba supplemented by Baudhayana. These texts were composed largely in the period c. 800–500 BCE, a middle portion of the first millennium BCE.

Probing beneath them one would locate the "pre-classical" level of the Rg Veda, Atharva Veda, and other Samhitas such as the Taittiriya of the Krishna Yajur Veda, compiled c. 1200–800 BCE. This stratum represents the Old Indo-Aryan speakers who entered India sometime after c. 1500 BCE. Deeper still, stratigraphic analysis would reveal the level of an earlier Proto-Indo-Aryan-speaking culture, one with a different dialect, a people who may have called themselves Dasas. They were pastoral nomads who migrated to India c. 2000–1500 BCE and fused with indigenous agrarian folk speaking a non-Indo-European language and inhabiting the broad area east of the Caspian Sea to the Indus River, the region known to linguists and historians as the Bactria Margiana Archeological Complex (BMAC). The Dasas may have built the forts described in the Rg Veda. And there are suppositions that the singular Veda of melodies, the Sama Veda, may have originated with these people speaking a language outside the Indo-European family.

This archaic level may have included the Vratyas, "known for their unorthodox aggressive behavior and raiding habits" as Jan Heesterman noted in his studies of the agonistic and cyclical dimensions of pre-classical Vedic ritual. While this archaic culture left no texts that precede the Rg Veda, the much later classical rituals, the *maha-vrata, asva-medha, pravargya,* and *vaja-peya,* for example, do carry survivals from that remote era, including the influence of Harappan religion in the last phases of the Indus Valley civilization c. 1200 BCE, in a continuing period of cultural fusion of non-Indo-European-speakers and Proto-Indo-Aryans. Of signal importance to emergent Vedic religion is the **sauma* cult of what appears to have been a mysterious plant, perhaps akin to ephedra, one that evolved into *haoma* for Indo-Iranian speakers to the west and *soma* for Rg Vedins in the centuries prior to the middle of the second millennium BCE. Some of these survivals from deep antiquity will be encountered in various segments of this chapter.[1]

6.1 Agni, Private and Extended

A blend of natural learning ability, recitation skills, and dedication to hard work creates a successful Veda pandit out of a *brahmacarin.* In Chapter 2 the Vedic student was seen to begin his lifelong bond with Agni by daily *agni-karya* that he learned on the second day of his initiation ritual. He collects kindling for his guru and looks after one or more fires, offering, for example, seventeen twigs from a branch of a *ravi* or *medi* tree with a mantra for each, waiting to see that each is entirely burned, doing an expiation if he has missed a day. Today his guru is most probably his father or grandfather and he is therefore doing routine household chores. But the hearth he cares for is not the ordinary kitchen one, although that may be an additional responsibility. Signs of the growing mystical liaison between *brahmacarin* and fire, the transforming power of Agni, occur in a moving passage in one of the two oldest Upanisads, Chandogya 4.6–15, dated perhaps to the seventh century BCE. When his guru is briefly away a student receives instruction in the highest knowledge from the fires he is tending. Upon return the teacher discovers splendor, a glow of wisdom in his student, and asks who it could be who has taught him during his absence. In reply the guru hears: "These (fires) look like this now, but they *were* different."[2] And it is the older Konasima pandits who confess to wondrous experiences during reveries sponsored by their fires. Baballa, for one, related two different luminous apparitions rising out of his fires, annunciations that he later understood to be the births of his son and, many years later, his second grandson. The emotions carried in such descriptions are quite unlike any others and reveal insights into the Agni-*yajamana* bond. The student begins to discover fire, to borrow Gaston Bachelard's phrase, as "one of the principles of universal explanation."[3]

When his basic education is concluded and his wife of several years is at last able to join him, a household fire for the couple may now be established either in a separate hearth in his parents' house or in a new residence. This *aupasana* fire receives the *sthali-pakana* cooked food (rice) offering and is now available for private domestic rituals such as *homa* offerings or life-cycle ceremonies. As described in Chapter 2 it cannot be used for *soma* or other *srauta* rites opened to the wider pandit community. It may be said that appreciation of the esoteric configurations of sacrifice arise later in life. Intimations of signal meanings, however, may occur in pre-teen years during *adhyaya*, as in the case of the Chandogya Upanisad student. Concentrating on retention of verses in order to feed them back correctly, he may also absorb the basic vocabulary of the *soma* sacrifice, for example, the minutiae of sacrificial elements, ritual tools, various deities, animals, priests, mystical constructions, and symbolic links between them all. His father or grandfather guru may be one who has done the ritual under study and "outside of class" favor him with accounts of the performance.

He may become intrigued by the mysteries of a particular sacrifice. The *asva-medha* horse sacrifice, for example, fascinated Kapilavayi Rama Sastri as a beginning *brahmacarin* learning TS 4.6.6–9, 4.7.15, and so on. Then after several more years he discovered the magnificent equine-cosmic catalogue that opens the Brhad-aranyaka Upanisad. It remains today his favorite ritual although, not being of royal lineage, one he cannot perform. Nor could he observe one or participate since it has been obsolete for centuries. It lingers as imaginative drama, a ritual of two years' duration with an appreciative day-dreaming audience of one.

Only a fraction of the certified Veda pandits and *patnis* of Konasima establish three fires, perform *agni-hotra* twice daily, and move on to their first *soma* sacrifice, the *agni-stoma*. A few may elect to perform *agni-hotra* on a single fire after *grhya adhana*. Upadhyayula Nagendram, for example, in a multigenerational family of *ahitagni* in Amalapuram, chose not to advance to *agni-stoma*. In this overview, however, all the featured *ahitagni* elected to perform *adhana* with multiple fires and proceed with *yajna* (*agni-stoma*). In some cases, Bulusu Vyaghresvara and Bulusu Kamesvara, for example, fire-setting and first *soma* rituals were scheduled on two successive days and within the year 1955 Mitranarayana did both. Normally, however, the distance between *adhana* and *agni-stoma* should be at least one year of *agni-hotra*. "The old tradition, doing them separately, is better," said Duvvuri Yajulu, and so he advised his relative in Iragavaram, Pisapati, who did *agni-stoma* in 1991.

6.2 *The* Adhana, *Setting the Fires for* Srauta Agni-hotra

A Vedic student's guru, usually his father or grandfather, determines the textual selection and pace of learning Veda. Parents select marriage partners when they are still children, sometimes even at birth. These two decisions, instruction schedules and marriage, are not personal ones. A commitment to set the fires for a career as *agni-hotrin* and co-sacrificing wife is different, and is perhaps the single most important decision in the lives of a Veda pandit and his spouse. It must be undertaken jointly and with deep consideration. This giant step expands upon a lifelong intimacy with fire that began for the boy with Agni maintenance as a *brahmacarin*. Now the liaison takes the form of twice-daily milk offerings and a demand for shared caretaker roles of constant fire tending with the proper implements.[4]

Small wonder that few pandits and wives project the hope of performing *adhana*, and still fewer actually go through with the ritual. One act of commitment is a three-day performance of *vaisa-deva* as a transition from domestic to *srauta* ritual life, a series of offerings to the All-gods to be described later under the *catur-masya* (part 6 of this chapter). Often the *adhana* is put off time and again until late middle age or beyond. Lanka, the foremost regional authority on *srauta*, delayed until his late forties and was prodded along by his son-in-law, Mitranarayana, who had set the fires at age twenty-two, two years earlier than his own father. Lanka, not the son of an *ahitagni* like Mitranarayana, had to sacrifice two animals in penance prior to *adhana*. Kapilavayi Rama Sastri is waiting until a retirement pension from TTD service begins, economic independence being a serviceable explanation for delay. Duvvuri Sarvesvara, Yajulu's eldest son, considered *adhana* late in life, his career being devoted to the worship of Siva and recitations of Puranas. He finally announced in 2007 that he would establish hearths and proceed to *agni-stoma*, a change of heart perhaps prompted by his younger brother, Surya Prakasa Avadhani, long ready to open this ritual gate, but one who could not proceed until Sarvesvara's sibling blockade was cleared away. Looming heavily in local lore is the earlier generation's case of Kapilavayi Yajnesvara Agnihotra Sastri, never able to perform *srauta* rituals because his older brother, Pedda Rama Sastri, had not set fires. Duvvuri Sarvesvara, however, never accomplished *adhana*.

The *adhana*, also known as *agny-adheya* or *adheya*, is a relatively uncomplicated ritual in a special room of the sacrificer's house. It requires a readiness to recite scores of mantras on demand, two full days beginning on a new- or full-moon day, usually in the spring, and four priests, *adhvaryu, hotr, brahman*, and *agnidhra*, the last an acolyte of the *brahman* who is, as his name suggests, closely connected to the ritual fires. In essence, *adhana* serves to "put in place" a set of clay hearths (*ayatana*) that will remain as sacred center for the couple, a cosmic, mystical space, until one of them dies. The room, not visible to outsiders, is entered twice daily for offerings and other times for fireplace maintenance. It should be large enough to seat four *rtvij* for *isti*. Three hearths are the focus of ritual action with a storage area (*vedi*) nestled between them. Another pair of hearths has outlying placement for this performance: the *sabhya* and *avasathya* are seldom re-employed. (See Plan 2.2. Ground plan of five fires for *adhana*.) Four are on the west-east line across the *agni-hotra* room with the *daksina* fire slightly to the south. The temporary *sabhya* and *avasathya* fires continue the eastward line outside the house.

ApSS 5.1–25 provides the program followed in Konasima. Determination of a proper asterism to govern the ritual must be done and this is a matter of some controversy in the Sutras.[5] The first day is devoted to bathing and nail-trimming the couple, shaving and tonsuring the *yajamana*, and obtaining sacrificial materials (*sambhara*). These include fire-sticks of various woods and several kinds of earth for hearth foundations collected in pots and baskets. Hearths are then shaped out of wet clay on the floor. The clay hearths

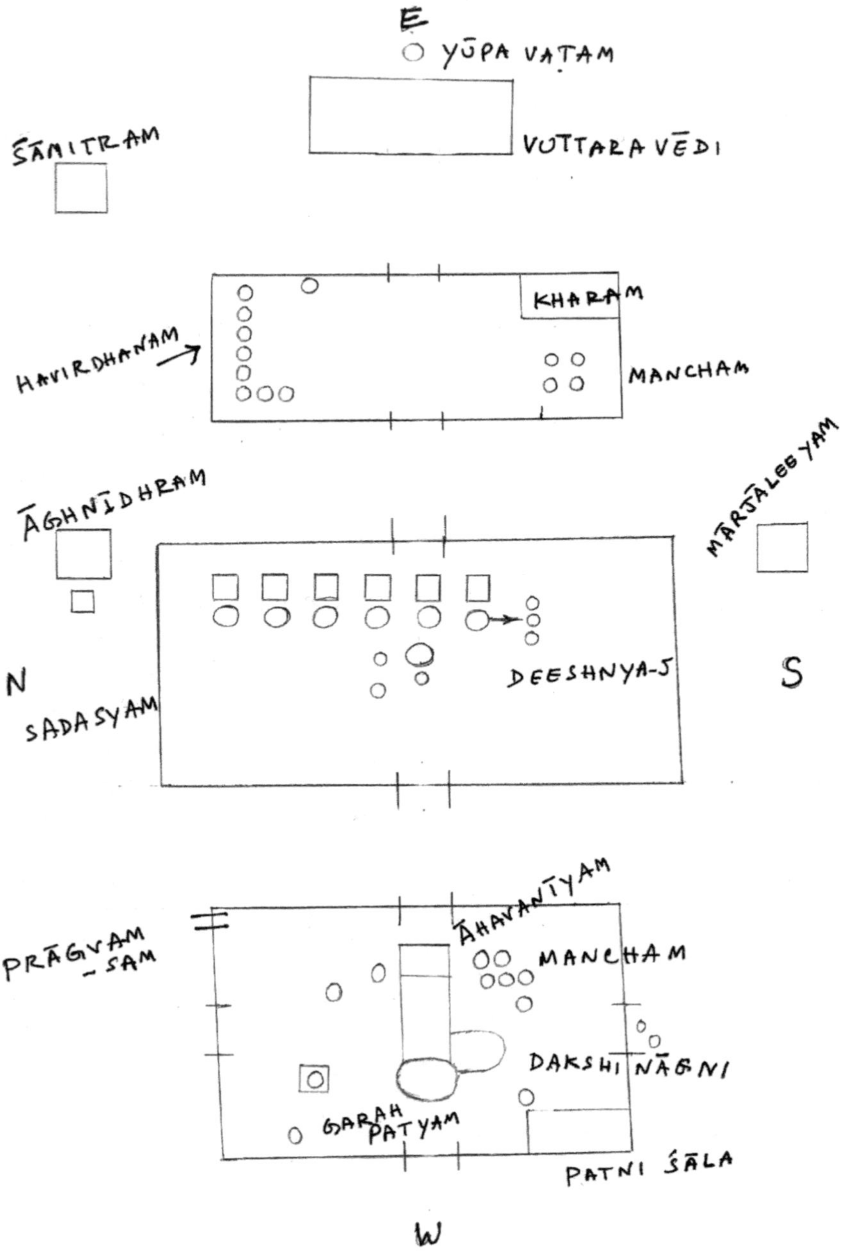

PLAN 6.1. Ground plan of an *agni-ksetra* "field of fire" projection of *agni-hotra* fires outside the house for an extended *srauta* ritual, drawn by Kapilavayi Venkatesvara, Simhacalam 2014, courtesy of M. V. Krishnayya.

of coastal Andhra usually have a softly contoured low profile, unlike the high, sharper edged configurations of western India.

Just west of the *garha-patya*, a fire is either churned or brought directly from the *aupasana* household fire; over it the *adhvaryu* cooks rice in water or milk. Again, it is important to remember that rice is "food" and without the help of Agni this life-sustaining substance is inedible. A portion is offered to this *brahmaudanika* fire and four plates are distributed so the priests may eat. Ashes of this temporary fire are cleared away and each hearth receives sprinkled water, then layers of sand, the collected soil (from a termite mound, a rat burrow, a boar rutting, and pond clay), the collected twigs of five different woods (*asvattha, udumbara, parna, sami,* and from any tree burned by lightning), and finally, as crowning layer, a piece of gold. The couple stays awake all night. As the sun rises the *adhvaryu* and *agnidhra*, in the presence of a horse,[6] heat the two fire-igniting *arani,* ritually present them to the sacrificer, then churn fire by pulling the rope back and forth, twirling the upright male spindle (*pramantha*) held in place between the wood blocks. A spine-tingling moment occurs, visualization of the first flame curling up from bone-dry wood shavings on the female block.

TB 1.2.1.15–16 is recited during this mystical production of Jatavedas, a constant epithet of Agni who knows all the human generations. He emerges from the semen (*retas*) in this womb (*yoni*) of the female block secure on the ground. A witness to this fire drilling, one deriving little inspiration from striking a kitchen match, may be forgiven a grip of emotion, a sense of being transported to the first such human generation of fire, documented some 400,000 years ago. A series of mantras from the RV and *saman* from the SV (themselves drawn from the RV) accompanies these steps. For example, SV 1.79, based on RV 3.29, compares Jatavedas within the kindling blocks to the human embryo in the womb. Phrases from the TA also declare homologies between the priests, ritual apparatus, and abstract powers such as speech, mind, and breath. Every opportunity is taken to employ correspondences (*nidana, bandhu*) proclaiming all the cosmic dimensions of Agni ritually brought to this household as the foundation of an advanced sacred career.

Now comes the all-important transfer of the newly kindled fire onto the layered hearths, the *adhvaryu* taking a fire pan to the *garha-patya* first and then to the *ahavaniya*, as the *agnidhra* priest next moves embers from the freshly lighted *garha-patya* onto the *daksinagni*. The sacrificer recites auspicious names of Agni and dispatches inauspicious, even destructive powers of the god in the direction of an enemy, *bhratrvya*, or rival, *sapatna*. In subsequent rituals this adversary, real or imagined, will be invoked frequently, often in astonishing ways. If he (and the enemy seems always to be male) is merely a phantom, these phrases are swiftly glossed over, but if one has a serious foe, a rival complicating one's ritual, political, or marital plans, that name is elevated to the status of designated target. If that rival is suspected of using *abhi-cara*, black magic, special defensive measures must be taken in counter-sorcery, often employing mantras from the Atharva Veda.[7]

The *adhvaryu* then takes embers from the *ahavaniya* to light the remaining hearths, *sabhya* and *avasathya*, until all five fires have been inaugurated. This pentadic layout is a harbinger of the far more elaborate five-layered fire altar of the *agni-cayana* ritual that may be undertaken by those who become *soma* sacrificers. In fact, the eastern direction out of the house presages extended sacrifices in the future. The cosmos being fivefold as well as threefold, Agni is thus omnipresent, here, now, in this home.

The *adhana* celebrant next recites in praise of each of the five while the *adhvaryu* bakes loaves on eight terra-cotta pans for Agni. In a ritual dice game the *yajamana* wins, to no one's surprise, with the best throw. More loaves are baked by the *adhvaryu* and his crew, this time on eleven sherds dedicated first to Agni and Visnu, then to Agni and Soma. This is the first invocation of Soma in the new fire complex. Again these ritual acts are accompanied by elaborate homologies between abstract agents and all the human and physical components of sacrifice. Ritual payments are presented to all priests by the sacrificer. The *yajamana* has already been called upon to recite mentally the morning and evening formulas for *agni-hotra*, and now, on the following morning, with considerable emotion, he and his wife perform the rite itself. The ritual of setting the fires has been completed, *agni-hotra* has been inaugurated, and the pentadic array may be reduced to a normative triad, *tretagni* (*treta-agni*) three fires.

Apastamba allows for the rekindling (*punar-adheya* or *punar-adhana*) of one or more sacred fires in case of accidental extermination, a death in the family, the loss of the *arani* fire-kindling woods after they have absorbed the fires, or if both sacrificer and wife must be away and cannot take the fires with them. If the lapse is extensive, one of three asterisms (Rohini, Punarvasu, or Anuradha) must govern this re-establishment. ApSS 5.26–29 gives details, including a placation of Agni by declining his name in various grammatical forms.[8]

6.3 *The* Agni-hotra, *Sunset and Sunrise Milk Offerings*

Because of multiple meanings, the term *agni-hotra*, literally "offering to Agni," often confuses those outside the sacrificial tradition, including educated Hindus. It is a liquid food offering to Agni, fresh milk or ghee poured twice daily from a *havani* ladle with a grooved "elephant's tongue" spout into the

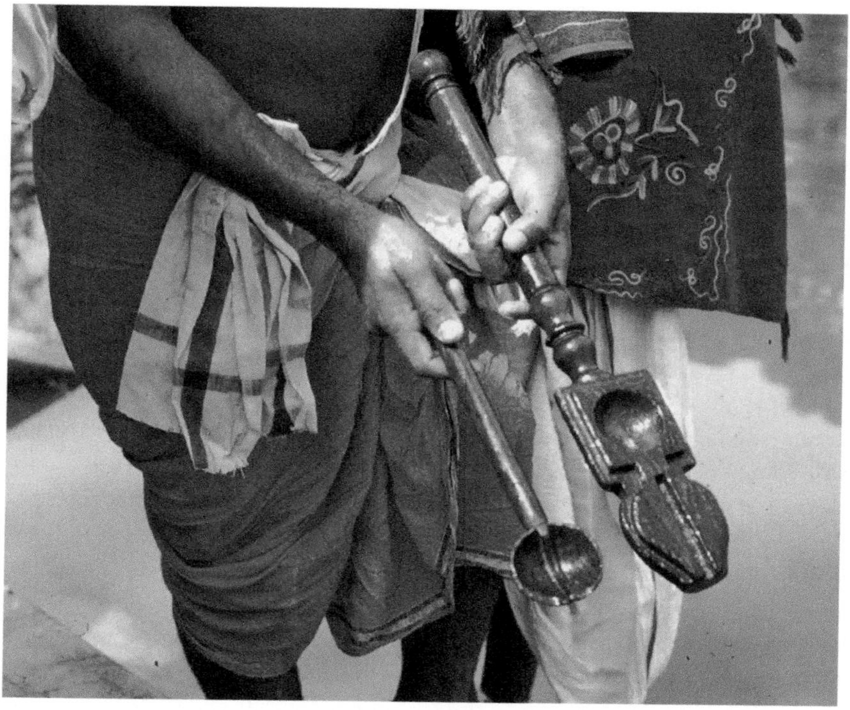

FIGURE 6.1. Ladles used to make offerings into Agni, Sriramapuram 1987.

ahavaniya fire. (This ladle appears on the right in Figure 6.1.) *Agni-hotra* is also the triadic complex of all three fire-hearths, one or more with active embers or cooling ashes. It may be, like other sacrificial terms, a personal name, as in the son of Kapilavayi Rama Sastri and Maruti, Agnihotra Sarma. But it is above all Agni himself, the god Agni-hotra who receives the libations. In that circular sense for dedicated *ahitagni* it is God receiving God.

Initially established with five hearths, the domestic *srauta* ritual complex is reduced to three at the close of fire setting. A decision is made about the degree of "permanence" to assign to each hearth. While some sutras require fires in all three, ApSS 6.2.13 provides relief, considering the vigilance, labor, and expense of keeping three sets of embers, by allowing for the *garha-patya* alone to be safeguarded and tucked in for the dark night. Therefore when the *yajamana* and *patni* are ready at sunrise, or later at sunset, *garha-patya* embers dropped into the *ahavaniya* ignite dry straw just long enough for the milk (already heated short of boiling point, then cooled) to be offered onto the flames. Drops remaining in the ladle are consumed by the couple as a share of what Agni has just received. These drops are literally his *ucchista*, leavings endowed with his powers. In a similar fashion, when the southern fire (*daksina-agni*) is required, *garha-patya* embers are distributed there.

In the evening *agni-hotra* mantras are addressed to Agni, then Prajapati, lord of sacrifice, while at dawn they go to Surya, the rising sun, and again to Prajapati. In both offerings preparatory gestures include the placement of blades of *darbha* grass and tosses of water from the fingers of the right hand of the sacrificer around the molded frames of the three hearths. In houses where there is more than one *nitya-agni-hotrin* the rites can be simultaneous, as in the case of the Dendukuri family in Vijayawada today where the hearth complexes in the spacious but well-trafficked *agni-hotra* room are only three feet apart. Baballa was one of six brothers, all of them *nitya-agni-hotrin* like their father, and he remembers an extraordinary array of hearths and murmurs of simultaneous mantras.

Sutras discuss the cooperation of an *adhvaryu* in *agni-hotra* but for most families the brief rite is private like the *sandhya-vandana* that accompanies it and no *rtvij* is required. Eligible sons or former students on occasion, however, might take the *adhvaryu* role in order to sit beside their fathers or gurus. The cooperation of *patnis* is normative but also optional, not requisite. Subbalaksmi, for example, went to the *puja* corner to perform *vaisva-deva*, a token offering of milk or curds for "all gods," both evening and morning while Bulusu Cayanulu simultaneously did *agni-hotra* alone inside the ritual room.

On the other hand, Renducintala Yajulu and Laksmikanta were so closely bound that late in life when he was crippled she held onto him, managed the fire, and ladled milk from the terra-cotta pot into the fire while he did the mantras. Early mornings are suitable for honoring the sun since Surya *namas-kara* (now familiar to tens of thousands of Westerners taking yoga classes) is a standard prayer greeting to the rising sun, as customary as the *sandhya-vandana*. If an offering is being made in the *agni-hotra* room then sunrise becomes an occasion for family worship, some inside the house, some outside.

Agni-hotra quickly becomes routine and may occur as many as 22,000 times in the thirty-year career of a faithful *ahitagni* and spouse. In *Bringing the Gods to Mind*, Laurie Patton employs her title to concentrate on the application of mantras in rituals. It might be said that Agni has never left the mind of the true *agni-hotrin*. In a cowshed attached to the house most *ahitagni* keep an "*agni-hotra* cow" for the two daily offerings. Although ghee may be offered, or even curds or barley gruel, the libation is usually milk, liquid food, precious to families today as it was for cattle herders in antiquity. It is shared in communion with Agni before any other food in the evening prior to the main meal and again in the morning to begin a new day. Henk Bodewitz understands the historic function of the *agni-hotra* as "a transference of the sun (the heated milk) into Agni," the evening or primary rite being a transport of the sun "already weakened at the end of the day, through the dangerous darkness and coolness of the night."[9] Konasima *ahitagni* appreciate this but their overwhelming interest is in serving the culinary needs of Agni just as they supply his body with kindling food and carry away from his sacred space the residue, his ashes.

If *agni-hotra* is not done for three days the fires are *vicchinna*, interrupted, literally cut or broken, and rekindling must be done with specific expiations, *prayascitta*, for the lapse. Legitimate occasions for a break in the routine include deaths or births in the family causing pollution (*asauca*, Telugu *maila*) when no ritual of any kind is permissible. Several provisions allow for a suspension of rules and these are invoked liberally today when travel is easier and families are more widely dispersed than a generation or two ago. As mentioned in Chapter 5, when the *ahitagni* is away from home he may perform *agni-hotra* in advance and his wife will maintain the hearths: *paksa homa* for a fortnight, *masa homa* for a month. If the husband is "out of station" for any extended period he must return for one or the other moon *isti* since the wife should not do this two-hour ritual alone. The use of expiation rites is frequent and these consist of silent or muttered recitations (*japa*), meditations, and offerings into the fire such as an *isti* known as *ijya*. The definition of a "continuous" or *nitya-agnihotrin* remains fuzzy since incapacitated elders who do mantras only and not the milk offering into the fire may be included in the prestigious category.

Agni's embers can be transferred not only hearth-to-hearth but also site-to-site. Three terra-cotta pots are hung from slings, marked by initials with names of each fire, and carried to the burning ground in a funeral procession, and the same procedure may be used by an *ahitagni* if he is traveling to a *sabha* or a son's marriage, for example. It is said that this occurs even on a train, albeit with surreptitious care! A less dangerous (and disputed) solution to the dilemma of maintaining *agni-hotra* while absent from home hearths is a mystical-ritual drawing of the fire up and into the churning sticks, the two *arani*, while they are held over it, or alternatively, into the body of the sacrificer himself, a technique known as *atma-rohana*. Either way the fires are then released elsewhere on prepared hearths.

As noted in Chapter 2, some in Konasima attribute this to outsider families "who have incorrect procedures." But ApSS 6.28.8–14 provides details about the effect of mantras from TB 1 and 2 causing fire to rise and descend. A homology between the churning sticks and the sacrificer's body is clear: both are temporary repositories of the fires. Perhaps here is the origin of the ubiquitous Hindu *puja* practice of open palms quickly touching fire and then one's face. This is Apastamba's directive to the sacrificer before going away overnight, breathing on them, praising them, touching them and then his face.

The benefits of *agni-hotra* are a frequent topic of conversation on pandit verandahs. As the planet Earth appears to ease from day to night and then back again at the two "joints" of twilight and dawn, so too the family home participates with conjunctive rituals of *sandhya-vandana* and *agni-hotra*. "Even if a house is full of faults or sins (*dosa*) from the perspective of geomancy (*vastu*), *agni-hotra* fires will guard it, absolving the faults of the day in the evening rite, the faults of night-time at dawn." This observation by Samavedam came with concern about his own house when neither he nor his Vedapandit sons aspired to setting fires. But the fact that three *agni-hotrin* neighbors were within sight of his verandah eased his mind.

The belief that nothing bad can happen in a house where *agni-hotra* is performed, with assured personal protection, resembles nearby non-Brahman folk who hang baskets containing the jute ropes of the neighborhood goddess Gangamma to protect their houses from all misfortune. "Death does not reach him . . . who offers *agni-hotra*," according to Vadhula Sutra 3.27.[10] It is small wonder that *ahitagni* and *patni* may spend thousands of hours in the hearth room feeding and caring for Agni, not only Lord of the house but protector of the entire neighborhood as well.

The *agni-hotra* should be done until physical incapacity prevents necessary movement in the ritual room. Without *kriyas*, however, the rite can still continue with mantras only. Until he lost his memory Lanka did such a mantra performance for years after his inability to stand up without pain. In their declining years Pullela Laksminarayana and Kamesvari rekindled for *agrayana* every autumn, continued normal *agni-hotra* every day until the next *amavasya* or *purnima*, then did mantras without *kriyas* as a daily pattern. This recalls the *adhana* in which a mental run-through of *agni-hotra* occurs even before fires are established.

Smoke from indoor fires may present problems. Baballa had very poor eyesight. Duvvuri Yajulu went completely blind during the course of interviews for this survey, although his wicked sense of humor continued to make Telugu puns on sneezing and being smoked, referring to *dhuuma*, smoke, as his constant companion. At the time of *agni-hotra* there is a rule that an *ahitagni* should not go beyond the village boundary and his wife should not go beyond the border of the property for their house.[11]

6.4 *Offerings to the New Moon, Full Moon, and Constellations*

Nocturnal life under the glare of electric lighting is a new experience for many in village India today just as it was a few generations ago in urban Delhi, New York, or London. After sundown, untold thousands of generations knew only the soft glow of an oil lamp supplementing light from stars and the fluctuating moon. The ease and power of an electric bulb, once made available to startle the night with human design and will, closed an era of cosmic dependence. It also erased a specific kind of knowledge, the awareness of where and when those spare sources of cosmic illumination appear. India, however, still remembers what industrialized societies have largely forgotten: lunar cycles and stellar rhythms.

Despite multiple ancient calendars, some solar, some lunar, there is a universal division in India between light and dark, waxing and waning, of the sun over the course of a year and the moon for the duration of each month, both holding consciousness of the human position within the flux. There is also in India still today near universal concern for astrological markers of stellar and planetary movements, recorded in birth and death horoscopes and in astrological pamphlets (*pancanga*) consulted daily by astrologers and priests for correct timing of events. Again, the Vedic tradition preserves a singular response to such cosmic rhythms, extensive sacrifices known as *naksatra isti* (*naksatresti*), offerings to twenty-eight constellations, one by one, requiring as many as forty days of performance.

To address first the lunar offerings, one of the landmark rituals of Vedic life in antiquity and today is the fortnightly tracking of the moon's progress. Every two weeks an *agni-hotrin* performs an offering known as *darsa-purna-masa*, "new- (or) full-moon (sacrifice)."[12] As the solar cycle is a routine easing from day to night and back again at the joints of sunset and sunrise, so also the lunar pattern, with an expansion from hours to days, impresses human awareness with a similar shift from bright to dark and back again. So important is this ritual observance of lunar swing that this *isti* became a paradigm (*prakrti*) for offerings in general, excepting only the animal and *soma* sacrifices.

As Agni and Prajapati receive the evening *agni-hotra* while Surya and Prajapati take the morning one, so too there are multiple recipients of *darsa-purna-masa*, the dual divinities Agni-Soma and Indra-Agni as well as Agni or Prajapati alone.[13] Offerings are melted butter (ghee) and *purodasa*, pounded rice flour mixed with water into dough and baked in clumps spooned onto pottery rings over open coals. The result is something of a cross between a small rounded loaf of bread and a pancake.

Four priests suffice—*hotr, adhvaryu, agnidhra,* and *brahman*—the sacrificer serving as one, sons and neighboring colleagues filling in the other posts. The wife, with several tasks and occasional brief lines to recite, is seated close by the *garha-patya*. Lanka noted a stopgap procedure in which it could be done alone, but help is considered appropriate and a full staff is desired when an *isti* is adjacent to a harvest festival or animal sacrifice. Every fortnight Duvvuri Surya Prakasa left his temple recitation duties in Rajahmundry for regular bus trips down to Sriramapuram and Vyaghresvaram to assist his father and then Bulusu Kamesvara, just as the latter reciprocated with Pullela Laksminaraya within the hamlet of Vyaghresvaram itself.

There is a difference between the two offerings as well as the divine recipients, and modifications for a *soma*-sacrificer. For some in Konasima the new-moon rite calls for milk and curds while the full moon involves the *purodasa* alone. Constant recitation of mantras, cleaning and heating sacrificial implements, tidying up the altar area, organizing kindling and enclosing sticks, and spreading sacred grasses take up most of the two hours and the offerings themselves are of brief duration. Requisite utensils include a sickle for cutting grasses, long-handled wooden paddle (*upavesa*) for managing the coals, a small wooden sword (*sphya*) for marking and digging the altar, and a winnowing fan (*surpa*), usually of woven reeds although Satyavati uses a beautiful brass one when she tosses the rice before sifting and pounding the grains to make dough. The *adhvaryu* braids and binds a sweeping-up brush of *darbha* grass, the *veda*, known mischievously in Konasima as "Brahma's moustache." As the *vedi* altar is female, so the *veda* brush is a masculine symbol. The brush is but one of an array of various grasses such as *barhis* that are essential, some of them bundled into batches (*prastara*) and strewn from point to point throughout the *isti*. The deep antiquity of these ritual procedures is borne out by the comparative significance of grass and twig bundles employed by ancient Iranian sacrificers.

Recipients of the main offerings—Agni, Soma, Indra, Prajapati—are all males. It should not be surprising, however, that a strong presence of goddesses and feminine powers along with featured roles for the wife lies just under the surface. The full and new moons have been addressed as goddesses from the time of the Atharva Veda (7.79 and 7.80, respectively, for *amavasya* and *paurnamasi* (*purnima*)). Polar events for a life-body, conception and death, draw together a complex symbol system of *soma*, the moon, impregnation, destinies of the unborn, the always hovering ancestors, and cooked food that is shared with invited deities.

The *pinda-pitr-yajna*, offerings to the ancestors, are included within the new-moon ritual (ApSS 1.7.1–10.15), although they are abbreviated today. In that sense the concatenation of birth, death, and rebirth has been loosened. But feminine powers play several roles. A special portion of a *purodasa* loaf is the *ida*, cut for the goddess Ida, soaked in ghee and offered to her, with remnants consumed by the priests and sacrificer (although not the wife). In the ritual known as *patni-samyaja* the wives of the deities (Indrani and others) are recipients of offerings, along with Soma, Tvastr, and Agni as lord of the household, made in the *garha-patya* by the *adhvaryu* while the sacrificer's wife touches his arm with a long blade of *darbha* grass.

Prajapati is not the only deity associated with conception and birth. If the sacrificer and wife seek to gain a son they may offer to Raka. Anasuya gave birth to seven consecutive sons after the first child, a girl. Satyavati produced six sons, and Surya, who conceived fourteen times, successfully raised five sons. Raka may well have been frequently sought. She is one of a trio of rather shadowy females—Raka, Sinivali, and Kuhu (Gungu instead of Kuhu in RV 2.32.8)—that joins the better-known goddess Anumati and the god Dhatr to serve as shapers or arrangers of childbirth in cosmic orientation. The quartet of feminine powers is divided for the lunar rites, eventually with Raka and Anumati on full-moon and preceding day, Kuhu and Sinivali on new-moon and preceding day (cf. TS 1.8.8.1; 3.3.11.13–20; 3.4.9.1; MSS 8.11). In other words, each lunar observance has two days, the fourteenth and fifteenth of a fortnight, the latter being completion of full or new moon (Raka or Kuhu), the former being an almost full or new moon (Anumati or Sinivali).

Their aggregate might be construed as Vedic midwives of destiny. The sketchy but revealing preoccupations of the original trio may indicate a Proto-Indo-European background that included the spinning and weaving of individual fate, even immortality. Raka, for example, sews with an unbreakable (or unstoppable) needle, a trait repeated from RV 2.32.4 through the Vedas to the sutras, perhaps in connection with garments of destiny or the thread of life itself. Sinivali, who places the embryo (*garbha*) in the womb (RV 10.284.2; AV 5.25.3) also shapes clay for the fire-pan carried by the sacrificer, a womb that gives birth to his new being of fire as he becomes Agni in the *agni-cayana*.[14]

The *patni* is highlighted when she sits, knees raised, to be encircled by the *agnidhra* and *adhvaryu* (ApSS 2.5.2–6) with a loop of three strands of *munja* grass. This *yoktra*, halter or yoke, suggests that she is now restrained like a domestic animal, and indeed in a different *sakha*, SB 1.3.1.13 understands the cord as such, as well as a dividing line between the pure upper half of her body and the impure lower half. This gloss points to a tension between seeing the auspicious wife as pure vessel destined to receive seed and produce children, and impure woman, unfit to direct her gaze toward the pot of ghee, a substance homologized to *retas*, male seed, semen.

The Taittiriya tradition, however, contains a positive valorization of this act in TB 3.3.3.2–3, directing comparative attention to the *upanayana* cord and initiatory symbolism.[15] It was in fact Subbalaksmi, first among others, who made the unsolicited connection between the grass belts of the *patni* and the *brahmacarin* (the latter described in Chapter 2). Both are initiations, she insisted, the boy into Veda learning, the wife into enhanced ritual life. Another occurrence of an encircling grass belt, noted in Chapter 5, is the bride being led by the groom to perform marital vows by the fire. Mircea Eliade noted that binding is a significant expression in the history of religions, carrying with it the antithesis, loosing.[16] The cord that restrains also sets free, and the freedom obtained by release becomes perhaps the cynosure of South Asian religious expression.[17] In this context, just as the girl-bride is momentarily bound, then released to become a woman-wife, so the wife in a *yoktra* sits in a posture of incipient power, about to become co-sacrificer. As noted earlier the *yoktra* belt may replace the wife for *agni-hotra* when her husband is away. Other examples of binding and loosing of inanimate as well as living components of sacrifice will appear in many of the rituals still to be discussed, as for example, drums in the *vaja-peya*.[18]

The wife stands after she loosens the grass belt and recites, addressing Agni first in the *garha-patya* fire and then the wives of the gods, prior to offerings to them (the *patni-samyaja*). These memorized phrases from the Taittiriya Samhita are the results of several sessions of instruction, usually by her husband. There is a special moment in either lunar rite or in iterations of this *isti* in other rituals, when the wife directs her gaze to the pot of offering ghee, closes her eyes, then opens them again. As Duvvuri Yajulu commented on the groom-husband taking a long time truly to *see* his bride-wife for the person she is (Chapter 3), so this sightless, wise pandit observed here: "She *sees* the ghee in the pot with closed eyes." It is particularly poignant that a female with a uterus (pot) so visualizes the contents (seed, new life) before anyone else.

Further attention to the symbolism of procreation, especially of a male child, is drawn when the *hotr* picks up the symbol of virility, the *veda* brush, "Brahma's moustache," and tosses it into the lap of the *patn*. She tosses it back until it is exchanged three times. The *hotr* recites and she replies that she loosened the grass belt to unite with her husband (and produce a child). Mitranarayana stressed the significance of this *veda* that is braided and later unbraided, that is, bound and released: "The offerings will not be actualized unless it is present. Once the karma is finished its stalks are undone and each one is strewn from the *garha-patya* to the *ahavaniya*. The rest of it is given to the *patni*. The *veda* has outlived its significance." Stephanie Jamison cites sutras other than Apastamba directing the wife to place some brush stalks between her thighs in an even more physical semblance of intercourse.[19]

Both lunar offerings and their alloforms in other rituals afford ample opportunities for the *adhvaryu* as well as the sacrificer to express certain personal desires other than children and prosperity. Regarding the pouring (*aghara*) of ghee from a ladle into the *ahavaniya* fire, ApSS 2.14.1–7 states the correct procedure and then follows with several alterations. For example, one who seeks heaven (*svarga, vyoman*) should pour more than the usual amount from a ladle held above the waistline, thus enhancing the result. In the other direction, a broken or diffuse flow of ghee instead of the proper continuous one, done with mental concentration, is a ritual-magical "mistake" presumed to promote the death of a rival sacrificer. In Chapter 3 rivaling families of *soma* sacrificers were mentioned and this frequent and paradigmatic lunar rite is an occasion for animosities to rise beyond imprecations into actions.[20] On a different plane, such offering of ghee may bring to the surface the special mysteries of outer sight and inner vision. "By closing the eyes while pouring and *then* looking," as Duvvuri Yajulu noted, "one perceives things as they really are."

In addition to tracking the daily course of the sun and monthly progress of the moon there is concern about *naksatra* and *graha*. The former are twenty-eight asterisms or constellations, ranging in size from a single star to the six stars of Krttika, the Pleiades, the whole series being the houses in which the changing moon briefly resides. The *graha* are the aggregate of nine planets, "seizers," including both the sun and the moon, the five visible planets, and Rahu and Ketu, invisible but notorious eclipse nodes.

Knowledge of all these celestial assemblies requires professional consultation of current *pancanga*, astrological manuals, readily available in paper pamphlets in bazaars but sufficiently cryptic to counter lay access. Lanka in Nedunuru and Baballa in Sriramapuram provided expertise and the latter at present is succeeded by grandson Prasad. Establishment of fires, life-cycle rites, lunar and harvest offerings, *soma* and other rituals must all be performed under appropriate constellations or expiations are required for improper timing. A newborn child is given a secret *naksatra* name, as ApGS 6.15.1–3 details. Like the planets of sharp concern to the general populace, *naksatra* have clear personalities, some known to be *ugra*, terrible, cruel, while others are *mrdu*, gentle and soft; in other words some are inauspicious, others are auspicious.

The *naksatra* are mentioned in the Rg Veda and Atharva Veda 19.7.2–5 names them all but it is the ritual tradition that best honors them. TS 4.4.10.1–3 lists twenty-seven from Krttika (the Pleiades) to Apabharani in the context of setting the fifth layer of bricks for the *agni-cayana*. A brick and deity are named for each, Agni first of all and Yama, judge of the dead, the concluding deity. Construction of the great altar of Agni is a *soma* sacrifice and of particular interest to the *ahitagni* is a belief that all the constellations together outline the body of Prajapati. It is Prajapati as well as Agni with whom the sacrificer is homologized.

Interestingly, it is the Brahmana text of the Taittiriyins that features twenty-eight *naksatra* with its addition of Abhijit to the Samhita list. TB 3.1.1–6 also changes several names such as the last one, Bharani instead of Apabharani, with reference to the bearers of the dead. And in fact half of the *naksatra*, numbers 15–28, are in the camp of Yama, lord of the dead, the first half, numbers 1–14, assigned to the Devas, the gods. Significant also is a change with respect to lunar powers, the full moon following the fourteenth *naksatra*, and the new moon, always a feature in death and ancestral rites, following the twenty-eighth *naksatra*. Dumont attributes these changes to a possible desire to reconcile the thirty-day solar month with the slightly shorter lunar month.[21]

It is Baudhayana who provides the sutra that is followed in Andhra, BSS 28.3–4 recommending that the sacrificer consign his fires to the *arani* and churn out new fire on another hearth. Just as the sacrificer in the *agni-cayana* identifies with Agni, Prajapati, the year, and the encompassed cosmos, so the performer of non-obligatory *isti* offerings to the *naksatra* declares the same homologies.

One by one, in the *naksatra-isti* sacrifice that requires approximately forty days, each constellation is praised and propitiated. The sacrificer pays close attention to the rising and setting of both sun and moon in order to keep proper timing. Kapilavayi Venkatesvara stated the purpose directly: "These *isti* are done to control and subjugate the *naksatra* so that all of them will be beneficial to the sacrificer." The *isti* to the *naksata* usually starts on Caitra new-moon day under a particular constellation and proceeds with a different *devata* each day, for example, Agni for Krttika, Brahma for Rohini, Soma the moon for Margasirsa, and so on. Baballa did this in the early 1960s. Lanka, Mitranarayana, and Kapilavayi Yajnesvara Agnihotra all supervised the lengthy rites that may include a goat sacrifice on the final day. Dendukuri Agnihotra was *yajamana* for his *naksatra-isti* in Hyderabad in 2001 when he was sixty-three. The *adhana* is prerequisite, not *agni-stoma*. The rite is usually done by older pandits with menopausal wives since a young or middle-aged wife would menstruate within the required thirty or forty days and no protection from *diksa* is afforded. The rite would then be broken and the performers damaged.[22]

6.5 *The* Agrayana *Harvest Sacrifices*

In some drought-stricken areas of Andhra and other states of South India hungry folk chastise their deities, even threaten to abandon their worship because they have withheld life-saving rains. Not so in Konasima's garden zone of abundant Godavari waters where first-fruit harvests are thrilling occasions and opportunities to reward the gods with first-taste offerings. The bagging of new rice, ripened in the autumn crop, brings a joyous festival when everyone thanks the goddess in Durga-*puja* and the Vaidika *ahitagni* perform *agrayana* in a *sala*, a bamboo screened area just outside each house. It is done on a new-moon day following much the same procedure as in the lunar rite that may either precede or succeed it. As noted in Chapter 5, aging and ailing *ahitagni* observe this new-rice ritual to the furthest limit of their capacities, rekindle fires and perform *isti* and expiations just for this quintessential ceremony. Baballa and Sundari managed their last *agrayana* in 1990 when he was eighty-seven and she was eighty-one. No one eats the new rice until it has been offered in sacrifice and then only in proper ritual attire and a state of purity. In the spring, barley is harvested in a minor version of *agrayana* and a third grain, *syamaka*, a rainy season millet, is also honored in first fruits with Soma the deity (cf. ApSS 6.29.10). Autumn *agrayana* involves new-rice dough *purodasa* made on twelve sherds offered to Indra-and-Agni, another one made on a single sherd for a second dual deity, Heaven-and-Earth (Dyava and Prthivi), and a cooked rice portion for the Visvedevas, the All-gods.

For many years before advancing to *srauta* lives Konasima pandits observed the domestic form of *agrayana* (cf. ApGS 7.19.6–7). This was on the *aupasana* fire with Agni Svistakrt, Agni as the maker of proper sacrifices, added to a quartet of recipient deities in the earlier *srauta* schedule laid out in ApSS 6.29.1–31.14. In the domestic rite new rice grains are cooked as *sthali-paka* in milk or water. At one point the sacrificer swallows a mouthful of new grains, then makes a ball (*pinda*) of cooked rice meant for the gods and tosses it up onto the roof of his house, perhaps for ancestors, perhaps to protect the dwelling and family from hungry ghosts who have a tendency to perch on roofs. Apastamba does not detail this practice but pandits say it is common before anyone in the family eats new rice.

Duvvuri Yajulu was fond of describing a special tradition he guarded well, one stretching back, he said, "many generations before my great-grandfather." A special yellow-green (*paccal*) millet, grown on rising upland soil dependent only on rain, not irrigation flooding, is offered along with the new rice or barley in *agrayana, homa* applying to both autumn and spring seasons permissible at the same time. He was asked: Why do you add this millet to rice or barley? "It promotes vigor (*pusti*) in one's semen (*indriya*)," he explained and continued in colloquial Telugu agrarian terms: "A lot of treatment is necessary and all the work on the grains has to be done by the *somi-devamma* alone. The deities of both seasons are always pleased by this offering!" Surya, who delivered fourteen infants, must have prepared this special grain quite properly. Again, as with the two lunar offerings, the *samskara*, and many other rituals, proliferation of children is at the forefront. The *samidheni* verses of the standard *isti* are increased from fifteen to seventeen, the sacred number of Prajapati, lord of procreation. And Soma, recipient of the millet offering, is both the deity and the sacred juice so readily homologized to *retas*, another Sanskrit word for semen.

An effortless method of performing *agrayana* is well known but not favored. The *agni-hotra* cow could be fed with new grain, then milked, and that milk offered in either evening or morning *agni-hotra*.[23]A firstborn calf suggested by Apastamba as *daksina* to the *adhvaryu* is scarcely realized today and an alternative, a piece of cloth or a dish of honey and curds suffices.[24] The *daksina* does not matter so much as the desire to live in harmony with the rhythms of nature as Baballa and Lanka, both lifelong cultivators, expressed it so many times. Laurie Patton has an appropriate summation: "The gods are given food and return it through their natural bounty; thus, the ecology of sacrificial food production and consumption is the central guiding metaphor for the survival of earthly and celestial worlds."[25]

6.6 The Catur-masya *Seasonal Rituals*

Another full set of rituals is the observation of a new three-month season every four months, the series known as *catur-masya*. In Konasima there is near uniformity of days and nights, twelve hours each, the sun rising or setting about six o'clock year round with none of the daylight and darkness fluctuations of climates farther north or south. The seasons change, however, each with a special character, the rapidly accelerating heat of the New Year from March to June (Caitra, Vaisakha, Jyestha), the breaking of heat with the monsoon rainy season (Asadha, Sravana, Bhadrapada), a cool-down for the autumn harvest (Asvina, Karttika, Margasirsa), and the coldest months giving way to spring and another New Year's festival on Ugadi (Pausa, Magha, Phalguna).

The formative period of Vedic India, developing in the northwest of the subcontinent, marked seasonal changes every four months (*catur masya*), with rites in the *isti* pattern connected to sowing and harvesting of crops in spring (*vasanta*), rains (*varsa*), and autumn (*hemanta*). The series is concluded with the *suna-siriya* ritual and offerings to Vayu, Indra Sunasiriya, and Surya. The two deities Suna and Sira occur in RV 4.57, an agrarian hymn addressed to them as well as to Ksetrapati, lord of the crop field, and Sita, the plowed furrow. There is also mention of Parjanya and Indra, responsible for necessary rains for fruitful harvests, and Pusan, bringer of prosperity, one closely related to the sun. Wealth in the form of plentiful harvests and herds appears to be the raison d'être of this early hymn and the seasonal rituals that ensued.

Although their seasons are at variance with the Rg Vedic series Konasima pandits are entirely familiar with all the deities and their forms of blessings. It must be said, however, that they have treated the seasonal rites with circumspection, performing the series once only or not at all and preferring to invest more energy and emotion in the *agrayana* harvest ritual. Baballa and Lanka did each of the *catur-masya* a single time while Bulusu Cayanulu, considerably vexed in later years about their absence from his record, seemed always to be planning implementation in the form of a single five-day ritual. In February 1992, five years before his sudden heart attack, Cayanulu's explanation hinged on the degree of difficulty involved: "They are not straightforward rituals like *agni-stoma*. They look at first like ordinary *isti* but under investigation one finds constant important links to maintain, intricate ones. A tough rite, it includes a sacrifice to the ancestors so it is the equivalent of going to Kasi or Gaya. It *should* be done at least once in one's life." He may or may not have known about procedures for folding all the rites into one or two days.

The *catur-masya* preserve a number of intriguing, presumably ancient features, of which there is opportunity here for barest mention. The three of them, spaced every four months on full-moon days, are *vaisva-deva*, Varuna-*praghasa*, and *saka-medha*, respectively, initiating spring, the rainy season, and autumn. The *vaisva-deva* ritual at the outset of the New Year with Caitya full moon begins a long series of offerings in recognition of Vaisvanara (Agni) and Parjanya, god of rain. It involves the pleasant task of eating honey, and concludes next day with the normal offering to the full moon.

The *vaisva-deva* rite occupies an important position in its own right, regardless of its role as first of the *catur-masya*. For ordinary householders it is a significant *grhya* (domestic) offering of cooked food to all the gods in a single ritual. Some see it as penance for acts of violence committed on a daily basis. It is a rite that Subbalaksmi did twice a day for most of her life. On the other hand, for Veda pandits and wives aspiring to a *srauta* career it may become the first step toward *adhana*, the setting of hearths for an *agni-hotra* career. In the latter case it is a full-blown *isti* with four *rtvij* and a duration of three days. Duvvuri Surya Prakasa Avadhani and Kanaka Durga took this step early in 2007 with Mitranarayana as *adhvaryu* and mentor. Both observed fasting with only hot milk and porridge at night. They anticipated *adhana* and *agni-stoma* in 2008 but in the end were unable to follow through. Kapilavayi Rama Sastri and Maruti did *vaisva-deva* in 2014 in anticipation of setting hearths in 2016. Rama Sastri compares *vaisva-deva* to the early childhood *samskara*, first feeding of rice, *anna-prasana*. Cooked rice is the medium for the baby's entry into a lifetime of eating *anna* every day. The ceremony of *vaisva-deva* is a preamble as well: *yajamana* and *patni* begin a pattern of daily offerings, one that should climax with *soma*.

To return to the *catur-masya* series, perhaps most magnetic of the three seasonal rites is the sharing of a barley meal offering to Varuna in hopes of evading his snares (*pasa*) and punishment for known or unknown sins. This second seasonal rite, Varuna-*praghasa*, involves five priests, *adhvaryu*, *prati-prasthatr*, *hotr*, *agnidhra*, and *brahman*. Small images of a ram and ewe are fashioned of barley flour paste and later sacrificed by the *adhvaryu* and *prati-prasthatr*, respectively. Abruptly, the *prati-prasthatr* asks the wife "How many lovers do you have?" and proclaims, having learned the names of each, that Varuna should snare them, evidently freeing the sacrificer from further cuckoldry. Other texts have the wife hold up the number of fingers or blades of grass that tally her amours. There is no hint that Varuna should punish the wife.

Much is made in commentarial literature about the cleansing effect of confession, sin being here removed not by punishment but rather by truthfulness. The inference that she indeed has lovers parallels the assumption that the sacrificer has enemies, sexual rivalry overlapping with ritual competition. Also fashioned of barley flour are tiny pots, one for each relative of the sacrificer plus an extra one for the unborn, containing gruel of course grains (*karambha*), all held in a winnowing fan (*surpa*) balanced on the head of the sacrificer or *patni*. Before offering into the *daksina-agni* both recite TS 1.8.3d. The *patni* unties the *yoktra* from her waist with TS 1.1.10g and together sacrificer and wife take a concluding bath.

There are numerous expressions from a cult of the dead in the *catur-masya* and one suspects that hesitation in performance of the full series may be reluctance to engage with Mrtyu. The *catur-masya* in the eighth segment of Apastamba's sutras flow as a continuum, *vaisva-deva* (1–4), Varuna-*praghasa* (5–18), *saka-medha* (9–12), straight into *pitr-yajna* (13–16) ancestor offerings. In Varuna-*praghasa* there are offerings into the southern fire, use of the winnowing fan, "dismemberment" of two flour-paste animals in lieu of real ones, communion shares of offerings with relatives and invited Brahmans, and special offerings of *karambha* to Pusan, pathfinder for the dead, one known to prefer mushy food like porridge. The third seasonal rite is the *saka-medha* that concludes with *pitr-yajna*, sacrifice to the ancestors who dwell in their heavenly world, *pitr-loka*. Again relatives are fed, this time with a rice mess instead of barley, and balls (*pinda*) of cooked rice and barley are offered to the paternal trio of father, grandfather, and great-grandfather, then the further trio of ancestors, and finally the Visvedevas, "all gods," served with rice that sticks to the offering hand. All of this occurs on a new screened-off altar with fire taken from the *daksina-agni*, mantras expressed soundlessly, sacred threads switched to left shoulders, circumambulations with left side toward the altar. The departed receive food, but with entirely different procedures.

Interesting to note are distinctions among those who do the *catur-masya* based on the sacrificial history of their *pitr*, ancestors. Those ancestors who performed no extended sacrifices after *adhana* are the *agnisvatta* fathers; those who performed only lesser sacrifices (*agrayana*, for example) are the *barhisad* fathers; while those who went on to the *agni-stoma* and offered *soma* are the *somavant* fathers. Thus in *catur-masya* performance Lanka, who had no *ahitagni* forbears, addressed a different aggregate of *pitr* from that to whom Baballa made offerings.

Subsequent to the trio of seasonal rites there is an offering to Tryambaka (Rudra) and then the *suna-siriya* ritual with offerings of milk to Vayu and *purodasa* for Indra Sunasiriya and Surya. A plow and various domestic animals are recommended as gifts to the priests. According to ApSS 8.7.5 and 11.7 a bull is given and cows should be sacrificed but of course this is not done today. Animal sacrifice with goats is one thing, cows are unthinkable. One of the two months designated for Varuna-*praghasa* is Sravana, the month when a goat sacrifice is required, the *pasu-bandha* that is independent of *soma* pressing. Interestingly, although flour-paste animals are "sacrificed" as part of the Varuna-*praghasa* no one suggests that such might be done with bovines as well.

To sum up the seasonal rituals, as in *agrayana*, prosperity in the form of bountiful harvests, milk, and wool appears to be the major focus, with strong attention to communication with the ancestors who are related to the seasons and indeed the full cycle of the year. Staying on the correct side of Varuna and other punishers such as the Maruts is an additional aim. Ganesh Thite makes the case that *catur-masya* have to do primarily with healing, seasonal changes signaling the arrival of various diseases.[26] Jan Heesterman, on the other hand, sees the ritual series as "a victorious course through the universe both in respect to time (seasons) and . . . space (the three worlds), by which the sacrificer encompasses and becomes the whole of the universe." In any case it appears that attention to ancestors is very much at the core of these seasonal rites.[27]

6.7 *The First* Soma *and Animal Sacrifice,* Agni-stoma

Baballa, so often equipped with the right phrase for the occasion, drew upon his experience as *soma-yaji, soma*-sacrificer, alongside his father and five *soma-yaji* brothers, and observed that this momentous step into *agni-stoma* permits the easy progress of a bullock cart on a well-grooved road. He belonged to an elite older generation that cherished the drinking of *soma* as a closed-circuit drama demanding only the purest and most accomplished of participants to serve the gods. As in his reluctance to accept *daksina* from students and his refusal of TTD employment, he frequently turned down invitations from local and regional pandits to be a priest in their sacrifices and accepted only the role of *sadasya* who does not drink *soma*. His dread was the possibility of error.

This ritual that Mitranarayana so energetically performed at age twenty-two and Mitranarayana's father-in-law Lanka later approached with some trepidation in midlife, is known as the praise (*stoma*) of Agni, honoring him with the juice of that heaven-born sacred plant *soma*. As noted in Chapter 2 this ritual has pride of place: *yajna*, the generic Sanskrit term for "sacrifice," is the reference in coastal Andhra to *agni-stoma*, almost as if there were no other sacrifice. Also known as *jyoti-stoma*, the praise of light, it is a sacrifice with a single day of pressing and offering *soma* but requires five busy days on an extended sacrificial arena with the full complement of the sixteen priests listed in Table 2.3 of Chapter 2. As the procedure for the two lunar *isti* offerings became the model for all sacrifices except *soma* and animal, so *agni-stoma* became the template for all additional *soma* sacrifices. A least one full year of *agni-hotra* is required of the householder pair before undertaking *agni-stoma*, although, as mentioned earlier, a few pandits abbreviated that schedule.[28]

This paradigmatic rite is an elaborate drama with thousands of preparations, major and minor offerings, chants, and recitations. Apastamba devotes 106 chapters to *agni-stoma* (ApSS 10.1 to 13.25), more attention than given to any other ritual. Another twenty-eight chapters (7.1–28) cover the independent *pasu-bandha*, the animal sacrifice, an analogue being a prominent feature of *agni-stoma*. And of course authorities squabble over which of their hefty compendia of inherited instructions will govern each procedure. There is space here only for selected highlights. In order to appreciate the spectacle of an *ahitagni*'s first *soma* and animal sacrifice, however, one must envision the stage, essentially a projection of the householders' *agni-hotra* room outdoors onto a spacious *maha-vedi* or great altar, including an *agni-ksetra*, field of fire. Orientation is extremely important, the eastern compass point being the primary direction.

In Plan 6.1 of this chapter, Kapilavayi Venkatesvara (KV) has drawn four rectangles to represent bamboo sheds over essential areas. Observing the chart's alignment from west (W) to east (E) these are the *prag-vamsa, sadas, havir-dhana,* and *uttara-vedi*. Measurements are done with the body of the *yajamana* as scale: the *aratni* yardstick or measuring rope is one-fifth of his height and two sacrificial poles, the *audumbari* in the center of the *sadas* and the *yupa*, a *vata* tree on the east border for the animal sacrifice, are exactly his height. For the *agrayana* harvest sacrifice a bamboo-and-straw-mat hut was constructed just outside the house and fires were transferred there. The same arrangement is made for *agni-stoma* except now the venue is an out-of-season crop field borrowed for the occasion, dimensions are far larger, and roofed structures for fires and participants are erected during initial days.

First is the *prag-vamsa* (or *pracina-vamsa*), a bamboo pole-and-rafter shelter to cover the three fires maintained in their house by the co-sacrificing husband and wife, these fires now being shifted outdoors onto brick hearths. The wife's corner (*patni-sala*) is in the southwest within reach of the cooking fire (round *garha-patya*) as well as *daksina-agni* (D-shaped southern fire). The square on Plan 6.1 on the east side (E) of the *prag-vamsa* represents the *ahavaniya* offering fire. South of the *ahavaniya* is the initial place of the *mancam*, a Telugu word for the movable bed that carries *soma* stalks, a litter conveyance also known as a *bandi*, cart, or *asandi*, throne. Doors to enter and exit the shelter are on the W to E line.

Next built is the *sadas* (or *sadasya*), erected to cover six priests (named S to N the *maitra-varuna, hotr, brahmanac-chamsin, potr, nestr*, and *acchavaka*). They work at six *dhisniya*,[29] fires ignited on low mud brick hearths, facing east (E) during the chanting of twelve *stotra* and reciting of twelve follow-up *sastra*. Flanking the *sadas* are two more fires ignited on raised earth excavated from a pit (*catvala*) dug off the northeast corner of the *agni-ksetra*. On the north (N) is the *agnidhriya* for the *agnidhra*, a kindling priest who distributes embers to various hearths and tends all fires. His fire makes the total of *dhisniya* seven. The other is the *marja-liya* for symmetry on the south side, a kind of kitchenette meant for cleaning implements. A rubbish dump, the *utkara*, is dug to collect debris such as used grasses and other sweepings. Just west of the *dhisniya* line is the *audumbari* pole.

The next construction (KV's third rectangle on Plan 6.1) is the *havir-dhana*, a *soma* factory with roofing to protect the stalks and pressing equipment (four stones, boards, animal skins) required for three preparations of *soma*. The bed (*mancam*) of cuttings that was prominently placed by the offering fire in the *prag-vamsa* is now carried onto the south side of the *havir-dhana* and readied for action. (KV has placed it twice on Plan 6.1.) Four holes (*uparava*) are excavated as sounding chambers beneath it. A curious moment occurs: the *adhvaryu* and sacrificer are on hands and knees, their right arms deep in these holes to touch fingers and test the correct depth. Earth from the holes serves as a small mound in the southeast corner, the *khara*, holding *soma* containers, eleven *camasa* (including one for the sacrificer) and twenty *graha* cups. The table is now set.

As they did the night before their *adhana* establishment of fires the couple remains awake, the sacrificer in the *havir-dhana* and his wife in the *patni-sala*. Directly east of the *havir-dhana* KV has marked the *uttara-vedi*, locus of the main altar, a new *ahavaniya* offering fire. In the middle of the east border, the farthest point east of the entire ritual field, stands the *yupa*, a second pole meant to tie the animal destined for sacrifice. It is a *vata* tree shaped by a carpenter into an octagonal post, exactly on the W-E line from the *garha-patya* fire through the centers of all the shelters. To the north is the *samitra*, the place where the *samitr* will smother the goat.

The result of all this labor is a magnification of the indoor *agni-hotra* room, preserving the same orientation, with a lateral spreading out of fires, now eight on the north-south axis, six *dhisniya* hearths under the *sadas* roof plus the two border fires. A transposition occurs among the essential three household fires: the *prag-vamsa* serves as a launching pad to make a *garha-patya*, cooking hearth, out of the former *ahavaniya* offering fire. This requires a new *ahavaniya* hearth to be established farther east on what is now called the *uttara-vedi*. A crucial moment is the shift of that offering fire eastward to the *uttara-vedi*.

Having established the arena and its parts, our attention is now drawn to the participants. A remarkable procedure on the first day is the *diksa* for the sacrificer and wife, a consecration ritual famous in anthropology and the history of religions for its initiatory structure and striking symbolism of rebirth. They sit on black antelope hides inside separate enclosures without speaking. Their *agni-hotra* are suspended but in a sense they are themselves fire (ApSS 10.13.1) and are maintained only by the offerings of *agni-hotra*: milk and perhaps ghee, a few grains cooked in milk, or curds. In other words, they are fasting. Their fists remain clenched as if they are embryos subsisting on mother's milk inside their womb-like huts. They may not bathe and in the fierce heat of April–May may scratch their heads and bodies only with an antelope horn.

Each is bound as in the *isti* described earlier for lunar rites, he with a *mekhala*, she with a *yoktra*, bonds that are loosened only when they have advanced to a higher state with the final bath. In Jan Gonda's words: "The initiatory birth which implies death to profane existence enables [them] to gain sacred knowledge and wisdom, a higher stage of existence and access to a heavenly life." They are in "a temporary state of higher sanctity."[30] The wife recites the mantra she has learned: "Praying for benevolence, offspring, good fortune, myself, in devotion to Agni, I gird myself for ritual and religious merit."[31] The sacrificer receives a staff of fig-tree wood (*udumbara*) similar to the one he used in his boyhood *upanayana* initiation and both don white cloth head covering.

This consecration readies them for *soma*, a deified plant with a storied past. The mythology and cult of a mountain or heaven-grown plant that provides poetic inspiration to priests, battle fury to warriors, and immortality to all may be of ancient Indo-European origin. Certainly the parallel Avestan *haoma* and Vedic *soma* cults indicate an Indo-Iranian development, a cult of drinking **sauma* associated with the warrior god Indra. A late phase of the Bactria and Margiana Archeological Complex (BMAC) that had begun in southern Central Asia early in the third millennium BCE resulted in assembly of the RV hymns between c. 1750 and 1500 BCE. The RV remains the best source with 120 hymns devoted to Soma, including the entire ninth *mandala*. RV 10.119 is Indra's famous boast of being high on *soma* and RV 4.26 and 27 depict the theft of *soma* from the highest heaven by an eagle, a myth that has a sparkling legacy in Sanskrit epics, Puranas, and other literary records as well as folklore.[32]

In Konasima *soma-lata* is the Telugu ritual name for a common green leafless creeper, *tiga* (*Asclepias acida*), purchased from one who harvests and carts it into the *agrahara*, then faces a brutal bargaining session that drives the reward down from a "*soma*-cow" to a bag of paddy. The seller is then formulaically beaten out of the *agrahara* as the stalks are bundled in white cloth and loaded onto a black antelope hide over the woven cords of the *mancam* destined for the *havir-dhana* by way of the *prag-vamsa*. The cuttings are sprinkled with water and pounded with stones over the *uparava* holes to make them swell as the four echo chambers reverberate. Their juices flow through woolen strainers into a wooden tub that serves as resource for all libations. Water, ghee, milk, curds, barley, or honey may be mixed in as the juice passes from tub to pot to cup. At one point priests form a moving serpentine line, crouching on haunches, each holding the shoulder of the one before, all chanting the *bahis-pavamana*, a *stotra* about the purity and brightness of milk-blended *soma* arriving at the altar. They see themselves as stealthy hunters of an antelope, stalking the very sacrifice they are now performing!

The *camasa* wooden cups have been crafted by a carpenter, each with distinctive shape or handle for the sacrificer and ten priests identified as cupbearers (*camasin*). Like the *soma-lata* creepers themselves these cups are believed to swell from the potent juice that is quaffed by the gods, Indra, Agni, Vayu, the Asvin pair, and others. These swollen cups also serve the ancestors, the *pitr*, Fathers, who arrive for their share.[33] At a certain moment in all the drinking of the remains of offerings to the deities (sacrificer and priests are actually receiving their *ucchista*, leftovers), the mysterious goddess Ida, a personification of sacrificial remnants, is toasted as the eleven *camasin* clink their cups together. The undiluted juice of coastal Andhra *tiga* is bitter. No one reports, even after the third pressing, hallucinogenic or stimulant effects. The age of poetic inspiration from drinking *soma* is recollected but not repeated.

There are strong associations between the drinking of *soma*, male virility, and female fecundity. Lanka pointed to the very first performance of an *agni-stoma* by Prajapati, lord of creatures, in order to bring life into the world. Several brief actions reinforce the procreative goals of *yajna* that mirror those of the lunar *isti*. The *veda* grass brush ("Brahma's moustache") that is featured in new- and full-moon rites appears again as a transient erotic symbol, sometimes on the lap of the sacrificer, sometimes on his wife's lap, and at times even hurled across the arena by her after presentation by the sacrificer. In her *diksa* mantra the wife requested offspring and later she is associated several times with water and bathing, at one point sitting with spread legs to pour water on her thighs in reference to her fertile womb and child-bearing capacity. Still later in the *agni-stoma* she will carefully bathe the sacrificial goat. And reference to the *soma* seat as a bed may be an oblique disclosure of the locus of semen production, *retas* being a frequent name for *soma* in the Rg Veda, replaced by ghee as another homology in the Brahmanas and ritual sutras.[34]

On the *agni-stoma*'s single pressing day (*sutya*) the drinking of *soma*, *soma-bhaksana*, occurs morning, midday, and afternoon-evening. Each pressing-offering-drinking event may be preceded by two other types of offerings, the *pravargya* and *upasad*. The *pravargya*, not necessarily part of *agni-stoma*, will be discussed at length below as it is a significant ritual in and of itself. The *upasad* have a history in the cosmic struggles between the gods and the Asuras, the gods eventually winning the day and becoming masters of the universe by laying successive sieges (*upasad*) to enemy redoubts and expelling Asuras from all three worlds. Immediately following discussion of the *pravargya* AB 1.4.6 relates that scene and proceeds with applications to ritual of these paradigmatic victories. In *soma* rites, however, *upasad* have another meaning, not assaults but reverent approaches—with multiple libations of ghee for Agni, Soma, and Visnu.[35]A special moment occurs during the third *soma* pressing (cf. ApSS 13.35.6) when the *udgatr* and his acolytes cover their ears and chant the *yajna-yajniya saman*, a string of verses drawn from the Rg Veda.

An essential part of *agni-stoma* is this animal sacrifice, *pasu-bandha*, meaning that the menu of this feast shared with the gods includes meat as well as cereal grain loaves and a *soma*-juice beverage. Like the *soma* narrative, animal sacrifice has an extensive genealogy in South Asia.[36] If Asko Parpola is correct in his interpretation of the Indus "fig-deity" seal from Mohenjo-Daro as the sacrifice of a *sarabha* or markhor goat (*Capra falconeri*) to a goddess in a tree ("a predecessor of Durga"), goat sacrifices in South Asia may be older than any known Vedic ritual.[37]

An animal sacrifice independent of *soma* rites is recommended for an *agni-hotrin* in the month of Sravana (July–August) and is usually called Sravana or *nirudha pasu*. Few if any, however, have done this prior to completing *agni-stoma* and only the rare Konasima pandit did it more than once after *yajna*. Reticence on the part of a few to discuss personal ritual history may stem from this disjuncture since Apastamba recommends that the *nirudha pasu* be sacrificed once a year or even every six months (ApSS 7.28.6). All pandits agree, however, on the absolute necessity of animal sacrifice within *soma* rites, including as many as thirty-two goats for a *vaja-peya*. In recent years the *pasu-bandha* involving large numbers of animals has often meant postponing the ritual until the final day and performing it within the guarded compound of a sympathetic land owner in order to avoid disturbance by animal-rights activists.

The *pasu-bandha* permits coastal Andhrans to believe that they are the sole remaining authentic Vedic sacrificers. Some in India and Nepal substitute vegetable for animal offerings. When shown a copy of color plate 98A in Frits Staal's *Agni*, eleven banana-leaf packages of rice flour lined up in a row as "animals" in the 1975 Nambudiri *agni-cayana* in Kerala, the Sriramapuram *ahitagni* laughed and asked "How can there be a sacrifice if no one dies?" They disdain the use of *pista-pasu* (flour-paste) figures of animals and continue to offer *soma* and a real *pasu* together.

On the pressing day of *agni-stoma* the Agni-Somiya male goat is dedicated to Indra and Agni. In the *samitra* space in the northeast corner on Plan 6.1 he is smothered rather than beheaded, as in the oldest known Vedic animal sacrifices,[38] by a Kummari, a Potter of the Sudra artisan caste taking the role of "pacifier" (*samitr*), one strong enough to hold a kicking goat. "It is the mantra that subdues the sacrificial victim; the Kummari only assists," say the Veda pandits. They are in agreement with the general Hindu populace—villagers who sacrifice thousands of goats to neighborhood goddesses—that a goat is the closest correspondent to a human body. Two legs, four legs do not matter: his forelegs are always called "arms." In ancient Rome Pliny the Elder, who was never near India, thought the elephant was closest to a human; in

India, land of elephants, an affection for the goat won the nod. In the pattern of Vedic correspondences, sacrificer and animal victim are one. Charles Malamoud observes, however, that the sacrificer wishes both to offer and avoid offering the animal; if their esoteric identity were total, the result would be the death of the sacrificer.[39]

Of the many segments of a goat's body, eleven are selected as main offerings, the heart *(hrdiya)* being singled out for special ritual attention. The most important part of the animal, however, is the omentum (*vapa*), as in TS 6.3.9.5, extracted as first offering. Today in the surrounding communities fierce goddesses demand blood and goats are "cut" in decapitation to feed them. Asphyxiation in Vedic *pasu-bandha*, on the other hand, preserves vital powers of breath within the animal; blood, left for demons and ghosts, is never an offering to *devata*. Preliminary rites in the two traditions, however, are identical. The he-goat is pledged as offering, tied to a post (the *yupa* on Plan 6.1), sprinkled with water, calmed, and prevented from bleating. The Vedic rite is apparently emotionally conflicted, more so than the neighborhood goddess rite. Both the Vedic sacrificer and *adhvaryu* (standing inside the square marked *uttara vedi* on Plan 6.1) turn away during immolation (as they avert eyes when felling the tree for the *yupa*).

Several mantras are muttered including TS 3.1.4.*h* insisting that the animal go as a *living* gift to the gods, Agni and Soma in this case. The wife's bathing of the dead but still warm goat is said to cause his body to swell and be strong, like the swelling *soma* stalks and wooden *soma* cups. Of this moment Stephanie Jamison observes that the animal, like *soma*, is welcomed as a guest in "a perverted hospitality ritual" and after its suffocation "the wife as progenitor causes the dead animal to be reborn."[40]

The omentum is knifed loose and drawn out through a hole in the abdomen and this fatty membrane, precious to Indra, is stretched across his chest by the *adhvaryu* as he struts and turns to every compass point for all to inspect, a procedure pandits admit is not in Sutras but adopted for dramatic effect. The *yajamana* touches this caul-like skein of flesh said to contain the essence (*medha*) of sacrifice. As Ganesh Thite has observed, it is homologized to semen and represents his immortality.[41] The *adhvaryu* declares TS 1.3.9.2*l* "For food!" It is a stunning moment reminiscent of the now rarely seen goddess festival known in Telugu Godavari dialect as *gavu* featuring a dancing male ritualist wearing a headless split goat, the *patta potu,* the special one of all the animals "sealed" to the goddess, splayed open to reveal the viscera, including the omentum.

In the Vedic rite the omentum is held momentarily over the *samitra* fire on a long fork where it flashes brightly before it is roasted on the *ahavaniya* as first offering in the morning, something of an appetizer for the gods. Several baked dough *purodasa* loaves for Indra and Agni accompany the goat in the midday *soma* pressing and goat limbs, butchered in the morning and either roasted or boiled in water or ghee in a pot, are offered at the third pressing of *soma* in the evening. Animal flesh and plant juice have reserved equal space on the banquet's menu.

As noted in Chapter 2, the parts of the animal are *avadana*, specific cuts designated as main offerings. Bulusu Cayanulu enthusiastically labeled pandits "surgeons" supervising the work of pristine double-edged knives wielded by the Kummari. He enjoyed the selection process: heart, roasted separately on a spit (*sula*) after slicing the omentum, tongue, liver, kidneys, lungs, breast, left foreleg, and right hindquarter. Agni Svistakrt receives second-choice cuts: right foreleg, left hindquarter, and a portion of the lower intestine. Telugu sensitivity about words for genitals means reluctance to discuss the fate of the penis and testicles although Apastamba (7.26.7) allots their remnants, after the gods' share, to the *hotr*, with the *agnidhra* and *brahman* respectively receiving leftovers of the lower intestines and breast. Even the tail, a phallic symbol, has quite a complicated denouement toward several recipients including the *patni* and the wives of the gods. The Kummari returns to receive the hide and head. The latter, supremely desired by neighborhood goddesses, has both mythic and ritual interest to Vedic gods but the *pasu-bandha* Sutra authors generally pass it over.

Duvvuri Yajulu was apathetic toward all of this, volunteering that he never once performed *nirudha pasu-bandha* because the whole process offended him, although for *soma* rites his consent was mandatory. Anasuya called him squeamish, the contrary of her husband Lanka, who was as much invigorated by the ritual as the bright-eyed Cayanulu. Kapilavayi Venkatesvara admitted that the sight of an animal killed by the roadside always saddens him while a sacrificed animal is totally different: *that*, he said, is a sacred act. Duvvuri Yajulu agreed, but he enjoyed most *anna-dana*, a gift of vegetarian food to the entire neighborhood. "When we performed our *yajna* 76 full bags of rice were consumed in seven days. Konasima, unlike Krishna District, is famous for generosity. Without *anna-dana* it is not a real *yajna*."

At the close of *agni-stoma*, yokes, both real and symbolic, are removed from the bullocks, *soma* carts, *soma*-pressing materials, wife (her *yoktra*), sacrificer (his *mekhala*) and all ropes, cords, and hides are thrown in the river along with all implements and containers that have been touched by *soma*. The gods, priests, and sacrificer have consumed *soma* together and no trace may remain. Although the wife does not drink *soma* her funeral will nevertheless require, as discussed in the final segment of this chapter, that her bones and teeth be re-cremated because she has absorbed the sacred substance by eating her husband's leftover food. The sacrificer and wife step into the river, now full of the abandoned architecture of *agni-stoma*, and repeatedly pour pots of water over each other until the *unnetr* priest leads them out. The sacrifice and its protective *diksa* are concluded, they are born anew with new names (Soma-yaji and Somi-devamma), and are now free to resume *agni-hotra* and entertain thoughts of any advanced *soma* rite.

6.8 The Pravargya

A ritual sometimes inserted into the *soma* sacrifices between the *diksa* and the three pressing days is the *pravargya*, basically an offering to the Asvins and a few other deities of hot milk (cow's and goat's) plus ghee and curds. It is often referenced as *gharma*, heat. Since it should be added during a second or third *soma* sacrifice, not the *soma*-initiating *agni-stoma* for the couple, it has an eccentric place in the sutras. The emphasis on heat brings to mind the cosmogonic theme of *tapas*, heat, emergent from the dark primordial waters, as in the famous late hymn of the Rg Veda, the *nasadiya sukta*, 10.129.3. In studied preparation for the *pravargya* the sacrificer is supposed to encourage his inner *tapas*. Both Tapas and Gharma are personalized as divine powers. The sun (Savitr, Surya), source of light as well as heat, is thought to be strengthened by this offering, just as in the two daily *agni-hotra*.

A focus, however, on one implement of crucial import seems almost predictive of later devotional Hinduism. That object, known as Maha-vira, "great hero," is a three-tiered terra-cotta pot resembling a seated figure with head, torso, and lower body. BSS has him created on the ritual ground from three clay *pinda*, suggestive of funerary or ancestral symbolism in some early version. ApSS 15.15.1 takes great pains to create a human effigy by careful placement of sacrificial tools against the clay pot to represent all the bodily features of Maha-vira: hair, ears, eyes, nose, mouth, right down to intestines, penis, muscles, and nerves. For example, the *veda munja*-grass brush ("Brahma's moustache") puts invisible hair on the unfired clay "head," a black antelope hide covers the pot with skin and body hair, curds and honey infuse blood, crumbs of two baked *purodasa* loaves make nerves, and so forth. Such an effigy calls to mind funerary texts, on one hand the cremation with sacrificial implements placed on the body (e.g. Baudhayana Pitrmedha Sutra 3.3),[42] and on the other hand the use of *pratima* or *prati-rupa* described in the construction of a temporary "carry-over" body for the naked *preta* spirit after death.[43]

The pot is briefly enthroned in the manner of the *soma* stalks before they are pounded and then Maha-vira is anointed with ghee. Special wooden tongs enfold and lift the molded three-leveled pot from the firing embers as the sacrificer addresses it: "I encompass you with heaven and earth." It is seated on *munja* grass on a disk of silver as a gold piece covers it. Maha-vira, also addressed as Gharma, is identified with the sun and called Prajapati, lord of creatures, and other supreme titles. The head serves as bowl above a central channel meant for the hot liquid offering to fill and then boil over "in all directions" and flash in the fire. AB 4.1–5 is a brief passage on the *pravargya* homologizing this moment to creation, milk as semen overflowing from priapic Maha-vira into Agni as birthplace of the gods.

In addition to milk and ghee, libations also include *dadhi-gharma*, hot curds. Two *purodasa* loaves are offered, the first to day, the second to night. The rite must be completed before sunset and no person should bring the sacrifice to a halt by casting a shadow on the pot. There is a BSS option for the sacrificer to be sole drinker of remnants after the offering but ApSS has them shared with the priests and Konasima aligns with the latter.

The wife, normally with specified mantras and *kriya* in sacrifices, has a limited role since the *patni sala* is screened from viewing preparation of Maha-vira. At the prompting of the *prati-prasthatr*, however, she recites TA 4.7.19 and in the closing ceremony outside the *sadas* she sings a *saman* along with the six priests involved, the basic three, *hotr, adhvaryu*, and *brahman*, plus *agnidhra, prati-prasthatr*, and *prastotr*, the last singing from the Sama Veda so that all four Vedas are present. When asked what happens to Maha-vira when the sacrifice is concluded Konasima Brahmans were not of one mind, mentioning immersion in the river, abandonment on an island, and delivery to the *uttara-vedi* as options.

Hans van Buitenen understood the *pravargya* as a mystery rite focusing on the central icon, Maha-vira, that he renders as "Large man." His exegesis uncovers not only a break with a Vedic aniconic tradition but also certain features unusual in *srauta* ritual, including the use of a special fire just north of the *garha-patya*, an implement of clay, not wood, made on the ritual ground, and the worship of an anthropomorphic figure, quite unlike the use of a gold man (*purusa*) in the *agni-cayana*. In his view the rite evolved from a simple libation of hot milk and ghee to the Asvins in the time of the RV and AV to the actual worship of the Maha-vira figure and incorporation into the *soma* schedule of six *pravargya*, morning and afternoon for three successive days, the intention being to encourage the sun's victorious emergence from the rainy season. The *pravargya* serves as well as an illustration of ritual expansion from simple to complex.[44]

6.9 *The* Soma-*sacrifice Schedule and Other Rituals*

Vedic ritual texts imagine an ideal progression through a number of sacrifices—extensive and quite expensive—after the *agni-stoma*. In the modern period there have been few *ahitagni* who managed more than the initial *soma* rite. A 1976 publication, *Veda Pandits in India*, volume 2, *Andhra Veda Pandits*, listed 401 names with photos, including numerous *ahitagni*, but largely without record of *srauta* careers.[45] A valuable 1983 survey by C. G. Kashikar and Asko Parpola is "Srauta traditions in recent times."[46] In the latter essay, the Krishna and East Godavari Districts together accounted for well over half (114) of the roughly 200 *ahitagni* listed historically for Andhra. It was at that time estimated that only 120 *ahitagni* in all of India and Nepal had performed two or more *soma* sacrifices, that is, *agni-stoma* plus any one of the other six variations in the list known as the *sapta-samstha*. Of these 120 more than half were Andhra pandits, and Konasima was well represented, although there being no available informant from the two Godavari districts not all were counted. In the three decades since that tally the Godavari sum has fallen while the Krishna number has risen markedly.

Of the Konasima (East Godavari) *ahitagni* featured in this current study, Duvvuri Yajulu, then age thirty-four, performed the *sarva-prstha* form of *agni-cayana* in 1949 and the *vyudha* form of *paundarika* in 1969, thereby receiving his full name, Duvvuri Yajnesvara Paundarika Yajulu. Baballa performed the *aruna-ketuka* in 1960. Mitranarayana was the sacrificer for *agni-cayana, sararvato-mukh*, and *ati-ratra*, all in the 1960s. At the age of fifty-four Bulusu Cayanulu performed his *agni-cayana* in 1969, the same year as Yajulu's *paundarika*, and thereby received his name. All four completed from one to three sacrifices beyond *agni-stoma*. Lanka, Bulusu Kamesvara, and Pullela Laksminarayana did not go beyond the first *soma* rite.

There is one legendary regional history, however, and another that is accumulating fame. The best known is Renducintala Yajulu, credited with compiling the most prolific *srauta* record in twentieth-century India and being a major stimulus for Konasima, the place of his birth. Among his twenty-some sacrifices were three *paundarika*, two *vaja-peya*, a *sarvato-mukha*, and seven courses of the *catur-masya*. His ritual history is a litany all the pandits can and do recite at every opportunity. He was a lifelong traveler, promoter of Veda and *srauta*, and pursuer of ever-more exotic rituals to be done with his own fires. After his passing an intriguing reflection was made by his wife, Laksmikanta, at her home in Vijayawada: "However playfully he may have felt about all those rituals connected with fire, I know they were as challenging to him as the taming of a tiger." His descendants have now forged ahead with their own performances.

It is the Dendukuri family of Vijayawada that is racing to earn honors equal to those of the Renducintalas by completing, even reduplicating the schedule, *vaja-peya, sarvato-mukha, aruna-ketuka,* and all. It is the nature of Vedic rituals to build interlocking systems, rituals within rituals, with mantras and *kriya* reappearing in different contexts. There is thus a tendency to solder together bits and pieces of a ritual life that sometimes appears as a Brahmanic counterpart to winning a page in the Guinness Book of Records, a frequent hobby of South Asians who grow the world's longest fingernails or beards.

There are several systems, by no means all in agreement, that classify further the Vedic rituals under review here. One is by the number of *soma*-pressing days, one day being an *ekaha* rite such as the *agni-stoma* with three pressings on a single day. An *ahina* is the designation of a sacrifice with two to twelve pressing days, although twelve-day rituals are also known as *dvadasaha*. A sacrifice lasting a year or more is a *sattra*. For example, the *maha-vrata* described later is one day in the middle of a year-long *sattra*. A sacrifice of Prajapati goes to outer limits with a duration of a thousand years, at least according to Apastamba (ApSS 23.14.11).

The array of seven *samstha* mentioned in Chapter 2 is another classification well known but not in mandatory order for observance after the initial one, the *agni-stoma*. The six after *agni-stoma* include the *vaja-peya*, discussed later, as well as *atyagni-stoma, ukhthya, sodasin, ati-ratra,* and *aptoryama*. Apastamba briefly describes four *soma* sacrifices (ApSS 14.1–4) in which adjustments are made in the pattern of *agni-stoma* by the addition of *stotra* for an animal sacrifice, distribution of *soma* cups, or in the case of the *ati-ratra*, the "overnight" sacrifice, by extending the ritual late into the night.

Yet a third ordering of rituals considers the material offerings themselves. One of course is *soma* while another is *havir-yajna*, a list of seven to match the seven *soma* sacrifices. These offerings are dairy products such as milk, ghee (butter), and curds, grains such as rice, barley, and millet, and animals (today the goat only, never the original bovines). Six of these rites have been covered earlier under *adhana, agni-hotra, darsa-purna-masa, pasu-bandha, catur-masya,* and *paka-yajna*, the last simply being a category of "cooked" food such as rice or barley. Still to be portrayed is a seventh *havir-yajna*, the *sautramani* offering to Indra with the fermented beverage *sura* replaced today by milk.

After the paradigmatic *agni-stoma* it is perhaps the *agni-cayana*, known locally simply as *cayana*, that carries the most weight in coastal Andhra. Its variations, extending as long as forty days in the *paundarika*, will now be addressed.

6.10 Variations of Agni-cayana, *Building a Fire Altar*

Baballa was delighted to see that his tortoise—the foundation "sacrifice" for his *aruna-ketuka* recounted in Chapter 3—had escaped during the night through the carefully crafted exit hole. He could then carry freely the pan of embers that identified him with Agni and Prajapati, Fire and Lord of creation. His venture was the construction of an imagined altar for Agni fashioned of "water bricks," *ab-istaka.* Duvvuri Yajulu also piled up sizable structures of a thousand actual clay bricks, 200 in each of five layers, and then twenty years later another with an additional thousand bricks. Both *ahitagni* knew they were returning to the beginning of Time with a compilation of all the visible and invisible parts of the universe. The water or clay bricks poured or laid down one by one with creative mantras by the sacrificer, the *adhvaryu,* and assistants are clouds, rivers, and grasses. They are bulls, asterisms, the new moon, full moon, *rsi* sages, meters. Some of them are breath, creation, "life" itself, "endless." The *coincidentia oppositorum* of an altar of fire made of water recalls the birth of Agni himself in the cosmic waters.

At the heart of the edifice as it gradually rises are tangible items that reveal the deep histories of arresting symbols, naturally perforated stones (*svayam-atrnna*), for example, conical aerated turrets of marvelous castles built by termites (*valnika*), and "space-fillers" (*loka-parna*), all of them declarations of an interplay between the material and the immaterial, the world that is manifest and the realm of the transcendent. As Mircea Eliade observed, "life cannot be *repaired,* it can only be *re-created* by a return to sources."[47] And the building of the altar is not merely a reconstitution of Agni, Prajapati, the universe in all its space and time, and the sacrificer who is identified with all of them, but also a recovery of that which has never been revealed. It is something like the astronomer peering into space to see the universe not as it is but as it *was* a hundred billion years ago.

The various forms of *agni-cayana* in today's Taittiriya tradition of Andhra vary considerably from the well-known Nambudiri rite that occurred in Kerala in 1975. The most striking difference is the dramatic horde of sacrificed animals, all of them goats. It is not quite the Roman-circus-like zoological spectacle of an *asva-medha,* but the array of bleating stand-ins for the horse, bull, ram, and others in the ancient version presents a bold contrast to the placid, soundless row of vegetable packets in Kerala.

Bricks assembled during the period of *diksa* for the *yajamana* and *patni* are carted to the construction site, a working crop field a with large trench excavated so that later the completed altar can be covered over and returned to production. The sacrificing couple may consult inherited copies of the Apastamba or Baudhayana Sulba Sutras[48] with various ground plans for altars (*citi*) in order to choose a design for their platform. Authors of these sutras possessed a spirited knowledge of geometry, sagely fitting kiln-fired bricks into intricate patterns for each layer. Their artistry even takes a playful dimension in the case of feathered wing tips for a soaring eagle or the outstretched legs of a tortoise who also appears to be flying to heaven! Mobility is again suggested in the *ratha-cakra citi*, chariot-wheel altar, either with spoked or solid wheels. In addition to the eagle that brings to mind the *syena* stealing *soma* from heaven in Rg Veda 4.26 and 27 (cf. TS 5.5.3.2), other birds can be constructed or the eagle may be stylized and built entirely of square bricks in a T-form with neither head nor tail. Others are in *drona* (*soma* cup or tub form), either circular or square, and still others are *mandala*, circular. Quite popular, however, is the soaring eagle, like the one sketched from memory by a Dendukuri grandson in Plan 6.2, the *brahmacarin* artist perhaps imagining his own *srauta* sacrifice in the future.

Construction demands a yardstick, supplied by a length of bamboo the height of the sacrificer with upraised arms. In addition to clay bricks of varying dimensions there are preparations of foundation soil. The *adhvaryu* plows the soil with one or more bullocks, waters it thoroughly, and sows seeds of sesame, rice, barley, wheat, legumes, and several wild plants. As well as the

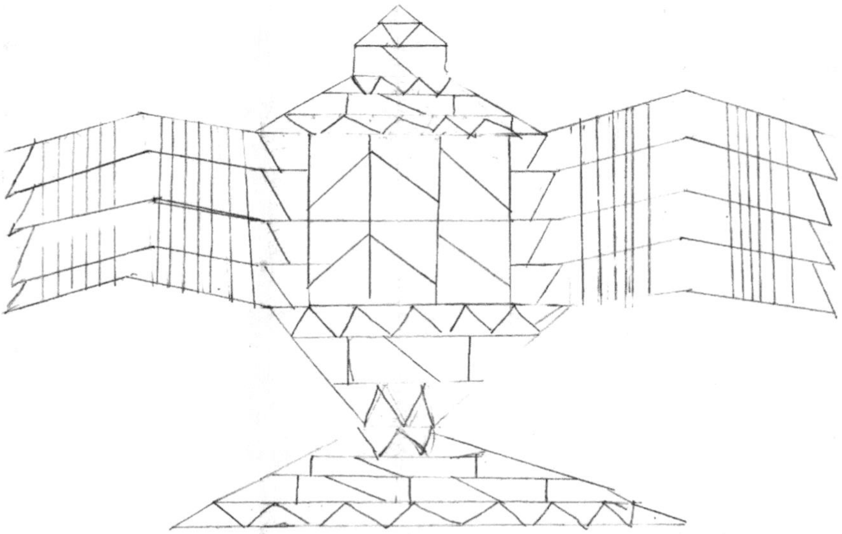

PLAN 6.2 Ground plan of a *syena-citi*, flying eagle altar for *agni-cayana*, drawn by Dendukuri Agnihotra Somayaji's grandson, Vijayawada 2005.

runaway tortoise two other reptiles are involved, a frog and a snake. A gold coin and a small gold human image (*hiranya-purusa*) are foundational, as are a naturally perforated stone, a divot of *darbha* grass, and a lotus leaf, all considered as "bricks" for the altar.

Pandits adhere to ApSS 16.1–17.26 in the first act of the standard *agni-cayana*, one that concerns the *ukha* fire-pot fashioned of clay, fired, cooled, filled with embers, and carried about by the sacrificer identified with this glowing heart of the altar under construction. It is symbolically bound (yoked) as are an ass, a horse that imprints with his right front hoof the major source of clay, and other featured elements of the sacrifice. The sacrificer visualizes, as he will throughout these proceedings, his ritual rival, that special person he hates.

The *ukha* is joined by a terra-cotta skull (substitute for the male Vaisya or Rajanya decapitated head in the ancient rite) and a termite turret containing, like a human head, seven holes. These two "heads" become the center of attention while verses are addressed to the Lord of the dead, Yama. They represent fore offerings, as signaled by the passage of fire around them, and there quickly follow the immolations of three goats impersonating the horse, bull, and ram of the ancient schedule, as well as two more that become the hornless goat and actual male goat (ApSS 16.7.1). Except for the clay dummy and the termite turret it is no longer the original festival of heads as there are no decapitations. Omenta are offered and *purodasa* loaves are baked on sherds and given to Agni Vaisvanara, "common to all men." The drama of the *ukha* fire-pan continues when the sacrificer raises it, takes the three Visnu strides that encompass the universe, enthrones it (just he did with *soma* stalks), then praises Agni who is kindled in it.

Once the initial foundation is constructed, four bricks initiate the new *garha-patya* hearth. Observers are instructed here with a significant point: bricks are not created until there is heard the resounding mantra that lays each in its place.[49] Just as a goat is not killed by the Potter acting as *samitr* but rather by the mantra, so it is not the Potter who creates each brick but a mantra. When Duvvuri Yajulu performed his first *cayana* it rose to knee height (and in the telling of it he here recited TS.5.6.8.d and Apastamba). His second one came up to his waist. Those who build a third attain the height of the mouth. Since each performance adds a thousand bricks, successive *cayana* are described by the number of *sahasra*, thousands. For example, Renducintala Yajulu performed several different *paundarika* forms of *cayana*, with a *dvi-sahasra* (2,000-brick) altar followed by *tri-sahasra* (3,000-brick) and *catur-sahasra* (4,000-brick) altars. Dendukuri Agnihotra performed his *prathama* or first *sahasra* in 1991, *dvi-sahasra* and *tri-sahasra* in 1994, all in Vijayawada.

At the conclusion of the sacrifice the *yajamana* stands and praises the altar, something he has done periodically throughout. More than a gesture, it is his opportunity to reflect upon the meaning of his cosmogonic effort. In the end the massive array of repeated correspondences in the *agni-cayana*—sacrificer = Agni = Prajapati = the year = the three worlds—points beyond merely gaining heaven toward that decisive statement of the Upanisads, *ya evam veda*, "who knows this (set of correspondences)" gains release. And yet, as we discover later in this chapter, he does not imagine *moksa* is his reward.

Popular as well as scholarly attention was drawn to the *agni-cayana* with the publication in 1882 of five volumes of the fifty-volume series, *The Sacred Books of the East*, these five being Julius Eggeling's translation of the Satapatha Brahmana with copious notes that remain incisive. Now, however, one turns first to Frits Staal's monumental two-volume project, *Agni: The Vedic Ritual of the Fire Altar* (1983, reprint 2001) with the cooperation of more than two dozen scholars and Kerala Veda pandits. Excellent color plates and diagrams from the 1975 performance in Kerala, as well as the 1977 film "Altar of Fire" provide unparalleled resources for the study of a single ritual. One of the few defects of the book is the lack of documentation on the *patni* who is virtually unmentioned. Of some 108 photographs of participants, the sacrificer's wife appears in only three, with head bowed under a parasol, suggesting she has no role.[50]

6.10.1 *Paundarika*

The most complex, demanding, even exhausting version of *agni-cayana* is the forty-day *paundarika*, considered the specialty of coastal Andhra, a rite featuring garlands of white lotus flowers (*paundarika*). It is usually an *ahina* with a core of eleven *soma*-pressing days in its *vyudha* form, by contrast with a variant *samudha* form with twelve, thirteen, or more pressing days.[51] There are prominent *srautin* who have performed both types. In all the scores of hours enjoyed in conversations with Duvvuri Yajulu the *paundarika*, one of his add-on names, remained his favorite topic. Large-scale preparation is necessary, as well as financial solvency since the recommended priestly fee (of course not observed today) is ten thousand cows (ApSS 22.24.8; KSS 23.1.9).

The capsule biography of Kapilavayi Rama Sastra in Chapter 3 included a narration of his uneasiness before his first *udgatr* role in a *paundarika*. This was the first performance in the area of a 3,000-brick *cayana* in the *vyudha* form of *paundarika*. His anxiety softened after his deceased father appeared in a dream to offer pertinent advice. Some of his stress may have been that his older brother Venkatesvara was *hotr*, the *adhvaryu* was Renducintala Krishna, son of Renducintala Venkatacala Yajulu, and his own son, Agnihotra, was assuming his first *rtvij* role as *prati-prasthatr* among the seventeen priests.

That particular *paundarika* began with twelve days of *diksa* and the sacrifice of a pure white goat for Vayu, the spotless goat having been procured in Hyderabad after a considerable search. He was first in the list of seventeen goats, the number belonging to Prajapati just as in the *vaja-peya* sacrifice. Days 13 to 25 scheduled an array of preliminary rites, including *prayaja*, fore-offerings involving Ida and other deities, the *pravargya*, and numerous libations of ghee. The centerpiece and fulcrum of the *paundarika*, as bricks were laid down in the manner described earlier, was eleven straight days of *soma* pressing, offering, and partaking along with goat sacrifices, one each day beginning on day 26 with the Agni-*somiya* goat. Ten of the goats were males, the sole exception being a nanny dedicated to the goddess Sarasvati on day 30. The last goat to be smothered was given over to Varuna on day 36 with its semen (*virya*, essence) extracted and offered as a *homa* into the *ahavaniya*.

Day 37 was a break in the dissecting of *pasus* when a goat dedicated to Tvastr was set free after circumambulation with the fire-pan. The final substantial sequence was a condensed version of the *sautramani* with milk substituting as usual for *sura* and a sacrifice to Indra of three goats at a single post, two of them serving as stand-ins for the bull and ram in the sutras. This was an overnight (*ati-ratra*) *soma*-pressing schedule on days 38 and 39. The long and arduous sacrifice conclude on day 40 with an offering of hot milk ladled onto cold curds before the final bath.

6.10.2 *Aruna-ketuka*

A quite different form of *agni-cayana* is the "water-brick" *aruna-ketuka* mentioned earlier in this chapter and in Chapter 3. It was a family tradition maintained by Baballa in August 1960 with Lanka as *adhvaryu*. At the ripe age of fifty-seven he first did a twelve-day neighborhood begging tour, *madhu-kara*, as if still a *brahmacarin* beginning his Veda career. He and Sundari observed *diksa* for a full year before commencing. This imaginative *cayana* establishes an "altar" of water, each ladle poured into his right palm and then into a clay pot being placement by mantra of an *ab-istaka*, "water brick." It is a perfect extension of the correspondences or connections (*nidana, bandhu*) that allow a brick to be a cloud, breath, or one of the meters.

TS 5.2.10.1–13 is the clue in establishment of the first layer of bricks for a standard *cayana*, with twenty *apasya* water bricks placed, five in each of in the cardinal directions. They are productive seed that brings offspring, cattle, and food. They also have prophylactic powers against demons and the dangers of unbridled fire. ApSS 16.28.4 follows suit by including rain water and river bricks (17.5.5; 7.1.1). The beauty of *aruna-ketuka* highlights the significance of water in all the sacrifices enumerated thus far, rituals that begin with the sprinkling of water, end with a bath in water, and entertain that essential element unobtrusively but frequently in the course of procedures.

In the *asva-medha,* to take one example, the horse sniffs water, both king and horse (the royal alter-ego and victim-as-offering-to-the gods) are sprinkled with water, a four-eyed dog is trampled by the horse in water, and at the conclusion a leper stands in water as an "altar" for a final offering. As much as any element, water is ubiquitous and it is not surprising to find a crucial identity regarding this cosmic foundation for Agni. Waters, either celestial or terrestrial, are described as the birthplace and home of Agni. In RV 10.51 Agni hides in the waters before he is discovered.

This primordial search for Agni therefore is replicated in the collection of different kinds of water to serve as bricks for *aruna-ketuka.* Baballa and Sundari saved water from rain that fell on a day with a bright, clear sun; from the nearby moving canal; from a standing pool; from the ocean (i.e., the Bay of Bengal); and last, the easiest source, from a learned Brahman's house, meaning their own courtyard well. The bricks were laid in courses, mostly in groups of one to eleven at a time, with appropriate mantras for Agni, Indra, Surya, Visnu, and a host of other deities. The foundational tortoise (recalling Kurma as source of the cosmos, its frontal plate, body, and carapace representing the three levels of the universe), lotus leaf, and gold man and plate were done according to the standard *agni-cayana.* Kurma, having found the escape tunnel, would live to plod along in the delta sun.

Attributed to the sage Aruna, the *aruna-ketuka* is one of a group of altar patterns ascribed to the Kathaka *sakha.* Five other altar constructions are listed by Apastamba (ApSS 19.11–15): *savitra-cayana,* according to Savitr or Surya, the sun; *naciketa-cayana,* ascribed to another sage, Naciketas; *catur-hota-cayana,* according to the RV formulas of the four *hotr* priests; *vaisva-srja-cayana,* the altar founded by universal creators; and finally an altar combining all of these styles. For his part Baudhayana (BSS 19.1–10) covers the same set of Kathaka altars, albeit with *brahma-cit* as the name of the one with multiple *hotr.* BSS 19.10 is the long segment followed by Baballa, one that concludes with the key statement that one who achieves *aruna-ketuka* reaches *brahma-loka,* the world of Brahma, and there is rewarded by being in the company of Brahma.

Charles Malamoud has noted that rites for these special kinds of fire altars are found in a segment of the Taittiriya Brahmana (10.1–10; 11.1–11; 12.1–9) with one exception, the *aruna-ketuka,* saved for the opening lines of the Aranyaka.

His suggestion is that the fashioning of water bricks was such an enigma, a paradox, that its proper locus for study and transmission was the forest.[52]

6.10.3 *Sarvato-mukha*

While the eleven *soma*-pressing days and forty overall days of *paundarika* make it the most extensive altar construction temporally, another variation of *agni-cayana* expands both space and personnel. That is the *sarvato-mukha*, a fire platform "facing all directions," four joined altars facing north, west, and south as well as east, the primary one of the cardinal directions. Such a prodigious undertaking demands an astonishing seventy-two *rtvij*, a number that consumes all available Telugu Veda pandits and still requires importation of outsiders from Tamil Nadu and as far away as Varanasi.

It is understandable that the rite is a rarity given the facts of ritual rivalry and a fear of damage either intentional or accidental. When a number of outsider pandits failed to appear for a *sarvato-mukha* that Lanka observed, the sacrifice was changed at the last moment into a *paundarika* requiring only seventeen *rtvij*. Nevertheless, there is a boldness in continuing performance and *sarvato-mukha* has been accomplished more than half a dozen times by pandits mentioned in this study, including Mitranarayana, as discussed in his capsule biography in Chapter 3. Renducintala Venkatacalu Yajulu was first in the region and later his eldest son Renducintala Canandrasekhara Yajulu was another in 1980 while Dendukuri Agnihotra was a recent *sarvato-mukha* performer in 1995.

6.11 The Vaja-peya *Drink of Strength*

The *vaja-peya*, "drink of strength," summarized in brief in Chapter 2, is sometimes chosen in Andhra for a second *soma* sacrifice. Along with Agni, Prajapati is the ever-conscious role model for a sacrificer. Prajapati's sacred number is the total or all-encompassing one of seventeen, one beyond the "complete" number sixteen, and it is not surprising therefore to find Apastamba declaring "the *vaja-peya* is all about seventeen."[53] Seventeen *sastra* and seventeen *stotra* are heard, seventeen cups of pressed *soma* are drunk on the seventeenth day by seventeen priests, seventeen animals are sacrificed, and in addition to *soma*, seventeen cups of *sura* are imbibed by the priests. *Sura*, a distant cousin to Japanese *saki*, was brewed from rice, barley, and millet left to ferment in milk for three days. The opening *diksa* days and closing *daksina* are also seventeen. The sacrificial pole (*yupa*) is seventeen *arati* in height. Seventeen bass drums are boomed to urge on horses drawing seventeen chariots on a race course measured at seventeen bow-shots to a goal post and back, a total distance that might be over two miles if the archer is given a decent bow.

The horse is celebrated for his strength (*vaja*), the first term in the name of the rite, and such power is acquired by the sacrifice. The horse-drawn war chariot figures obliquely when a wheel with seventeen spokes is set up with its hub on a short post. The wheel becomes a seat for the *brahman* priest when he does the "chant of the horses" commanding the steeds to win heaven while the *adhvaryu* revolves the wheel three times. All the horses had been bathed and made to approve rice cooked in milk by smelling it. And . . . they're off! But no charioteer may round the turning post and return to the finish line before the sacrificer. The horses smell the rice again, drums are unbound, and immediately the sacrificer, having won an earthly victory, achieves heaven by climbing a ladder braced against the sacrificial pole. The ladder of course has seventeen rungs. Apastamba has him ascend alone after three exchanges of verses with his wife whereas some sutras authorize her partial ascent; halfway up the sacrificer announces "We have now become the children of Prajapati!" At the top he declares "We have now *both* become immortal!"

The cosmic symbolism of the race may be expressed in the circuit itself with a turning post (*kastha*, similar to the Roman circus *meta*) as well as the revolving chariot wheel-seat for the chanting *brahman*. Here Asko Parpola has supplied several cogent insights into the *vaja-peya*: the turning post could be construed as world pillar or axis mundi; one type of fire altar construction is the *ratha-cakra*, chariot wheel; and the divine horsemen twins, the Asvin, may be representatives of the routine chariot drives of the sun and the moon in day and night, respectively.[54]

Gold is featured many times, in gold chain necklaces for the priests, a piece on which the sacrificer places his right foot, and in *daksina*. The sixteen charioteers who completed the main event are given cups of *sura* (but not *soma*) and they join in the feast of meat from the sacrificed animals, including, in addition to the seventeen for Prajapati, a cow for the Maruts and a ram and ewe for Sarasvat and Sarasvati, respectively.

Thus the ancient program. Today's *vaja-peya* is less spectacular, the wooden-wheeled bullock-drawn *ratha* (chariot) "race" is not about to challenge Ben Hur, and the sacrificer, his wife holding on to him, may keep one foot on earth while he "climbs" to heaven with the other. It is also less stimulating as *sura* has become milk. Nevertheless, it is an authentic *soma* and *pasu* sacrifice (without cow or ram) with all the mantras and *kriya* and as many as thirty-two goats in a recent one. Lanka supervised several, including two in his home village of Nedunuru in 1975 and 1979. A charming photo of the former *vaja-peya* shows him in a wooden-wheeled *ratha* surmounted by a parasol. Mitranarayana was *brahman* singing the chant of the horses in the first one, *udgatr* in the other, and Bulusu Kamesvara also took priestly roles. Dendukuri Agnihotra performed *vaja-peya*, as his older brother, Candrasekhar, had done previously. Dendukuri Agnihotra commenced on Telugu New Year's Day, Ugadi, March 20, 1996, only three months after he performed his gigantic *sarvato-mukha*.

Forty years earlier Hans van Buitenen filmed a *vaja-peya* with the last *ahitagni* in Pune who still maintained three fires, Sri Bapat, who followed Hiranyakesi Srauta Sutra. A number of Sukla Yajurvedins were attendants but not participants and a crowd estimated at 25,000 observed. The first day took place in the *agni-hotra* room, the second on the *prag-vamsa*, third on the *maha-vedi*, the space being a sports field of S. P. College. The *soma* was pressed and drunk, a goat was tied to the sacrificial pole but never sacrificed. Again the Andhra pandits, when told of this event, considered it an inappropriate and incomplete *yajna* if no animal was offered and shared. As in ancient versions, a modern sacrificer concludes with a verse addressed to Brhaspati, the god who aided him in winning the chariot race.[55]

6.12 The Maha-vrata *Great Vow and* Go-sava *Bull Imitation*

The great majority of rituals covered in this chapter are solemn affairs, everyone striving to avoid errors, the alert *brahman* paying as close attention as possible to every syllable and action, the *adhvaryu* and crew moving rapidly from point to point, outside onlookers observing restraint. Joy, exuberance, vivacity are not common expressions, with the possible exception of pleasure during an *agrayana*. At its height, however, one ritual evokes a festive response with musical instruments, singing, dance, and transgressive performance arts. That occasion is the *maha-vrata*, "great vow," in the middle of a sacrificial session (*sattra*) known as the *gavam-ayana*, "path of the cows." According to the sutras the one-day festival is preceded and succeeded by 180 days of the *sattra* in which priests take multiple roles in pressing *soma*, offering a goat to Prajapati (or Surya), and building the fire altar. Shorter versions of *sattra* from a fortnight to forty-nine days are possible, and of course the other extreme is also presented, including a *sattra* lasting a hundred years.[56]

The *maha-vrata* is the keystone of the *sattra* described in ApSS 21.15–25. No Konasima pandit living today has performed it but some have participated in one by invitation. Each priest has a place and functions often unique in his experience. The *adhvaryu* sits on a wooden bench, the *udgatr* on a high chair of *udumbara* wood, and the *hotr* on a swing-seat suspended like a glider from a cross bar, a type of seat seen in affluent Andhra homes today. An accomplished person using a bamboo pluck plays an extraordinary *vina*, a lute with ten holes, each with ten *munja* strings. Wives sit on distributed grasses and occasionally sing, play flutes, or blow on conches, while girls sing and perform dances that one might imagine to be ancient precursors of classical Kuchipudi. Four "earth drums" are constructed of hides drawn over pits in the ground. They have the wonderfully onomatopoeic name *bhumi-dundubhi*. Chariots roll onto the *maha-vedi* and archers shoot arrows into rawhide targets. Martial arts in ritualized combat take place, similar to nocturnal street pageants among non-Brahmans today, although the Vedic version features a match between Sudras and Brahmans under showers of abusive phrases not otherwise heard. In other words, it is a celebratory occasion for transgressive release.

Erotic display is not omitted. Behind a screen on the *maha-vedi* a man "from Magadha" has intercourse with one prostitute (*pumscali*) while a Vedic student under a vow of celibacy engages in a ribald dialogue, reminiscent of *asva-medha* exchanges, with another. Some sutras are far more explicit here than Apastamba. The *maha-vrata* has elicited response from pandits as well as scholarly commentators, the former back-pedalling away from what they see as licentious elements, the latter pointing to those same aspects as well known in the history of religions for promoting fecundity in earth, animals, and humans. Many have seen swinging and a tug of war over a rawhide facsimile of the sun as annual solar rituals. Asko Parpola's suggestive analysis, uncovering deeper layers of the pre-classical Vedic religion, sees the goddess Vac (=Durga) as the central deity in the *maha-vrata* and he understands the *bhumi-dundubhi* as war drums in keeping with the archers, ritualized combat, and fiercer aspects of the goddess.[57]

Long ago Renducintala Yajulu performed a *maha-vrata* in Gungalakurru, on the canal just south of Nedunuru, employing a *vesya* (Telugu: prostitute) and a Brahman bachelor in lieu of a *brahmacarin* for the sexual act, and Dendukuri Agnihotra has more recently added the rite to his impressive resume. Duvvuri Yajulu, performer of a *paundarika* in 1969, knew that the *maha-vrata*, with requisite prostitute, was to be performed on the next-to-last day. "A couple was available in Guntur," he said, Guntur being "Magadha," far away where things are done improperly, "but I did not seek them. No one would watch them perform, so who could verify that 'it' was actually done! So with *darbha* grass we made a male and a female doll (*bomma*) and threw them both up on the platform out of sight!" On another occasion he suggested that "it" might have entered the ritual to remind the sacrificer and wife, celibate for forty days in a *paundarika*, how "it" is done!

There appears to be no limit to Vedic ritualists' imagination regarding the voluptuous interplay of human, animal, and plant kingdoms, what Dylan Thomas called "the force through which the green fuse drives the flower." In a later segment of this chapter the *asva-medha* is explored, an extensive rite in which the king-sacrificer is homologized to a living stallion, both remaining celibate for one year. The queen ritually accepts into her body the pent-up sexual forces of productivity from the sacrificed horse-king. In another ritual, the *go-sava*, the sacrificer, not a royal one, is homologized to a bull, and in direct opposition to the king-horse, enjoys the freedom to mount anything that moves. In fact, this libertarian venture grants license to incest, transgression of a nearly universal taboo. Behaving bull-like, for one year the sacrificer should mount his own mother, sister, and (directly countering marriage rules) a woman from his own *gotra*. Also bull-like, he should be free to urinate and defecate anywhere and anytime he chooses.

Apastamba (ApSS 22.12.17–20; 13.1–3) and Baudhayana (BSS 18.7) rely on TB 2.7.6.1–3 but come up with quite different details on this one-pressing-day *ukthya* type of *soma* sacrifice that admits the sacrificer to *svarga*, heaven, and requires a *daksina* of 10,000 cows. Baudhayana omits transgressive acts and any mention of bulls or cows other than the *daksina*. There is understandable reluctance on the part of pandits following Apastamba to discuss what is seen as outrageous behavior. Age-old musings on human-bovine rapport carry no weight. Outside the Taittiriya *sakha*, however, there is one amusing tale to inject a note of levity. The Jaiminiya Brahmana (JB 1.113) includes the experience of an old man who performed the *go-sava*, in the course of which, in a crowd of people, he lost control of his bladder. This comes naturally to bulls so he pronounced the *go-sava* to be properly an old man's ritual, a *sthavira yajna*. Perhaps the narrative also defuses sexual transgressions (with troubling echoes of the sins of Prajapati with his daughter and Yama with his sister) as no more than the empty gestures of an old bull put out to pasture.[58]

6.13 The Sautramani *Offering to Indra the Protector*

An addendum to the now discontinued *raja-suya*, or the *vaja-peya* or the *agni-cayana*, including the *paundarika*, is a four-day *soma*, *sura*, and animal sacrifice known as the *sautramani,* addressed to Indra Sutraman, the king of the gods as protector. Actually, the deities are threefold and a ram was once sacrificed to Sarasvati and a goat for the Asvin twins along with a bull to Indra. Today the offerings are all goats, a female going to the goddess. Sarasvati and the divine twins are known for their healing powers and the trio figures in the origin myth of the rite. More than any other god, Indra is famed as *soma-pa,* drinker of *soma.* He had an early start as is mother served him the sacred juice as a newborn baby (RV 3.48.2–3). But at one time an over-indulged Indra had what could be described as a bad trip: he came completely undone and lost his vital powers, including the splendor and fiery energy that enabled him to rise above all other gods. The curative ritual, offerings to Indra of more *soma,* sounds like a "hair of the dog that bit you" remedy. It worked, apparently due to *sura,* Indra became his powerful self again, and the *sautramani* has been recommended ever after for Brahmans unable to hold their *soma.* Apastamba and other sutra writers repeatedly address this matter of the sacrificer or priest who vomits *soma* and is in need of special attention.[59]

There are two versions of the rite and coastal Andhrans follow that of Kakali rather than Caraka. The *sura* fermented grain concoction of the *vaja-peya* appears again in the *sautramani* with special cups for the deities in addition to *soma* cups. Eagle feathers are involved, perhaps a reminder of the eagle that first brought *soma* from heaven. A wilder *sura* recipe occurs in the Caraka version where the hairs of a lion, leopard, and wolf are placed in the deities' cups. A way to avoid these dangerous predators, however, is simply for the sacrificer and two priests to visualize them. Kane has an observation here: "The prowess, impetuosity, and fury found in those wild beasts" is the symbolic point.

Once again in today's performance the sacrificer and priests drink milk as substitute although a goat-hair sieve is employed as if this "*sura*" required purification by straining in the fashion of *soma* production. The sacrificer offers a *sura* cup to Indra while the *adhvaryu* and *prati-prasthatr* present cups to the Asvins and Sarasvati, respectively. (The *prati-prasthatr* for this *sautramani,* incidentally, was Kapilavayi Rama Sastri's son, Agnihotra, enjoying his first *rtvij* role). After the initial omenta are removed, the three animals are dissected, cooked, and offered with *purodasa.* The hoof and vestigial "hoof" of one goat are covered with fat scooped from the surface of the cooking water and offered into the *ahavaniya,* all the *sura* cups are dumped in the water meant for the concluding bath of sacrificer and wife, *daksina* are distributed, and the *sautramani* is concluded.[60]

6.14 The Asva-medha, *Sacrifice of the Royal Horse, the* Purusa-medha, *and the* Raja-suya

Of all the Vedic rituals surveyed here it is perhaps only the *agni-cayana* that has drawn as much attention from scholars outside of India as the horse sacrifice. This is due in part to the huge spectacle of the year-long rite with its cast of many hundreds, an Indic Noah's ark collection of wild and domestic animals (as many as 636 in one account), and the cachet of a handsome stallion wandering free to seek new pastures and conquer new territory for the king in the bargain. Mostly, however, its notoriety west of India is gained from apparent Indo-European roots and knowledge of counterparts in the Roman October horse, ancient Scandinavian myths and rites, and Celtic and Greek mare sacrifices. Jaan Puhvel notes that the *asva-medha* represents "the sum of Ancient Indic pageantry" and Wendy Doniger, an ardent lover of horses, observes in the introduction to her translations of Rg Vedic hymns about the *asva-medha* (1.162 and 163): the horse is three things at once, a material creature, a race horse, and "a precious sacrificial victim."[61]

As noted previously, the *asva-medha* is the favorite ritual of Kapilavayi Rama Sastra although he knows he can never see or participate in one, the last performance being some three centuries ago. Its mantras and *kriya*, however, are alive in his imagination. And most pandits are familiar—although it is not in the Taittiriya syllabus—with the wondrous opening lines of the Brhadaranyaka Upansad in which all parts of the sacrificial horse are linked to cosmic space and time, even his neigh being speech. Sanskrit epics and Puranas occasion numerous performances of the horse sacrifice and Chapter 1 noted that several rulers of Andhra dynasties celebrated *asva-medha* to mark successful wars, expanded kingdoms, and their new roles as *cakra-vartin*, universal sovereigns. One of the last recorded performances was that of the *raja* of Amber, Savai Jayasing, early in the eighteenth century CE.

Rama Sastra's acquaintance with the horse sacrifice began in his first two years of sitting with his father to hear mantras from *kanda* 3 and 4 of the Taittiriya Samhita. These mantras about the sacred horse were put in perspective when he later came to the Taittiriya *brahmana* portion. Finally, when he neared the end of his *brahmacarin* years, he learned the full program of the drama in ApSS 20.1–23. Other than BAU 1.1 he is not acquainted with the Vajasaneyi mantras and the Satapatha Brahmana version that have been major sources for many scholars.

In his mind's eyes and ears Rama Sastra sees and hears the scenes develop from the selection of an outstanding stallion, often white but not necessarily so, to the king whispering to the horse's right ear the appellations of a champion, then on to the release of the royal horse for a year of wandering in the company of a hundred warriors, perhaps even 400 including 300 charioteers. Although the king remains at home he turns over rulership to the *adhvaryu* who is acknowledged as putative king as well as executive priest making daily ghee libations into a footprint of the absent horse. The sacrificer-king listens as the *hotr* recites and lute players accompany singers recounting famous exploits by kings past and present. These evening narrations will continue for a full year of *pari-plava* cycles changing every ten days. After almost a year the horse is guided home to his stable, provided that no defending army has killed or captured him.

Soma pressings and various animal sacrifices accompany the building of the *maha-vedi,* great altar. The four major priests symbolically receive not only the four quarters of space but also the four queens in hierarchical order, the chief queen (*mahisi*) going to the supervising *brahman,* the favorite (*vavata*) to the *hotr,* the displaced one (*parivrkti*) to the *udgatr,* and the message-bearer wife (*palagali*) to the *adhvaryu.* The wives of the gods are addressed and a host of the *adhvaryu* assistants distribute food to gathered observers throughout the night.

The second of three pressing days is the main event. The victorious horse and two other animals are dedicated to Prajapati. A hornless goat is to go as pathfinder-announcer to the gods, as in RV 1.162.4, and a gayal (*gomrga, bos frontalis*) is given a role in special offerings. Then a vast crowd of other animals is driven or carted in for dedication to a variety of deities, some creatures tied to different parts of the starring horse that is bound to the central sacrificial pole. In a single row ten poles flank each side of the median post and animals are bound to each. TS 5.6.11–20 enumerates 180 animals tied to these twenty flanking poles. Captive wild animals, including a boar and various birds, are stationed between thee poles as scores of goats of every description bleat anxiously in the midst of all the unruly creatures straining at cords on the dusty, dung-strewn arena of sacrifice.

Three of the wives, each with a hundred female assistants, come forward according to rank to wash the horse and string gold, silver, or pearl beads into his mane, tail, and other hairy parts and smear him with ghee. The *adhvaryu* hitches the stallion with flanking horses to the royal chariot, the king-sacrificer equips himself with armor and bow and mounts it while expressing reverence to his ancestors and respect to the horses, chariot, and charioteer. The horse sniffs water and is released, then drinks water. The *agnidhra* brings Agni in a pan, circles first the horse, then all the wild creatures so the latter can be freed along with four selected mares and goats. The arena becomes markedly calmer with only domestic victims still bound.

The climax of the ritual year comes with the immolation of the stallion, hornless goat, and gayal, all by asphyxiation, the horse smothered with a blanket, the other two strangled by cords. The *prastotr* sings a *saman* for the ears of Yama and the *prati-prasthatr* brings the queens to the dying horse to circle him nine times while fanning him, moving clockwise or counterclockwise with their hair braided or flowing loose, slapping right or left thighs, changing these gestures as they alternate directions. As the lesser queens sit close by, the chief queen lies down and entwines her legs with the stallion as the *adhvaryu* guides the massive penis against her vagina. It is a graphic evocation of channeling the pent-up sexual powers of the king-horse toward the sought-for birth of a new king. Although the horse wandered freely, care was taken to prevent mares from attracting his attention, and simultaneously the king observed chastity for that year while sleeping in the arms of his favorite wife. Erotic forces are also aroused by juicy exchanges between priests and the king's wives who were earlier granted to them, dialogues of a sort that would never occur in life outside the protective canopy of consecrated ritual space and time.[62]

The three queens, again according to rank, stitch the horse with gold, silver, and copper or lead needles to mark butchering lines, then do the same on the hornless goat and *gomrga* before the extraction of omenta. It is said that a horse has no *vapa* (omentum) so a layer of belly fat is stripped in its place. The king-sacrificer cuts off the right ear of the horse, the one into which he earlier whispered eulogies. Omenta are cooked and apportioned as the many victims are dismembered, the blood and right front hoof of the horse being set aside for cooking and then *svistakrt* sacrifice into the throat of the gayal. The king-sacrificer ascends his throne to sit on a lion or tiger skin where he is sprinkled repeatedly with water as the Purusa *sukta* is recited.

Then comes a striking ritual that has the ring of ancient Central Asian horse sacrifices, perhaps even Paleolithic ancestry. The *adhvaryu* takes the dismembered parts of the three chief victims and assembles them on the ground as if they were alive, the head of the pathfinder goat facing west, the other two heads facing east. All are then gathered up and offered into the *ahavaniya*. The *adhvaryu* makes three additional offerings into the gayal's throat, on the right front hoof of the horse, and into an iron bowl. Animal sacrifices continue, as they have throughout the ritual.

The *asva-medha* opened with a curious ritual involving a "four-eyed" dog. It now closes with an equally odd offering on to the bald head of a buck-toothed, yellow-eyed leper from the lineage of Atri. Both rites involve pools of water, the featured horse made to trample the dog in water, the leper made to stand in water. Throughout the ritual water has sprinkled both horse and king and again water is the medium for the concluding bath for the king-sacrificer and presumably one or more of his queens.[63]

Konasima pandits are as uncomfortable parsing the *purusa-medha*, human sacrifice, as were some ancient commentators. Apastamba provides only seventeen phrases immediately following the horse sacrifice. Accounts closely follow the *asva-medha* schedule, including an extraordinary number of human victims and selection of a primary man who, like the stallion, is granted a year of privileges while remaining chaste until his asphyxiation and copulation with the chief queen. There is no inscriptional or other record that a *purusa-medha* was ever performed, leading some scholars to suggest it was simply invented to round out sacrificial possibilities. And yet there it is in the list of requisite sacrifices. The Vajasaneyi Samhita—Satapatha Brahmana—Katyayana Srauta Sutra sequence of White Yajur Veda texts contains the most details, 184 human victims in the SB account, 158 in KSS, all of them bound to sacrificial posts, then circumambulated by fire. Parallel to the *asva-medha* a host of wild animals is released. The significance of the entire enterprise is compromised when SB 13.6.2 presents a deus ex machina, an ethereal voice that intervenes to halt the proceedings: a sacrificer always eats the victim, man would therefore eat man, not an acceptable act, ergo, no performance.[64]

The *raja-suya*, consecration of a king, died out like the *asva-medha*. Although of considerable interest to scholars it draws scant attention from the pandits and will be passed with brief mention here. It is treated in the Taittiriya corpus including ApSS 18.8–25.22. Featured in addition to *soma* pressing and drinking are several king-as-warrior pursuits, a chariot drive, the king shooting arrows from his bow, and a brief cattle "raid." There is a recitation of the tale of Sunahsepa, the boy who was nearly sacrificed to Varuna on behalf of the sonless king Hariscandra. Also included is a game of throwing dice by which the king is reborn and enthroned and the cosmos is regenerated. In his thorough monograph on the *raja-suya* Jan Heesterman concluded by noting that the presiding deity of the ritual is the king, identified with the cosmos and its processes.[65]

6.15 Final Absorption into Agni: Funeral Rites

In the Harappan civilization of the third and second millennia BCE, successive funeral traditions included burial in the ground, then cremation, and then urn burials of the ashes from cremation. So too the Rg Veda included hymns for ritual burials as well as cremations. Ultimately, however, Agni prevailed for normative funerals. Henceforth it was Agni Kravyad, eater of flesh, who was invoked rather than Bhumi, the gracious and mothering earth goddess who still today safeguards the departed in many non-Brahman communities.

Virtually every human has the desire to live a long life, postpone death, and hear about concepts of fate and an afterlife hallowed by long tradition. Such yearning has been resonant throughout this chapter, every ritual reflecting some aspect of personal end time. The recruitment of ancestors in proceedings is also essential since they form a community everyone will someday join. A review of the rituals in the order described here may be instructive.

When Agni is established in his fivefold and threefold representations the *daksina* southern fire is in the quarter of death and attention to ancestors and its embers will be employed in *pitr-yajna*, offerings to the Fathers. The twice-daily *sandhya-vamdana* is a moment for a *brahmacarin* or an *ahitagni* to declare his place in an ancestral lineage. For the *ahitagni* it is accompanied by an evening or morning *agni-hotra* that includes mantras recognizing these Fathers now in the company of the Vasus, Rudras, and Adityas, the celestial generations to which *pitr-yajna* go, along with the more remote and generalized ancestors with the Visvedevas, All-gods.

The lunar *isti* include some of the same mantras and by long tradition new-moon day, more than full-moon day, is a special occasion for providing satisfaction to ancestors. As for the *agrayana*, the perpetuation of nutritive life is celebrated in the first-fruit offerings of new rice, barley, and millet. Some families also offer seeds of bamboo, *vamsa*, a word that means lineage as well, the tall measured stalk expressing a line of descent. The seasonal offerings, the third (*saka-medhas*) in particular, involve the *surpa* winnowing fan, a funereal emblem, offerings into the southern fire, discreet offerings to Pusan, pathfinder to the other world, and a link into *pitr-yajna*. It was suggested earlier that one reason for laxity in performance of the threefold *catur-masya* could in fact be such preoccupation with Mrtyu, lord of the dead, the maxim "let sleeping dogs lie" coming to mind.

In addition to fashioning three *maha-vira* "great hero" or "large man" pots for the remarkably iconic *pravargya* ritual, a human effigy is created complete with symbolic body parts. Ritual implements are placed, as if predictive of what will happen later in last rites: first comes adornment of the deceased's body with all the paraphernalia of ritual life and then a temporary transitional body is fashioned for the *preta*, transient spirit of the deceased.

Turning to the first *soma* sacrifice, the requisite *diksa* is a symbolic death and rebirth for both sacrificer and wife. The *agni-stoma* will include as well an actual victim, the goat, going to the gods as a "living" gift. His omentum (*vapa*) representing the immortality of the sacrificer will be the first offering to the deities before it is cooked and shared in what amounts to the goat's funerary banquet. The Sravana-*pasu* independent goat sacrifice is also a real rite of passage, again involving identification of the sacrificer with that animal closest to a human, now transported from this world to the other.

As for the additional *soma* sacrifices, the construction of the fire altar in *agni-cayana* or any of its variations is predictive of funeral observances for an *ahitagni* or his wife, whoever dies first. The *smasana citi* or *losta citi* is the construction of an altar on the site of the funeral pyre that consumed all the ritual implements employed by the couple throughout years of *agni-hotr*a and other sacrifices. In smaller compass it is a recapitulation of *cayana*. With successful conclusion of the *vaja-peya* "drink of strength" sacrifice it may be recalled that the sacrificer and wife symbolically climb a ladder to *svarga*, heaven or the sun, as he proclaims: "We have now both become immortal!"

The *maha-vrata*, despite episodes of merriment and the arousing of powers of fertility, also has animal sacrifices. In the full course of a *sattra* goats are everywhere stand-ins for the bulls, cows, calves, and ewes specified in the sutras. And finally, to complete this review of rituals in this chapter, the *sautramani* that parallels the independent goat sacrifice and includes such immolation, contains an offering of "*sura*" (i.e., milk) onto a termite mound with its folkloric connections to the other world, and ends with sacrifice to the ancestors. A rite intending to fortify the body of a one who cannot tolerate *soma*, the *sautrmani* concerns a sacrificer who could be denied the attainment of heaven without benefit of the sacred beverage.

Apart from all these details in the full array of rituals, there are special sutras known as *pitr-medha* that cover funerals for *ahitagni* (as well as single-fire sacrificers and those who have not set fires). Just as manuals for the final *samskara, antyesti*, are written by hand or published separately from other life-cycle rites, so the touchy subject of ancestors, meaning the dead, is covered by texts uncoupled from both *srauta* and *grhya* sutras.[66] They are largely unknown to Brahmans except for the special class of Apara Brahmans and *ahitagni* who must consult books to perform last rites for one of their own tiny circle.

Chapter 3 noted the deaths of numerous *ahitagni* and *patni*, and some funeral procedures for Baballa, Cayanulu, and Surya were detailed. Three significant features were mentioned there and these require further elaboration. First is the fact that an *ahitagni*, alone among all Hindus, does not die until the beginning of the special funeral Taittiriyins know as *brahma-medha*. A second matter pertains to a *soma* sacrificer, and therefore drinker, who must receive *punar-dahana*, a re-cremation of pulverized bones and teeth in order to eliminate all traces of the sacred substance, and this rule extends to his co-sacrificer wife. And third, an *ahitagni* who has performed any type of *agni-cayana* fire-altar building is entitled to the rite of *losta-citi* (or *losta-cayana)*, construction of an altar of mud or sod bricks on the spot of the cremation pyre. Perhaps the best way to illustrate these different funerary procedures is to relate events in a single *agrahara*.

Samavedam lived most of his life in the Sriramapuram *agrahara* as a successful Veda pandit, one who did not choose to establish sacrificial fires and perform *agni-hotra*. After his abrupt departure from this life he was soon shaved, washed, and garlanded at home and carried to the burning mound just fifty yards from the hamlet, a site never referred to as *smasana* but simply "there" or "that place." Although a short journey, the bamboo bier was set on the ground for the requisite three stops, each for three circumambulations by mourners before reaching a prepared pyre. The wood was ignited by embers from the Samavedam household's *aupasana* fire. An Apara Brahman, a priest who specializes in obsequies for Brahmans, came from Amalapuram to supervise the ceremonies. Venkatarama Ghanapathi and Bhaskara Ghanapathi, Samavedam's two Veda pandit sons, participated and were then tasked with the *masika*, monthly observances, including *astaka*, offerings on "the eighth" day of the new moon, continued on the following day, as well as the anniversary ritual (Telugu *abdika*) occurring a year later.

Samavedam's next-door neighbors, however, included three *ahitagni*, Baballa, Cayanulu, and Duvvuri Yajulu, whose respective funerals required the extended procedures of Taittiriya tradition. Akondi Suryanarayana, the same Apara Brahman, attended but could not direct; other *ahitagni* took over, consulting books with special mantras and *kriya* for which Akondi was not qualified. These three *ahitagni* required different procedures. Baballa was stretched out on blocks of ice placed in his *agni-hotra* room, awaiting the arrival from Pune of his student Ramam (Chirravuri Srirama Sarma) to assist in the ceremonies at Baballa's request. In their *guru-sisya* relationship Ramam was a surrogate son, Baballa's own disabled son a dying cancer patient at this point. Cayanulu was laid face up across the *vedi* between his hearths as if he were one more implement in sacrifice. And indeed his body *was* the sacrifice, *antyesti*, the last *isti* to be performed before the clay hearths were scraped away.

In both situations there was no death until the *brahma-medha* started. Twice each day their bodies were washed, as if they were still bathing, and fires were aroused, as if they were still doing *agni-hotra* evening and morning. Colleagues did mantras and *kriya*, including *isti* and *prayascitta* expiations. The breathless bodies lying so close to the fires seemed to be cooking, slowly melding with Agni, interiorizing him even before final absorption on the cremation pyre. The significance of an *ahitagni*, about to travel, mystically drawing the fires up into his body for safekeeping, is realized: a journey to the other world is imminent.

On the third day the bodies of Baballa and Cayanulu were carried to the same *smasana* mound used years later for Samavedam, their processions to respective pyres leaving about 8 AM for rituals lasting almost until sundown. Mourners carried three terra-cotta pots on slings labeled "a," "d," and "g," one for each of the three fires brought from the *agni-hotra* rooms. A fourth pot behind carried coals from the *aupasana* fire to be maintained separately. Ritual implements brought from the *agni-hotra* room were smeared with ghee and placed on each body after it was laid across the wood, the *havani* ladle for *agni-hotra* on the mouth, *upabhrt* ladle in the left hand, wooden knife (*sphya*) under the back, winnowing baskets (*surpa*) at the sides, wooden yoke-pin (*samya*) on the genitals, metal pots for *agni-hotra* milk and ghee at the feet.

Embers from the *ahavaniya* ignited straw at the head, *daksina-agni* and *garha-patya* igniting torso and right thigh, respectively. Only the *arani* fire-churning woods, the *juhu* ladle, and *ukhala* and *musala* mortar and pestle were withheld from the flames, these five to be used for secondary cremation. The microcosmic layout of the body—head, torso, feet—is recognized in the ritual as the body is returned via Agni to Purusa-Prajapati, the macrocosm embracing heaven, midspace, and earth.

Women are sometimes gatherers of charred bone and tooth fragments a day or two later, dropping them one at a time into a pot without looking at it. This important task is succeeded by the rite of *punar-dahana*, re-burning of these fragments after they have been ground into chalky powder in the mortar and pestle, then stirred with ghee into a paste. The *juhu* ladle serves to offer the mixture, including the last traces of twice-burned *soma*, into a separate fire maintained with embers from the initial cremation.

After *brahma-medha* and re-cremation the procedures for Baballa and Cayanulu differed only slightly in mantra and *kriya*. As performers of two different versions of *agni-cayana* both were entitled to *losta-citi*, the stacking of small sod or earth (*losta*) blocks in layers to commemorate their fire-altar building. The blocks are called bricks (*istaka*) even though unfired, and at times small stones may suffice. Baballa had performed *aruna-ketuka* with water bricks while Cayanulu (as his honorary name reveals) had done *cayana* in a more conventional style nine years later. After thorough sweeping and washing, the spot of cremation became the site of the memorial *citi*, one that in both cases soon crumbled and disappeared in the rainy season. Ashes to ashes, dust to dust.

With the losses of Baballa and Cayanulu, Sundari Somidevamma and Subbalaksmi Somidevamma were left as white-covered widows confined to their houses. Duvvuri Yajul's wife Surya Somidevamma, on the other hand, died suddenly nine years before him and her last rites had to meet three requirements not faced by the other *somi-devamma*. First, because Surya's death left Yajulu alive the *musi-vayanam* ritual had to be performed for the auspicious wife who dies first. A *brahma-muttaiduva* Brahman funerary priestess was brought from Amalapuram to locate Surya's spirit and send it to Gauri-*loka*, the heaven of goddess Gauri. Ten flower-adorned women attended this female-directed ritual by the canal close to Sriramapuram and each received Surya's blessing in the form of *prasada* to take home. This is the ritual that was done for Cayanulu's first wife, Rama Suryakanta, when she died of typhoid fever in 1945. Second, their ritual utensils, excepting implements for re-cremation, were burned on Surya's pyre with embers from their *agni-hotra* fires. The Duvvuri hearths then were permanently cold when Yajulu returned home. And third, the *punar-dahana* re-burning was necessary for Surya, just as it was for Baballa and Cayanulu.

Over in Vyaghresvaram a similar situation unfolded in the same year with the death of Kamesvari Somidevamma, wife of Laksminarayana, leaving another *ahitagni* a widower two years before his own passing. It was necessary to reserve a portion of her cremation fire, grind bone fragments, re-burn, and offer the ashes with the proper mantras because, like Surya, her body contained *soma*. This raises a question: neither Surya nor Kamesvari ever drank *soma* from a *graha* cup in *soma-bhaksana*, *soma* drinking in a sacrifice. How then did their bones accumulate *soma*?[67] To explain, some background in the long history of funeral traditions is necessary.

Significant agrarian symbols, along with pastoral ones, are expressed in last rites from the earliest Vedas. The bone-collection rite (*asthi-samcayana*) still today follows standard cremation. Requests to Agni to permit the deceased to join a new body are accompanied by the sprinkling of water on bone fragments in Rg Veda 10.16.5–6 (cf. AVS 18.2.10; KausS 82.28), suggesting regeneration of life. It is possible that *sesa* in verse 5 may be the "remnant" *soma* the poet declares in verse 6 to be "in" *brahmana* such as the deceased. The practice of plowing, seeding, and watering furrows (*karsu*) on or next to the cremation mound, then "planting" bones in these beds, is known from TS 5.2.5.2–5 (cf. SB 13.8.2.1–3) and this appears to be the intention of a different version of *losta-citi* which bypasses re-cremation in favor of burial of the entire bone pot. Further, there may be a direct homology between three *soma*-pressing days and a vague three-day journey of the deceased expressed in RV 10.14.16.[68]

There are several possible solutions to the puzzle of the *soma*-retaining wife who did not drink it. Stressed throughout this book is the fact that the *ahitagni* and *patni* pair is a co-sacrificing unit. Although of different ages at birth, in the *diksa* for *agni-stoma* and every subsequent *soma* rite they are symbolically born again at the same moment, bound together by this transformation. A second consideration is the belief of some that a bride takes her husband's blood at marriage.[69] Is blood exchange a possible avenue for *soma* to journey from the body of the *ahitagni* to the body of the *patni*? *Soma* drinking took place, however, some decades after the marriage qualification and only *soma* inherited by a previous generation of sacrificers would be relevant. If the *musi-vayanam* ritual performed for Surya and Kamesvari returned the two deceased wives to their bridal moments, pre-pubescent girls with natal family blood, they both would have been *soma*-free.

Perhaps the question is too esoteric to consider further but there is another explanation that satisfies more than one *somi-devamma* family. A wife eats the leftovers of her husband's food and over the course of many years *soma* is transferred into her bones. In the case of Surya, a marriage of fifty-one years after *agni-stoma* meant a considerable period of *soma* accumulation.

6.16 Becoming an Ancestor

Ancestors are everywhere. It is not only the *rsi* sages who hover within the river mists of Konasima. Past generations are still present requesting recognition and offerings in rituals that keep their names and accomplishments in mind. American college students, from evidence in classroom questioning, seldom supply the full name of a single one of their eight great-grandparents. *Ahitagni* may provide five to ten generations of names. Connections are reinforced by daily worship (*pitr-tarpana*), the new-moon-day offerings of water and rice balls (*pinda-dana*), and many other rites intended to give satisfaction (*trpti*) to the Fathers residing, ever watchfully, in *pitr-loka*. An important symbiosis is operative here: ancestors survive on human offerings of food routinely linked to the lunar cycle, just as humans achieve long life, children, and prosperity from the beneficence of forefathers.

Everyone remembers that a person has three debts (*rna*) in life: to the *rsi* sages, the gods, and the ancestors, paid respectively by reciting Veda, performing sacrifices, and raising children. As constant reminders, Samavedam, whose grandfather performed *agni-stoma*, always wore two silver rings with ruby stones on his right forefinger, known in Telugu as *tarjanilu*, also the name of the two rings, each engraved with ancestors' names in *deva-nagari* letters.

Despite the ubiquity and neediness of ancestors, there is decided ambivalence about an individual's fate after death, as is true for the Vedic-Hindu tradition in general. Contradictions can be controversial even in in the course of a ritual and some have already been mentioned. For example, wives who die before their husbands and receive the female-directed *musi-vayanam* ritual are dispatched on the tenth day to Gauri-*loka*, realm of the goddess Gauri. Two days later, however, male-directed rituals promote them into *pitr*-hood via their husbands' or their own parental ancestors, designating an altogether different celestial company. And always contentious is the question of *ista-purta*, merited results gained from the performance of sacrifices and other deeds.[70]

It may be recalled from his capsule biography in Chapter 3 that Duvvuri Yajulu learned from an old stranger that his achievement of *agni-stoma* would become worthless when he reached his eighties. He connected this prediction to the prior death of Surya who took their *agni-hotra* with her on the cremation pyre. In his mind, the merit from *yajna* is not permanent. Regarding rebirth, he said, a record of multiple *soma* sacrifices, however great, is not enough to escape the cycle. Accomplished deeds are for cleansing of one's consciousness (*citta-suddhi*) and for the pleasure of Paramesvara, the highest god. An *ahitagni*, still a householder, cannot escape the route from ancestor to rebirth. Only the world renouncer has a chance at release.

Cayanulu took another approach, arguing that merit from sacrifices could be rewarded with a kind of immortality, not merely with long life and prosperity. This is a frequent topic in *sabha* debates: whether or not *amrta*, immortality, is more than the popular desire to see a hundred autumns or a thousand full moons and whether *svarga-loka*, heaven, or *brahma-loka*, the heaven of Brahma, are permanent or temporary states. Rg Veda 10.14.8 is cited in which the deceased is invited to receive a new body, join his ancestors with Yama in the highest heaven, and enjoy the rewards of his sacrifices and good works. Woven into discussion is a related subject, *tyaga*, "abandonment" to the gods of the results (*phala*, fruit) of one's ritual labor rather than cashing them in for eternal reward.

One expression that surfaces compares the temporary pleasures of heaven to a holiday resort: a vacationer may enjoy himself as long as his wallet is full. When the money runs out he has to go home. Brian Smith mines texts to describe the sacrificial journey to heaven as a round trip. Whether it is by bird, cart, ship, or chariot, it is "just long enough to mark out and reserve a space for the next life."[71] Baballa, in his dying days, appreciated the fact that his *aruna-ketuka* sacrifice would reward him with a visit to *brahma-loka* and, however briefly, the company of Brahma.

As mentioned earlier in the discussion of ancestors in the *catur-masya* (part 6) those *ahitagni* who went on to become *soma* sacrificers are aware of the privileging of *soma-vant* ancestors, those who offered and therefore drank *soma*. TS 2.6.12.2 reveals two other classes of *pitr, barhisad* and *agni-svatta*, respectively, those who sat on the sacred *barhis* grass to offer cooked food and those consumed by Agni in cremations, designations that occurred already in RV 10.15.4, 11.[72] Pandits almost without exception agree that the path to the Fathers lies ahead. Already when learning the Taittiriya Brahmana they knew of successive existences beyond the present.[73] And yet it is not easy to become an ancestor. If proper rituals are lacking after cremation the deceased's disembodied spirit (*preta*, one who has "departed" from the body) may become a wandering, troublesome ghost, a *bhuta*. The Apara Brahman goes to work precisely to ensure passage to the other world in a ritual program building a temporary body for the deceased, one to cover the naked, vulnerable spirit that exited the used body on the pyre. This requires ten days, a gestation of sorts, just as the embryo in its mother needs ten lunar months before birth, and the baby and mother stay ten days secluded in the birthing room before entering the social world.

The invisible transitional body is constructed a step at a time from head to internal powers by ten days of mantras with rice ball (*pinda*), sesame seed (*tila*), and water offerings. The carry-over (*ati-vahika*) body having safely covered the *preta*, rituals may now eliminate all the material objects in which the *preta* might have sought momentary refuge. These include a small stone (*preta-sila*) worshipped by all in the mourning family; a shroud piece worn by the chief mourner, usually a son; the rice *pinda* and the crows who arrive to peck at leftovers; *kusa* grass planted and watered; nine different grains (*nava-dhanya*) seeded, watered, and fed cooked food daily; a goat either sacrificed or set free to wander in lieu of immolation; an effigy of leaves, sticks, or powders; and of course the bone and tooth fragments recovered from the cremation ashes. On the tenth day all face abandonment (*visarjana*). One by one each is thrown in a river or canal, including the sprouting *nava-dhanya* basket. An exception is the jar of an *ahitagni*'s or *patni*'s twice-burned bone and tooth fragments that is planted in a plowed furrow. The ashes of all others go into the water.[74]

The eleventh day is devoted to feeding *bhokta*, a degraded subset of Brahmans willing to be "eaters" of food for the deceased, as in other rituals they accept *dana* (gifts) to appease malicious planets such as Sani, Saturn. The chief mourner, usually a son, serves a full-course feast to eleven of them in a row, representatives of the eleven Rudras. The twelfth day is another crucial one in which the *sapindi-karana* conveys the deceased to join ancestors in *svarga*, heaven, a journey of a twelve-month year in the older texts but later condensed to a symbolic twelve days, perhaps in concern that a ritual surrogate might die during the lengthy period.

That surrogate today is a selected *bhokta* Brahman who assumes the guise of the deceased and accepts provisions for the year-long journey, an array of uncooked food that may include ten bags of paddy, a bed, bed linens, clothes for all seasons, an umbrella, cane, shoes, and gold or cash. It is traditional that his personification of the dead about to depart this world expresses persistent demands for more and more supplies. This degraded Brahman leaves and should not be seen again. He must perform long *santi-karma* himself to eliminate the dreadful effects of such dangerous gifts.

Once there is secure reception among the *pitr* the deceased becomes an ancestor to the living, bouncing prior ancestors, male or female, up a rung of the ladder of Vasus, Rudras, Adityas, the closest three generations, with the Visve-devas, the All-gods, residing in the remote space beyond. As Baballa said repeatedly, employing his own gendered terms, the self (*atman*) is situated on the middle rung of a seven-fold lineage, three generations ahead (father, grandfather, great-grandfather), three more below (son, grandson, great-grandson). All those "above" are entitled to *sraddha* rituals of a daily, monthly, and annual character, with far more attention paid to closer Fathers. The remote ancestors receive only token nourishment, rice grains that stick to the offering hand, since they are in the process of dissolving among the All-gods before returning to this world in other life forms.

Specific rules apply, however, regarding the one who "leaves water" for the departed and the frequency of such performance. As Baballa lay dying he feared that his cancer-ridden son might die before he did, thus preventing this crucial son-to-father offering. But Bullebayi lived just long enough to leave water for Baballa before he himself died and his own son, Yajnesvara Prasad, could continue. As remarked earlier, it is noteworthy that ancestors show up at *soma* rites to receive their share of the beverage.[75]

The thirteenth day is usually devoted to an assembly of regional Veda pandits in a memorial session of respectful debates and encomia to honor the deceased. With the fortnight of rituals completed the *agrahara* or hamlet returns to routines of the living. The house of the deceased, as in the cases of Lanka, Cayanulu, and others, may be closed for a year to clear it of "dust and wind," a generic Telugu term for hauntings by evil spirits. Mrtyu is asked to remain at a reasonable distance.[76]

Epilogue

BECOMING "MODERN"

CHILDREN BORN IN the United States 1982–2002, the period bracketing the turn of the millennium, are known as Millennials, as those born in the decade after World War II, 1945–55, were dubbed Baby Boomers. Seeking labels for the generations of Andhra pandits discussed here we might call the oldest set Traditionalists, a group that included Baballa, Lanka, Duvvuri Yajulu, Bulusu Cayanalu, and Gullapalli Sita Ram Sastri, as well as Renducintala Venkatacalu Yajulu, Kapilavayi Yajnesvara Agnihotra Sastri, and others. They had all grown up with what Chinese culture esteems as filial piety, particularly with regard to the father-son relationship, which in Vedic Brahmanical terms usually means guru-student. For them there was strict adherence to the rules for *sandhya-vandana, adhyaya,* marriage and other rites of passage, *yajna,* and subsequent sacrifices when they chose to perform them. With few exceptions, parental will and authority were obeyed without question. Baballa, one of six *ahitagni* brothers, is an example of generational fidelity to the path of his *ahitagni* father and his father's ancestors.

In turn, the sons and daughters of Traditionalists came of age in a period of shifting cultural norms, a time when choices that seemed inconceivable to their parents gradually became available. All seven of Lanka and Anasuya's sons, all six of Bulusu Kamesvara and Satyavati's sons, and both sons of Bulusu Cayanulu chose careers outside the Vaidika path of their parents. Of the five sons of Yajulu and Surya, the eldest, Sarvesvara, prepared for, but eventually declined, the ritual path of his father, and three other sons chose worldly careers, leaving only Surya Prakasa Avadhani as a potential sacrificer. That role he and Kanaka Durga eventually abandoned for health reasons in 2014. On the other hand, all five of Sita Ram Sastri's sons, unburdened by pursuit of a sacrificing legacy, became highly successful Veda pandits to continue the teaching heritage of their distinguished parent. Two of the four sons of Samavedam achieved similar aims. This second generation had a checkered pattern and could be called the Selecters, those who chose between options, Vaidika and *laukika,* a preference that many of their parents did not deem possible.

The next generation in this delta narrative brings us into the age of computers and information technology, yet a further distancing from the traditions of the early and mid-twentieth century. In fact, the "IT" generation, like "TV" a recognizably pan-Indian English acronym, is not an inappropriate label since a few of the Traditionalists' grandsons left India to accept computer services employment abroad. Perhaps Opportunists is a better tag for those leaping into careers totally apart from both parental and grandparental generations. There are several aspects of modern changes with which to explore the distinctions between these generations.

E.1 A New Cash Economy

> *The standard of living has changed. Money is necessary to live now, not the exchange of services between Brahmans and others.*
>
> DHUPALA RAMACANDRA SASTRI, Head of Veda-Agama Pathasala, November 17, 1980

Baballa, Lanka, Mitrnarayana, and other older pandits spoke frequently of their disillusionment with the *dabbu* (money) culture of modern India. On the other hand, Samavedam was not at all displeased to receive paper rupees instead of paddy or vegetables for his services reciting *asir-vacanam* blessings and welcomed the opportunity to buy personal items or turn the cash into dowry payments. Dowry debt, in fact, has always been one of the crippling features of economic life, an obstacle to financial solvency. Lanka paid Rs. 400 *katnam* (dowry fee) when giving his daughter Anasuya to Mitranarayana. "No land," he said, "just cash. And I have been in debt my whole life." An arrangement such as the Gullapalli-Duvvuri exchanges of sons and daughters discussed in Chapter 5 is one method of alleviating indebtedness. For another, it may be recalled that Cayanulu taught Veda to a son of his friend Renducintala in exchange for a dowry-less marriage with his daughter. The boy, Renducintala Satyanarayana Avadhani, lived in the house with Cayanulu, Subbalaksmi, and his future bride for the years of *adhyaya* until marriage in Vijayawada when he was fifteen and the girl was ten.

Attitudes toward money do in fact reveal a separation between generations. It was their loathing of *veda-vikraya*, the selling of Veda, that kept Traditionalists such as Baballa and Lanka from accepting any *parayana* position with the TTD. Selecters and Opportunists, who had no such qualms, welcomed the steady income from a monthly check and a future pension plan. Financial independence for the family became more important than the strict distancing from rupee transactions so cherished by some elders, those who regarded salaries for Veda pandits as filthy lucre. The Traditionalists were fiercely guarded in many ways. Lanka, for example, remarked that any milk from the *agni-hotra* buffalo left over from daily offerings and family consumption was always given away. "Selling milk just once," he said with a bizarre analogy, "is the karmic equivalent of torturing fish for a year." Such dogmatic circumspection, like Lanka's refusal to use chemical fertilizers or hybrid seeds on his croplands, has all but disappeared today.

E.2 Mobility

In the past we did not stir out of our villages. Now we receive constant invitations to go to other places, Hyderabad, Delhi, Ujjaini, elsewhere. And in the past there was contentment, satisfaction with life. Now there is no contentment.

MITRANARAYANA, April 22, 1989

Another striking feature of the new era is mobility, a freedom to move farther and more frequently from the *agrahara*. Routine boat traffic on the canals, bullock carts, horse tongas, and man-pulled rickshaws are quaint memories or tall tales for most people today. Buses rumble by on more or less regular schedules, the occasional taxi is available for an emergency or special event, and for longer distances a relatively short bus ride provides access to the gargantuan Indian railway system. Cars that changed American society with the arrival of Henry Ford's Model T are now on the market for India's middle class. The Tata Nano, unveiled in New Delhi in January 2008 at the rupee equivalent of $2,000, appeared exactly a century after Ford's "Tin Lizzie" and may have much the same effect on Indian society. For those four rubber tires, not wooden bullock cart wheels, the National Highways Development Project provided the beginnings of the Golden Quadrilateral, 3,625 miles of four-and-six-lane highways crossing thirteen states. A portion of the Kolkata-Chennai segment runs through the delta near Ravulapalem. Still today, however, most residents of the delta, with the exception of the lucky few in a hired taxi for a wedding party, have never been in a car. In 1992 one of Lanka's successful *laukika* sons was the first in any *ahitagni* family to own a car, a Maruti.

Public transportation by train, bus, or shared taxi means of course rubbing shoulders with outsiders, an immense hurdle for *ahitagni* and awkwardly distasteful for teaching Veda pandits managing *madi*, ritual purity. This is a leading reason for limited movement. And yet both groups, for whom long-distance journeys were rare before the 1960s, have indulged in travel to an increasing degree over the decades. As discussed in Chapters 2 and 6, *agni-hotrin* found ways to cope with hearth maintenance and requisite *isti* performance while absent. Recruitment of someone to serve as *adhvaryu, brahman*, or other *rtvij* role could mean travel to another state, usually Tamil Nadu, or attendance at a major *sabha*, perhaps in Kanci, or all-expense paid trips for special occasions such as the sixtieth and seventieth birthdays of Satya Sai Baba, in which cases wives were included in the festivities. Mentioned earlier is the case of Samavedam and his two sons, traveling anywhere by whatever conveyance, as long as an honorarium and travel expenses were forthcoming for their recitations. In the Tirupati temple in 1980, the Foreigner and his wife were delighted to encounter four Gullapalli brothers, Samavedam, and other Konasima friends among the sixteen Veda pandits belting out antiphonal *ghana* in a Varuna *puja*, an attempt to bring rain to the Seven Hills. The pandits' train journey south from Rajahmundry was successful and temple dignitaries were all pleased that mantras defeated the drought.

The most recent development is air travel. Lanka was flown to Delhi in May 1994 to receive a citation from the president of India. He was the only one of the *ahitagni* to travel in an airplane, an experience he never dreamed would happen. On the other hand, Duvvuri Sita Ram Sastry, one of Yajulu's computer science grandsons, did relate his nocturnal dream of flying to Kennedy Airport in New York where he was met by President Clinton and his secretary of state, Madeleine Albright. The flight was a dream soon realized, although it lacked such a grand welcoming party.

E.3 Huna-vidya: *A Rival Form of Education*

Reading and writing I acquired in the course of time. I never went to school. There was no activity other than Veda.

DUVVURI Yajulu, March 28, 1992

The spirit of Vedic life has disappeared. Now huna-vidya, vocational proficiency, livelihood, are all that matters to the younger generation, not rituals.

MITRANARAYANA, March 26, 1992

Yajulu spoke in the old coinage: 12 pice to an anna, 16 annas to a rupee. He loved to tell a story from his youth when a boatman shortchanged him with pice in a broken coconut shell after he paid to cross the Godavari River. The boatman showed up later with the balance, saying it was a test to verify what he suspected: the boy could not count. Like others of the old school Yajulu took pride in a record of learning Veda *before* reading, writing, and arithmetic. Late in his life he tried to help negotiate marriage arrangements for a granddaughter in a time when a typical newspaper ad sought a "Fair beautiful MSc. Software handling bride." "She has no B.A.," he lamented, "and cannot go out and earn the money that parents want for their sons now."

Mitranarayana's comment broaches the vexing and complicated matter of an English curriculum in public schools mentioned in several previous chapters. Labeled by the older Veda pandits *huna-vidya*, literally "the practice of the Huns," that is, British invaders/colonizers, the English curriculum was abhorred for its interference in traditional Vedic *adhyaya*. According to the elders, learning in the *agrahara* should begin at dawn or earlier, even 4 AM, and if the boy is expected to be in an outside school at eight o'clock the schedule is untenable. More important than timing was the matter of content, of what constitutes learning. The boy's mind, says the old generation, should be fresh and open to retain the flow of the Taittiriya syllables, not stuffed with ephemera like math and other subjects that can always be learned, as *they* learned them, later. The younger generation, having witnessed the advantages and wider perspectives of learning English and computer skills, among other subjects, has distanced itself, respectfully, from grandparental views. The middle generation is stuck somewhere between these viewpoints, having seen mediocrity or outright failure as the result of a boy's divided mind.

The English-speaking world represents to the elders a *laukika* world that is intrusive and divisive. The Traditionalists and Selecters speak no English while Opportunists have become accustomed to hearing some English in school and even more via TV-TV (as it is called), particularly after the appearance of Star TV with programs available in English. Bookstore aisles contain English texts on biology, chemistry, math, physics (never anthropology, history, religious studies, sociology), all in preparation for the Indian Council for Secondary Education, SAT and GRE exams. The sons of Surya Prakasa Avadhani (grandsons of Duvvuri Yajulu) were the first to learn any English in their school in the large town of Rajahmundry, the eldest, Phani, being the only youngster in this entire survey to learn Veda and English simultaneously. The net effects of English education in India are increasing yearly, although still it is true that only a tiny fraction of the populace speaks or reads the language.

E.4 The Powers That Be

All people should not be equal!

LANKA, December 29, 1991

Although *agrahara* life is decidedly not the same as existence in a typical Andhra village or town there is no lack of awareness of what goes on in the outside world. Cayanulu, for example, cycled daily to recite in a temple in nearby Vyaghresvaram village and Duvvuri Surya Prakasa lives in Rajahmundry, recites in a temple, and teaches in his orchard compound. In Sriramapuram and Nedunuru, people from all social strata come to supply and service *agrahara* residents and inform them of current events, local, statewide, and national. Radio was there for the oldest generation after electricity arrived, and television was available for the two recent ones. Suddenly a single "TV-TV" appeared on Main Road in Rajahmundry, drawing crowds of shoppers to stare at what seemed like a lighted bird house atop a tall pole. Soon the crowds shifted to lanes where homes of the wealthy glowed with magical blue light and locked steel gates provided ladders for distant gawkers. When visiting pandit homes in the 1990s the TV, like that initial single dangling light bulb for an earlier generation, seemed always to be on for the ladies in an interior room. "But we don't have color" became an apologetic refrain, at least until they did have color.

Although no pandit would admit to having gone there, a single cinema, Jaya Prakasa Talkies, was visible for many years across the canal from Sriramapuram. With the advent of TV in nearly every house in the late 1990s it suddenly disappeared. In January 1987 *agrahara* residents joined their fellow citizens nationwide in the devotional event of watching the great epic Ramayana, a serial television broadcast on Sunday mornings, a drama that for many legitimized the suspect medium itself. The silver screen in cinema hall form had already claimed the devotion of millions of Andhrans with the appearances of N. T. Ramarao (NTR) as Krishna or Rama in epic films; he starred in more than 300 from 1949 on. When NTR turned to politics in 1982 and led the Telugu Desam Party in defiance of Indira Gandhi he successfully won office as chief minister, the first person outside the Congress Party to hold the state's highest post. He died of a sudden heart attack in 1996 and the entire state shut down in mourning for the screen deity turned politician. Several agonized fans committed suicide. A *samadhi* was established in Hyderabad, as for a saint, and his ashes were ceremonially deposited with Vedic mantras throughout Andhra, including the Godavari at Muktesvaram in Konasima and Kotlinga *revu* in Rajahmundry.

With so many available forms of communication, any distancing from the external world is therefore self-chosen. Lanka once interrupted a discussion of *dharma* to pose his own query: "Who is in power now?" He meant the central government in Delhi. At the time he most certainly knew it was Congress Party but his expression of disdain for any form of worldly politics was as important to him as his estrangement from a constantly changing democratic system in Delhi. More than once he praised the days of British rule. "They did nothing bad to us and they encouraged merit. Now it is *our* government that is bad." At the same time his comment "All people should not be equal!" displays his adherence to *varanasrama dharma*, the classical system of hierarchy and stage of life, everyone in place according to birth, age, profession, and gender.

One common thread in *agrahara* conversations was a new sense of the growing powerlessness of Brahmans in society in general. Brahmans, by a "natural" hierarchy in accordance with scripture from the Rg Veda's Purusa Sukta to Dharma Sastra, should be on top, prestige-wise if not always in terms of economics or polity. The Indian constitution and decades of Indian's version of affirmative action, however, tweaked the old rules. In 1980 at the start of research for this book, the Delhi government's Mandal Commission submitted its report recommending a 27 percent quota system for large portions of the population, "Backward Classes," "Scheduled Castes," "Scheduled Tribes"—all those disadvantaged by "the Hindu social scheme." Gradually, over time, the masses had real weight and competitive opportunities. Brahmans could no longer count on posts in village, state, and central governments, seats in college and university departments, shares of governmental largesse. This leveling of the playing field was unsettling to Veda pandits. Some pointed to distressing news of self-immolations of upper caste protestors against the report. Later, however, they displayed a measure of pride in 1993 when India's prime minister, P. V. Narasimha Rao, a much-respected fellow Andhran, announced implementation of the report some thirteen years after its composition.[1] The school at the end of Sriramapuram's single lane was opened to all castes and this was accepted without agitation.

It is perhaps the newest generation, the Opportunists, that has the most favorable opinions of the ruling powers of state and nation. Already discussed in Chapters 3 and 5 is one example, the significant change regarding family planning. From the Traditionalists' point of view contraception is unnatural and contrary to Dharma Sastra. A strong battery of Vedic texts is quickly recited touting the purpose of marriage as the production of children to continue the lineage, governmental attempts at planned parenting being a meddling with family values. As in other ways the Selecters were divided while the Opportunists wholeheartedly embraced the national slogan "We are two, we have two." Duvvuri Phani and Laksmi (Nagalaksmi) added two sons to their union in 1996 and 1998, declaring the second to be "the final" child. It could be said that Dharma Sastra rules were outweighed by the economic advantage of being a small family. The days of ten- or twelve-child families were numbered well before the turn of the millennium.

E.5 "America": Polarities and Dreams

What is it all about, this 'going to America'? Anasuya, February 24 2000

From a distance the mountains look soft. Lanka, March 22, 1995

Anasuya, a lifelong Traditionalist whose father, grandfather, great-grandfather, and husband Lanka were all *ahitagni,* was perplexed when *ahitagni* descendants, including one of her sons, began leaving *agrahara* for that strangely menacing other-worldly place called "America." Lanka, who failed to teach Veda to a single one of their seven sons, assessed that departing son's chances of succeeding abroad with a grim proverb: a closer look at his foreign home will reveal rugged, forbidding peaks. Anasuya, capitulating to the loss, lamented: "When they go, they don't come back."

The pandit community's opinions of "America" comprise a fascinating and complicated subject that morphed in various ways over the research period. A small part concerns the researcher himself, this white Foreigner (*tela-dora*) who knows much about Vedas, sacrifices, *samskara,* and recites mantras learned, *mirabile dictu,* in Kasi, one who repeatedly appears to pose questions about their lives. Samavedam expressed the sentiments of many: "It is wonderful that someone from America is so dedicated to our traditions." Baballa went further and expressed a belief shared with Yajulu and others: "He belongs to our country, our region, our place. Only to propagate Veda was he born in that other place."

A wider perspective with which to begin, however, is the Dharma Sastra dictum that a Brahman should not live in inauspicious lands, places where *mlelccha* (barbarians) might contaminate him. Manu 3.158 condemns those who travel by sea and Bhaskara Misra admonishes those who incur the sin or fault (*dosa*) of being in an inauspicious country.[2] In 1980 the Foreigner enjoyed long discussions on the Atharva Veda with Tangiral Balagangadhara Sastri, one of Lanka's gurus, in his Sarvaraya Veda *Patha-sala* in the bucolic village of Kapilesvarapuram. He was one of the six Veda pandits teaching twenty-five students. In 1993 Sastri-garu was encountered again at an Atharva Veda Conference in Manhattan where he recited from his seldom heard Veda. There in New York City, adjacent to the United Nations headquarters among gigantic skyscrapers, so unimaginable to one secluded on the north bank of the Gautami-Godavari in Konasima, he confessed his trepidation about crossing the ocean. To the surprise of all the Veda pandits, Sastri-garu returned as the same person, apparently undamaged by American soil, food, customs, and evil eyes. It was the beginning of a slow transformation of opinion regarding that dangerous and remote land of iniquity.

Transcripts from sessions with pandits in the 1980s glitter with negative views of America, a place of magic, mystery, and money, full of people who drink alcohol excessively, communicate by sorcery over wrist watches like Dick Tracy or James Bond, carry cameras that cause photographed objects to burst into flames, and frolic as spendthrifts with fabulous wealth. Lanka once asked: "How is it that Americans are so wealthy? Is there a lot of gold just lying about?"—a remark that called to mind Herodotus' gold-mining ants that made the people of India so rich.

As mentioned earlier, in the late 1980s the Foreigner and the Andhra University professor began to read to the younger pandits letters the youth had received from Hindu temples in Chicago, Pittsburgh, Atlanta, Houston, and other cities, invitations via the TTD to recite daily as Yajur Veda pandits. The letters were all in English and of course had gone unread. After hearing the invitations no one responded, all citing fear of excommunication by older pundits, including fathers and grandfathers, their gurus. Yajulu was among the fathers who simply forbade such thoughts of foreign employment. "Selling the Veda," said Lanka, terminating discussion. Samavedam's son Bhaskara might have been a likely candidate. But he was fond of narrating two accounts, one of a Brahman from Gangalakurru who returned from America and found that no one would eat in the same line with him, while another Brahman was in America when his father's funeral took place without him, a horrendous thing to do to a guru and parent.

Opposition to such travel did shrink, however, when long-term effects of a 1965 change in US immigration laws became apparent. Young men sought employment in the United States, came home to marry, and soon added parents to their new American homes. It seemed that someone from every village in Andhra dropped anchor in the United States and reported back a quite different perspective from received knowledge. Over-the-counter medicines became popular gifts; plain aspirin, available in India at one-tenth the price, was proudly shown to the Foreigner as if it cured cancer. In America, it was said in hushed tones, everyone receives free life-saving injections and lives to be ninety years old. News soon came that not only were there Hindu temples in America but that some were staffed with Telugu priests who served Venkatesvara while other Brahmans recited Vedas! It was of course the "I.T." phase that led the march, the outsourcing of computer technologists who at first manned telephones in Hyderabad or Bangalore and then began to emigrate. Dollars were no longer the tainted wealth of filmi stories but now a valuable asset. By 2008 it was reported that Indian citizens working in the United States had the highest annual amount of dollar remittances to the home country of all foreign nationals: $27 billion.[3]

Several descendants of *ahitagni* were reported in earlier chapters to be computer specialists trained in Hyderabad before emigrating to the United States. One is Duvvuri Sita Ram Sastry, grandson of Yajulu and also of Gullapalli Sita Ram Sastri, now living with his wife and two children in Hartford, Connecticut. A failure at learning Veda, he devoted himself to providing financial support for his family in Andhra. A cousin who is also a grandson of Yajulu performs similar computer technology services in Milwaukee. As for Yajulu himself, after the Foreigner's leave-taking one sunbaked afternoon in Sriramapuram, the blind and halting nonagenarian mischievously shouted: "Tell them in America I am looking for employment!"

All Veda pandit family histories have revealed multiple changes in transitions from the older to the middle to the new generations and from the age of man-pulled rickshaws to flat-screen TVs and laptops. None has retained the features of life in the early twentieth century. Baballa's descriptions of his Konasima childhood life at the outset of the twentieth century seem quite mythic to residents of the same hamlets today. They are seeing the results of one hundred years of ballooning populations; expansion of towns, roads, communications, and amenities; political and social tinkering with the caste system; intrusion of the British curriculum and some of its language into public education; presentations of the wider world on radio, television, and film; firsthand accounts from those who had defied Manu, traveled over the great oceans, and somehow returned alive, well, and worldly wise.

The narrow dirt track that Lanka walked in the dark to and from his daily lessons is long gone, replaced by an asphalt road for motor vehicles. The servant courier walking with spoken messages for another village has been swapped for a cell phone. The many coins that added up to a rupee have been replaced by large denominations on paper or a bank check. While not the "digital natives" of American Millennials, Indian students are entirely familiar with the *meaning* of the Internet and the new social media. Certain aspects of domestic ritual life have been abbreviated, a few *samskara*, for example. Girls and women of the household are not as artistic as they used to be in creating the predawn threshold designs (*muggu*) of rice or lime powder, if there is time to do them at all. And people are living longer. About the middle of the research period for this book came the report that life expectancy in India had risen from thirty-two years in 1947, when Duvvuri Yajulu was exactly thirty-two, to fifty-nine in 1991, an astonishing increase of twenty-seven years. Yajulu lived to be ninety.

In taking the measure of a Veda pandit life that is supported by convention, stamina (*opika*), sobriety, dharmic responsibility, and above all, adherence to ritual schedule and detail, it is important to discern the impact of "modernity."

The sense that the Vedic tradition is being consumed by modernity has been afloat for much of the past three decades. It is a misleading apprehension, however, and is shared mostly by those families whose sons failed to learn Veda, or never tried, and settled for worldly careers.

Families with successful sons actually believe that their numbers have increased. And when sons achieved certification and entered into temple employment the steady income meant a considerable improvement over former times.

The accelerated pace of modern changes received an enormous boost in the period 2010 to 2014, something like a jet-assisted cultural take-off. Kapilavayi Rama Sastri in Annavaram is a good illustration, driving a car, living in a new multi-floor private house glistening with electronics to match the most up-to-date American home: flat-screen TV, laptops, I-pads, I-pods, and possibly I-things that are yet to appear in Silicon Valley. And brother Venkatesvara over in Simhacalam, also bearded, also wealthy, first to own a motorcycle, is now driving his own car. One might think that Glinda had floated in from Oz to endow the delta with all the treasures of the New Age.

Many aspects of life, however, remain unchanged. When the sun rises or sets each day it is just about six o'clock. The distinctive colorations of rice fields that line the roads, asphalt or dirt, transform as always with every season, and the expert coconut picker still shinnies barefoot up the bristly trunks with ankles bound in rope. But above all, the lessons that Baballa and Lanka heard and repeated back so many years ago are exactly the same today, as are the basic procedures of an *ahitagni* ritual life.

In the early 1990s the delta was opened to drilling by the ONGC, India's Oil and Natural Gas Company. Large-scale road construction enabled massive equipment to reach the littoral of the Bay of Bengal. Then a spectacular "blowout" occurred in well number 19 on January 8, 1995, at Pasarlipudi and dangerous horizontal flames shot hundreds of feet in all directions, lighting up Konasima and frightening everyone in the delta. No one had seen anything like it. Vedic Brahmans began to recite mantras. Astrologers were consulted about this eerie phenomenon and one with Veda pandit ancestry assured the Foreigner that *sabda,* sacred sound, either mantras or *slokas,* "both are the same," would solve the problem. One day a group of hulking Texans, complete with spurs, Stetson hats, and bulging beer bellies, appeared on the road outside Amalapuram, as inconspicuous as a squadron of Martians landing in town. They set to work first turning the flames into a vertical inferno a thousand feet in the air, then capping the well with a robot. When the fire finally fizzled and went out after burning sixty-five days, the Vedic Brahmans announced that their mantras had been the correct ones. The Brahman astrologer demurred and proclaimed that certain planets whose paths he routinely stalks had fortunately changed course on March 10, as he predicted. Others said the well fire had burned itself out, "as do most fires." No one gave the Martians credit and they all flew back to Texas.

There is something to be said here regarding the persistence of worldviews in the face of altered cultural landscapes. The softly uttered morning and evening Gāyatrī prayer, Ṛg Veda 3.62.10, once heard only in India, is now comfortably at home in Hartford, Milwaukee, San Diego.

> ***oṃ tat savitur vareṇyaṃ / bhargo devasya dhīmahi / dhiyo yo naḥ pracodayāt oṃ***
>
> May we achieve the divine splendor of Savitṛ; may he illumine our minds.

Glossary

All words are Sanskrit unless noted (T) for Telugu.

ābdika, (T) death anniversary ritual; giving water to the deceased.
abhicāra, magic, sorcery.
abhiṣeka, sprinkling with water in a ritual.
ab-iṣṭakā, water brick in the āruṇa-ketuka sacrifice.
acchāvāka, priest in a śrauta ritual assisting the hotṛ.
ādhāna, ritual setting of three household fires.
adhikāra, authority; eligibility.
ādhvaryava, text for the adhvaryu.
adhvaryu, major priest with executive roles; may have three assistants.
adhyāpana, instruction, teaching.
adhyāya, lesson, learning of Veda, a student's repetition of his guru's recitation.
adhyayana, study.
āghāra, pouring or sprinking ghee.
agni-cayana, one of seven soma sacrifices after agni-ṣṭoma; building of the great fire altar.
āgnī-dhra, priest in a śrauta ritual assisting the brahman.
agni-hotra, twice-daily offering of milk or ghee to Agni; name for the three fires.
agni-hotrin, one who performs agni-hotra.
Agni-hotruḍu (T), an āhitāgni's personification of three fires as principal deity; cf. Yajñeśvaruḍu.
agni-kṣetra, field of fire, arena for extended sacrifices.
agnī-ṣomīya, for Agni and Soma, e.g. the animal victim.
agni-ṣṭoma, initiatory soma sacrifice; known also as "yajña."
agni-ṣvātta pitṛ, esteemed ancestor consumed by Agni in a cremation fire.

agny-ādhāna, agny-ādheya, synonyms for the ādhāna ritual.
agrahāra, Brahman hamlet.
āgrayaṇa, first fruits sacrifice, annual harvest rite.
āhavanīya, offering fire.
ahīna, sacrifice with two to twelve soma-pressing days.
āhitāgni, Vedic Brahman with one or more ritual fires for agni-hotra in the home.
āhvāna-patrika, invitation, e.g., to a sacrifice.
akṣara, syllable, letter of the alphabet.
akṣarā-bhyāsa, ritual of a child's first instruction in writing.
amāvāsyā, new-moon day.
amṛta, immortality, non-death
an-ādi, without beginning or origin, eternal.
an-adhyāya, a day without teaching or learning Veda.
añjali, folded hands in prayer or cup form.
anna, rice, food.
anna-prāśaṇa, life-cycle rite, first feeding of rice to a baby.
antyeṣṭi, last iṣṭi, i.e., the body as offering to Agni.
apara, the future; (T) funerary tradition, rites requiring a special apara-brahman priest.
aparigraha, non-acceptance, not taking, e.g., honoraria; refusing gratuities.
a-patnika, one without a wife.
a-pauruṣeya, without human authorship, i.e., the Veda.
aptor-yāma, one of seven soma sacrifices starting with agni-ṣṭoma.
ārāma, pleasure garden, grove.
araṇī, (dual) a pair of aśvattha woods used for churning fire, an upper male (uttarāraṇi) connected by a spindle (pramantha) to a lower block (adharāraṇi), usually unnamed as it is the female yoni on the ground.
āraṇyaka, forest-book; a segment of each śākhā, e.g., Taittirīya Āraṇyaka.
aratni, measuring rod; one-fifth the height of the sacrificer.
arthavāda, explanation.
ārugu, (T) verandah or front porch of a house, a social space.
āruṇa-ketuka, a form of agni-cayana with water offerings in lieu of bricks.
asakti, (T) curiosity, desire, eagerness, intention.
āsandī, wooden throne with four legs for soma installed as king; mancan, (T) bed, cot.
a-śauca, impurity, pollution.
āśīr-vācana, (T) blessing, benediction; recitation by a Veda pandit for personal or community welfare.
āśrama, stage of life.

aṣṭakā, eighth day of the new moon, a time for offerings to ancestors.

asthi-sañcayana, collection of bone fragments from cremation ashes with eventual ritual disposal, usually in a river.

a-śuddha, impure, polluted.

aśva, horse.

aśva-medha, horse sacrifice.

aśvattha, *Ficus religiosa* tree.

ati-rātra, an "overnight" ritual; one of seven soma sacrifices starting with agni-stoma.

ātithyā, offering to a guest, e.g., guest appearance of a ṛtvij.

ati-vāhika, temporary carry-over (body) for the preta in transition.

ātman, self; core of the fire altar flanked by wings and tail if in eagle form.

ātma-rohaṇa, technique of absorbing ritual fires into one's body.

atukulu, (T pl.) patches of mantras stitched together from disparate sources.

atyagni-ṣṭoma, one of seven soma sacrifices starting with agni-ṣṭoma.

audgātra, text regarding the Sāma Veda for the udgātṛ and staff.

audambarī, an udumbara tree erected in the sadas, shaped as a sacrificial pole the height of the yajamāna.

aupāsana, single household ritual fire; also known as a smārta fire.

avabhṛtha, river bath for sacrificer, wife, priests to consecrate a soma sacrifice.

avadāna, a cut portion of a sacrificed animal, puroḍāśa, or iḍā.

āvasathya, an additional (fifth) fire during the ādhāna rite.

avatāra, incarnation, e.g., as of Viṣṇu or Śiva.

avayava, limb, member, part; avayava-homa, offering of parts of a dismembered animal (goat).

āyatana, layout of clay hearths for ritual fires in the house.

bālya-vivāha, (T) child marriage.

bandhu, homology, correspondence, identity.

baṇḍi, (T) cart.

barhis, kuśa grass spread out as seat for deities, priests, implements.

barhiṣad pitṛ, ancestors who sat on sacred barhis grass and offered cooked food.

bhāṣya, commentary, explanation.

bhaya, fear, dread.

bhiṣaj, healer; the brahman priest when he corrects errors or breaks in proceedings.

bhokta, eater; (T) invited Brahman who eats food for the dead.

bhrātṛvya, relative and ritual rival.

bhūmi-dundubhi, ritual drum half buried in the ground used in the mahā-vrata.

bhūta, ghost, lingering preta.

bomma, (T) doll, puppet.

brahma, (T) family priest, purohita.

brahmacārin, celibate Vedic student.

brahmacarya, the vow of chastity of a Vedic student.

brahma-loka, the heaven of Brahma.

brahma-medha, special funeral for an āhitāgni.

brahma-muttaiduva, (T) female Brahman ritualist in a mūsi-vāyanam funeral.

brahman (masculine, accent second syllable), a major priest with an overseer's role; may have three assistants.

brahman (neuter, accent first syllable), verbal power; in Upaniṣads identified with the absolute.

brāhmaṇāc-chaṃsin, priest in a śrauta ritual assisting the hotṛ.

brahma-sthāna, place of the Brahmans.

brahma-tva, Brahman-hood, being a Brahman.

brāhm-audanika, temporary fire for cooking rice during the ādhāna ritual.

caitya, assembly hall for Buddhists, Jains.

cakra, wheel of a cart or chariot.

cakra-vartin, universal emperor, sovereign of the world.

camasa, wooden cup.

camasin, a priest who drinks soma from a camasa.

caraṇa or cāraṇa, belonging to the same śākhā, branch, of Veda.

cātur-hotra-cayana, a special form of agni-cayana with cātur-hotra mantras.

cātur-māsya, four-monthly seasonal rites, spring, rainy season, autumn.

cātvāla, pit for earth off NE corner of the mahā-vedi.

cayana, fire altar, citi; abbreviated name for the agni-cayana ritual.

ceta-baḍi, (T) spell, charm, invocation of evil spirits, sorcery.

chandas, meter.

citi, fire altar, a cayana.

citta-śuddhi, cleansing of the mind or consciousness.

cūḍa, or cūḍā, top-knot, tuft of hair remaining after tonsure, a life-cycle rite.

dabbu, (T) money.

dadhi, curds.

dakṣiṇa, on the right side, to the south, southern, the Deccan region.

dakṣiṇā, payment or fee for services in a ritual.

dakṣiṇa-agni, southern fire in the agni-hotra room.

dāna, gift, donation; ritual offering.

dāna Brahman, one who accepts gifts such as food for the dead or offerings to maleficent planets and is therefore unclean.
daṇḍa, ritual staff.
darbha, grass spread around hearths; also known as kuśa.
darśaṇa, sight, as of a deity.
daśāvatāra, the ten avatāra of Viṣṇu.
darśa-pūrṇa-māsa, new- and full-moon rites.
deśa, land, region.
deśa-doṣa, the transgression of being in an inauspicious land.
deva, a deity, god.
deva-nāgarī, script for Sanskrit in particular; currently for other Indic languages.
deva-pūjā, worship of a god.
devatā, a deity, god.
devatārcana, honoring, praising a god.
devuḍu, (T) god.
dharma, law, duty, custom.
dharma-sandeha, doubts about the law.
dharma-śāstra, dharma-sūtra, dharma texts appended to Vedic śākhā.
dhiṣṇiya, row of hearths on piled earth or mud bricks on the mahā-vedi for a śrauta sacrifice.
dīkṣā, consecration of sacrificer and wife for a soma sacrifice, symbolic death and rebirth.
dora, (T) foreigner.
doṣa, fault, transgression, sin; negative consequence.
droṇa, tub for pressed soma juice; square soma cup with handle.
droṇa-citi, square or circular fire altar with "handle" like a soma cup.
dūrvā, darbha grass.
dvādaśāha, twelve-day soma sacrifice, classified as either ahīna or sattra.
dvāra, door, gate.
dviṣa, foe, enemy, rival.
eka-bhojana, eating cooked food only once a day; (T) eka-bhokta, one who eats once a day.
ekāha, sacrifice with a single soma-pressing day.
gāli, (T) wind; ghost, evil spirit.
gāna, Sāma Veda melodies.
garbha, embyo.
garbhā-dhāna, impregnation, a life-cycle rite.
gārha-patya, round cooking fire in the agni-hotra room.
gavām-ayana, path of the cows, a one-year satra sacrifice.
gavu, (T) goat sacrifice to a goddess.

gāyatrī, a meter; the mantra RV 3.62.10, also known as the sāvitrī.
ghana, ghana-pāṭha, braided recitation of Veda.
ghana-pāṭhī, one who has mastered ghana.
gharma, heat; hot milk in the pravargya rite.
ghṛta, clarified butter, ghee.
go-mṛga, gayal.
go-sava, a one-year soma ritual featuring the sacrificer's bull imitation.
gotra, clan, lineage in descent from a ṛṣi.
graha, wooden cup for soma; a pouring of a liquid (soma, ghṛta); a planet, cf. nava-graha.
grāva-stut, priest in a śrauta ritual assisting the hotṛ.
gṛha, house.
gṛha-pati, lord of the house, a householder.
gṛhastha, householder stage of life.
gṛhya-praveśa, house warming, inauguration of a new dwelling.
gṛhya, domestic, as opposed to śrauta, extended fire, ritual, or manual for such.
guru-kula, residence of the guru for oral teaching.
hautra, text for the hotṛ.
havaṇī, ladle for offering agni-hotra.
havir-dhāna, two soma-stalk carts in enclosure east of the sadas on the mahā-vedi.
havir-yajña, set of seven sacrifices apart from soma rites.
hemanta, winter, cold season.
hiraṇya, golden.
homa, offering.
hotṛ, a major priest, reciter of the RV; may have three assistants.
hotraka, assistant to the hotṛ.
hotrīya, hearth for the hotṛ.
hṛdiya, the heart.
hūṇa-vidyā, (T) foreign ways, alien practice; pejorative reference to "English education."
hūṇuḍu, (T) Hun, barbarian.
iḍā, offering to the goddess Iḍā, a personification of sacrificial remnants.
iḍlī, (T) steamed rice pancake.
ijyā, an expiation iṣṭi.
indriya, semen.
iṣṭakā, brick.
iṣṭā-pūrta, merit from sacrifices, good works.
iṣṭi, fortnightly offering on new- and full-moon days.

janma-cakra, janma-patrikā, astrological birth chart.
janman, birth; janman rahita, absence of (re)births, liberation.
japa, muttering, a repetitive prayer or praise.
jāta-karma, life-cycle rite, childbirth.
jatā-pāṭha, a style of recitation of Veda.
jāti, caste.
jīrṇa, digestion; jīrṇaḍu, (T) being digested by time, old age.
jñāna, knowledge.
jīva, life, spirit.
juhū, ladle.
jyotir-liṅga, twelve forms of Śiva's divine light.
jyotiṣa, science of astronomy and astrology.
kakṣa, (T) rivalry; spite, enmity, malice.
kalā, a small part, a sixteenth.
kāla, time.
kala-kari, (T) coastal Andhra technique of painting vegetable dyes on cloth.
kāmya, optional, e.g., a ritual of choice.
kanyā-dāna, father's gift of a daughter to the groom during marriage ritual.
kāpala mokṣa, breaking deceased's skull the on a funeral pyre, allowing the preta to escape.
karma, act, work, ritual.
karmādhikāra, authority in rituals.
karma-kāṇḍa, texts pertaining to rituals.
karma-kāṇḍin, priest who specializes in rituals, usually meaning domestic ones.
karṇa-vedha, ear-piercing, a life-cycle rite.
karṣū, plowed furrow.
kartā, kartṛ, one who acts ritually, as sacrificer or chief mourner in a funeral.
kāṣṭhā, turning post on a chariot race course.
kāvya, classical poetry.
keśānta, tonsure and shaving a boy, a life-cycle rite.
khāṇḍa, chapter, portion.
khara, small square mound of earth excavated from uparava holes; holds soma cups.
krama-pāṭha, step-by-step recitation of Veda.
krama-pāṭhi, one certified in krama-pāṭha.
kravyād, epithet of Agni as eater of flesh in the cremation ritual.
kriyā, ritual act, a karma.
kṛṣi, (T) labor, cultivation of crops.
kṛṣṇā-jina, black antelope hide used ritually.
kṣatriya, military varṇa.

kṣūdra-vidyā, (T) mean practice, black arts, sorcery.
kūḍulu, (T) cooked rice.
kūrma, tortoise.
kuśa, grass spread around hearths; also known as darbha.
lakṣaṇa, mark, sign, symbol.
lanka, (T) island.
lata, (T) green creeper substitute for soma; cf. tīga.
laukika, worldly, secular; Brahman who is not vaidika.
lepa-bhāgin, remote ancestor who receives only rice sticking to the hand in śrāddha.
liṅga, phallic symbol of Śiva.
loka, world.
loka-pṛṇā, space-filler item in various cayana including loṣṭa-cayana.
loṣṭa-cayana, loṣṭa-citi, an āhitāgni's funeral mound commemorating agni-cayana.
loṭā, water jug or pot.
madhu-kāra, "honey maker," brahmacārin's mendicant begging house to house collecting food like a bee, flower to flower; cf. vāralu, an alternative.
madhu-parka, honey and curds offered to a guest.
madhyānna, (T) midday, noon.
maḍi, (T) state of ritual purity; demands pure clothes when reciting or learning Veda, worshipping, eating cooked food.
māhātmya, magnaminity, greatness, power.
mahā-vedi, great altar for extended sacrifices such as soma.
mahā-vīra, great hero; three-tiered pot in pravargya ritual.
mahā-vrata, great vow; soma sacrifice including numerous transgressive features.
mahiṣī, chief queen in the aśva-medha.
maila, (T) pollution, ritual defilement.
maitrā-varuṇa, priest in a śrauta ritual assisting the hotṛ.
makara, crocodile.
mancam, (T) bed, cot; seat or throne (āsandī) for soma.
maṇḍala, circle, area.
mantra, Vedic verse or formula.
mār-jālīya, kitchenette for cleaning ritual implements on south line of the mahā-vedi.
marri, (T) banyan tree, *Ficus indica.*
māsa, moon, month.
māsika, monthly, as in rites for one recently deceased.
maṭha, meditation center, monastery, religious center.
medha, essence, marrow, sap; sacrificial victim.

medhā, wisdom, intelligence; vigor; medhā-janana, instilling wisdom in a baby, part of a life-cycle rite.
meḍi, (T) *Ficus glomerata* tree.
mekhalā, grass belt on the yajamāna.
menarika, (T) cross-cousin marriage; a boy with mother's brother's daughter, a girl with father's aunt's son.
mīmāṃsā, analysis of rituals, a philosophical school.
mleccha, barbarian, one who speaks no Sanskrit.
mokṣa, liberation from rebirths.
mṛdu, gentle, soft.
mṛtyu, death.
mṛtyu-cakra, astrological death chart.
mudda kūḍulu, (T) fist-sized rice balls in a ceremony for a baby who first makes fists.
muggu, (T) auspicious rice powder or lime design created daily by women at the front entrance of the house.
muhūrta, auspicious time reckoned for a ritual.
mūla, root or original text, without commentary or alteration.
muñja, a species of grass used ritually.
mūrti, image of a deity.
musala, wooden pestle for grinding grain.
mūsi-vāyanam, (T) funeral for an auspicious wife who dies before her husband.
nāciketa-cayana, a form of agni-cayana attributed to Naciketas.
nakṣatra, constellation, asterism.
nakṣatreṣṭi, iṣṭi offering to each of the twenty-eight nakṣatra.
nāma-karaṇa, name-giving to a baby, a life-cycle rite.
nava-dhānya, nine grains. nava-grahas, nine planets (sun, moon, five visible planets, Rāhu, Ketu).
nāyakuḍu, (T) leader, chief, hero.
neṣṭr, priest in a śrauta ritual assisting the adhvaryu.
nidāna, homology, correspondence, identity.
nirūḍha paśu, animal sacrificed in Śrāvaṇa month; independent of soma rites.
niṣ-kramaṇa, first "stepping out" of a baby from the house, a life-cycle rite.
nitya, obligatory, as in a required ritual, e.g., nityāgni-hotra, required agni-hotra.
nomu, (T) vow, especially a woman's vow.
nyāsa, touching parts of one's body during sandhyā-vandana devotions.
opika, (T) stamina, endurance.
paccal, (T) greenish yellow.
pada-pāṭha, word-by-word recitation of Veda.
pāka-yajña, offering of cooked food.

pakṣa, fortnight, two weeks.
pālāgalī, message-bearer queen in the aśva-medha.
pāla-piṭṭa, (T) a brilliant blue bird.
palāśa, *Butea frondosa* tree.
panasa, (Classical T) portion of Veda, lesson; = Sanskrit praśna.
pañca-aṅga, astrological manual.
pañca-āyatana, an altar or temple for worship of five deities.
pañca-bhūta, five forms of Śiva.
pañca-gavya, five bovine products used ritually, milk, butter, curds, urine, dung.
pārā-yaṇa, (T) "going over" a portion of Veda; scheduled recitation by a Veda pandit in public.
parāyatta, (T) dependent, as portions of Veda dependent on the Saṃhitā.
pari-graha, taking, accepting, e.g., fees, honoraria.
pāri-plava, year-long cycle of royal narratives in the aśva-medha.
pariṣad, organization, committee.
parīṣṭa, supersession, one whose younger brother performs marriage, ādhāna, agniṣṭoma, etc., before him.
parīṣṭa-doṣa, the transgression (doṣa) of parīṣṭa.
pari-vṛktā, displaced queen in the aśva-medha.
parṇi, *Butea frondosa* tree.
parokṣa, hidden, secret.
parvan, break, joint, division, section (of text); season of the year.
paryāhita, supersession; cf. parīṣṭa.
pāśa, snare, bond, fetter.
paśu, animal.
paśu-bandha, animal sacrifice.
pāṭha, recitation, one of several patterns for reciting Veda.
pāṭha-śāla, school for teaching Veda.
pati, husband, lord, sovereign.
patnī, wife.
patnī-śālā, secluded space for the sacrificer's wife during certain rites, e.g., pravargya.
patnī-saṃyāja, offering to the wives of the gods.
patrika, (T) invitation, e.g. to a sacrifice; = Sanskrit pattra.
pauṇḍarīka, special form of agni-cayana popular in coastal Andhra.
paurāṇika, one who recites Purāṇas.
pava-māna, pure soma after filtering.
pavitra, filter of wool or grass used to strain and purify soma or water; a soma sacrifice.
phala, fruit, result.

phala-hārā, (T) light snack of fruit or leftover cooked food suitable during a lengthy ritual or for one traveling away from controlled food at home.
pilaka, (T) top-knot, tuft of hair on a male; cūḍā.
piṇḍa, cooked rice ball as an offering.
piṇḍa-dāna, rice-ball offering to the deceased and ancestors.
piṇḍa-pitṛ-yajña, sacrifice to ancestors (pitṛ) of rice balls.
piṣṭa-paśu, flour-paste animal as substitute for a real one.
pīṭha, seat, chair, throne.
pīṭhādhipati, authority who occupies a pīṭha, important chair.
pitṛ, father, deceased one, ancestor.
pitṛ-loka, the heavenly world of ancestors.
pitṛ-medha, funeral rites for āhitāgni and patnī.
pitṛ-tarpaṇa, water offering to an ancestor.
polimera, (T) boundary of a village.
potṛ, priest in a śrauta ritual assisting the brahman.
prācīna-vaṃśa or prāg-vaṃśa, enclosure for the fires of an extended sacrifice.
praghāsa, the Varuṇa-praghāsa, the second or rainy season cātur-māsya ritual.
prakṛti, paradigm, model, template, e.g., agni-ṣṭoma for other soma sacrifices.
pramantha, spindle connecting the two araṇī.
prāṇa, breath.
prasāda, grace; remnant of an offering to a deity, returned to the one who offered.
praśna, question, topic, lesson; (T) panna.
prastara, bundle of darbha grass.
prastotṛ, priest in a śrauta ritual assisting the udgātṛ.
prathama, first.
prati-hartṛ, priest in a śrauta ritual assisting the udgātṛ.
pratimā, effigy, image.
prati-prasthātṛ, priest in a śrauta ritual assisting the adhvaryu.
prati-rūpa, effigy, image.
pravara, declaration of three ancestral names in sandhyā-vandana.
pravargya, śrauta ritual focused on the mahā-vīra pot.
prayā-ja, a fore-offering in a sacrifice, e.g., eleven in the animal sacrifice.
prāyaś-citta, rite of expiation.
preta, disembodied spirit of a deceased person.
pṛṣṭha, back, spine; particular arrangement of sāmans.

pūjā, worship, making offerings.
pūjāri, priest in a temple or shrine.
puṃsavana, life-cycle rite, turning an embryo into a male child.
puṃścalī, prostitute.
punar-ādhāna, punar-ādheya, rekindling fire.
punar-dāhana, re-burning, a second cremation in order to eliminate traces of soma.
puṇḍarīka, white lotus flower.
puṇya, good, auspicious; virtue, merit.
pūrṇimā, full moon; paurṇamī, day of the full moon.
puroḍāśa, loaf of rice-flour dough baked on terra-cotta rings.
purohita, priest, family chaplain.
puruṣa, man, human; generation; Puruṣa, Lord of creation, Prajāpati.
puṣkara, twelve-year cycle of festivals on India's greatest rivers, including the Godavari.
puṣpavatī, (T) girl who has "flowered," i.e., attainted puberty and is ready to bear fruit.
puṣṭi, prosperity; strength, vigor.
rahasya, secret, mystery.
rāja, rājan, king.
rājā-sandī, wooden stool for the god Soma installed as king.
rāja-sūya, consecration (lit. birth) of a king, a śrauta sacrifice lasting more than two years.
rajasvalā, menstruating, therefore marriage-ready girl.
rākṣasa, demon.
rāṇī, queen.
rāśi, astrological house.
ratha, chariot.
ratha-pāṭha, chariot-style recitation of Veda.
rāvi, (T) pīpal tree, *Ficus religiosa.*
retas, semen.
revu, (T) riverside steps for bathing, worship.
ṛṇa, debt.
ṛṣi, sage, seer, one of the seven original seers of the Veda.
ṛtvij, officiating priest in a sacrifice, one to eighteen in number.
sabhā, assembly of Veda pandits and brahmacārins.
sabhya, an additional (fourth) fire during the ādhāna rite.
sadas, bamboo-screened arena for extended sacrifices.
sadasya, seventeenth priest in certain soma sacrifices.
sādhu, ascetic, renunciant, wandering mendicant.
sāgni-citya, referring to the ati-rātra form of agni-cayana.

sahasra,	a thousand.
sahasra-nāma,	reciting the thousand names of a deity.
sahas-rika,	death anniversary.
sāka-medha,	autumn ritual, third of the cātur-māsya sacrifices.
śākhā,	branch or school of Vedic tradition, e.g., Taittirīya.
sālā,	temporary enclosure for a sacrifice.
salakṣaṇa,	(T) reputable, of good quality.
sallekhanā,	Jaina fast to death.
sāman,	verse put to melody, chant, portion of the Sāma Veda.
samā-ropaṇa,	uploading fire into the two araṇī.
samarta,	(T) menarche, a girl's pubescence, readiness (for childbearing).
samā-vartana,	return of a Vedic student from his guru.
sambhāra,	items collected for a sacrifice, e.g., kinds of earth.
sambhāvana,	(T) honorarium, payment for ritual services.
saṃhitā,	collection of verses, recitations.
śamī,	*Mimosa suma* tree.
samidh,	kindling stick.
sāmidhenī,	verses recited from the RV while kindling Agni.
śamitṛ,	officiant responsible for smothering and butchering sacrificial animals.
śāmitra,	hearth belonging to the śamitṛ.
saṃnyāsa,	the state of renunciation, abandonment of society.
saṃnyāsin,	ascetic, renunciant, world renouncer, one who has attained saṃnyāsa, liberation.
sampradāya,	lineage of a school or sect.
saṃsāra,	worldly existence, the cycle of births and deaths.
saṃskāra,	life-cycle rite, one of some twelve to sixteen rites of passage.
saṃsthā,	a type of soma sacrifice, seven in all (sapta-saṃsthā).
samūḍha,	a form of pauṇḍarīka.
sandhyā-vandana,	devotions at the "joints" of day/night, i.e., sunrise and sunset.
saṅ-kramaṇa,	day of solar passage from one to another rāśī, astrological house.
śānti,	peace, tranquility.
sapatna,	rival, enemy.
śapha (dual),	pair of curved wooden tongs for lifting the hot ukhā fire pot.
sapiṇḍī-karaṇa,	twelfth-day funerary rite of sending the deceased to heaven.
śarabha,	post-Vedic composite beast with eight legs.
sarva-pṛṣṭhā,	soma sacrifice with all (six) pṛṣṭha saman chanted.
sarvato-mukha,	a grandiose form of agni-cayana with altars facing all four compass points.
ṣaṣṭhi-pūrti,	ṣaṣṭhyābda-pūrti, (T) sixtieth birthday.
śastra,	RV verses recited by the hotṛ et al.

śastriṇa, the hotṛ and his three assistants who recite śastra.
sat-kāram, honoring, felicitation, usually with a cash honorarium.
sattra, a sacrifice lasting a year or more.
satyā-graha, Gandhi's "truth force," militant non-violent political action.
śauca, purity.
***sauma,** hypothetical Indo-Iranian name for the plant known as Vedic soma, Avestan haoma.
sautrāmaṇi, sacrifice to Indra Sutraman as protector.
savana, pressing of soma stalks for juice.
sāvatra-cayana, a form of agni-cayana addressing Savitṛ or Sūrya.
sāvitrī, the mantra RV 3.62.10, also known as the gāyatrī.
śamyā, yoke pin on a bullock cart.
śilā, stone.
sīmanton-nayana, life-cycle rite, upward parting of the wife's hair by the husband to promote safe delivery of a baby.
śiṣya, student or disciple of a guru.
smārta, relating to smṛti as opposed to śruti; name of a domestic fire, text, priest, etc.
śmaśāna, cremation ground.
smṛti, "that which is remembered"; post-Vedic texts including Vedāṅgas, sūtras, epics, Purāṇas.
snāna, ritual bath.
ṣoḍaśin, one of seven soma sacrifices starting with agni-ṣṭoma; dedicated to Indra; sixteenth.
soma, sacred plant and its pressed juice, possibly ephedra; the god Soma.
soma-bhakṣaṇa, drinking of soma.
soma-lata, soma-tīga, (T) names for the green creeper used for soma.
soma-pa, a drinker of soma.
soma-pravāka, organizer of a soma rite, procurer of ṛtvij crew.
soma-vant pitṛ, ancestor who offered and therefore drank soma.
soma-yāji or soma-yājulu, (T) new name for a soma sacrificer after agni-ṣṭoma.
somi-devammā or somi-devī, (T) new name for a patnī after agni-ṣṭoma.
sphya, wooden sword used to outline spaces in rituals.
śraddhā, faith.
śrāddha, funerals and rituals for ancestors.

śrauta, extended, as opposed to gṛhya (domestic) fire, ritual, or manual for such.

śrautin, one performing śrauta rituals, a fire sacrificer.

śrāvaṇa-paśu, animal (goat) sacrificed in Śrāvaṇa month (July–August).

śruti, "that which is heard," i.e., the Veda.

sthālī, cooking pot.

sthālī-pākana, food offering, e.g., rice or barley boiled in milk.

sthāvira, stable; old person.

stoma, arrangement of stotras for a particular soma sacrifice.

stotra, verses chanted by the udgātṛ et al. prior to śastra recitations by the hotṛ.

stuti, chant in a soma sacrifice; a synonym for stotra.

śu-bhakārya, auspicious ceremony.

su-brahmaṇya, priest in a śrauta ritual assisting the udgātṛ.

śūla, skewer.

śūla-gavya, sacrifice of an ox to Rudra-Śiva.

su-maṅgalī, auspicious married woman.

śunā-sīrīya, concluding ritual of the three cātur-māsya.

surā, ritual beverage of fermented rice, barley, millet.

śūrpa, winnowing fan; implement in rituals.

sūtikā-agni, protective fire or lamp burning after childbirth.

sūtra, thread; rule, manual, handbook of rules, e.g., gṛhya-, śrauta-, or dharma-sūtra.

sutyā, a day for pressing soma.

svadhiti, double-bladed knife for butchering sacrificed animals.

svar, sunshine, light, heaven.

svarga, heaven, abode of light and the gods.

svasti, svasti-vācana, group recitation of RV 1.89.

svayam-ātṛṇṇa, naturally perforated stones in agni-cayana.

sviṣṭa-kṛt, "maker of good," i.e., Agni; offering meant for Agni.

śyāmaka, rainy season millet.

śyena, eagle that fetched soma from heaven; shape of the bricks for an agni-cayana.

tapas, heat; ascetic practice.

tarjanilu, (T pl.) two rings on right forefinger (tarjani), the threatening finger, worn for conducting ancestor rites and for protective purposes.

tarpaṇa, satisfying the deceased and ancestors with offerings of water.

tāta, tāta-garu, (T) grandfather.

tavaḍu, (T) outer cover of rice grain after husking, bran.

tela-dora, (T) white foreigner.

tējassu, (T) brilliance, splendor.

tīga, (T) soma-tīga, *Asclepias acida*, a green creeper, substitute for soma; cf. lata.

tila, sesame.

tīrthaṅkara, Jaina saint.

tretāgni, the three-fire complex, the agni-hotra (plural).

tṛpti, satisfaction.

tyāga, sacrificing, abandoning, e.g., renunciation of the fruit of rituals.

ucchiṣṭa, saliva pollution, food or drink touched by the mouth of another; the gods' leavings after the offerings.

udgātṛ, a major priest, chanter of sāman from the Sāma Veda; may have three assistants.

udumbara, *Ficus glomerata* tree for sacrificial poles and other ritual implements.

ugra, powerful, mighty; terrible, fierce, wrathful.

ugra-dāna, a ritual payment unacceptable to some Veda pandits, e.g., a cow.

ukhā, terra-cotta fire pot.

ukthya, one of seven soma sacrifices starting with agni-ṣṭoma.

ulūkhala, wooden mortar for grinding with a pestle.

unnetṛ, priest in a śrauta ritual assisting the adhvaryu.

upabhṛt, a ladle.

upanayana, ritual initiation of a Vedic student when first he hears the Gāyatrī mantra and receives a sacred thread.

uparava, four holes in the ground of the havir-dhana; connected by tunnels they magnify the sound of soma stalks being pounded above them.

upā-rohaṇa, downloading fire from the two araṇī onto fresh kindling.

upasad, an iṣṭi series of offerings for Agni, Soma, and Viṣṇu after dīkṣā, before soma pressing.

upaveṣa, wooden poker for tending fires.

utkara, rubbish bin.

uttara-vedi, projected new altar at the east end of the mahā-vedi.

vaidika, Veda person or family; Brahman who learns Veda; opp. laukika, a secular Brahman.

vaiśva-deva, cooked food offerings to Viśve-devā, all gods; spring ritual, first of the cātur-māsya sacrifices.

vaiśva-sṛja-cayana, a special form of agni-cayana.

vāja-peya, "drink of strength"; one of seven soma sacrifices starting with agni-ṣṭoma.

valmīka, anthill, termite mound.

vāma-devya, name of a sāman.

vamśa, lineage, genealogy.
vana, forest.
vāṇa, harp played in vāja-peya and mahā-vrata sacrifices.
vāna-prastha, forest dweller; vāna-prasthin, one who has retired to the forest.
vaṇṭa-brahman, (T) Brahman cook, e.g., during sacrifices.
vapā, omentum of a sacrificed animal.
vāralu, (T pl.) days of the week; a brahmacārin's food provisions from a different family each day; an alternative to madhu-kāra.
varṇ a, class.
varṇāśrama-dharma, laws governing class and stage of life.
varṣā, rainy season.
varuṇa-praghāsa, second of the cātur-māsya seasonal rites.
vasanta, spring season.
vāstu, proper siting of a house or sacrifice.
vauṣaṭ, exclamation seeking Agni's aid in delivering offerings to the gods.
vaṭa, banyan tree, *Ficus indica.*
vāvātā, favorite; the king's special wife in the aśva-medha.
veda, small muñja-grass brush used to sweep hearth areas.
Veda, the entire corpus of Vedic texts; within a śākhā, the body of texts including Saṃhitā, Brāhmaṇa, Āraṇyaka, and Upaniṣads.
veda-adhyāya, lesson in learning the Veda.
veda-bhāṣya, commentary on Veda.
vedhava, (T) widow; also a term of abuse; Sanskrit vidhavā.
vedi, hourglass space for utensils between gārhapatya and āhavanīya hearths.
veśyā, prostitute.
vicchinna, interrupted, as in offerings, fires, generations; a break in the lineage.
vidhi, injunction, rule.
vihāra, enclosure for the three fires; Buddhist monastic quarters.
vikraya, sale, selling; veda-vikraya, accepting money for any Vedic purpose.
vikṛti, modification, as in alterations of the text for various recitation styles.
vīṇā, lute.
virāṭa-krama, five mantras addressed to the fires during ādhāna.
vīrya, strength, power; semen.
visarjana, abandonment.
vivāha, marriage, a life-cycle ritual.
vrata, vow.

vṛddhi, retired, pensioned.
vyākaraṇa, grammar, analysis.
vyasana, (T) passion, obsession; devotion, attachment, even addiction.
vyoman, heaven.
vyūḍha, a form of pauṇḍarīka.
yāga, sacrifice, offering, oblation; less commonly used than yajña.
yāga-bhikṣā, begging to obtain money for a ritual.
yajamāna, performer of yajña, sacrifice.
yajña, sacrifice; (T) a name in coastal Andhra for agni-ṣṭoma.
yajñā-yajñīya, a sāman and stotra prominent when the dhiṣṇiya fires are established; the udgātṛ and assistants cover their ears while chanting.
Yajñeśvara, Lord of Sacrifice; Yajñeśvaruḍu, (T) an āhitāgni's personification of principal deity; cf. Agnihotruḍu.
yājñika, performer of yajña.
yajñopavīta, sacred thread for a Brahman.
yajus, mantra muttered as directive in rituals.
yava, barley.
yoga, (T) fate, destiny, fortune.
yoktra, cord or belt that ritually binds a person or item.
yoni, female genitals; lower block of wooden fire-churning pair of araṇī.
yūpa, sacrificial pole shaped from a palāśa or other tree to the height of the yajamāna.

Notes

CHAPTER 1

1. "The Dry Salvages."
2. The crocodile is an enduring symbol. Asko Parpola makes the case for the crocodile cult of the Indus civilization still existing among Gujarati tribals four thousand years later (2012c, 2012b: 9).
3. Kashikar and Parpola (in Staal 1983.2: 204–5) provide evidence, chiefly from *Epigraphica indica*, of other Vedic rituals documented from inscriptions discovered in Andhra.
4. Thapar 1966–67 1: 173 with reference to Pallavas, Calukyas, and Rastrakutas; Kulke and Rothermund 2010: 74.
5. Talbot 2001: 22. There is considerable elasticity in historical references to "Vengi," variously indicating the village-becoming-a-town near Eluru midway between the Krishna and Godavari deltas, or the capital of the Eastern Calukas that formerly was situated at Pithapuram, or the entire coastal zone between the great deltas; cf. Mangalam 1980: 106–7 with maps and Gopalachari 1976. A series of chieftains bearing the name Sankayana, possibly related to a Vedic lineage, ruled from Vengi for about a hundred years until they were displaced by Visnukundins early in the fifth century.
6. Satyanarayana 1975–83: 2, 25.
7. Rath 2012: 189 and plate XV.
8. Nilakanta Sastri 1976: 4, 453–56.
9. Jawaharlal 1994: 45–53; Jaini 1979: 281. Jawaharlal notes that Jaina antiquities have been excavated in twenty-two villages in the two Godavari Districts (105–6).
10. Dundas 1992: 102.
11. Narayana Rao and Shulman 2002: 81.

12. Narayana Rao 1990: 7.
13. Cf. Nilakanti Sastri 1976: 166.
14. The lingering effects of endemic filarial worms, smallpox, and malaria, all thought to be goddess-produced, gave an uncanny atmosphere to the town in 1980: scores of temple priests and other residents dragged grotesque elephantiasis feet about the lanes.
15. Richard Eaton (2005) tracks the career of this exceptional sovereign as the first of eight lives he artfully employs to portray the vicissitudes of Deccan culture and politics from the fourteenth through the eighteenth centuries. And Cynthia Talbot (2000) explores a text composed c. 1490–1550 she regards as the first Telugu historiography, the Pratiparudra Caritamu, the Story of Pratipa Rudra, with a version of Kakatiya dynastic events that varies considerably from that of Indo-Muslim historians.
16. Satyanarayana 1975–83: 2, 94–5. A thorough and convincing study by Richard Eaton (2000) of temple desecration during the Indo-Muslim period of 1192–1728 does not mention in his list of eighty destroyed temples the replacement of the Rajahmundry temple of Venugopal by a mosque under the reign of Muhammad Tughluq. Sounding a note of caution regarding the view in Indo-Muslim accounts (as well as later Hindu nationalist perspectives) of constant Muslim destruction of temples, he builds a case for Indo-Muslim support and protection of Hindu temples once a region had been subjugated. His argument is that temples were political institutions with shared sovereignty of a king and the deity within a royal temple. Since resident deities were closely connected to ruling authorities, Hindu as well as Muslim warring kings removed temple images in order to defuse or co-opt their powers.
17. Stein 1989: 18.
18. Regarding the temple styles of the sixteenth century, see Mitchell 1992; Mitchell and Zebrowski 1999.
19. Wolpert 1993: 165.
20. Richards 1995: 214.
21. Pathak 1960: 126–27.
22. Merchants from Sweden and the Austrian Ostend Company also played minor roles in trade.
23. Burton Stein reports its population to be 100,000 at the end of the sixteenth century (1989: 127).
24. Prakash 1998: 208–9; cf. 260–1. Not as successful as the Dutch and English on the Coromandal coast, the Danish Company was dissolved in 1650. Two successor companies were formed but by 1807 Danish presence had ended.
25. Prakash 1998: 164.
26. Prakash 1998: 244.
27. Stein 1989: 127.

28. Prakash 1998: 136.
29. Ludden 1999: 182.
30. See Figure 1.1, this chapter, Mukkamalla Lock sluice gate on the canal system designed by Cotton. Sources for Cotton's projects in the deltas include Cotton 1854 and 1968. Cotton's was of course not the first attempt to tame the Godavari, levees and tanks having been constructed as early as the Pallava and Calukya periods; cf. Stein 1989: 21, 24;Schmitthenner 2011.
31. P. R. Rao 1980: 76.
32. When the American researcher first heard this common expression he was shocked: Huns were the dreaded Germans of his childhood, barbarians whose lust for empire started both World Wars. In India, however, the Huns are not limited to invaders of the Punjab in the fifth century CE but also include British aggressors who established a universal system of education that—in the eyes of traditional Veda pandits—was incompatible with Vedic learning.
33. Jones 1989: 161–62.
34. On Kandukuri Virasalingam, see his autobiography translated from Telugu by V. Ramakrishna Rao and T. Rama Rao (Rajahmundry: Adepally, n.d.); the biography by John G. Leonard 1979; A. A. Rao, 2010: 49–51, 96–98; Forbes 1996: 23–25; P. R. Rao 1980: 76–80.
35. On Radhakrishnan, see Gopal 1989; Minor 1987; A. A. Rao, 2010: 141–44.
36. On Sitaramayya, see P. R. Rao 1980: 221–22. In his useful and well-illustrated history of Kakinada Allam Appa, Rao includes an overview of thirty-two other Godavari political leaders (2010: 147–69).
37. P. R. Rao 1980: 142–47; on the history of the Nizams of Hyderabad, see Ramusack 2004: Index.
38. *Alphabetical List of Villages in the Taluks and Districts of the Madras Presidency* (Madras: Government Press, 1914), 129–41, lists 120 in Amalapuram Taluk but omits many well-known villages including Munganda.
39. As will be noted in Chapter 3, several Veda pandits rented out portions or all of their crop fields as "gentleman farmers," with actual farmers honoring oral agreements and paying in produce. Writing of earlier centuries, David Ludden credits coastal Andhra village elders who supervised rental transactions in oral contracts linked to market prices (1999: 178).
40. Talbot 2001: 98, 116.
41. On Gangamma in Tirupati, see Flueckiger 2013.
42. Thousands of devotees trekked barefooted to a tiny village in a northern tract of East Godavari District to see and hear a pre-pubescent goddess before she suddenly died, some say as victim of *cetabadi* (sorcery) from a jealous woman possession ritualist (Knipe 2005: 100–104 and 2004a).
43. In addition to citations listed earlier, other sources for the political, social, and cultural history of the region include Asher and Talbot 2006; Irschick 1994.

CHAPTER 2

1. *Srauta*, based on *sruti*, "that which is heard," i.e., the Veda, is not easily distinguished as a ritual category. Jan Gonda and other scholars have defined *srauta* rituals as "solemn" or "public" but neither term is satisfactory. More accurate in both time and space, "extended" describes this complex schedule of rites advanced beyond the *grhya* domestic program.
2. These portions are known in Telugu as *panna* and in Sanskrit as *prasna*, literally "questions" or "lessons." Chapter 4 expands further on the student's Vedic textual absorption.
3. This is not to suggest that Vedic Brahmans alone are capable of prodigious feats of memory. Before immigrating to Wisconsin from Scotland at the age of eleven, John Muir, the naturalist of Rocky Mountain fame, had memorized the entire New Testament and nearly half the Hebrew Bible (Old Testament), having been beaten into compliance by his father. Numerous Muslims memorize the entire Qur'an, Jaina monks often have phenomenal memories, and adherents of other faiths as well as secular folk such as numerologists are further examples. In 2013, a student from an Indian immigrant family was the American national champion speller, a thirteen-year-old Telugu speaker in seventh grade, Arvind Mahankali, who placed third in the contest in 2010 and 2011 (*New York Times* June 1, 2013, p. A1).
4. The *upanayana* is detailed in Chapter 4.
5. The ritual of marriage, *vivaha*, is described in Chapter 5 covering the lives of householders.
6. Kane rejects Ram Gopal's arguments for a North Indian home for Apastamba and suggests the school may have originated in "Andhra and the territory about the mouth of the Godavari" (Kane 1968–75, 1.1:67; cf. Gopal 1983a: 94–98). Textual scholars date the ApSS to c. 500 BCE, the ApGS to perhaps two centuries later, and a third Apastamba Sutra, the Dharma Sutra, to c. 300 BCE. To be kept in mind is the vast span of centuries between assembly of the hymns of the RV in the period c. 1750–1500 BCE and the application of mantras and chants in the Brahmana-texts and Sutras.
7. This offering is *sthali-pakana*, the cooking of rice in a pot (*sthali*) as an *isti* performed every new-and-full moon day. Tachikawa and Kolhatkar 2006 provide an excellent portrayal of every step of the *sthali-paka* with 110 photos of performances by Ganeshashastri Shende (1899–1992) in Maharashtra according to AsvGS. There is also a brief introduction and text and translation of a ritual manual including mantras from the RV and injunctions from the TB and both Asvalayana Sutras.
8. On the Sama Veda, D. Arkasomayaji, at the TTD office in Tirupati noted November 13, 1980: "I have heard Sama Veda recitations in Konasima and they are unlike the other three, Jaiminiya, Kauthuma, and Ranayaniya. Konasima

has preserved one of the many *other* ancient *sakha*." On the other hand, Western scholars, including Parpola and Heesterman, perceive only two recensions, Jaiminiya and Kauthuma-Ranayaniya, the latter pair approximately identical. Howard (1977) observes distinctions between Kauthuma and Ranayaniya and notes that the "Kauthuma" of Tamil Nadu is actually Ranayaniya. Cf. Renou 1947: 85–129. It is not surprising that disagreements persist since there are thousands of *ganas* and musical notations are variable. Further field recording and study is clearly warranted.

9. Staal 1983: 1: 45f; 2: 201–55.
10. This triadic classification is not in the Vedas although, as Frederick Smith (1987: 122–224) explains it, TS 2:1–4 essentially makes such a separation.
11. The *patni* (wife) does not drink *soma* in the ritual but obtains it by eating the leftovers of her husband's food. After her death and cremation a "re-burning" or secondary cremation is required to remove traces of *soma* from her bones. Chapter 6 provides further details on this important circumstance.
12. Staal 1983; the 40-minute film *Altar of Fire* was produced by Frits Staal and directed by Robert Gardner, Berkeley: University of California Media Center, 1977.
13. The *daksina* that should go to each priest as a share of the sacrifice, are notoriously open-ended, often extravagant. Dividing up a thousand cows is a recurrent notation. ApSS 13.5.1–13 is an example of variability, including the sacrificer's entire estate with an exception of an inheritance share for the first son. On one hand is a demonstrative potlatch enterprise. On the other hand is the intriguing directive to the sacrificer (13.6.6) to divide body and soul as *daksina*, his mind to the *brahman*, breath to the *adhvaryu*, eye to the *udgatr*, even his *atman* to the *sadasya*, seventeenth priest, a remarkable presentation to this minor but symbolically significant actor, the number seventeen being that of Prajapati, lord of sacrifice.
14. This "plus one" formula is discussed in Knipe 1975:1–18 and 1991:40–42. Abstract numbers occur in many contexts as, for example, the "totality" of sixteen surmounted by Prajapati as seventeen, discussed by Gonda 1984 index. Cf. also Proferes 2007: 23–76, "Ritual fires and the construction of sovereignty."
15. Fuller 1992: 57.
16. Among elements evoking intense human responses, fire has a special place in the history of religions. See Knipe 2004b and 1975: 45–89; Bachelard 1964a; Heesterman, 1983, 1993: 86–141; Falk 2002; Patton 2005: 104–111.
17. On the Zoroastrian cult of fire in ancient Iran, see Boyce 1986, 1975, 1979. On *soma* see Jan Houben 2003 with a substantial bibliography; Parpola 1995, 2012a: 247–51; the botanist Harri Nyberg 1995; Falk 1989; Staal 1983 1: 105–13; McClymond 2008: 101–11. On expansion of the BMAC (Bactria Margiana Archaeological Complex) see Chapter 1 this volume and Parpola 2002a, 2012a; on the post-Vedic history of the *soma* plant see the essay by Wendy Doniger

O'Flaherty in Wasson 1968: 95–147; on the background of the *soma*-theft myth, Knipe 1967.

18. An obsession with the dangerous impurity (*asauca, asuddha*) and inauspiciousness of menstrual blood seems strange to the contemporary West until one looks into some bizarre attitudes and concepts of nineteenth-century Europe and America. For the affluent, paper-rich West, "feminine napkins" have been available to women for over a century, the even more discreet mini-tampons being a more recent innovation. No banishment from kitchen or dining areas and, with electric washing machines a standard household item, no embarrassing garment stains in the laundry. But for occasional guarded TV ads, the monthly change for perhaps a third of the population goes without remark by male Western culture. India, with an entire "unclean" caste of men and women laboring in rivers and streams to wash clothes, takes a closer look at this female "disease" as if it were dangerously infectious and, ritually speaking, it is traditionally considered to be exactly that.
19. This bodily assumption of sacred fires is described at the close of TS 3.4.10 with reference to the sacrificer as the birthplace of Agni and therefore a proper temporary container outside of the hearths. The term *atma-rohana* is not accepted by some Konasima authorities although ApSS.6.28.10-11 describes the procedure of bodily assumption immediately after transfer into *arani*. On the wood for *arani, asvattha* grown on a *sami* tree, see ApSS 5.1.2. Frederick Smith 1987: 92–96 details the techniques of both churning and consignment of fire; cf. Heesterman 1993: 94ff.
20. Frederick Smith 1987: 49 and n.168 describes the 1977 *paundarika* sacrifice. A similar event occurred in coastal Andhra during a neighborhood festival when the featured goddess's ritual pole suddenly fell to the ground. In the ensuing pandemonium a German scholar-observer seen running for cover was blamed for carrying off the goddess in his beard.

CHAPTER 3

1. Further details on wives, marriage, children, and the householder's life are discussed in Chapter 5.
2. More details on *antyesti*, the offering of the body, *sraddha*, ancestor rituals, and afterlife are discussed in Chapter 6.
3. The *musi-vayanam* is detailed in Chapter 5. For an extensive discussion of this special coastal Andhra funeral with a female Brahman ritualist, see Knipe 2003.
4. Avadhani or Avadhanulu is an honorific (from Sanskrit *avadhana*, "attention, attentiveness") signaling special ability to remember important matters, in this case, Veda. It is commonly affixed to Veda pandit names of those who have achieved the status of *krama-pathi*.

5. Manu 5.167–68 allows for remarriage and rekindling of fire; cf. Kane 1968–75, 4: 225.
6. A correction to the 1997 essay, "Becoming a Veda in the Godavari Delta" is acknowledged here: whereas both of his sons became *ghana-pathi* Samavedam senior did not achieve that rank.
7. Cf. Stephanie Jamison's remarks on hospitality 1996:182–84.
8. The quiet, virtually anonymous presence in Kakinada, the bustling headquarters of East Godavari District, of an *ahitagni* well known among Vedic Brahmans across South India was revealed by M. V. Krishnayya to the vice chancellor of Jawaharlal Nehru Technical University in Kakinada, Professor Alam Appa Rao. The vice chancellor published his sumptuously illustrated book *Kakinada. The Making of a University City* (Hyderabad: Geographica 2010) with biographical details on the educational, political, and cultural lights of the area with no mention of Mitranarayana or his famous predecessor, now deceased, Uppuluri Ganapati Sastri. Amends were made late in 2010 with a videotaped celebratory meeting and portrait photography of Mitranarayana and his wife Anasuya.
9. See Chapter 2, n. 8.
10. Only Bulusu Kamesvara's wife Satyavati was comparable. It is most probable that Venkatesvara' late wife, Sita Rama Laksmi, was equally well informed; less research time, however, was spent in Simhacalam than in Annavaram. Other *patni* might have contributed had they been allowed to speak freely, particularly in the early 1980s when their *srauta* lives were still fresh in mind. Laksmi Narasamamba was able to interview Anasuya, Lanka's wife, privately in the house, in 1991. Otherwise, on the rare occasion when she was present, Lanka would always answer questions directed to her. Widows (Sundari, Anasuya, Subbalaksmi, others) were always open and forthcoming.
11. See Knipe 2004a on "ritual subversion."
12. Being familiar with Indian books and the many creatures who dine on them, these elders would appreciate a comment by Frits Staal: "Books bound in India continue to fall apart but the Vedic Oral Tradition is still there" (2008: 252).

CHAPTER 4

1. On the Vedic textual tradition in general see Gonda 1975; Witzel 1987, 1997b; Parpola 1997, 2002b: 44–48; Patton 1994a, 1994b, 2004a; Holdrege 1994a, 1994b.
2. Bachelard 1964a, 1964b, 1969. This is also *in illo tempore*, "in that time," the "great" time (Eliade 1959: 80–113) when cosmically foundational events occurred, an age newly recovered and entered by living believers. By intuiting Veda the great *rsis* established both sacred text and ritual; those today who "enter" Veda live in that time writ large and even speak of themselves as

legatees of *rsis* whose names they recite twice daily and are believed to watch over them.

3. Staal 1989: 48.
4. On the *upanayana* and career of the *brahmacarin*, see Kane 1968–74, 2.1: 268–415; Brian Smith 1989: 92–101; Pandey 1969:111–40.
5. Pandits insist on Vedic oral transmission *ab origine*. It has been put forth that limited early writing of a Veda may have occurred, for example, in the *pada-patha* legacy; see Bronkhorst 1982; contra Falk 1993. On "orality and memory culture" and an aversion to written transmission of sacred texts see the important essay by Houben and Rath 2012.
6. On dating Vedic texts see n.1 above; Olivelle 1996: xxxvi–xxxvii on the Upanisads; Gonda 1977 and Lingat 1973: 20–23 on Apastamba's Sutras.
7. Bachelard 1969: 20.
8. Ricoeur 1995: 164; cf. 162–66.
9. On *sama-vartana* see further Heesterman 1968; Kane 1968–75, 2.1: 405–15; Pandey 1969: 146–52.
10. This Andhra specialty has afforded more than one pandit mentioned in this survey with nearly a fulltime career.
11. On *sakha* see Gonda 1975; Witzel 1987, 1997b; Renou 1947; Patton 2005: 31–36.
12. Of 401 names in one catalogue of Veda pandits in Andhra (Jeeyar 1976) only nine are listed as Rg Vedins with Asvalayana Sutra.
13. Jeeyar 1976 has only a single pandit listed for Andhra: "Kauthuma *sakha*, Sama Veda, Drahyayana Sutra." Three are given as "Ranayaniya *sakha*, Sama Veda," but with Asvalayana Sutra; possibly they acquired the Sama Veda after the Rg Veda.
14. Jeeyar 1976 lists ten Sukla Yajur Veda pandits for Andhra, all with Katyayana as Sutra, three of them in Madhyandina *sakha*, seven in Kanva *sakha*. Of the Kanvas three are in Kothapeta, East Godavari District.
15. A different tale accounting for this epithet came from another Taittiriya pandit: "Madhyandina students once challenged their guru and in anger he reciprocated 'You Candalas!' The curse of a guru cannot be reversed, only ameliorated. They pleaded for mercy and the guru relented. So exactly at noon for half an hour they are Untouchable Candalas. So they are excluded, have no right to eat with others due to caste pollution. We may not even talk to them! They have to keep to themselves!"
16. On the Vidhana texts for various *samhita* and the use of *vidhi* see Patton 2005: 27–34.
17. Still in use today in the Delta is another term for an assembly of learned Brahmans, *parisad*, one found in the earliest Upanisads. Cf. Olivelle 1993: 210 where he cites ApDhS 1.3.11.38.

CHAPTER 5

1. *The Cloudsplitter* (New York: HarperCollins 1998), 37.
2. Sanskrit *masa,* moon, month; *masika,* monthly; cf. English menses, from Latin *mensis,* month, Greek *men,* month, *mene,* moon.
3. That is to say, she disappears to the rear of the house. Velcheru Narayana Rao (1994: 128) precisely describes the Andhra Brahman house with its division into three areas, men in the front, women in back including the kitchen and the backyard with a well where women gather and servants enter. In between is a neutral zone where genders meet, the men entering discreetly by coughing or summoning a female to signal intended arrival. Cf. Marjatta Parpola (2000: 142–43) on Naputiri "ownership of territory and privacy."

   Regarding the period of impurity and seclusion, Holly Reynolds (1978: 100–113) reports on Madurai District, Tamil Nadu (including certain influence from Telugu Brahmans) that it is three to seven days, the first three being maximum pollution; also on Tami Nadu, Gabriella Eichinger Fero-Luzzi (1974); on the Namputiris in Kerala, M. Parpola (2000: 181). On an eighteenth-century ritual manual, Julia Leslie (1989: 283–87). Frederique Apffel-Marglin (1985: 56f, 72f, 234f) gives details from Puri, Orissa, where the female period is four days, including that of the goddess earth who menstruates once a year on Raja Sankranti in Jyestha, the hot season of May–June; during those four days no farmer may plow or use a cart and there must be no human sexual intercourse. Regarding lunar symbolism it might be observed that after its absence the moon is reborn on the fourth night.
4. ApSS 9.2.1-3. In Konasima this has been reported but not observed.
5. Knipe 1997 and 2003.
6. Cf. Kane (1968–75 2.1: 518 and n. 1208) citing the exact same ApDhS passage quoted from memory by Lanka. Trikandamandana 1.80c-81b, permitting the wife whose husband is away to perform *agni-hotra* with the aid of another, is cited by Frederick Smith (1987: 164f.). According to Konasima pandits the replacement could be, for example, a qualified son or nephew. Recent scholarly studies have illuminated the role of the *patni*. Stephanie Jamison (1996: 289 n.295, 292 n.20) translates a mantra from Maitrayani Samhita 1.4.3 addressed to the husband and wife during an *isti*: "You two have become the yoked team of the worship." Ellison Banks Findly marshals texts highlighting "the naturalness of the marital unit" in Vedic rituals (2002: 21) and Mary McGee (2002) convincingly summarizes the wife's *adhikara* to perform *srauta* rituals. Cf. also Leslie (1989: 102ff, 176ff.); H.-P. Schmidt (1987).
7. T. N. Madan 1985: 20.
8. Bruce Lincoln 1975; see also John Brough 1953; G. S. Ghurye 1972; Kane 1968–75 2.2: 479–501. On *pravara* see SKE 1.2: 979–1032.

9. Puberty rituals among Aiyar Brahmans in Kanyakumari District, Tami Nadu, are well described with case studies in Vasumathi Duvvury (1991: 111–32); she distinguishes between *vaidika* and *laukika* traditions and employs the methodology of van Gennep to understand puberty as separation, marriage as transition, childbearing as incorporation into the community of auspicious married women (*su-mangali*). From her perspective a female is not "fully auspicious" (Tamil *naranja su-mangali*) until she attains menopause and sees all her children married and settled (215f). On puberty and first menstruation among Namputiri in Kerala, M. Parpola (2000: 180–89). Cf. also N. N. Bhattacharyya 1980.
10. Further details on marriage rituals may be found in Kane (1968–75 2.1: 427–541); R. B. Pandey (1969: 153–233); M. Parpola's 2000 study of a Namputiri family in Panjal, Kerala, is the most thorough ethnography of a living Vedic community yet published; marriage and the lives of married women are covered on pp. 191–209; Duvvury (1991: 132–83); Ram Gopal (1983: 204–54); R. S. Khare (1976: 189–240); Baidyanath Sarasvati (1977: 114–205); Padfield (1908: 94–118), covering Brahman and other marriages in Telugu-speaking areas at the close of the nineteenth century.
11. Patrick Olivelle (1993: 45–53) discusses another version of this triple debt, Satapatha Brahmana 1.7.2.1–6, one that also treats *rna* payments as *avadana*. Analyzing a "theology of debts," citing Charles Malamoud (1980: 41–43, tr. 1996) and others, he notes that *rna* can mean a fault, crime, or guilt as well as debt. The association of debt and guilt in this context may have origins in the Rg Veda. On the wider context of debt see Donald Davis (2010).
12. On the ritual and theoretical details of these ten-day parallels see Knipe (2007) in German and the original English version, "Constructing a provisional body for the *preta* in Hindu funerals," delivered at Heidelberg University, 2004, in Knipe (forthcoming); also Knipe (2007: 184–86).
13. On *samskara* in general prior to death rites see Kane (1968–75: 2.1: 188–582); Pandey (1969); McGee (2004); Gavin Flood (1994); Lakshmi Kapani (1992: 1: 81–165); Sarasvati (1977: 82–113); Nicholas and Inden (1977: 35–66) on Bengali rites; Knipe (1991: 120–28). Gonda (1956) is a model study of the *simantonnayana*. Death and the final *samskara* are pursued at the close of this chapter and again in Chapter 6 concerning special rites for *ahitagni*.
14. R. Soma Reddy (1984: 154).
15. Taittiriya Upanisad 3.10.6; cf. 2.2.1 and food in the chain of the famous five-fire doctrine of Brhadaranyaka Upanisad 6.2.11-12 and Chandogya Upanisad 5.6-7. Some contents of this segment of Chapter 5 are forthcoming in Knipe, *Ritual and Folklore in the Godavari Delta*: "Jirna: Reflections of Andhra *ahitagni* on old age and dying."
16. United Nations World Population Prospects for 2005–2010, 2006, Table A.17, provided statistics for India in the period of the last *ahitagni* deaths in

Konasima: an average longevity of 66.4 years for women, 63.2 years for men. India was then ranked 139 of 195 nations. Modern medicine, a better diet, and proliferation of hospitals and clinics have sharply increased longevity; between 1980 and 2000 there was an astonishing 90 percent increase in the number of people in India who lived beyond 70.

17. Olivelle (1993: 161–82) makes clear the distinction between an early system of career choice of one *asrama* from among the four and a "classical" system that replaced it, with an individual moving sequentially through each one, student, householder, forest dweller, renouncer. In the classical system, reduplication in the last two, both of them meaning abandonment of house and village, essentially eliminated the forest dweller stage of life, one that is seldom mentioned by Konasima pandits.
18. ApDhS 2.9.21–23 details rules for the *samnyasin* with no fire and the forest hermit with one fire, both of them homeless wanderers begging for food.
19. Agehananda Bharati, an experienced renouncer-scholar, offers his own assessment (1961: 161f.); cf. Ghurye (1964: 220–37).
20. Olivelle's suggestion (1993:177).
21. Kane (1968–75 2.2: 843ff).
22. B. K. Smith 1989: 109.
23. Heesterman 1993: 71.
24. Madan 1985: 20.
25. Kane (1968–75 2.1: 583–93) discusses texts regarding widows; cf. M. Parpola (2000: 239–40); Julia Leslie (1989: 298–30); Vanaja Dhruvarajan (1989: 91–95). Regarding the Tamil Aiyar Brahman widow, Duvvury (1991: 224–27) details the pre-dawn stripping of the marriage thread on the eleventh day after her husband's death rather than the day of his cremation.
26. On details and case studies of the *musi-vayanam*: Knipe (2003). The report from Tamil Nadu (Duvvury 1991: 226–27) concerns the funeral for an auspicious Aiyar Brahman wife who dies before her husband, is dressed like a bride in a bright colored sari, covered with flowers, and considered to be Mahalaksmi. However, unlike the Godavari rite in which the deceased is sent to Gauri's heaven, the Aiyar rite described by Duvvury has no Brahman funerary priestess possessed by the spirit of the deceased and no presentations from natal and marital female relatives who are the only attendees.

CHAPTER 6

1. Regarding the Vratyas the citation is Jan Heesterman 1985: 52; cf. also his 1962, 1987, and 1993 publications. Groundbreaking observations since Heesterman have come from Asko Parpola 2012a, 2012b; cf. also his 1983 essay "The pre-Vedic Indian background of the *srauta* rituals," and his 1997, 1999, 2002 works;

Michael Witzel 2000; cf. 1987, 1997a; James Mallory 1989. Other secondary sources for the general study of Vedic ritual are plentiful; monographs on specific rituals are cited in notes below as each is discussed. The *Srautakosa* (SKE and SKS for English and Sanskrit sections, respectively) ed. by C. G. Kashikar and R. N. Dandekar was published in two "volumes," 1958–95, each with multiple "parts," for a total of eight books. The third and fourth projected volumes did not appear. Kane's *History of Dharmasastra* (1968–75) provides encyclopedic coverage in five volumes, some also with two parts. Ranade 2006 has expanded Sen 1978 and Renou 1947 with indispensable photos, line drawings, and textual citations. Among older general works that remain insightful resources are Hillebrandt 1897; Bergaigne 1878–83; Levi 1898; Hubert and Mauss 1898 (Eng. tr. 1964); Oldenberg 1923; Keith 1925; Dumont 1927, 1939; Rodhe 1946. More recent general studies include Potdar 1953; Renou 1954; Gonda 1965a, 1977, 1980; Kashikar 1968; Thite 1975; Knipe 1975; Malamoud 1976; Moody 1980; Krick 1982; Gopal 1983; Staal 1983; F. M. Smith 1987; B. K. Smith 1989; Sparreboom and Heesterman 1989; Patton 1994a, 1994b, 2004a, 2005; Minkowski 1991; Oberlies 1998–99; Staal 2008; McClymond 2008.

2. 4.14.2a, Patrick Olivelle's translation 1996: 134, emphasis added.
3. Bachelard 1964a: 7. Agni has been described by Jan Heesterman as the sacrificer's "external soul" (1987: 223), his "alter ego" (1993: 27, 29).
4. On the implements used in *grhya* and *srauta* rites see the excellent photographs and descriptions in *Yajnayudhani*, the Vaidika Samsodhana Mandala publication edited by T. N. Dharmadhikari in 1989; also Ranade 2006, an alphabetic list by Sanskrit name; Tachikawa et al. 2001: 41–47 and many photos; Sen 1978: 171–75; Ranade 1978 with photos and sketches following p. 447.
5. On the *naksatra* and *adhana* see the detailed analysis of Hertha Krick 1982: 9–38. The *naksatra* are discussed further in segment 4 of this chapter.
6. No animal is sacrificed in the *adhana*, but present are both a yoked white horse and a cart or "chariot" wheel that is rolled from the *garha-patya* to the *ahavaniya* as embers are transferred. Jan Heesterman sees vestiges of a more ancient program in which Agni was transported by chariot, perhaps indicating "a warlike expedition, especially when the accompanying mantras (referring to unnamed enemies) are taken into consideration" (1987: 232); cf. Sparreboom 1985: 65ff.; Krick 1982. As shown later, chariots play significant roles in several major sacrifices; cf. also Parpola 2005; 2012a: 249–50: Anthony 2007.
7. On the bondage of mutual hatred between sacrificers consider TS 1.1.9.8; 1.3.1.3; 1.5.7.6; 2.5.11.7; 2.6.4.2–4; etc.; cf. AV 10.6.1–35. ApSS 22.13 prescribes the performance of the *vighnana* (hammer) sacrifice to kill an enemy and elsewhere Apastamba provides numerous methods of using sorcery (*abhicara*) against rival sacrificers as well as defensive techniques (cf. ApSS 2.20.1; 3.14.1–3). In *The Broken World of Sacrifice* Jan Heesterman observes, regarding

ancient sacrifice, it is "from beginning to end a conflict." Competition among sacrificers, he notes, reflects the continuing redistribution of material goods necessary for life (1993: 33–41). On ritual rivalry, known by the Delta pandits as *srauta-kaksa*, the naming of enemies, and a comparative study of Vedic sacrificers and non-Brahman possession ritualists in the Godavari Delta, see Knipe, "Ritual subversion . . ." 2004a. Cf. B. K. Smith 1996.

8. On the *adhana* (also known as *agnya-dhana* or *agnya-dheya*) see Krick 1982; Sparreboom and Heesterman 1989; Moody 1980; Kane 1968–75: 2.2: 986–97; Hillebrandt 1897: 105–6; Keith 1925: 316–18; SKE 1.1: 1–84; on *punar-adheya* Krick 1982: 314ff; Hillebrandt 1897: 109; Kane 1968–75: 2.2: 997–98. Theodore Proferes (2007: 62–75) explores connections between the five peoples or tribes of the RV and other texts and the five fires, races of humans, and directions (four cardinal points plus the center).
9. Bodewitz 1976: 3; cf. 34–40, 144–46, 162–64. Bodewitz notes here the identification of sacred fires with breath, *prana*, both cosmic and human; inhalation and exhalation owning counterparts in sunrise and sunset.
10. Cited by Asko Parpola (1998: 227) in Bodewitz's translation (1976: 157).
11. On *agni-hotra*, in addition to Bodewitz's three volumes, see Parpola 1998: 227–28; Brian Smith 1989: 5, 156–57; SKE 1.1: 85–198; Dumont 1927, 1964; Kane 1968–75: 2.2: 998–1008; Hillebrandt 1897: 109–11; Keith 1925: 318–19; McClymond 2008: 97–101.
12. The term *darsa* refers to the first "appearance" of the emerging new moon, while a fortnight later the moon is *purna*, "full." Monographs on these two *istis* include Rustagi 1981, with sketches of ritual implements in chapter 10, and Hillebrandt 1880. Cf. SKE 1.1: 211–501; Keith 1925: 319–21; Kane 1968–75: 2.2: 1009–90 (including *pinda-pitr-yajna*); Dumont 1957–61; Jamison 1996: index; Brereton 2004; Frederick Smith 1987: 478–83. Tachikawa, Bahulkar, and Kolhatkar (2001) discuss with photos a *pavitresti*, modified form of *darsa-purna-masa*, performed in Pune in 1979.
13. On these dual deities functioning as one see Gonda, 1974: 363–88, 271–309.
14. Knipe 2006: 321; 1981.
15. Jamison 1996: 46.
16. Eliade 1961: 92–124, "The 'god who binds' and the symbolism of knots."
17. That is to say, *moksa*, liberation, or *nirvana*, cessation. Consider, among others, Rodhe 1946: 37–42 on freedom from the *pasa*, snare, bond, fetter.
18. On the significance of the grass belt around the wife see Stephanie Jamison's detailed discussion, "Making the wife ritually fit" (1996: 42–50); for a different interpretation, see Frederick Smith 1991. Ranade 2006: 269 has a photo of the *yoktra* loop being placed over the seated wife.
19. Jamison 1996: 61.
20. See note 4 earlier.

21. Dumont 1954: 205; this introduces Dumont's translation of TB 3.1.1–6.

22. Asko Parpola has aptly defined *naksatra* as "lunar marker stars" (1998: 239) along with arresting insights on several asterisms including Rohini, marker of the vernal and autumnal equinoxes, the festival times for Durga. Already in 1985 he had begun to connect Indus Valley seal symbols with Vedic patterns such as the *dhisniya* fires, seven sages, and seven stars of *Ursa major* (1985: 60, 122–40).

    The Taittiriya ritual use of *naksatra* is outlined in TB. 3.1.4–6; BSS 28.3–4 including a recommendation that *naksatra-isti* should be done at least three times in a life. Secondary sources on *naksatra* include Kane 1968–75: 5.1: 486–536; Krick 1982: 3–38; Dumont 1954; SKE 1.1: 591–93. Regarding the nine planets, *nava-graha* are discussed in Markel 1989 and Knipe 1995, the latter with attention to Godavari Delta beliefs and practices among Hindus in general. Several Veda pandits mentioned troublesome *grahas*; few praised beneficent ones for their favors.

23. Cf. ApSS 6.30.14. Frederick Smith (1987: 168) notes that this may be done in the absence of the sacrificer; Konasima pandits treasure this ritual enormously and would not miss its delights.

24. On the *agrayana* see Meyer 1937 and the brief overviews of Kane 1968–75: 2.2. 827–29 (*grhya*), 1106–7 (*srauta*) and Ram Gopal 1983: 427–29 (*grhya*), 542 (*srauta*); Keith 1925: 323–24; Hillebrandt 1897: 119–20; SKE 1.1: 502–15. Extraordinarily obtuse is Keith's remark (1925: 2.323): "That [the *agrayana*] was felt to be in any way sacramental, or even as inducing a special sense of community, is not to be seen in the Vedic evidence." The *agrayana* festival at the time of Durga-puja is in fact the most cohesive of all ritual times for Veda pandits and the wider Hindu populace and it is difficult to imagine this was not the case in the ancient period.

25. Patton 2000b: 43.

26. Thite 1969: 19.

27. The Heesterman quote is 1957: 29. On the *catur-masya* see also SKE 1.2: 646–767; Einoo 1988; Bhide 1979 based on Hiranyakesi Srauta Sutra and its Prayoga of Mahadeva Somayajin and including useful charts of hearth arrangements with multiple *vedis* for the three different rites, 214–16; Thite 1969 and 1975: 55–76; Kane 1968–75: 2.2: 1091–106; Keith 1925: 321–23; Hillebrandt 1897: 115–19. Although Matthew Sayers does not take up the *catur-masya* rites he convincingly situates the *pinda-yajna* and the earlier *pinda-pitr-yajna* in the broad context of developing Vedic texts, including the Taittiriya *srauta* and *grhya* series (2013: 40–69); cf. D. R. Shastri 1963: 54.

28. Sources on the *agni-stoma* include Caland and Henry 1906; Kane 1968–75: 2.2: 1132–203 with a diagram of fires and priests on the first page; Keith 1925: 326–32; Hillebrandt 1897: 124–34; Thite 1975: 49–55; SKE 2.1–3 covers first the *agni-stoma* in Parts 1 and 2, pp. 1–435 and pp. 439–894, respectively,

and then the other *soma* sacrifices in Part 3, pp. 1–200 with appendices on the sutras following, 201–80. V. G. A. Somayajulu, an industrious scholar at Andhra University, Vishakhapatnam, completed his PhD thesis in 1991 under the direction of Professor Akkubhatla Sharma. Somayajulu interviewed all the *ahitagni* discussed here and others in Hyderabad as well as Krishna and Guntur Districts. His thesis, submitted in cursive Sanskrit, remains unpublished, the author having retired to live in Hyderabad.

29. Plan 6.1 has "deeshnya-s" instead of the correct *dhiṣṇiya*, and "mancham" instead of the correct *mancam*.
30. Gonda 1965a: 316; cf. 315–462; on *diksa* in general Kane 1968–75: 2.2: 1136–41; Hillebrandt 1897: 124–34; Eliade 1958: 54–59; Thite 1970a; Proferes 2007: 120–24.
31. TS. 1.1.10e in Gonda's translation (1965a: 370).
32. On *soma*, including the motif of theft by an eagle, see the references in Chapter 2 n. 17.
33. See Heesterman 1997: 250.
34. O'Flaherty [Doniger] 1980b: 25–27, 46, 49.
35. On *upasads* see also SB 3.4.4.1–27 and Kane 1968–75: 2.2. 1151ff.
36. On *pasu-bandha* in general the monograph by Schwab 1886 covers details; Kane 1968–75: 2.2:1109–32 introduces some Sutras and commentaries not used by Schwab; cf. SKE 1.2: 770–898; Thite 1970b and 1975: 139–51; Malamoud 1988: Ram Gopal 1983: 542ff.; Dumont 1962, 1969; Keith 1925: 324–26; Hillebrandt 1897: 121–24; Jamison 1991: 103–106; Knipe 1997: 314ff. Other *sakha*, not consulted in Konasima, provide more details, e.g., SB 3.6.4.1–9.2.17. On the goat among other animal or human victims, cf. Brian Smith 1989: 176ff.
37. Parpola 2002a: 284–89; 1994: 256ff, and fig. 14.35; 1989.
38. Before asphyxiation became standard practice decapitation was normative. Later in this chapter the *agni-cayana* is described with its foundation sacrifice of male heads, originally placed in the first layer of the fire altar. A termite mound turret and a clay replica of a human head now serve as fore-offerings, followed by asphyxiated goats substituting for the decapitated man, horse, bull, ram, and goat.
39. Malamoud 1988: 3.
40. Jamison 1996: 146–49.
41. Thite 1970b: 245ff.; 1975:141ff.
42. Malamoud 1996: 146–49.
43. See Knipe 2007 and 2008a.
44. On the *pravargya* see ApSS 15.11.10-13 with Ganesh Thite's translation and notes; BSS 9.1–20 with C. G. Kashikar's translation and notes; SKE 2.1; Houben 1991, 2000a, 2000b, and the detailed fifty-nine-minute film by Jan Houben and Nandini Bedi, *The Vedic Pravargya Ritual*, performances in Delhi,

December 1996; Van Buitenen 1968; Kramrisch 1975; Thite 1975: 125–32; Keith 1925: 332–33; Kane 1968–75: 2.2: 1147–51; Rönnow 1929; Hillebrandt 1897: 134–36. On the origin and development of the cult of the Asvins and their role in the *pravargya* see Parpola 2005.

45. Jeeyar 1976.
46. Staal 1983: 1. 199–251.
47. Eliade 1963: 30; cf. Eliade 1954: 81. On naturally perforated stones, see Staal 1983: 2: 142–43 (plate 6) and index.
48. On the Manava as well as these two Sulba Sutras see the concise 1987 monograph by R. P. Kulkani; cf. also Seidenberg 1983 and Somiyajapad et al. 1983.
49. Frits Staal (2004: 553) noted that mantras "seal" the bricks in place.
50. For reviews of Staal 1983, see Brian Smith 1985a; Schechner 1981, 1986; Knipe 1986. Additional resources for study of the *agni-cayana* include Mus 1935; Converse 1974; Hillebrandt 1897: 161–65; Keith 1925: 354–56; Kulkarni 1987; Dumont 1951; Thite 1975: 83–98; Proferes 2007: 118–37.
51. Rg Vedins with KSS employ these two terms quite differently with respect to meters transposed in *sastra* recited by the *hotr (vyudha)* and a routine metrical arrangement (*samudha)*.
52. Malamoud 2004: 452. See Dumont 1951. For his twenty-day *aruna-ketuka* Baudhayana was followed by Baballa but considerable reliance was upon family *paddhati* for details. At the end of his *raja-suya* section Baudhayana 12.8 has a larger collection of sixteen waters, including water from dew, a whirlpool, and bovine products such as milk, curds, ghee, and the aul of a cow.
53. On the numeral *sodasin*, 16, and the fraction *kala*, 1/16th, see Gonda 1965a: 115–30 and on Prajapati's number 17 see Gonda 1984 and 1986.
54. Parpola 2005: 34–42; 2012: 311–12.
55. Other sources on the *vaja-peya* include Weber 1892; Kane 1968–75: 2.2: 1204–6; Thite 1975: 76–83; Keith 1925: 339–40; Hillebrandt 1897: 141–43; SKE 2.3: 45–119. Hans van Buitenen distributed an unpublished thirteen-page commentary on his film of the 1956 *vaja-peya* in Poona.
56. Asko Parpola sees the 180-day intervals of the year-long *sattra* as equinoxes, turning points of the sun, culminating on the Vivasvat (Sun) day and the *maha-vrata* day. He also suggests that the *maha-vrata* and the *asva-medha* may originally have been one ritual (1983: 49, 51).
57. Parpola 1999b: 120–31; cf. 2002a: 278–86.
58. Other sources on the *maha-vrata* include Rolland 1973; Gonda 1961 and 1963c; Meyer 1937; Jamison 1996: 96–98 and *passim*; Thite 1975: 100–103; Kane 1968–75: 2.2 1239–46; Keith 1925: 349–52. Sources on the *go-sava* include Thite 1975: 97–100; Keith 1925: 338, 475–76; Kane 1968–75: 2.2: 1212 n. 2644 dismisses it as "very strange" and probably "make-believe."
59. The episode of Indra shattered by drinking *soma* stolen from Tvastr occurs in TS 2.3.2.5–8. Not familiar to Konasima pandits are the details of VS 19–21 (e.g.,

19.93 where Sarasvati and the Asvins reconstruct Indra) and SB 5.5.4.1; 12.7.1–9.3.16. Although they are distinctly different in substance and ritual preparation TB 1.3.3.2 makes a united pair of male *soma* and female *sura*, a coincidentia oppositorum also of light and darkness. Apastamba recommends an extra goat sacrifice to Brhaspati in case the *yajamana* has previously vomited *soma* (ApSS 19.2.2); on the full *sautramani* see ApSS 19.1–10. Contemporay use of *soma-lata* appears to pose no threat of stomach illness. When tasted the *dora* found it to be a bitter, nasty juice unless laced with honey and one with no psychotropic effect.

60. Sources on the *sautramani* include Thite 1975: 83–89; Kane 1968–75: 2.2: 1224–28; Jamison 1991: 98–102; Rönnow 1929; Gopal 1983a: 166–67, 544–45; Keith 1925: 362–54; Dumont 1965; Hillebrandt 1897: 159–61; SKE 1.2: 899–943.
61. Puhvel 1970: 160; O'Flaherty [Doniger] 1980b: 85. Cf. also the exegeses of myths, symbols, and sexual mystereries behind the *asva-medha* in O'Flaherty [Doniger] 1980b: 149–64, 239–41, and *passim*.
62. Usually these dialogues are labeled by translators "obscene." Stephanie Jamison (1996: 73) rightly prefers to call them "sexual riddles" and notes: "We must treat these riddle dialogues as deeply serious attempts to approach and verbally harvest the mysterious forces released in sexual activity."
63. Asko Parpola, the leading authority in comparative studies of the Indus Valley seals and the Vedas, sees the Harappan water-buffalo sacrifice as the origin of the later Vedic horse sacrifice (2012b: 11; 2004: 483–85, 494–507; cf. Hitebeitel 1978. In addition to *asva-medha* sources already cited, see Koppers 1936; Kane 1968–75: 2.2: 1228–1239; Puhvel 1955 and 1970; Thite 1975: 89–97; Keith 1925: 343–47; Dumont 1948; Hillebrandt 1897: 149–53; Proferes 2007: 169–71; cf. also Lincoln 1986: 41–64 on sacrifice.
64. Sources on the *purusa-medha* include Weber 1864; Keith 1925: 347–48; Dumont 1963; Hillebrandt 1897: 153; Sauve 1970; Thite 1975: 23–28, 143; Parpola 2002b: 11–12.
65. Heesterman 1957: 225; other sources on the *raja-suya* include Falk 1986 on the significance of dice games; Kulke 1992, Kane 1968–75: 2.2: 1214–1223; cf. also Keith 1925: 340–43; Hillebrandt 1897: 141–47.
66. This separation is not complete. For example, ApSS 8.13 contains *pinda-pitr-yajna* to be done in the *saka-medha* portion of seasonal rituals. BSS 3.10 and 4.32 include *pinda-pitr-yajna* between attention to *agni-hotra* and *agrayana*. Nevertheless, both Apastamba and Baudhayana have separate *pitr-medha* sutras, the former closely following that of Bharadvaja. Cf. Gonda 1977: 616–21; Sayers 2013.
67. Analysis of this curious circumstance was presented to the Twelfth World Sanskrit Conference in Helsinki 2003: "*Somidevamma*: The wife who consumes *soma* in the Andhra Vaidika tradition." This will appear in Knipe, *Ritual and Folklore in the Godavari Delta.*
68. On RV 10.16.16 see O'Flaherty [Doniger] 1981: 46 nn. 17–18. There are textual variants of *losta-citi* in the *pitr-medha* sutras containing practices reminiscent

of the *maha-vrara* and *asva-medha*, including sexually and socially transgressive dialogue, musical instruments, singing, dancing, slapping the right thigh, loosening hair, and fanning (in this case, the urn of bones). No living memory supplies information regarding coastal Andhra performance of this version. Kane 1968–75: 4: 251–53 volunteers that the rite was assurance to the deceased of his wife's continuing fidelity, a curious observation since the wife agreed to sleep with a Sudra man for one or more nights. In the context of regenerating life in bones a better explanation might be the arousal of powers of fertility by realizing suppressed (and forbidden) desires. Once again it may be that certain features from the pre-classical era have endured in last rites. Finally, it is always important to note that women of the household insert numerous non-textual procedures into rites for the dying and the dead.

69. Knipe 2003: 77, 91 n45; Harman 1989: 134.
70. See Chapter 5 and n21.
71. Brian Smith 1989: 109; cf. 104–19.
72. Cf. ApSS 7.15.15–19. On the changing classifications of *pitr* in Vedic and post-Vedic texts see Kane 1968–75: 4: 343–48; Sayers 2013: 70–85 and *passim*.
73. For example, TB 3.12.1.20, a passage that Dumont (1951: 660) considered to be one of the oldest references to the doctrine of transmigration.
74. For further details of the ten-day construction, see Knipe 2007 and 2008a.
75. For coverage of the twelfth-day *sapindi-karana* and the ranking of ancestors, see Knipe 1977; Sayers 2013: 1–20.
76. On funeral rites and *sraddha* for ancestors in general, see Sayers 2013; Knipe 2007; Caland 1893 and 1896 (1967); Shastri 1963; Kane 1968–75: 4: 179–551; Pandey 1969: 234–74; Malamoud 1999; Padfield 1908: 193–245; Parry 1994; Schömbucher and Zoller 1999; SKE 1.2: 1033–132.

EPILOGUE

1. J. W. Elder 2006: *Encyclopedia of India* 3: 96–98.
2. On Bhaskara Misra's warnings, see Frederick M. Smith 1987: 205–207.
3. *New York Times*, March 17, 2008, pp. 1, 9. In 2014 it was reported that Indian Americans earned almost double the average annual American household income, $90,000 versus $50,000, higher than any other immigrant category, *New York Times*, January 26, 2014, p. SR 1.

Bibliography

SANSKRIT TEXTS AND TRANSLATIONS WITH ABBREVIATIONS

AB Aitareya Brahmana, ed. by T. Aufrecht (Bonn 1879); ed. by S. Samasrami, 4 vols. (Calcutta 1895–1906); tr. by A. B. Keith (Cambridge, MA, 1920).

AiA Aitareya Aranyaka, ed. by A. B. Keith (Oxford 1909).

ApDhS Apastamba Dharma Sutra, ed. by U. C. Pandey (Varanasi 1971); ed. and tr. by P. Olivelle (Delhi 2000); tr. by G. Buhler (Oxford 1886).

ApGS Apastamba Grhya Sutra, ed. by M. Winternitz (Vienna 1887); ed. by U. C. Pandey (Varanasi 1971); tr. by H. Oldenberg (Oxford 1886).

ApSS Apastamba Srauta Sutra, ed. by R. Garbe, 3 vols. (Calcutta 1882–1902; New Delhi 1983); tr. by W. Caland, 3 vols. (Groningen & Amsterdam 1921–28); ed. and tr. by G. Thite, 2 vols. (New Delhi 2004).

AsvGS Asvalayana Grhys Sutra, ed. by A. F. Stenzler (Leipzig 1864); tr. by H. Oldenberg (Oxford 1896); ed. and tr. by N. N. Sharma (Delhi 1976).

AsvSS Asvalayana Srauta Sutra, ed. by R. Vidyaratna (Calcutta 1874); partial tr. by H. G. Ranade (Poona 1981).

AV Atharva Veda Samhita (Saunaka), ed. by V. Bandhu, 5 vols. (Hoshiarpur 1960–64); tr. by W. D. Whitney, rev. ed. by C. R. Lanman, 2 vols. (Cambridge, MA, 1905); tr. by M. Bloomfield (Oxford 1897); K. L. Joshi et al., ed. and tr., 3 vols. (Delhi 2000); (Paippalada) ed. by V. Raghavan, 20 vols. (Lahore 1930–42).

BAU Brhad Aranyaka Upanisad, ed. by V. P. Linaye and R. D. Vadekar (Poona 1958); tr. by R. E. Hume (Oxford 1931); tr. by P. Olivelle (Oxford 1996).

BDS Baudhayana Dharma Sutra, ed. by E. Hultzsch (Leipzig 1929); ed. by U. C. Pandey (Varanasi 1972); ed. and tr. by P. Olivelle (Delhi 2000); tr. by G. Buhler (Oxford 1879).

BGS Baudhayana Grhya Sutra, ed. by R. Sarma Sastrai (Mysore 1920).

BhGS Bharadvaja Grhya Sutra, ed. by H. J. W. Salomons (Leiden 1913).

BhSS Bharadvaja Srauta Sutra, ed. and tr. by C. G. Kashikar (Poona 1964).

BSS Baudhayana Srauta Sutra, ed. by W. Caland, 3 vols. (Calcutta 1907–24); ed. and tr. by C. G. Kashikar, 4 vols. (Delhi: 2003).

ChUp Chandogya Upanisad, ed. by V. P. Linaye and R. D. Vadekar (Poona 1958); tr. by R. E. Hume (Oxford 1931); tr. by P. Olivelle (Oxford 1996).

GB Gopatha Brahmana, ed. by D. Gaastra (Leiden 1919).

HGS Hiranyakesi Grhya Sutra, ed. by J. Kirste (Vienna 1889).

HSS Hiranyakesi Srauta Sutra, ed. by K. S. Agase and S. S. Marulakara, 10 vols. (Poona 1907–32).

JB Jaiminiya Brahmana, ed. by Raghu Vira and L. Chandra (Nagpur 1954); partial tr. by H. Bodewitz (Leiden 1973, 1990).

JGS Jaiminiya Grhya Sutra, ed. and tr. by W. Caland (Lahore 1922).

JSS Jaiminiya Srauta Sutra, ed. by P. Sastri (Delhi 1966).

KausS Kausika Sutra, ed. by M. Bloomfield (*JAOS* 14 [1890] Delhi 1972).

KB Kausitaki Brahmana, ed. by B. Lindner (Jena 1897); ed. by H. Bhattacharya (Calcutta 1970); tr. by A. B. Keith (Cambridge, MA, 1920).

KGS Kathaka Grhya Sutra, ed. by W. Caland (Lahore 1925).

KKS Kapisthala Katha Samhita, ed. by Raghu Vira (Lahore 1932).

KS Kathaka Samhita, ed. by L. von Schroeder, 3 vols. (Leipzig 1900–10).

KSS Katyayana Srauta Sutra, ed. by A. Weber (Berlin: 1859); ed. and tr. by H. G. Ranade (Pune n.d. [c. 1978]); ed. and tr. by G. U. Thite, 2 vols. (Delhi 2006).

M Mantrapatha, ed. by M. Winternitz (Oxford 1897, Delhi 1985).

Manu Manava Dharma Sastra, ed. by J. H. Dave, 5 vols. (Bombay 1971–82); tr. by G. Bühler (Oxford 1886); tr. by W. Doniger and B. K. Smith (London–New York 1991); tr. by P. Olivelle (Oxford 2004).

MGS Manava Grhya Sutra, ed. by R. H. Shastri (rpt. Delhi 1982).

MSS Manava Srauta Sutra, ed. and tr. by J. M. van Gelder, 2 vols. (Delhi 1961–63).

MS Maitrayani Samhita, ed. by L. von Schroeder, 4 vols. (Leipzig 1881–86).

PB Pancavimsa Brahmana [also known as Tandyamahabrahmana], ed. by P. A. Chinnaswami Sastri and P. Pattabhirama Sastri, 2 vols. (Benares 1935–36); tr. by W. Caland (Calcutta 1931).

RV Rg Veda Samhita, ed. by T. Aufrecht, 2 vols. (Bonn 1877); tr. by K. F. Geldnrer, 4 vols. (Cambridge, MA, 1951); tr. by L. Renou, 17 fasc. (Paris 1955–69); tr. by R. T. H. Griffith, 2 vols. (London 1896), 2d ed. by J. L. Shastri (Delhi 1973); partial tr. by W. Doniger O'Flaherty (London–New York 1981); tr. by S. W. Jamison and J. Brereton, 3 vols. (New York 2014).

SB Satapatha Brahmana (Madhyaindina recension), ed. by A. Weber (Berlin 1855); (Kanvilya recension), ed. by W. Caland and R. Vira (Lahore 1926); (Madhyandina recension) ed. by Y. K. Mishra (Varanasi 2004); tr. by J. Eggeling, 5 vols. (Oxford 1882–1900).

SGS Sankhayana Grhya Sutra, tr. by H. Oldenberg (Oxford 1896); ed. and tr. by S. R. Sehgal (Delhi 1960); ed. and tr. by S. G. Rai (Varanasi 1995).

SSS Sankhayana Srauta Sutra, ed. by A. Hillebrandt, 2 vols. (Calcutta 1888); tr. by W. Caland (Nagpur 1953); partial tr. by J. Gonda (Amaterdam 1982).

SV Sama Veda(Jaiminiya) ed. by W. Caland (Breslau 1907); (Ranayaniya) tr. by J. Stevenson (London 1842, Varanasi 1961), tr. by R. T. H. Griffiths, 4th ed. 1893, Varanasi 19630).

TA Taittiriya Aranyaka, ed. by R. L. Mitra (Calcutta 1872); Ananda Sanskrit Series (Poona 1898); ed. by T. N. Dharmadhikari (Delhi 1984).

TB Taittiriya Brahmana, ed. by N. S. Godbole and H. Apte, 3 vols. (Poona 1934–38); ed. by A. M. Sastri (Mysore 1908–12, Delhi 1985); tr. by R. L. Mitra, 4 vols. (Calcutta 1885, Osnabrück 1981).

TS Taittiriya Samhita, ed. by A. Weber, 2 vols. (Leipzig 1871–72); ed. 8 vols. Poona 1978); tr. by A. B. Keith, 2 vols. (Cambridge, MA, 1914).

TU Taittiriya Upanisad, ed. by V. P. Linaye and R. D. Vadekar (Poona 1958); tr. R. E. Hume (Oxford 1931); tr. by P. Olivelle (Oxford 1996).

VadhGS Vadhula Grhya Sutra, ed. by Raghu Vira (Lahore 1932).

VadhSS Vadhula Srauta Sutra, ed. by W. Caland and Raghu Vira (Lahore 1933).

VaikhGS Vaikhanasa Grhya Sutra, ed. by W. Caland (Calcutta 1927); tr. by W. Caland (Calcutta 1929).

VaikhSS Vaikhanasa Srauta Sura, ed. by W. Caland (Calcutta 1941).

VarGS Varaha Grhya Sutra, ed. and tr. by P. Rolland (Aix-en-Provence 1971).

VarSS Varaha Srauta Sutra, ed. by W. Caland and Raghu Vira (rpt. Delhi 1971).

VS Vajasaneya Samhita, ed. by A. Weber (Berlin 1852); tr. by R. T. H. Griffith (Banaras 1899); ed. and tr. by Devi Chand (Delhi 1980).

Yajnavalkya Yajnavalkya Dharma Sasta, ed. and tr. by A. F. Stenzler (Berlin 1849).

OTHER ABBREVIATIONS

BhORI Bhandarkar Oriental Research Institute

EJVS *Electronic Journal of Vedic Studies laurasianacademy.com*

HR *History of Religions*

JAOS *Journal of the American Oriental Society*

PAPS *Proceedings of the American Philosophical Society*

SKE English section of Kashikar, C. G. and R. N. Dandekar, eds. 1958–95. *Srautakosa: Encyclopaedia of Vedic Sacrificial Ritual. 5 vols. Poona: Vaidika Samsodhana Mandala.*

SO *Studia Orientalia*

SUNY *State University of New York Press, Albany*

ZDMG *Zeitschrift der Deutschen Moregenländische Gesellschaft*

SECONDARY SOURCES

Alam, Muzaffar. 2000. "*Sharia* and governance in the Indo-Islamic context." In David Martin and Bruce Lawrence, eds., *Beyond Turk and Hindu*, 216–245.

Allchin, F. R. 1995. *The Archaeology of Early Historic India*. Cambridge: Cambridge University Press.

Anthony, David. 2007. *The Horse, the Wheel, and Language: How Bronze-age Riders from the Eurasian Steppes Shaped the Modern World*. Princeton, NJ: Princeton University Press.

Apffel Marglin, Frederique. 1985. *Wives of the God-King. The Rituals of the Devadasis of Puri*. Delhi: Oxford University Press.

Apffel Marglin, Frederique and John B. Carman, eds. 1985. *Purity and Auspiciousness in Indian Society*. Leiden: E. J. Brill.

Apte, V. M. 1939. *Social and Religious Life in the Grhya Sutras*. Ahmedabad: Virvijaya.

Asher, Catherine B. and Cynthia Talbot. 2006. *India before Europe*. Cambridge: Cambridge University Press.

Bachelard, Gaston. 1964a. *The Psychoanalysis of Fire*. Tr. by Alan C. M. Ross. Boston: Beacon.

Bachelard, Gaston. 1964b. *The Poeics of Space*. Tr. by Maria Jolas, Boston: Beacon.

Bachelard, Gaston. 1969. *The Poetics of Reverie*. Tr. by Daniel Russel. Boston: Beacon.

Bayly, C[hristopher] A. 1988. *Indian Society and the Making of the British Empire*. New Cambridge History of India 2:1. Cambridge: Cambridge University Press.

Bentour, Yael. 2000. "Interiorized fire rituals in Indian and Tibet." *JAOS* 120.4: 594–613.

Bergaigne, Abel. 1878–83. *La religion védique après les hymnes du Rig-Veda*. 3 vols. Paris: F. Vieweg.

Bhandarkar, D. R. 1946. "Were women entitled to perform srauta sacrifices?" *Proceedings of the All-India Oriental Conference*, Varanasi.

Bharati, Agehananda. 1961. *The Ochre Robe*. London: George Allen and Unwin.

Bhattacharyya, Narendra Nath. 1980. *Indian Puberty Rites*. 2d ed. New Delhi: Indian Studies Past and Present.

Bhide, V. V. 1979. *The Caturmasya Sacrifices with Special Reference to Hiranyakesi Srautasutra*. Pune: University of Poona.

Biardeau, Madeleine and Charles Malamoud. 1976. *Le sacrifice dans l'Inde ancienne*. Paris: Presses Universitaires.

Bloomfield, Maurice. 1899. *The Atharva Veda*. Strassburg: Trubner.

Bloomfield, Maurice. 1890. *The Kausika Sutra of the Atharva Veda*. New Haven, CT: American Oriental Society.

Bloomfield, Maurice. 1906. *A Vedic Concordance*. Cambridge, MA: Harvard University Press.

Bloomfield, Maurice. 1908. *The Religion of the Veda*. New York: Putnam.

Blumenthal, James, ed. 2005. *Incompatible Visions: South Asian Religions in History and Culture. Essays in Honor of David M. Knipe.* Madison, WI: Center for South Asia.

Bodewitz, Henk W. 1973. *Jaiminiya BrahmanaI.1-65, Translation and Commentary, with a Study of Agnihotra and Pranagnihotra.* Leiden: Brill.

Bodewitz, Henk W. 1976. *The Daily Evening and Morning Offering (Agnihotra) according to the Brahmanas.* Leiden: Brill.

Bodewitz, Henk W. 1983. "The fourth priest (the Brahman) in Vedic ritual." In Ria Kloppenburg, ed., *Selected Studies in the Indian Religions. Essays to D. J. Hoens.* Leiden: Brill, 33–68.

Bodewitz, Henk W. 1990. *The Jyotistoma Ritual. Jaiminiya Brahmana I, 66-364. Introduction, Translation, and Commentary.* Leiden: Brill.

Bosch, F. D. K. 1960. *The Golden Germ. An Introduction to Indian Symbolism.* The Hague: Mouton.

Boyce, Mary. 1975. "On the Zoroastrian temple cult of fire." *JAOS* 95: 454–465.

Boyce, Mary. 1979. *Zoroastrians: Their Religious Beliefs and Practices.* London: Routledge and Kegan Paul.

Boyce, Mary. 1986. "On the sacred fires of the Zoroastrians." *Bulletin of the School of Oriental and African Studies* 31: 52–68.

Brereton, Joel P. 1981. *The Rgvedic Adityas.* New Haven, CT: American Oriental Society.

Brereton, Joel P. 1986. "'Tat tvam asi' in context." *Zeitschrift der Deutschen Moregenländische Gesellschaft* 136: 98–109.

Brereton, Joel P. 1991. "Cosmographic images in the Brhadaranyaka." *Indo-Iranian Journal* 34: 1–17.

Brereton, Joel P. 1999. "Edifying puzzlement: Rgveda 10.29 and the uses of enigma." *JAOS* 119: 248–60.

Brereton, Joel P. 2004. "On the composition of the new and full moon rites." In Maitreyee Deshpande, ed., *Problems in Vedic and Sanskrit Literature,* 55–78.

Bronkhorst, Johannes. 2007. *Greater Nagadha: Studies in the Culture of Early India.* Leiden: Brill.

Bronkhorst, Johannes and Madhav M. Deshpande, eds. 1999. *Aryan and Non-Aryan in South Asia.* Cambridge, MA: Harvard University Press.

Brough, John. 1953. *The Early Brahmanical System of Gotra and Pravara.* Cambridge: Cambridge University Press.

Bryant, Edwin and Lauie Patton, eds. 2002. *The Indo-Aryan Controversy. Evidence and Inference in Indian History.* Richmond: Curzon.

Bühnemann, Gudrun. 1988. *Pūjā: A Study in Smārta Ritual.* Vienna: Institut für Indologie der Universität Wien.

Caland, Willem. 1893. *Altindischer Ahnencult. Das Sraddha nach den vorschiedenen Schulen dargegestelt.* Leiden: Brill.

Caland, Willem. [1896] 1967. *Die Altindischen Todten- und Bestattungsgebräuche.* Amsterdam: J. Müller.

Caland, Willem and V. Henry. 1906–1907. *L'Agnistoma: description complète de la forme normale du sacrifice de Soma dans le culte védique.* 2 vols. Paris: E. Leroux.

Carpenter, David. 1994. "The mastery of speech." In Laurie L. Patton, ed., *Authority, Anxiety and Canon. Essays in Vedic Interpretation.* Albany: SUNY Press, 19–34.

Charpentier, Jarl. 1920. *Die Suparnasage. Untersuchungen zur altindischen Literatur- und Sagengeschichte.* Uppsala: Akademiska Bokhandeln.

Clooney, Francis X. 1990. *Thinking Ritually.* Vienna: De Nobili.

Converse, H. S. 1974. "The Agnicayana rite: Indigenous origin?" *HR* 14: 81–95.

Coomaraswamy, A. K. 1941. "Atmayajna: Self-sacrifice."*Journal of Asian Studies* 6: 358–398.

Cotton, Arthur. 1854. *Public Works in India, Their Importance.* London: Richardson Brothers.

Cotton, Arthur. 1968. *Lectures on Irrigation Works in India* (Delivered at the School of Military Engineering, Chatham, December 1874), ed. by Uddaraju Ramam. Hyderabad: Jyothi Press.

Dandekar, R. N. 1979. *Vedic Mythological Tracts.* Delhi: Ajanta.

Dandekar, R. N. 1987 "Vedas." In M. Eliade, ed., *Encyclopedia of Religion.* NewYork: Macmillan, 15: 214–217.

Dandekar, R. N. 1962. "Some aspects of the Agni-mythology in the Veda." *Journal of the Oriental Institute of Baroda* 12: 4: 347–370.

Dange, Sadashiv A. 1971. *Vedic Concept of "Field" and the Divine Fructification.* Bombay: Bombay University.

Dange, Sadashiv A. 1979. *Sexual Symbolism from the Vedic Ritual.* Delhi: Ajanta.

Dange, Sadashiv A. 1982. *Vedic Myths in Social Perspective.* Hoshiarpur: Punjab University.

Dange, Sadashiv A. 1985. *Hindu Domestic Rituals.* Delhi: Ajanta.

Davis, Donald R. 2010. *The Spirit of Hindu Law.* Leiden: Cambridge University Press.

Desai, P. B. 1957. *Jainism in South India and Some Jaina Epigraphs.* Sholapur: Jaia Samskrti Sangha.

Deshpande, Madhav. 1990. "Changing conceptions of the Veda: From speech acts to magical sounds." *Adyar Library Bulletin* 54: 1–41.

Deshpande, Maitreyee, ed. 2004. *Problems in Vedic and Sanskrit Literature.* Delhi: New Bharatiya.

Devi, Konduri Sarojini. 1990. *Religion in Vijayanagara Empire.* New Delhi: Sterling.

Dharmadhikari, T. N., ed. 1989. *Yajnayudhani (An Album of Sacrificial Utensils with Descriptive Notes).* Pune: Vaidika Samsodhana Mandala.

Dhavalikar, Madhukar K. and Shubhangana Atre. 1989. "The fire cult and virgin sacrifice: Some Harappan rituals." In J. M. Kenoyer, ed., *Old Problems and New*

Perspectives in the Archaeology of South Asia. Madison: Wisconsin Archaeological Reports 2, 193–205.

Dhruvarajan, Vanaja. *Hindu Women and the Power of Ideology*. 1989. Granby, MA: Bergin and Garvey.

Diehl, Carl Gustav. 1956. *Instrument and Purpose: Studies on Rites and Rituals in South India*. Lund: Gleerup.

Doniger, Wendy. 1988. *Other People's Myths*. New York: Macmillan.

Doniger, Wendy. 1998. *The Implied Spider. Poetics and Theoology in Myth*. New York: Columbia University Press.

Doniger, Wendy. 2005. "The Clever Wife in Indian mythology." In James Blumenthal, ed., *Incompatible Visions*, 185–203.

Doniger, Wendy. 2009. *The Hindus. An Alternative History*. New York: Penguin.

Drury, Naama. 1981. *The Sacrificial Ritual in the Satapatha Brahmana*. Delhi: Motilal Banarsidass.

Dumont, Paul-Emile. 1927. *L'Asvamedha: description du sacrifice solennel du cheval dans le culte védique d'après les textes du Yajurveda blanc*. Paris: P. Geuther.

Dumont, Paul-Emile. 1939. *L'Agnihotra. Description de l'agnihotra dans le ritual védique après les srautasutras*. Baltimore, MD: Johns Hopkins University Press.

Dumont, Paul-Emile. 1948. "The Horse-sacrifice in the Taittiiya-Brahmana." *PAPS* 92: 447–503.

Dumont, Paul-Emile. 1951. "The special kinds of agnicayana (or special methods of building the fire altar) according to the Kathas in the Taittiriya Brahmana." *PAPS* 95: 628–675.

Dumont, Paul-Emile. 1954. "The istis to the naksatras in the Taittiriya Brahmana." *PAPS* 98: 204–223.

Dumont, Paul-Emile. 1957–61. "The full-moon and new-moon sacrifices in the Taittiriya-Brahmana." *PAPS* 101: 216–243; 103: 584–608; 104: 1–10; 105: 11–36.

Dumont, Paul-Emile.1962. "The animal sacrifice in the Taittiriya Brahmana." *PAPS* 106: 246–263.

Dumont, Paul-Emile. 1963. "The human sacrifice in the Taittiriya Brahmana." *PAPS* 107: 177–182.

Dumont, Paul-Emile.1964. "The Agnihotra (or fire-god oblation) in the Taittiriya Brahmana." *PAPS* 108: 337–353.

Dumont, Paul-Emile.1965. "The Kaulika-sautramani in the Taittiriya Brahmana." *PAPS* 109: 309–341.

Dumont, Paul-Emile.1969. "The Kamya animal sacrifice in the Taittiriya Brahmana." *PAPS* 113: 34–66.

Dundas, Paul. 1992. *The Jains*. London: Routledge.

Duvvury, Vasumathi K. 1991. *Play, Symbolism and Ritual. A Study of Tamil Women's Rites of Passage*. New York: Peter Lang.

Eaton, Richard M. 2000. "Temple desecration and Indo-Muslim states." In David Martin and Bruce Lawrence, eds. *Beyond Turk and Hindu*, 246–281.

Eaton, Richard M. 2005. *A Social History of the Deccan 1300–1761. Eight Indian Lives.* Cambridge: Cambridge University Press.

Eichinger Ferro-Luzzi, Gabriella. 1974. "Women's pollution periods in Tamilnad (India)." *Anthropos* 69: 113–161.

Einoo, Shingo. 1988. *Die Caturmasya oder die altischen Tertialopfer dargestellt nach den Vorschriften der Brahmanas und der Srautasutras.* Tokyo: Institute for the Study of Languages and Cultures of Asia and Africa.

Einoo, Shingo and Jun Takashima, eds. 2005. *From Material to Deity: Indian Rituals of Consecration.* New Delhi: Manoharlal.

Eliade, Mircea. 1954. *Cosmos and History. The Myth of the Eternal Return.* Tr. by Willard R. Trask. New York: Harper.

Eliade, Mircea. 1958. *Birth and Rebirth. The Religious Meanings of Initiation in Human Culture.* Tr. by Willard R. Trask. New York: Harper.

Eliade, Mircea. 1959. *The Sacred and the Profane.* Tr. by Willard R. Trask. New York: Harper.

Eliade, Mircea. 1960. *Myths, Dreams, and Mysteries.* Tr. by Philip Mairet. New York: Harper.

Eliade, Mircea. 1961. *Images and Symbols.* Tr. by Philip Mairet. London: Harvill Press.

Eliade, Mircea. 1963. *Myth and Reality.* Tr. by Willard R. Trask. New York: Harper.

Eliade, Mircea. 1964. *Shamanism. Archaic Techniques of Ecstasy.* Tr. by Willard R. Trask. New York: Bollingen.

Elizarenkova, Tatiana. 1995. *The Language and Style of the Vedic Rsis.* Albany: SUNY Press.

Erdosy, George. 1968. *Urbanisation in Early Historic India.* Oxford: British Archaeological Reports.

Erdosy, George, ed. 1995. *The Indo-Aryans of Ancient South Asia.* Berlin: Walter de Gruyter.

Falk, Harry. 1986. *Bruderschaft und Würfelspiel. Untersuchungen zur Entwicklungsgeshichte des Vedischen Opfers.* Freiburg: Hedwig Falk.

Falk, Harry. 1989. "Soma I and II." *Bulletin of the School of Oriental and African Studies*, 52: 77–90.

Falk, Harry. 1993. *Schrift im alten Indien.* Tübingen: Gunter Narr.

Falk, Harry. 2002, "How his *srauta* fires saved an *ahitagni*." *JAOS* 122.2: 248–251.

Findly, Ellison Banks. 1978. *Aspects of Agni: Functions of the Rgvedic Fire.* PhD Dissertation, Yale University.

Findly, Ellison Banks. 1979. "The 'child of the water': A revaluation of Vedic Apam Napat." *Numen* 26.2: 164–184.

Findly, Ellison Banks. 1981. "Jatavedas in the Rgveda: The god of generations." *ZDMG* 131: 349–373.

Findly, Ellison Banks. 2002. "The housemistress at the door: Vedic and Buddhist perspectives on the mendicant encounter." In Laurie L. Patton 2002a, 13–31.

Flattery, David S. and Martin Schwartz. 1989. *Haoma and Harmaline.* Berkeley: University of California Press.

Flood, Gavin. 1994. "Hinduism." In Jean Holm with John Bowker, eds., *Rites of Passage.* London: Pinter, 66–89.

Forbes, Georgine. 1996. *Women in Modern India.* New Cambridge History of India 4:2. Cambridge: Cambridge University Press.

Flueckiger, Joyce. 2013. *When the World Becomes Female: Guises of a South Indian Goddess.* Bloomington: Indiana University Press.

Freeman, John R. 1991. *Purity and Violence: Sacred Power in the Teyyam Worship of Malabar.* 2 vols. PhD Dissertation, University of Pennsylvania.

Fujii, Masato. 2012. "The Jaiminiya Samaveda traditions and manuscripts of South India." In Saraju Rath, *Aspects of Manuscript Culture*, 99–118.

Gai, G. S., ed. 1988. *Subject-index to the Annual Reports on Indian Epigraphy (from 1936 to 1972).* K. V. Ramesh, General ed. New Delhi: Archaeological Survey of India.

Gengnagel, Jorg, Ute Hausken, and Srilata Ramanujan, eds. 2005. *Words and Deeds. Hindu and Buddhist Ritual in South Asia.* Wiesbaden: Harrassowitz,.

Ghadially, R. 1988. *Women in Indian Society: A Reader.* New Delhi: Sage.

Ghurye, G. S. 1964. *Indian Sadhus.* 2d ed. Bombay: Popular Prakashan.

Ghurye, G. S. 1972. *Two Brahmanical Institutions: Gotra and Charana.* Bombay: Popular Prakashan.

Gonda, Jan. 1956. "The simantonnayana as described in the Grhyasutras." *East and West* 7: 12–31.

Gonda, Jan. 1960–63. *Die Religionen Indiens.* 2 vols. Stuttgart: Kohlhammer.

Gonda, Jan. 1961. "Ascetics and courtesans." *Adyar Library Bulletin* 25: 78–102.

Gonda, Jan. 1963a. *The Vision of the Vedic Poets.* The Hague: Mouton.

Gonda, Jan. 1963b. "The Indian mantra." *Oriens* 16: 242–297.

Gonda, Jan. 1965a. *Change and Continuity in Indian Religion.* The Hague: Mouton.

Gonda, Jan. 1965b. *The Savayajnas (Kausikasutra 60–68).* Amsterdam: North-Holland.

Gonda, Jan. 1966a. *Loka: The World of Heaven in the Veda.* Amsterdam: North-Holland.

Gonda, Jan. 1966b. *Ancient Indian Kingship from the Religious Point of View.* Leiden: Brill.

Gonda, Jan. 1965c. *The Ritual Functions and Significance of Grasses in the Religion of the Veda.* Amsterdam: North-Holland.

Gonda, Jan. 1965d. "Bandhu in the Brahmanas." *Adyar Library Bulletin* 29: 1–29.

Gonda, Jan. 1969. "The meaning of the Sanskrit term *ayatana.*" *Adyar Library Bulletin* 33: 1–79.

Gonda, Jan. 1970. *Notes on Names and the Name of God in Ancient India.* Amsterdam: North-Holland.

Gonda, Jan. 1974. *The Dual Deities in the Religion of the Veda.* Amsterdam: North-Holland.

Gonda, Jan. 1975. *Vedic Literature.* Wiesbaden: Harrasowitz.

Gonda, Jan. 1976. *Triads in the Veda.* Amsterdam: North-Holland.

Gonda, Jan. 1977. *The Ritual Sutras.* Wiesbaden: Harrasowitz.

Gonda, Jan. 1979a. "A propos of the mantras in the pravargya section of the Rgvedic Brahmanas." *Indo-Iranian Journal* 21: 255–271.

Gonda, Jan. 1979b. "Agni in Rgveda-samhita 9.66-67." *Journal of the Royal Asiatic Society* 2: 137–152

Gonda, Jan. 1980. *Vedic Ritual. The Non-solemn Rites.* Leiden: Brill.

Gonda, Jan. 1981. *The Vedic Morning Litany (Prataranuvaka).* Leiden: Brill.

Gonda, Jan. 1984. *Prajapati and the Year.* Amsterdam: North-Holland.

Gonda, Jan. 1986. *Prajapati's Rise to Higher Rank.* Leiden: Brill.

Gopal, Ram. 1983a. *India of Vedic Kalpa Sutras.* 2d ed. Delhi: Motilal Banarsidass.

Gopal, Ram. 1983b. "Vedic gods and the sacrifice." *Numen* 30.1: 1–34.

Gopal, Sarvepalli. 1989. *Radhakrishnan: A Biography.* New Delhi: Oxford University Press.

Gopalachari, K. 1976. *Early History of the Andhra Country.* 2d ed. Madras: University of Madras.

Gottschalk, Peter. 2000. *Beyond Hindu and Muslim. Multiple Identity in Narratives from Village India.* New York: Oxford University Press.

Gottschalk, Peter. 2013. *Religion, Science, and Empire. Classifying Hinduism and Islam in British India.* New York: Oxford University Press.

Goudrian, Namboodiri, V. 2002. *Srauta Sacrifices in Kerala.* Calicut: University of Calicut.

Griffiths, Arlo and Jan E. M. Houben (eds.). 2004. *The Vedas. Texts, Language and Ritual.* Groningen: Egbert Forsten.

Hancock, Mary E. 1995. "The dilemmas of domesticity: Possession and devotional experience among urban Smarta women." In Lindsey Harlan and Paul Courtright, eds., *From the Margins of Hindu Marriage: Essays on Gender, Religion and Culture.* New York: Oxford University Press, 60–91.

Hanumantha Rao, B. S. L. 1973. *Religion in Andhra.* Guntur: Welcome.

Harman, William. 1989. *The Sacred Marriage of a Hindu Goddess.* Bloomington: Indiana University Press.

Heesterman, J. C. 1957. *The Ancient Indian Royal Consecration.* The Hague: Mouton.

Heesterman, J. C. 1958. "Reflections on the significance of the daksina." *Indo-Iranian Journal* 3: 241–258.

Heesterman, J. C. 1962. "Vratya and sacrifice." *Indo-Iranian Journal* 6: 1–37.

Heesterman, J. C. 1968. "The return of the Veda scholar (*samavartana*)." In *Pratidanam* (The Hague: Mouton), 436–447.

Heesterman, J. C. 1983. "Other folk's fire." In Frits Staal, ed., *Agni. The Vedic Ritual of the Fire Altar.* Berkeley: Asian Humanities, vol. 2, 76–94.

Heesterman, J. C. 1985. *The Inner Conflict of Tradition. Essays in Indian Ritual, Kingship, and Society.* Chicago: University of Chicago Press.

Heesterman, J. C. 1987. "Vedism and Brahmanism." In Mircea Eliade, ed., *Encyclopedia of Religion.* New York: Macmillan 1987, vol. 15, 217–242.

Heesterman, J. C. 1993. *The Broken World of Sacrifice. An Essay in Ancient Indian Ritual.* Chicago: University of Chicago Press.

Heesterman, J. C. 1997. "Ritual and ritualism: The case of ancient Indian ancestor worship." In Dick van der Meij, ed., *India and Beyond. Aspects of Literature, Meaning, Ritual and Thought. Essays in Honour of Frits Staal.* Leiden: International Institute for Asian Studies, 249–270.

Heesterman, J. C. 1997. "Vedism and Hinduism." In Gerhard Oberhammer, ed., *Studies in Hinduism.* Vienna: Der Osterreichischen Akademie der Vissenschaften, 43–68.

Hillebrandt, Alfred. 1880. *Das altindische Neu- und Vollsmondsopfer.* Jena: Gustav Fischer.

Hillebrandt, Alfred. 1897. *Ritual-litteratur. Vedische Opfer und Zauber.* Strassburg: Trübner.

Hillebrandt, Alfred. 1927–29. *Vedische Mythologie.* 2 vols. Breslau. Tr. by S. R. Sarma, 1980. *Vedic Mythology,* Delhi: Motilal Banarsidass.

Hiltebeitel, Alf. 1978. "The Indus Valley 'Proto-Siva.'" *Anthropos* 73: 767–797.

Hiltebeitel, Alf. 1988–91. *The Cult of Draupadi.* 2 vols. Chicago: University of Chicago Press.

Hoch, Hans Heinrich. 1999. "Through the glass darkly." In J. Bronkhorst and M. M. Deshpande, eds., *Aryan and Non-Aryan in South Asia,* 145–174.

Hoch, Hans Heinrich, ed. 2014. *Vedic Studies: Language,Text, Culture and Philosophy.* New Delhi: Printworl.

Holdrege, Barbara A. 1990. "Ritual and power." *Journal of Ritual Studies* 4: 2.

Holdrege, Barbara A. 1994a. *Veda and Torah. Transcending the Textuality of Scripture.* Albany: SUNY Press.

Holdrege, Barbara A. 1994b. "Vedas and Brahmanas: Cosmogonic paradigms and the definition of canon." In L. L. Patton, ed., *Authority, Anxiety and Canon,* 35–66.

Holdrege, Barbara A. 1998. "Meaningless ritual, agonistic sacrifice, or ritual taxonomy?" *Critical Review of Books in Religion.* Bellingham, WA.

Hopkins, E. Washburn. 1908. "The mediatorial office of the Vedic Fire-god." *Harvard Theological Review* 1.4: 507–512.

Houben, Jan E. M. 1991. *The Pravargya Brahmana of the Taittiriya Aranyaka: An Ancient Commentary on the Pravargya Ritual.* Delhi: Motilal Banarsidass.

Houben, Jan E. M., ed. 1996. *Ideology and Status of Sanskrit. Contributions to the History of the Sanskrit Language.* New York: Brill.

Houben, Jan E. M. 1999. "To kill or not to kill the sacrificial animal (*yajna-pasu*)?" In J. E. M. Houben and K. R. van Kooij, eds., *Violence Denied.* Leiden: Brill.

Houben, Jan E. M. 2000a. "The ritual pragmatics of a Vedic hymn: The 'riddle hymn' and the pravargya ritual." *JAOS* 120.4: 499–536.

Houben, Jan E. M. 2000b. "On the earliest attested forms of the Pravargya: Vedic references to Gharma-Pravargya." *Indo-Iranian Journal* 43: 1–25.

Houben, Jan E. M. 2001. "The Vedic horse-sacrifice and the changing use of the term *ahimsa*." In Klaus Karttunen and Petteri Koskikalio, eds., *Vidyarnavandanam*, 279–290.

Houben, Jan E. M. 2003. "The *soma-haoma* problem." *EJVS*.

Houben, Jan E. M. 2009. "Transmission sans ecriture dans l'Inde ancienne: Enigme et structure rituelle." *Ecrire et Transmettre en Inde Classique*, 81–105.

Houben, Jan E. M. and Saraju Rath. 2012. "Introduction: Manuscript culture and its impact in 'India.'" In Saraju Rath, ed., *Aspects of Manuscript Culture*, 1–54.

Howard, Wayne. 1977. *Samavedic Chant*. New Haven, CT: Yale University Press.

Howard, Wayne. 1986. *Veda Recitation in Varanasi*. Delhi: Motilal Banarsidass.

Hubert, Henri and Marcel Mauss. 1964. *Sacrifice: Its Nature and Function*. Tr. from 1898 edition by W. D. Halls. Chicago: University of Chicago Press.

Ikari, Yasuke. 1983. "Ritual preparation of the mahavira and ukha pots." In Frits Staal, ed., *Agni*, 168–177.

Irschick, Eugene. 1994. *Dialogue and History: Constructing South India, 1795–1895*. Berkeley: University of California Press.

Irwin, John C. 1982. "The sacred anthill and the cult of the primordial mound." *HR* 21: 339–360.

Jain, Jyoti Prasad. 1964. *The Jaina Sources of the History of Ancient India, 100 B.C.–A.D. 900*. Delhi: Munshi Ram Manohar Lal.

Jaini, Padmanabh S. 1979. *The Jaina Path of Purification*. Berkeley: University of California Press.

Jamison, Stephanie W. 1991. *The Ravenous Hyena and the Wounded Sun. Myth and Ritual in Ancient India*. Ithaca, NY: Cornell University Press.

Jamison, Stephanie W. 1996. *Sacrificed Wife / Sacrificer's Wife. Women, Ritual and Hospitality in Ancient India*. New York: Oxford University Press.

Jamison, Stephanie W. 2005. "Vedic Hinduism." In Arvind Sharma, ed., *New Focus on Hinduism*. Delhi: DK Print World.

Jamison, Stephanie W. and Joel P. Brereton. 2014. *The Rigveda: The Earliest Religious Poetry of India*. 3 vols. New York: Oxford University Press.

Jawaharlal, G. 1994. *Jainism in Andhra (as depicted in inscriptions)*. Hyderabad: A. B. Suvarna Jaina Sea Fund.

Jeeyar, Tridandi Srimannarayana Ramanuja, compiler. 1976. *Veda Pandits in India. Volume 2 (Andhra Veda Pandits)*. Srirangam-Hyderabad: Published by the compiler.

Johansson, Karl Ferdinand. 1910. *Solfågeln i Indien. En Religionshistorisk-Mytologisk Studie*. Uppsala: Akademiska Bokhandeln.

Johansson, Karl Ferdinand. 1917. *Über die altindische Göttin Dhisana und Verwandtes.* Uppsala: Akademiska Bokhandeln

Johnson, Willard. 1980. *Poetry and Speculation in the Rg Veda.* Berkeley: University of California Press.

Jones, Kenneth W. 1989. *Socio-religious Reform Movements in British India.* New Cambridge History of India, 3:1. Cambridge: Cambridge University Press.

Joshi, J. R. 1972 "Prajapati in Vedic mythology and ritual." *Annals of the BhORI* 53: 101–125.

Kaelber, Walter G. 1989. *Tapta-Marga: Asceticism and Initiation in Vedic India.* Albany: SUNY Press.

Kane, P. V. 1968–75. *History of Dharmasastra.* Rev. ed. 5 vols. Poona: BhORI.

Kapani, Lakshmi. 1992. *La Notion de samskara dans l'Inde Brahmanique et Bouddhique.* 2 vols. Paris: Edition-Diffusion de Boccard.

Kapferer, Bruce. 1997. *The Feast of the Sorcerer. Practices of Consciousness and Power.* Chicago: University of Chicago Press.

Kashikar, C. G. 1968. *A Survey of the Srauta-sutras.* Bombay: University of Bombay.

Kashikar, C. G. 1973. "Apropos of the Pravargya." *Journal of the Center of Advanced Sanskrit Studies* 1: 1–10.

Kashikar, C. G. and R. N. Dandekar, eds. 1958–95. *Srautakosa: Encyclopaedia of Vedic Sacrificial Ritual.* 5 vols. Poona: Vaidika Samsodhana Mandala.

Keith, A. B. 1925. *Religion and Philosophy of the Veda and Upanishads.* 2 vols. Cambridge, MA: Harvard University Press.

Keith, A. B. and A. A. Macdonell. [1912] 1967. *Vedic Index of Names and Subjects.* Delhi: Motilal Banarsidass.

Kelting, Whitney M. 2001. *Singing to the Jains: Jain Laywomen, Mandal Singing, and the Negotiations of Jain Devotion.* New York: Oxford University Press.

Khare, R. S. 1976. *The Hindu Hearth and Home.* New Delhi: Vikas.

Knipe, David M. 1967. "The heroic theft: Myths from Rgveda IV and the ancient Near East." *HR* 6: 328–360.

Knipe, David M. 1975, rpt 1980. *In the Image of Fire. Vedic Experiences of Heat.* Varanasi: Motilal Banarsidass.

Knipe, David M. 1977. "*Sapindikarana*: The Hindu rite of entry into Heaven." In Frank E. Reynolds and Earle H. Waugh eds., *Religious Encounters with Death. Insights from the History and Anthropolgy of Religions.* University Park and London: Pennsylvania State University Press,111–124.

Knipe, David M. 1981. "Midwives of destiny." Part of a paper presented to the Annual Meeting of the American Academy of Religion, San Francisco, unpublished.

Knipe, David M. 1986. Review symposium on *Agni: The Vedic Ritual of the Fire Altar. Journal of Asian Studies* 45: 355–363.

Knipe, David M. 1987. "Priesthood, Hindu." In Mircea Eliade, ed., *The Encyclopedia of Religion.* New York: Macmillan, 11: 539–542.

Knipe, David M. 1989: "Night of the growing dead: A cult of Virabhadra in coastal Andhra." In Alf Hiltebeitel, ed., *Criminal Gods and Demon Devotees. Essays on the Guardians of Popular Hinduism.* Albany: SUNY Press, 123–156.

Knipe, David M. 1991. *Hinduism: Experiments in the Sacred.* San Francisco: Harper.

Knipe, David M. 1995. "Softening the cruelty of god: Folklore, ritual and the planet Sani (Saturn) in southeast India." In David Shulman, ed., *Syllables of Sky: Studies in South Indian Civilization. In Honour of Velcheru Narayana Rao.* New Delhi: Oxford University Press, 206–248.

Knipe, David M. 1997. "Becoming a Veda in the Godavari Delta." In Dick van der Meij, ed., *India and Beyond. Aspects of Literature, Meaning, Ritual and Thought. Essays in Honour of Frits Staal.* Leiden: International Institute for Asian Studies, 306–332.

Knipe, David M. 2001. "Balancing *raudra* and *santi*: Rage and repose in states of possession." In Klaus Karttunen and Petteri Koskikallio, eds., *Vidyarnavavandanam. Essays in Honour of Asko Parpola.* Helsinki: SO, 343–357.

Knipe, David M. 2003. "When a wife dies first: The *musivayanam* and a female Brahman ritualist in coastal Andhra." In Liz Wilson, ed., *The Living and the Dead: The Social Dimensions of Death in South Asian Religions.* Albany: SUNY Press, 51–93.

Knipe, David M. 2004a. "Ritual subversion: Reliable enemies and suspect allies. In A. Griffiths and J. E. M. Houben, eds., *The Vedas: Texts, Language and Ritual.* Groningen: Egbert Forsten, 433–448.

Knipe, David M. 2004b. "Sowing for the grim reaper: Gardens of the *preta*." In Maitreyee Deshpande, ed., *Problems in Vedic and Sanskrit Literature,* 50–57.

Knipe, David M. 2004c. "Fire." In *The Encyclopedia of Religion.* 2d ed. New York: Macmillan.

Knipe, David M. 2005. "Rivalries inside out: Personal history and possession ritualism in coastal Andhra." *Indian Folklore Research Journal* 2: 5, 1–33.

Knipe, David M. 2006. "Devi." In Stanley Wolpert, ed., *Encyclopedia of India.* New York: Scribner, 1: 319–324.

Knipe, David M. 2007. "Zur Rolle des 'provisorischen Körpers' für den Verstorbenden in hinduistischen Bestattungen." In Jan Assmann, Franz Maciejewski, and Axel Michaels, eds., *Der Abschied von den Toten. Trauerrituale im Kulturvergleich.* 2d ed. Göttingen: Walstein, 62–81.

Knipe, David M. 2008a. "Make that sesame on rice, please! Appetites of the dead in Hinduism." *Indian Folklore Research Journal* 5: 27–45.

Knipe, David M. 2008b "Hindu eschatology." In Jerry L. Walls, ed., *The Oxford Handbook on Eschatology.* New York: Oxford University Press, 170–190.

Knipe, David M. Forthcoming. *Ritul and Folklore in the Godavari Delta.*

Kochhar, Rajesh. 2000. *The Vedic People. Their History and Geography.* Hyderabad: Orient Longman.

Koppers, Wilhelm. 1936. "Pferdopfer und Pferdekult der Indogermanen." *Wiener Beitrage zur Kultgeschichte und Linguistik* 4: 202–409.

Kramrisch, Stella. 1975."The Mahavira vessel and the plant putika." *JAOS* 95: 222–235.

Krick, Hertha.1982. *Das Ritual der Feuergrüdung (Agnyadheya)*. Ed. G. Oberhammer. Vienna: Ősterreichische Akademie der Wissenschaften.

Krishna, B. V. 1973. *History of the Eastern Chalukyas of Vengi*. Hyderabad: Andhra Pradesh Sahitya Academy.

Krishnamacharlu, C. R. [1940] 1988. *Subject Index to the Annual Reports on Indian Epigraphy from 1887 to 1936*. New Delhi: Archaeological Survey of India.

Krishnamurti, Bhadraraju. 1995. "A shift of authority in written and oral texts: The case of Telugu." In David Shulman, ed., *Syllables of Sky*. Delhi: Oxford University, 76–102.

Krishnamurthy, Salva. 1994. *A History of Telugu Literature from Early Times to 1100 AD*. Madras: Institute for Asian Studies.

Krishnarao, B. V. 1973. *History of the Eastern Chalukyas of Vengi*. Hyderabad: Andhra Pradesh Sahitya Academy.

Krishnayya, M. V. 2005. "Dattatreya worship in the popular Hinduism of coastal Andhra." In James Blumenthal, ed., *Incompatible Visions*, 171–183.

Kuiper, F. B. J. 1960. "The ancient Aryan verbal contest." *Indo-Iranian Journal* 4: 217–281.

Kuiper, F. B. J. 1975. "The basic concept of Vedic religion." *HR* 15: 107–120.

Kulkarni, Raghunatha Purushottama. 1987. "Layout and construction of citis according to Baudhayana-, Manava-, and Apastamba-sulbasutras." Poona: *BhORI*.

Kulke, Hermann. 1992. "The rajasuya: A paradigm of early state formation?" In A. W. van den Hoek, D. H. A. Kolff, and M. S. Oort, eds., *Ritual, State, and History in South Asia. Essays in Honour of J. C. Heesterman*. Leiden: Brill, 188–198.

Kulke, Hermann and Dietmar Rothermund. 2010. *A History of India*. 5th ed. London: Routledge.

Leonard, John G. 1970. *Kandukuri Viresalingam 1848–1919: A Biography of an Indian Social Reformer*. PhD Dissertation, University of Wisconsin.

Leslie, I. Julia. 1989. *The Perfect Wife. The Orthodox Hindu Woman according to the Stridharmapaddhati of Tryambakayajvan*. Delhi: Oxford University Press.

Leslie, I. Julia, ed. 1991. *Roles and Rituals for Hindu Women*. Madison, NJ: Fairleigh Dickinson University Press.

Levi, Sylvain. 1898. *La doctrine du sacrifice dans les Brahmanas*. Paris: Ernest Leroux.

Lincoln, Bruce. 1975. "Indo-Iranian *gautra." *Journal of Indo-European Studies* 3: 161–171.

Lincoln, Bruce. 1986. *Myth, Cosmos and Society. Indo-European Themes of Creation and Destruction*. Cambridge, MA: Harvard University Press.

Lingat, Robert. 1973. *The Classical Law of India*. Tr. by J. Duncan M. Derrett. Berkeley: University of California Press.

Lipner, Julius. 1994. *Hindus. Their Religious Beliefs and Practices*. New York: Routledge.

Long, Charles H. 1986. *Significations. Signs, Symbols and Images in the Interpretation of Religion*. Philadelphia: Fortress.

Lubin, Timothy. 1994. *The Domestication of the Vedic Sacrifice*. PhD Dissertation, Columbia University.

Lubin, Timothy. 2001. "Vedas on parade: Revivalist traditions as civic spectacle." *Journal of the American Academh of Religion* 69.2: 377–408.

Lubin, Timothy, D. R. Davis, and J. Krishnan. 2010. *Hinduism and Law: An Introduction*. Cambridge: Cambridge University Press.

Ludden, David. 1999. *The Agrarian History of South Asia*. New Cambridge History of India 4:4. Cambridge: Cambridge University Press.

Lyle, Emily B. 1984. "The circus as cosmos." *Latomus* 43: 827–841.

Macdonald, Kenneth S. [1897] 1979. *The Brahmanas of the Vedas*. Delhi: Bharatiya Books.

Macdonell, A. A. [1897] 1963. *Vedic Mythology*. Varanasi: Indological Bookhouse.

Macdonell, A. A. and A. B. Keith. [1912] 1967. *Vedic Index of Names and Subjects*. 2 vols. Delhi: Motilal Banarsidass.

Madan, T. N. 1985. "Concerning the categories *subha* and *suddha* in Hindu culture: An exploratory essay." In Frederique Appfel Marglin and John Carman, *Purity and Auspiciousness in Indian Society*, 11–29.

Madan, T. N. 1991. "Secularism in its place." In T. N. Madan, ed., *Religion in India*. Delhi: Oxford University Press, 394–411.

Mahony, William K. 1998. *The Artful Universe. An Introduction to the Vedic Religious Imagination*. Albany: SUNY Press.

Malamoud, Charles. 1976a."Terminer le sacrifice." In Madeleine Biardeau and Charles Malamoud, ed., *Le sacrifice dans l'Inde ancienne*. Paris: Press Universitaire, 155–204.

Malamoud, Charles. 1976b. *Village et forêt dans l'idéologie de l'Inde brahmanique*. Paris : Archives européennes de sociologie.

Malamoud, Charles. 1977. *Le svadhyaya: récitation personelle du Veda. Taittiriya-Aranyaka, livre II*. Paris: Editions de Boccard.

Malamoud, Charles. 1980. "Theologie de la dette dans les Brahmana." *Purusartha: Science Sociales en Asie du Sud* 4: 39–62.

Malamoud, Charles. 1988. "Paths of the knife: Carving up the victim in Vedic sacrifice." In Richard F. Gombrich, ed., *Indian Ritual and Its Exegesis*. Delhi: Oxford University, 1–14.

Malamoud, Charles. 1996. *Cooking the World: Ritual and Thought in Ancient Indi*. Tr. David G. White. Delhi: Oxford University Press.

Malamoud, Charles. 1999. "Le sacrifice des os." In Elisabeth Schömbucher and Claus Peter Zoller, eds., *Ways of Dying*, 135–149.

Malamoud, Charles. 2004. "A note on abistaka (Taittitiya Aranyanka I)." In A. Griffiths and J. E. M. Houben, eds., *The Vedas: Texts, Language and Ritual.* Groningen: Egbert Forsten, 449–455.

Mallory, James P. 1989. *In Search of the Indo-Europeans: Language, Archaeology and Myth.* London: Thames and Hudson.

Mangalam, S. J. 1980. "Vengi: A study of its history and historiography." *Bulletin of the Deccan College Research Institute* 40: 96–107.

Marriott, McKim. 1976. "Hindu transactions; diversity without dualism." In Bruce Kapferer, ed., *Transaction and Meaning.* Philadelphia: Institute for the Study of Human Issues, 109–142.

Marriott, McKim and Ronald B. Inden. 1974. "Caste systems." In *Encyclopaedia Brittannica,* 3: 982–991.

Markel, Stephen A. 1989. *The Origin and Early Development of the Nine Planetary Deities (navagrahas).* PhD Dissertation, University of Michigan.

Martin, David G. and Bruce B. Lawrence, eds. 2000. *Beyond Turk and Hindu. Rethinking Religious Identities in Islamicate South Asia.* Gainesville: University Press of Florida.

Maurer, Walter Harding, tr. 1986. *Pinnacles of India Past: Selections from the Rgveda.* Amsterdam: John Benjamin.

McClymond, Kathryn. 1999. *In the Matter of Sacrifice. A Comparative Study of Vedic and Jewish Sacrifice.* PhD Dissertation, University of California.

McClymond, Kathryn. 2008. *Beyond Sacred Violence: A Comparative Study of Sacrifice.* Baltimore, MD: Johns Hopkins University Press.

McGee, Mary. 1998. "Religious studies: Vedic and classical Hinduism." In J. W. Elder, E. C. Dimock, and A. Embree, eds., *India's Worlds and U. S. Scholars: 1947–1997.* New Delhi: Manohar, 419–431.

McGee, Mary. 2002. "Ritual rights: The gender implications of *adhikara.*" In Laurie L. Patton, 2002a: 32–50.

McGee, Mary. 2004. "Samskara." In Sushil Mittal and Gene Thursby, eds., *The Hindu World.* New York: Routledge, 332–356.

Meyer, J. J. 1937. *Trilogie altindischer Mächte und Feste der Vegetation.* 3 vols. Zurich-Leipzig: May Niehan.

Michaels, Axel. 2005. "Samkalpa. The Beginnings of a Ritual." In J. Gengnagel, U. Hausken, and S. Ramanujan, eds., *Words and Deeds,* 45–64.

Michell, George. 1992. *The Vijayanagara Courtly Style.* New Delhi: American Institute of Indian Studies.

Michell, George. 1995. *Architecture and Art of South India.* New Cambridge History of India 1:6. Cambridge: Cambridge University Press.

Michell, George and Mark Zebrowski. 1999. *Architecture and Art of the Deccan Sultanates.* New Cambridge History of India 1:7. Cambridge: Cambridge University Press.

Minkowski, Christopher Z. 1991. *Priesthood in Ancient India. A Study of the Maitravaruna Priest.* Vienna: Sammlung De Nobili.

Minor, Robert N. 1987. *Radhakrishnan: A Religious Biography.* Albany: SUNY Press.

Moody, Timothy F. 1982. *The Agnyadheya: Establishment of the Sacred Fires. Ottawa: National Library of Canada.*

Moser, Heinke. 2012. "From palm leaves to a multimedia database . . ." In Saraju Rath, *Aspects of Manuscript Culture,* 139–156.

Muller, Klaus-Werner. 1992. *Das Brahmanische Totenritual nach der Antyestipaddhati des Narayanabhatta.* Stuttgart: Steiner.

Mus, Paul. 1935. *La Barabadur.* Hanoi: Extreme-Orient.

Narayana Rao, K. V. 1973. *The Emergence of Andhra Pradesh.* Bombay: Popular Prakasam.

Narayana Rao, Velcheru, translator. 1990. *Siva's Warriors. The Basava Purana of Palkuriki Somanatha.* Princeton, NJ: Princeton University Press.

Narayana Rao, Velcheru, 1994. "A Ramayana of their own: Women's oral tradition in Telugu." In Paula Richman, ed., *Many Ramayanas.* Berkeley: University of California, 114–136.

Narayana Rao, Velcheru and David Shulman. 2002. *Classical Telugu Poetry. An Anthology.* New Delhi: Oxford University Press.

Neoh, Kok-Boon. 2013. "Termites and human society in Southeast Asia." *International Association for Asian Studies Newsletter,* 66 Winter, 30–31.

Nicholas, Ralph W. and Ronald B. Inden. 1977. *Kinship in Bengali Culture.* Chicago: University of Chicago Press.

Nyberg, Harri. 1995. "The problem of the Aryans and the Soma: The botanical evidence." In G. Erdosy, *The Indo-Aryans of Ancient South Asia,* 382–406.

Oberlies, Thomas. 1998-99. *Die Religion des Rgveda.* 2 vols. Wien: Instit für Indologie der Universität Wien.

O'Flaherty, Wendy Doniger. 1976. *The Origins of Evil in Hindu Mythology.* Berkeley: University of California Press.

O'Flaherty, Wendy Doniger, ed. 1980. *Karma and Rebirth in Classical Indian Traditions.* Berkeley: University of California Press.

O'Flaherty, Wendy Doniger. 1980b. *Women, Androgynes, and Other Mythical Beasts.* Chicago: University of Chicago Press.

O'Flaherty, Wendy Doniger. 1981. *The Rig Veda.* New York: Penguin Classics.

O'Flaherty, Wendy Doniger. 1984. *Dreams, Illusions, and Other Realities.* Chicago: University of Chicago Press.

O'Flaherty, Wendy Doniger. 1985. *Tales of Sex and Violence: Folklore, Sacrifice and Danger in the Jaiminiya Brahmana.* Chicago: University of Chicago Press.

O'Flaherty, Wendy Doniger. 1988. *Other People's Myths. The Cave of Echoes.* New York: Macmillan.

Oldenberg, Hermann [1923]. *Die Religion des Veda.* 3d–4th ed. Stuttgart: J. G. Cottasche. Tr. by S. B. Shrotri as *The Religion of the Veda.* 1988. Delhi: Motilal Banarsidass.

Olivelle, Patrick. 1982. *Samnyasa Upanisads: Hindu Scriptures on Asceticism and Renunciation.* New York: Oxford University Press.

Olivelle, Patrick. 1993. *The Asrama System. The History and Hermeneutics of a Religious Institution.* New York: Oxford University Press.

Olivelle, Patrick. 1996. *Upanisads.* New York: Oxford University Press.

Orr, Leslie C. 2000. *Donors, Devotees and Daughters of God: Temple Women in Medieval Tamilnadu.* New York: Oxford University Press.

Padfield, J. E. 1908. *The Hindu at Home.* 2d ed. Madras: S.P.C.K. Depository

Pandey, Raj Bali. 1969. *Hindu Samskaras.* 2d ed. Varanasi: Motilal Banarsidass.

Parpola, Asko. 1968. *The Srautasutras of Latyayana and Drahyayana and Their Commentaries: An English Translation and Study, I.1.* Helsinki: Societas Scientiarum Fennicia.

Parpola, Asko. 1980. *Från Indus religion till Veda: Studier i de äldsta indiska religionerna.* Helsinki: Finnish Oriental Society.

Parpola, Asko. 1983. "The Pre-Vedic Indian background of the srauta rituals." In Frits Staal, ed., *Agni.* Berkeley: Asian Humanities, 2: 41–75.

Parpola, Asko. 1985. *The Sky-Garment. A Study of Harappan Religion and Its Relation to the Mesopotamian and Later Indian Religions.* Helsinki: Finnish Oriental Society.

Parpola, Asko. 1988. "The coming of the Aryans to Iran and India and the cultural and ethnic identity of the Dasas." *SO* 64: 193–302.

Parpola, Asko. 1989. "The 'fig deity seal' from Mohenjodaro: Its iconography and inscription." In Catherine Jarrige, ed., *South Asian Archeology 1989.* Madison, WI: Prehistory Press, 227–236.

Parpola, Asko. 1994. *Deciphering the Indus Script.* Cambridge: Cambridge University Press.

Parpola, Asko. 1995. "The problem of the Aryans and the Soma: Textual-linguistic and archaeological evidence." In G. Erdosy, ed., *The Indo-Aryans of Ancient South Asia,* 353–381.

Parpola, Asko. 1997. "The Dasas and the coming of the Aryans." In Michael Witzel, ed., *Inside the Texts, Beyond the Texts, New Approaches to the Study of the Vedas* (Cambridge, MA: Harvard Oriental Series), 193–202.

Parpola, Asko. 1998. "Savitri and Resurrection." In A. Parpola and Sirpa Tenhunen, eds., *Changing Patterns of Family and Kinship in South Asia* Helsinki: SO, 267–312.

Parpola, Asko. 1999a. "The formation of the Aryan branch of Indo-European." In Roger Blench and Matthew Spriggs, eds., *Archaeology and Language III: Artefacts, Language and Texts.* London: Routledge, 180–207.

Parpola, Asko. 1999b. "Vac as a goddess of victory in the Veda and her relation to Durga." *ZINBUN* (Memoirs of the Research Institute for Humanistic Studies, Kyoto University), 34.2: 101–143.

Parpola, Asko. 2000. "The religious background of the Savitri legend." In R. Tsuchida and A. Wezler, eds., *Haranandalaha.* Reibeck: Verlag für Orientalistische, 193–216.

Parpola, Asko. 2002a. "Proto-Indo-Iranians of Afghanistan and Initiators of Sakta Tantrism." *Iranica Antiqua* 37: 233–322.

Parpola, Asko. 2002b. "From the dialects of Old Indo-Aryan to Proto-Old-Indo-Aryan and Proto-Iranian." In N. Sims-Williams, ed., *Indo-Iranian Languages and Peoples*, 43–100.

Parpola, Asko. 2004. "From archaeology to a stratigraphy of Vedic syncretism." In A. Griffiths and J. E. M. Houben, eds., *The Vedas*, 479–515.

Parpola, Asko. 2005. "The Nasatyas, the chariot, and Proto-Aryan religion." *Journal of Indological Studies* 16–17: 1–63.

Parpola, Asko. 2012a. "The Dasas of the Rgveda as Proto-Sakas of the Yaz I-related cultures. With a revised model of the protohistory of Indo-Iranian speakers." In M. E. Huld, K. Jones-Bley, and D. Miller, eds., *Archeology and Language: Indo-European Studies Presented to James P. Mallory* Washington, DC: JIES Monograph Series No. 60, 221–264.

Parpola, Asko. 2012b. "Indus Civilization (–1750 BCE)." *Brill's Encyclopedia of Hinduism*. Leiden: Brill, 3–18.

Parpola, Asko. 2012c. "Crocodile in the Indus civilization and later South Asian traditions." In T. Osada and H. Endo, eds., *Current Studies in Indus Civilization*. New Delhi : Manohar, 9: 1–58.

Parpola, Marjatta. 1995. *Intialainen Kylä. A Village in India*. Helsinki: National Board of Antiquities.

Parpola, Marjatta. 2000. *Kerala Brahmins in Transition: A Study of the Namputiri Family*. Helsinki: Finnish Oriental Society (*SO* 91).

Parry, Jonathan. 1994. *Death in Banaras*. Cambridge: Cambridge University Press.

Pathak, V. S. 1960. "Vedic rituals in early medieval period: An epigraphic study." *Annals of the BhORI* 40: 218–230.

Patton, Laurie L., ed. 1994a. *Authority, Anxiety and Canon. Essays in Vedic Interpretation*. Albany: SUNY Press.

Patton, Laurie L, ed. 1994b. *Arguing the Vedas*. Albany: SUNY Press.

Patton, Laurie L. 1996a. *Myth as Argument: The Brhaddevata as Canonical Commentary*. Berlin: Degruyter Mouton.

Patton, Laurie L. 1996. "Myth and money: The exchange of words and wealth in Vedic commentary." In L. L. Patton and W. Doniger, eds., *Myth and Method*. Charlottesville: University Press of Virginia, 208–246.

Patton, Laurie L., ed. 2000a. *The Jewels of Authority: Women and Text in the Hindu Tradition*. New York: Oxford University Press.

Patton, Laurie L. 2000b. "Nature romanticism and sacrifice in Rgvedic interpretation." In Christopher K. Chapple and Mary E. Tucker, eds., *Hinduism and Ecology. The Intersection of Earth, Sky, and Water*. Cambridge, MA: Harvard University Press.

Patton, Laurie L. 2004a. "Veda and Upanisad." In S. Mittal and G. Thursby, eds., *The Hindu World*. New York: Routledge, 37–51.

Patton, Laurie L. 2004b. "When the fire goes out the wife shall fast: Notes on women's agency in the Asvalayana Grya Sutra (AGS)." In Maitreyee Deshpande, ed., *Problems in Vedic and Sanskrit Literature*, 294–305.

Patton, Laurie L. 2005. *Bringing the Gods to Mind. Mantras and Ritual in Early Indian Sacrifice*. Berkeley: University of California Press.

Patton, Laurie L. and Wendy Doniger, eds. 1996. *Myth and Method*. Charlottesville: University Press of Virginia.

Phillip, Kavita. 2003. *Civilising Nature: Race, Resource, and Modernity in Colonial South India*. New Delhi: Orient Longman.

Possehl, Gregory L. 2012. *The Indus Civilization: A Contemporary Perspective*. Altamira, CA: Walnut Creek.

Potdar, K. R. 1953. *Sacrificein the Rgveda*. Bombay: Bharatiya Vidya Bhavan.

Prakash, Om. 1998. *European Commercial Enterprise in Pre-colonial India*. New Cambridge History of India 2:5. Cambridge: Cambridge University Press.

Prasher-Sen, Aloka; B. Subrahmanyam; Imani Sivanagireddi; B. S. Hanumantha Rao. 2004. *Kevala-Bodhi. Buddhist and Jain History of the Deccan*. 2 vols. New Delhi: Bharatiya Kala Prakashan.

Proferes, Theodore N. 2003a. "Poetica and pragmatics in the Vedic liturgy for the installation of the sacrificial post." *JAOS* 123: 317–350.

Proferes, Theodore N. 2003b. "Remarks on the transition from Rgveda composition to srauta compilation." *Indo-Iranian Journal* 46: 1–21.

Proferes, Theodore N. 2007. *Vedic Ideals of Sovereignty and the Poetics of Power*. New Haven, CT: American Oriental Society.

Puhvel, Jaan. 1955. "Vedic asvamedha and Gaulish Iipomiidvos." *Language* 31: 353–354.

Puhvel, Jaan. 1970. "Aspects of equine functionality." In Jaan Puhvel ed., *Myth and Law among the Indo-Europeans*. Berkeley: University of California Press, 159–172.

Raghavan, V. 1962. *The Present Day Position of Vedic Recitation and Vedic Sakhas*. Kumbhakonam: Veda Dharma Sabha.

Ramusack, Barbara N. 2004. *The Indian Princes and Their States*. New Cambridge History of India 3:6. Cambridge: Cambridge University Press.

Ranade, H. G. 1978. *Katyayana Srauta Sutra*. Pune: H. G. Ranade and H. R. Ranade.

Ranade, H. G. 2006. *Illustrated Dictionary of Vedic Rituals*. New Delhi: Indira Gandhi National Centre for the Arts.

Rangacharya, V. 1919. *A Topographical List of Inscriptions of the Madras Presidency (Collected till 1915), with Notes and References*. 3 vols. Madras: Government Press.

Rao, A. A. 2010. *Kakinada. The Making of a University City*. Hyderabad: Graphic Printers.

Rao, P. R. 1980. *History of Modern Andhra*. New Delhi: Sterling Publishers.

Rapson, E. J., W. Haig, H. H. Dodwell et al., eds. 1922–58. *Cambridge History of India.* 6 vols. Cambridge: Cambridge University Press.

Rath, Saraju, ed. 2012. *Aspects of Manuscript Culture in South India.* Leiden: Brill.

Rath, Saraju. "Varieties of Grantha script." In Saraju Rath, ed., *Aspects of Manuscript Culture,* 187–206.

Reddy, R. Soma. 1984. *Hindu and Muslim Religious Institutions. Andhra Desa, 1300–1600.* Madras: New Era.

Renou, Louis. 1947. *Les écoles védiques et la formation du Veda.* Paris: Imprimerie Nationale.

Renou, Louis. 1949. "La valeur du silence dans le culte védique." *JAOS* 69: 111–118.

Renou, Louis. 1954. *Vocabulaire du rituel védique.* Paris: Librairie C. Klincksieck.

Renou, Louis. 1955–69. *Études védiques et paninéennes.* 17 fascs. Paris: Edition-Diffusion de Boccard.

Renou, Louis. 1965. *The Destiny of the Veda in India.* Delhi: Motilal Banarsidass.

Reynolds, Holly. 1978. *"To Keep the Tali Strong." Women's Rituals in Tamilnad, India.* PhD Dissertation, University of Wisconsin.

Ricoeur, Paul. 1995. *Figuring the Sacred. Religion, Narrative and the Imagination.* Tr. by David Pellauer; ed. by Mark I. Wallace. Minneapolis: Fortress.

Richards, John F. 1995. *The Mughal Empire.* New Cambridge History of India 1:5. Cambridge: Cambridge University Press.

Robinson, Francis. 2000. *Islam and Muslim History in South Asia.* New Delhi: Oxford University Press.

Rodhe, Sten. 1946. *Deliver Us from Evil. Studies on the Vedic Ideas of Salvation.* Lund: Gleerup.

Rolland, Pierre. 1973. *Le Mahavrata: Contribution à l'etude d'un rituel solennel védique.* Göttingen: Vanderhoeck und Ruprecht.

Rönnow, K. 1927. *Trita Aptya. Eine vedische Gottheit.* Uppsala: Lundequist.

Rönnow, K. 1929. "Zur Erklarung des pravargya, des agnicayana, und der sautramani." *Le Monde orientale* 23: 113–173.

Rustagi, Urmila. 1981. *Darsapurnamasa : A Comparative Ritualistic Study.* New Delhi: Bharatiya Vidya Prakashan.

Sarasvati, Baidyanath. 1977. *Brahmanic Ritual Traditions. In the Crucible of Time.* Simla: Indian Institute of Advanced Study.

Sarbacker, Stuart R. 2005a. *The Numinous and Cessative in Indo-Tibetan Yoga.* Albany: SUNY Press.

Sarbacker, Stuart R. 2005b. "The future of creative hermeneutics in the history of religions." In James Blumenthal, ed., *Incompatible Visions,* 227–249.

Sastri, K. A. Nilakanta. 1976. *A History of South India.* 4th ed. Madras: Oxford University Press.

Satyanarayana, K. 1975-83. *A Study of the History and Culture of the Andhras.* 2 vols. New Delhi: People's Publishing House.

Sauve, James L. 1970. "The divine victim: Aspects of human sacrifice in Viking Scandinavia and Vedic India." In Jaan Puhvel, ed., *Myth and Law among the Indo-Europeans.* Berkeley: University of California Press, 173–191.

Sayers, Matthew R. 2013. *Feeding the Dead: Ancestor Worship in Ancient India.* New York: Oxford University Press.

Scharfe, Helmut. 2002. *Education in Ancient India.* Leiden: Brill.

Schechner, Richard. 1981. "Restoration of behavior." *Sudies in Visual Communication* 7.3: 2–45.

Schechner, Richard. 1986. Review symposium on *Agni: The Vedic Ritual of the Fire Altar. Journal of Asian Studies* 45: 355–363.

Schmalz, Matthew N. and Peter Gottschalk. 2010. *Engaging South Asian Religions: Boundaries, Appropriations, and Resistance.* Albany: SUNY Press.

Schmidt, Hanns-Peter. 1968. *Brhaspati und Indra.* Wiesbaden: Harasowitz.

Schmidt, Hanns-Peter. 1987. *Some Women's Rites and Rights in the Veda.* Poona: BhORI.

Schmitthenner, Peter L. 2011. "*Colonial hydraulic projects in South India.*" In: Deepak Kumar, V. Damodakam, R. D'Souza eds., The Environmental and Cultural Legacy of Colonial Hydraulic Projects in Two South Indian Deltas (New York: Oxford University Press) 183–201.

Schömbucher, Elisabeth and Claus Peter Zoller, eds. 1999. *Ways of Dying. Death and Its Meanings in South Asia.* Delhi: Manohar.

Schwab, Julius. 1886. *Das altindische Thieropfer.* Erlangen: A. Deichert.

Seidenberg, A. 1983. "The geometry of the Vedic rituals." In Frits Staal, ed., *Agni,* 2: 95–126.

Sen, Chitrabhanu. 1976. *A Dictionary of the Vedic Rituals.* New Delhi: Concept.

Sewell, Robert. 1882. *Archaeological Survey of Southern India.* Vol. 1. Madras: Government Press.

Shastri, Ajay Mitra. 1999. *The Age of the Satavahahas.* 2 vols. New Delhi: Aryan Books International.

Shastri, Dakshina Ranjan. 1963. *Origin and Development of the Rituals of Ancestor Worship in India.* Calcutta: Bookland.

Shende, S. J. "Agni in the Brahmanas of the Rgveda." *Annals of the BhORI* 46: 1–28.

Shulman, David D. 1980. *Tamil Temple Myths. Sacrifice and Divine Marriage in the South Indian Saiva Tradition.* Princeton, NJ: Princeton University Press.

Sims-Williams, Nicholas. 2002. *Indo-Iranian Languages and Peoples.* Oxford: Oxford University Press.

Sircar, D. C. 1998. *Inscriptions of Asoka.* Delhi: South Asia Books.

Smith, Brian K. 1985a. "Vedic Fieldwork." Review of Frits Staal, *Agni. Religious Studies Review* 11: 136–145.

Smith, Brian K. 1985b. "The unity of ritual: The place of the domestic sacrifice in Vedic ritualism." *Indo-Iranian Journal* 28: 70–96.

Smith, Brian K. 1986. "Ritual, knowledge and being: Initiation and Veda study in ancient India." *Numen* 33: 65–89.

Smith, Brian K. 1989. *Reflections on Resemblance, Ritual, and Religion.* New York: Oxford University Press.

Smith, Brian K. 1994. "The Veda and the authority of class: Regarding structures of Veda and *varna*." In L. L. Patton ed., *Authority, Anxiety and Canon,* 67–96.

Smith, Brian K. 1996. "Ritual perfection and ritual sabotage in the Veda." *HR* 35: 285–306.

Smith, Brian K. and Wendy Doniger. 1989. "Sacrifice and substitution: Ritual mystification and mythical demystification." *Numen* 36.2: 189–224.

Smith, Frederick M. 1987. *The Vedic Sacrifice in Transition. A Translation and Study of the Trikandamandana of Bhaskara Misra.* Poona: BhORI.

Smith, Frederick M. 1987. "Agni's body." *Adyar Library Bulletin* 51: 79–103.

Smith, Frederick M. 1991. "Indra's curse, Varuna's noose and the suppression of women in Vedic *srauta* ritual." In Julia Leslie, ed., *Roles and Rituals for Hindu Women.* Delhi: Motilal Banarsidass, 17–45.

Smith, Frederick M. 1994. "Puranaveda." In L. L. Patton, ed., *Authority, Anxiety and Canon,* 97–138.

Smith, Frederick M. 2000. "Indra goes West: Report on a Vedic soma sacrifice in London in July 1996." *HR* 39: 247–267.

Smith, Frederick M. 2001. "The recent history of Vedic ritual in Maharastra." In K. Karttunen and P. Koskikallio, eds., *Vidyarnavandanam.* Helsinki: Finnish Oriental Society, 43–63.

Smith, Frederick M. 2006. *The Self in Possession. Deity and Spirit Possession in South Asian Literature and Civilization.* New York: Columbia University Press.

Smith, Frederick M. and S. J. Carri. 1994. "The identity and significance of the *valmikavapa* in the Vedic sacrificial ritual." *Indo-Iranian Journal* 38.1: 30–61.

Somayajipad, C. V., M. Itti Ravi Nambudiri, and F. Staal. 1983. "The five-tipped bird, the square bird, and the many-faced domestic altar." In Frits Staal, ed., *Agni.* 2: 343–358.

Somayajulu, V. G. A. 1991. *A Study of the Performance of Agnistoma Yaga (according to Andhra Tradition).* Unpublished PhD Dissertation in cursive Sanskrit, Andhra University, Visakhapatnam.

Sparreboom, M. 1985. *Chariots in the Veda.* Leiden: Brill.

Sparreboom, M. and J. C. Heesterman. 1989. *The Ritual of Setting Up the Sacred Fires according to the Vadhula School.* Vienna: University Press.

Sreekrishna Sarma, E. R. 1999. *Vedic Tradition in Kerala.* Calicut: University of Calicut.

Srinivasan, Doris. 1973. "Sandhya: Myth and ritual." *Indo-Iranian Journal* 15: 161–178.

Staal, Frits.1961. *Nambudiri Veda Recitation.* The Hague: Mouton.

Staal, Frits.1982. *The Science of Ritual.* Poona: BhORI.

Staal, Frits. 1983. *Agni. The Vedic Ritual of the Fire Altar*. 2 vols. Berkeley: Asian Humanities.

Staal, Frits.1988. *Rules without Meaning: Essays on Ritual, Mantras, and the Science of Man*. New York: Peter Lang

Staal, Frits.1989. "Vedic mantras." In Harvey P. Alper, ed., *Mantra*. Albany: SUNY Press, 48–95.

Staal, Frits.1990. "Jouer avec le feu. Pratique et théorie du ritual védique." *Publications de l'Institut de Civilisation indienne* 8.57. Paris: Boccard, 1–107.

Staal, Frits.2004. "From pranmukham to sarvatomukham. A thread through the srauta maze." In A. Griffiths and J. E. M. Houben, eds., *The Vedas: Texts, Language and Ritual*. Groningen: Egbert Forsten, 521–553.

Staal, Frits.2008. *Discovering the Vedas: Origins, Mantras, Rituals, Insights*. New Delhi: Penguin.

Stein, Burton. 1989. *Vijayanagara*. New Cambridge History of India 1:2. Cambridge: Cambridge University Press.

Steiner, Karin. 2005. "Proposal for a multi-perspective approach to Srauta ritual," *Ethno-Indology: Studies in South Asian Ritual* 1: 221–237.

Tachikawa, Musashi. 1985. *The Indian Homa Ritual*. Nagoya: Nagoya University Press.

Tachikawa, Musashi, Shrikant Bahulkar, and Madhavi Kolhatkar. 2001. *Indian Fire Ritual*. Delhi: Motilal Banarsidass.

Tachikawa, Musashi and Madhavi Kolhatkar. 2006. *Vedic Domestic Fire-Ritual: Sthalipaka*. New Delhi: New Bharatiya Book Corporation.

Talbot, Cynthia. 2000. "The story of Pratiparudra. Historiography on the Deccan frontier." In David Martin and Bruce Lawrence, eds., *Beyond Turk and Hindu*, 282–299.

Talbot, Cynthia 2001. *Precolonial India in Practice: Society, egion, and Identity in Medieval India*. New York: Oxford University Press.

Talbot, Cynthia and and Katherine B. Asher. 2006. *India before Europe*. New York: Cambridge University Press.

Tapper, Bruce. 1987. *Rivalry and Tribute. Society and Ritual in a Telugu Village in South India*. Delhi: Hindustan.

Thapar, Romila. 1966–84. *A History of India*. 2 vols. Vol. 2 with Percival Spear. Baltimore, MD: Penguin.

Thapar, Romila. 1987. *The Mauryas Revisited*. Kolkata: K. P. Bagchi.

Thapar, Romila. 2004. *Early India: From the Origins to AD 1300*. Berkeley: University of California Press.

Thieme, Paul. 1957. *Mitra and Aryaman*. New Haven, CT: Yale University Press.

Thite, Ganesh U. 1969. "Caturmasya-Sacrifices Researched." Poona: *Publications of the Centre of Advanced Study in Sanskrit* A31: 57–79.

Thite, Ganesh U. 1970a. "Significance of diksa." *Annals of the BhORI* 51: 163–173.

Thite, Ganesh U. 1970b. "Animal-sacrifice in the Brahmana texts." *Numen* 17:143–158.

Thite, Ganesh U. 1975. *Sacrifice in the Brahmana-Texts.* Poona: Poona University.

Tsuchiyama, Y. 2005. "Abhiseka in the Vedic and post-Vedic rituals." In Shingo Einoo and Jun Takashima, eds., *From Material to Deity,* 51–93.

Tull, Herman W. 1989. *The Vedic Origins of Karma. Cosmos and Man in Ancient Indian Myth and Ritual.* Albany: SUNY Press.

Vajracharya, Gautam V. 2013. *Frog Hymns and Rain Babies: Monsoon Culture and the Art of Ancient South Asia.* Mumbai: Marg.

Van Buitenen, J. A. B. 1956. "Vajapeya: English commentary." Unpublished 13-page typescript accompanying his film of the Vajapeya in Poona.

Van Buitenen, J. A. B. 1962. *Maitrayaniya Upanisad.* The Hague: Mouton.

Van Buitenen, J. A. B. 1962. "The Large Atman." *HR* 4: 103–114

Van Buitenen, J. A. B. 1968. *The Pravargya: An Ancient Indian Iconic Ritual Described and Annotated.* Poona: Deccan College.

Vesci, Uma Marina. 1985. *Heat and Sacrifice in the Vedas.* Delhi: Motilal Banarsidass.

Wagoner, Phillip B. and John H. Rice. 2001. "From Delhi to the Deccan: Newly discovered Tughluq monuments at Warangal-Sultanpur and the beginnings of Indo-Islamic architecture in Southern India." *Artibus Asiae* 61.1: 77–117.

Wasson, R. Gordon. 1968. *Soma. Divine Mushroom of Immortality.* New York: Harcourt Brace Jovanovich.

Weber, A. 1864. "Über Menschenopfer bei den Indern der vedische Zeit." *ZDMG* 18.

Weber, A. 1892. *Über den Vajapeya.* Berlin: Verlag der Königl. Akademie der Wiss.

Wheelock, Wade T. 1969. "The Mantra in Vedic and Tantric ritual." In Harvey P. Alper, ed., *Mantra.* Albany: SUNY Press, 96–122.

Wheelock, Wade T. 1978. *The Ritual Language of a Vedic Sacrifice.* PhD Dissertation, University of Chicago.

Wheelock, Wade T. 1980. "A taxonomy of the mantras in the new- and full-moon sacrifice." *HR* 19: 349–369.

Wheelock, Wade T. 1982. "The problem of ritual language." *Journal of the American Academy of Religion* 50: 49–70.

White, David G. 1996. *The Alchmical Body. Siddha Traditions in Medieval India.* Chicago: Universiy of Chicago Press.

Witzel, Michael. 1979. *On Magical Thought in the Veda.* Leiden: Leiden University.

Witzel, Michael. 1987. "On the localization of Vedic texts and schools." In G. Pollet, ed., *India and the Ancient World: History and Culture before AD 650.* Leaven: Department Orientalistiek, 174–213.

Witzel, Michael. 1993. "Toward a history of the Brahmins." *JAOS* 113.2: 264–268.

Witzel, Michael. 1995. "Rgvedic history: Poets, chieftains, and politics." In G. Erdosy, ed., *The Indo-Aryans of Ancient South Asia,* 307–335.

Witzel, Michael, ed. 1997a. *Inside the Texts, beyond the Texts: New Approaches to the Study of the Veda*. Cambridge, MA: Harvard University Press.

Witzel, Michael. 1997b. "The development of the Vedic canon and its schools." In Michael Witzel, ed., 1997a: 257–345.

Witzel, Michael. 2000. "The home of the Aryans." In Almut Hintze and Eva Tichy, eds., *Anusantatyai*. Dettelbach: J. H. Rolle, 283–338.

Wolpert, Stanley. 1993. *A New History of India*. 4th ed. New York: Oxford University Press.

Yazdani, G. 1982. *The Early History of the Deccan*, 2 vols. London: Oxford University Press.

Zimmerman, Francis. 1987. *The Jungle and the Aroma of Meat*. Berkeley: University of California Press.

Zysk, Kenneth G. 1985. *Religious Healing in the Veda*. Philadelphia: American Philosophical Society.

Zysk, Kenneth G. 2012. "The use of manuscript catalogues as sources of regional intellectual history in India's early modern period." In Saraju Rath, *Aspects of Manuscript Culture*, 253–288.

Index

abhicara (black magic), 128, 193–194, 288*n*7
Acchuta Rama Somayajulu (ancestor of Baballa), 58
adhana (setting of three fires), 42, 50, 190–194, *192*, 204, 288*n*6, 290*n*22
adhvaryu (major priest), 45, 47, *48*, 200, 235, 236
adhyaya (recitation lesson), 29, 96. *See also brahmacarin/brahmacarya*
Agni (the deity fire), 35, 43–44, 46, 49–52, 142, 169, 199, 200, 201, 204, 213, 214, 216, 222, 227, 240, 241, 242
Agni, process of becoming, 187–246
  overview, 187–190
  adhana, 190–194, *192*, 204, 288*n*6, 290*n*22
  agni-cayana, 222–228, *223*, 291*n*38
  agni-hotra, 194–198, *195*
  agrayana, 205–206
  asva-medha, 188, 234–237, 293*n*62
  becoming an ancestor, 243–246
  catur-masya, 206–209
  final absorption and funeral rites, 237–243, 293*n*68
  first *soma* and *agni-stoma*, 210–218, 291*n*38
  maha-vrata and *go-sava*, 188, 230–232, 292*n*56
  offerings according to lunar cycles and stellar rhythms, 199–204
  pravargya, 218–219
  sautramani offering to Indra, 232–233, 292*n*59
  soma schedule and other rituals, 220–221
  vaja-peya, 188, 228–230
agni-cayana (fire altar), 46, 50, 194, 201, 220, 222–228, *223*, 240, 291*n*38
agnidhra (priestly helper), 47, 200, 235
agni-hotra (three fires)
  and becoming Agni, 194–198, *195*, 238
  and bonding with Agni, 49–52
  house floor plan for, *42*
  in householder offerings, 41, 42–43, 50
  outdoor complex, 44–45, *44*
Agnihotra (title), 119, 195
agni-hotrin (performer of *agni-hotra*), 41, 43
agni-karya (daily fire maintenance), 30, 127, 136, 143, 189
Agni Kravyad (deity), 49, 238
agni-ksetra (outdoor multi-fire complex), 44–45, *44*, 50, 211–212
agni-manthana (churning of fire), *51*
Agni-Soma (deity), 44, 199

agni-stoma (initiatory *soma* offering)
becoming Agni, 210–218, 238–239
description of, 44–49, 281*n*11, 291*n*38
in early centuries, 10
importance of, 44–46
Lanka on, 65, 103
priests and helpers, 47–48, *48*
Agni Svistakrt (deity), 169, 205, 217
Agni: The Vedic Ritual of the Fire Altar (Staal), 215, 225
Agnivata Naga Laksmi Sastri (daughter of Kapilavayi Rama Sastri), 125, *126*
agrahara (Brahman hamlet), 4. *See also* Iragavaram Village; Kakinada Town; Kamesvari *Agrahara*; Sriramapuram *Agrahara*; Vyaghresvaram Village
impact of mobility on, 249–250
livelihood within, 176–179
search for, 23–27, 279*n*42
agrayana (harvest sacrifice), 178–179, 205–206
ahavaniya (offering fire in east), 42, 43, 49, 52, 64, 66, 67, 193–195, 202, 203, 211, 212, 216–217, 226, 233, 236, 241
ahitagni (Vedic Brahman with *agni-hotra* fires in home). *See also vedamlo unnaru* (existing in Veda); *specific individuals and rites*
four generations of, *139*
losta-cayana (funeral mound for in *agni-cayana*), 185, 240
pitr-medha (funeral rites for), 67–68, 239
Akella Subha Avadhani, 59
Akondi Suryanarayana, 67, 240
"Altar of Fire" (film), 46, 225
altars. *See agni-cayana* (fire altar); *maha-vedi* (great altar); *ratha-cakra citi* (chariot-wheel altar); *syena-citi* (flying eagle altar)
Ambedkar, B. R., 18
Anasuya (wife of Lanka), *100*, 101–102, 103, 104, 106, 158–159, 161, 163, 165, 170–171, 178, 180, 217, 254
Anasuya (wife of Mitranarayana), 102, 111, 115, 165, 171, 248
ancestors (*pitr*). *See also specific individuals*
becoming, 243–246
continued role in afterlife, 146
debts to, 29, 61–62
honored in homes, 38
offerings to, 208–209
pinda-pitr-yajna (offerings), 200
pitr-loka (heaven of), 209, 243
status of *pitr*, 68
Andhra Pradesh. *See also* Tirumala Tirupati Devasthanam (TTD); *specific agrahara* and villages
Department of Religious Endowments, 63
Hyderabad, 15, 22
as language state, 22
maps of, xxi–xxii
population of, 23
statehood, 38–39
Andhra Pradesh Charitable Act, 179
Andhra Veda Pandits (book), 220
animal sacrifice, 45, 47, 65–66, 170, 191, 209, 215–217, 222, 226, 229, 230, 232–233, 235, 236, 238–239, 288*n*6
antyesti (cremation), 66, 78, 155, 175, 184, 239, 240
Anumati (goddess), 201
Apastaba Dharma Sutra, 36, 280*n*6
Apastamba Grhya Sutra, 32, 36, 87, 144, 145, 148, 165, 168, 169, 170, 173–175, 203, 280*n*6
Apastamba Srauta Sutra, 30–31, 32, 36, 37, 46, 47, 87, 119, 144, 145, 164, 181, 188, 191, 193–195, 197–198,

208, 210, 218, 221, 224, 227, 230, 280*n*6, 282*n*19
aptoryama (*soma* sacrifice), 46
arani (woods for churning fire), 51, 52, 67, 78–79, 193, 194, 197, 204, 241
Arkasomayaji, D., 280*n*8
Arnold, Harold, 53
Aruna (sage), 227
aruna-ketuka (rite), 58, 62, 110, 131, 186, 220, 221, 222, 226–228
asakti (curiosity), 146
asauca (impurity), 49, 67, 160, 197
ascetics, 182
asrama (stages of life), 28–38, *29*. *See also brahmacarin/brahmacarya*; householders
astrology, 40, 105, 163, 167, 175, 180, 184–185, 199, 203–204, 257–258
Asvalayana Grhya Sutra, 170
Asvalayana Srauta Sutra, 149
asva-medha (royal horse sacrifice)
  and becoming Agni, 188, 189–190, 227, 232, 234–237, 292*n*56, 293*n*62
  in early centuries, 8, 10, 14
Asvin (twin deities), 213, 218, 219, 229, 233
Atharva Veda, *37*, *47*, 99, 120, 124, 125, 145, 149–150, 151, 169, 188, 203
atiratra (overnight *soma* sacrifice), 46
atman (self), 11, 246
aupasana (household fire), 35, 42–43, 67, 135, 138, 189, 193, 205, 240, 241
Avadhani/Avadhanulu (title), 79, 282*n*4
Avesta (Zoastrian text), 45, 145

Baballa (Bhamidipati Yajnesvara), xv, *xvi*, 56–71, *57*, *88*, *95*, 117, 167–168
  on afterlife, 186, 244
  agrayana, 179
  aruna-ketuka, 220, 222, 226, 227
  on *atman*, 246
  catur-masya, 89, 207
  comments on Knipe (*tela-dora*), 254
  comments on rites, 203, 204, 205, 209, 210
  and decline of traditions, 114
  family of, 68–71, *69*, 171
  fulfillment in *srauta*, 61–62
  funeral of, 66–68, 78, 240, 241
  as gatekeeper of *agrahara*, 159
  as gentleman farmer, 177–178
  on honoraria as *veda-vikriya*, 99, 154, 156, 179, 248
  on importance of *patni*, 160
  lineage of, 56–61, *59*, 87, 102, 143, 164, 182
  marriage of, 163
  moves to Sriramapuram, 62–66
  on mysticism of fires, 189
  as *nitrya-agni-hotrin*, 196
  in old age, 180, 198
  and sequential family deaths, 184
  and student examinations, 61
  as Traditionalist, 247
Bachelard, Gaston, 141, 189, 283*n*2
Bactria Margiana Archeological Complex (BMAC), 188, 213
Balayogi of Mummidivaram, 182
balya-vivaha (child-marriage), 164–165
bandhu (identity), 142, 193, 226
Banks, Russell, 159
Bapat, Sri, 230
Bhamidipati Brahmibuta Acarya (ancestor of Baballa), 58, 182
Bhamidipati Chinna Subrahmanya Somayajulu (father of Baballa), 58, 72, 149
Bhamidipati Mitranarayana. *See* Mitranarayana (Bhamidipati Mitranarayana Sarvatomukha Somayaji)
Bhamidipati Sesadri Somayaji, 110–111
Bhamidipati Somasekhara (grandson of Baballa), 58

Bhamidipati Yajnesvara Prasad (grandson of Baballa), 58–59, 60–61, 67, 68–70, *69*, 167, 172, 203, 246
Bhaskara Misra, 254
bhokta (ritual eater of food for the dead), 245–246
bhuta (ghost), 245
birthday celebrations, 175
black magic. *See abhicara* (black magic)
Black Yajur Veda, 29, *37*
Bodewitz, Henk, 197
bodily assumption of sacred fires, 51–52, 282*n*19
brahma (household/family priest), 87, 89
brahmacarin/brahmacarya. *See also Veda*, process of becoming
  and becoming Agni, 188–190
  begging for food (*madhu-kara*), 30, *31*
  examinations, 34–35, 61, 65, 144, 156
  and guru, 29, 32, *33–34*, 34, 146–147
  marriage arrangements, 31–32, 34, 163
  memorization and recitation phase, 32, 34
  upanayana ceremony, 29–30
  in Veda *patha-sala* in Kapilesvarapuram, *32*
brahma-loka (heaven of Brahma), 75, 162, 186, 227, 244
brahma-medha (funeral rites), 66–68, 114, 237–243, 246, 293*n*68
brahman (major priest), 47, *48*, 200, 235
Bringing the Gods to Mind (Patton), 196
Buddhism, 11
Buitenen, Hans van, 219, 230
Bullebbayi (Bhamidipati Subrahmanya Somayaji), 58, 66, 67, 68, 159, 246
bullock carts, *3*
Bulusu Kamesvara. *See* Kamesvara (Bulusu Kamesvara)
Bulusu Somayajulu, 65
Bulusu Vyaghresvara Soma-yaji, 107, 190

cakra-vartin (sovereign of world), 234
calendars, 114, 144
cash economy. *See* India and modernity
catur-masya (seasonal rites), 89, 206–209
cayana. *See agni-cayana* (fire altar)
Cayanulu (Bulusu Vyaghresvara Cayanulu), *xvi*, 85–91, *87–88*, 92, 95, 117
  agni-cayana, 220
  agni-hotra, 196
  brahma-medha, 66, 67, 110
  catur-masya, 207
  comments on rites, 217
  dowry debt, 167
  family of, 171, 247
  funeral of, 240, 241, 246
  on immortality, 244
  livelihood of, 178, 179
  as *purohita*, 152
  and recitations with Sathya Sai Baba, 183
  remarriage of, 169–170
  and sequential family deaths, 184, 185
  as Traditionalist, 252
  and TTD service, 182
Cayanulu (title), 174
ceta-badi. *See abhicara* (black magic)
Chandrasekhar, M., 119
children and life-cycle rites, 170–175
Cigna Insurance Company, 84
coconut palms, 7, 176
Cotton, Arthur, 18–20
cows, in ritual life, 43, 94, 196, 206
cuda-karana (first tonsure), 174, 175

dabbu (money), 104, 178
daksina (ritual payments), 46, 281*n*13

daksina-agni (southern fire), 42, *43*, 196, 208, 209, 211, 241
dana (ritualized donations), 94
danda (staff), 30, 142
darbha (grass), 66, 173, 174, 196, 200, 201, 224, 231
darsa-purna-masa (new-or-full-moon offering), 44, 199–204, 221
death and dying. *See* funeral rites
Dendukuri Agnihotra Somayaji, 129–131, *129*, 224, 228, 230, 231
Dendukuri Candrasekhar (older brother of Dedukuri Agnihotra), 230
Dendukuri family, 53, 127–132, *129–130*, 138, 150, 153, 196, 221, 230
Dendukuri Laksminarasimha Somayajulu (son of Dedukuri Agnihotra), 129–130, *129*
devata (deities), 43–44, 204, 216. *See also specific deities*
devudu (god), 79, 105
dharma (law), 65, 176, 253. *See also specific texts by name*
Dharma Sastras, 94, 99, 118, 144, 152, 178, 182, 254
Dhatr (deity), 201
dhisniya (hearths for *srauta*), 211, 212
diksa (death-and-rebirth consecration), 45, 46, 50, 62, 160, 161–162, 204, 212, 214, 222–223, 226, 228, 238, 243
Dokka family, 24, 177
Doniger, Wendy, 234
dora (foreigner), 52–53, 282*n*20
dosa (sin/fault), 62, 198, 254
dowries for daughters, 54, 75, 76, 87, 96, 102, 163, 167, 172, 248
Draksarama temple, 13, 26
Dumont, Paul-Emile, 204, 294*n*73
Dundas, Paul, 11
Duvvuri Girija Sankar (grandson of Duvvuri Yajulu), *78*, *81*, 84, 137, 138
Duvvuri Hari Prasad (grandson of Duvvuri Yajulu), *78*, *81*, 137, 138
Duvvuri Karttikeya (great-grandson of Duvvuri Yajulu), 84, 175
Duvvuri Phani Yajnesvara Yajlulu (grandson of Duvvuri Yajulu), 71, *72*, 80, *81*, 82–83, 113, 137, 138, 149, 156, 172, 251, 253
Duvvuri Sarvesvara Somayajulu Ghanapati (son of Duvvuri Yajulu), 76, 77, *78*, 191
Duvvuri Sita Ram Sastry (grandson of Duvvuri Yajulu and grandson of Gullapalli Sita Ram Sastri), xvii, 74–75, *81*, 83–85, 129, 165, 175, 250, 256
Duvvuri Venkata Surya Prakasa Yajulu Avadhani (son of Duvvuri Yajulu), 66, 72, 77, 79–85, *81*, 137, 164, 167, 175, 178, 184, 191, 200, 247, 251, 252
Duvvuri Yajnesvara Paundarika Yajulu, *xvi*, *33*, 71–85, *72*, 88, 91, *95*, 111
  agni-cayana, 220, 224, 225
  agrayana, 205–206
  brahma-medha, 110
  brahmancarin period, 149
  catur-masya, 207–208
  comments on America, 97, 256
  comments on rites, 175, 190, 202, 203, 217
  and Dendukuri family, 128–129
  on detachment of Lanka, 104
  on early education of, 250–251
  family of, xvii, 66, 71, *72*, 74–77, 79–85, *81*, 170–171, 247
  floor plan of house, *42*
  fulfillment in *srauta*, 73–75
  funeral of, 231

Duvvuri Yajnesvara Paundarika Yajulu (*Cont.*)
guru of, 59–60
on *kesma* (welfare of land), 177–178
last rites, 78–79
lineage of, 78, 117, 164
livelihood of, 179
losta-citi, 67
on marriage, 162
marriage of, 75–76, 163
on Mitranarayana, 113
in old age, 151, 180, 181, 198
performance of *agrayana*, 179
on rebirth, 244
on renunciation, 183
sabha in name of (2005), 153
and sequential family deaths, 184
as *soma-pravaka*, 133
as Traditionalist, 114, 255
tradition of *sabha*, 154–155
and Veda, 72–73
viewpoints of, 89–90
Duvvuri Yajnesvara Yajulu (son of Duvvuri Sarvesvara), 84

East India Company, 16, 18
Eaton, Richard, 278*nn*15–16
Eggeling, Julius, 224
Eliade, Mircea, 202, 222
Eliot, T. S., 5
expiation rites. *See prayascitta* (expiations)

family planning, 82–83, 171–172, 253
fires. *See also adhana* (setting of three fires); *agni-hotra* (three fires); *agni-karya* (daily fire maintenance); *agni-ksetra* (outdoor multi-fire complex); *ahavaniya* (offering fire in east); *aupasana* (household fire); *daksina-agni* (southern fire); *garha-patya* (cooking fire in west); *punar-dahana* (second cremation fire); *srauta* (extended fire rites/texts); *tretagni* (three-hearth fire)
absorption into Agni, 237–243
Baballa on mysticism of, 189
bodily assumption of sacred, 51–52, 282*n*19
Fuller, Christopher, 49
funeral rites. *See brahma-medha* (funeral rites); *pitr-medha* (funeral rites for *ahitagni/patni*); *sapindi-karana* (twelfth-day funeral rite); *sraddha* (funeral rite)

Gandhi, 18, 23
Gangamma (goddess), 25, 198
garbha (embryo), 201
garbha-dana (impregnation), 172, 174
Gardner, Robert, 46
garha-patya (cooking fire in west), 42, 43, 44, 49, 51, 67, 181, 193, 195–196, 200, 201, 202, 211, 212, 219, 224, 241
Gauri (goddess), 185–186
Gauri-*loka* (heaven of Gauri), 186, 242, 244
gayatri (mantric meter), 29, 94, 142, 143, 258
gentleman farmers, 100–103, 177
ghana (braided recitation), 40, 73, 76–77, 82, 95, 96–97, 135, *135*, 149, 155, 175, 250
ghana-pathi (master of *ghana*), 35, 38, 77, 82, 84, 90, 110, 124, 133, 138, 149
Girija Syamala (wife of Duvvuri Sita Ram Sastry), 84, 137, 175
goats. *See* animal sacrifice
Godavari Delta, 5–27. *See also* Andhra Pradesh
agrahara and temple pilgrimages, 23–27, 279*n*42

arrival of Europeans, 16–18
domestication of, 18–21
dynasties of regional kings, 9–11
early centuries, 7–9
emergence of Telugu literature, 7, 12
and Islam, 13–14, 278*n*16
Kakatiya dynasty, 12–13
as modern Telegu langauge state, 21–23
riverine lifelines, 5–7
rule of Vijayanagara, 14–16
Godavari Mandala Parisad, 79
Godavari River, *1*
Gonda, Jan, 212–213
go-sava (bull imitation), 232
gotra (clan), 31, 163–164
Grantha (script), 10
grha (house), 29
grhastha (householder), 34–36. *See also* householders
grhya. *See aupasana* (household fire)
Gullapalli Butchi Rama Sarma Avadhani (son of Gullapalli Sita Ram Sastri), *135*, *167*
Gullapalli Chinna Anjaneya Ghanapathi (son of Gullapalli Sita Ram Sastri), *135*, *167*
Gullapalli family, *34*, 132–140, *135*, 153, 158, 178
Gullapalli Ramakrishna Avadhani (son of Gullapalli Sita Ram Sastri), *135*, *167*
Gullapalli Sita Ram Sastri Avadhanulu, *34*, 77, 134–138, 149, 164, *167*, 171, 247
Gullapalli Venkata Naga Srirama Avadhani (son of Gullapalli Sita Ram Sastri), *135*, 137, *167*
Gullapalli Venkata Rama Suryanarayana, 82
Gullapalli Venkata Surya Subrahmanya Avadhanulu, *135*, *167*
Gungu (goddess), 201
Guru. *See also brahmacarin/brahmacarya; specific individuals*
for *brahmacarins*, 29, 32, *33–34*, 34, 146–147
and husband/wife relationship, 75
and mantras, 142

havir-dhana (shed for soma-stalk carts), 211, 212, 213
heaven. *See loka* (world)
Heesterman, Jan, 184, 188, 209, 237, 288*n*6
Hindu Religious Institutions and Endowments Act, 179
Hiranyakesi Srauta Sutra, 230
homa (daily offerings), 35, 42–43, 64, 66, 143, 189, 205, 226
honoraria. *See sambhavana* (honoraria)
hotr (major priest), 47, *48*, 200, 202, 231, 235
householders, 157–186. *See also specific individuals*
agni-stoma events, 44–47
children and life-cycle rites, 170–175
death and beyond, 184–186
fire offerings, 42–43, *43*
livelihood among, 176–179
marriage, 160, 162–170
old age/retirement/renunciation, 180–184, 287*n*17
renaming of, 45
voices of women, 157–162
huna-vidya (foreign ways), 21, 69, 114, 250–251, 279*n*32

Ida (goddess), 201, 214
immortality, 44, 45
India and modernity, 247–250
cash economy, 40, 97, 156, 176–177, 248–249
dollar remittances to, 255

India and modernity (*Cont.*)
and emigration to America, 254–258
huna-vidya as rival education, 250–251
life expectancy increases, 256
mobility in new era, 249–250
power shift for Brahmans, 251–253
television, 251, 252
Indian Express, The, on Kapilavayi Yajnesvara Sastri, 119
Indra (deity), 200, 206, 213, 215, 216, 226, 232–233, 292*n*59
Indra-Agni (dual deity), 44, 199
Indra Sutraman (deity), 233
Iragavaram Village, 132–138
establishment of, 25
profiles of *ahitagni* from. *See* Gullapalli family
Islam, 13–14
istaka (bricks), 46
isti (new-and-full moon offerings), 36, 44, 47, 56, 62, 67, 70, 74, 78, 80, 89, 110, 111, 131, 132, 152, 161, 191, 197, 199, 200, 202, 206–207, 212, 214, 238, 240, 250–251

Jainism, 11
Jamison, Stephanie, 203, 216, 293*n*62
janma-rahita (absence of rebirths), 183
japa (repetitive prayer), 63, 94, 105, 197
jata-karma (birth-rite), 173–174
jata-patha (recitation pattern), 35, 149
Jatavedas, 193
Jayendra Sarasvati Swami, 183
Jay Prakasa Talkies, 252
jiva (spirit), 174
jnana (knowledge), 113
Jones, Kenneth, 21
jyoti-stoma. See agni-stoma (initiatory *soma* offering)

Kakinada Town, 110–116, *115–116*, 117
establishment of, 25
profiles of *ahitagni* from. *See* Mitranarayana (Bhamidipati Mitranarayana Sarvatomukha Somayaji)
Kalyani (great-granddaughter of Baballa), 68, *69*
Kamala (wife of Samavedam), *92*, 96, 171
Kambhampati Laksmana Avadhani, 134
Kamesvara (Bulusu Kamesvara), *43*, 91, 106–109, 117
agni-hotra, 200
family of, 160, 170–171, 247
marriage of, 163
in old age, 114
as *rtvij*, 110
shows *agni-hotra* hearth, 74
soma, 160, 190, 220
vaja-peya, 230
Kamesvari (wife of Pullela Laksminarayana), 109–110, 117, 137, 164, 171, 198, 242
Kamesvari *Agrahara*, 97–106
establishment of, 24–25, 177
profiles of *ahitagni* from. *See* Lanka (Lanka Venkatarama Sastri)
Kampan (poet), 12
kamya (rite for personal desire), 41
Kanaka Durga (wife of Duvvuri Surya Prakasa), 72, 77, 79, 80, *81*, 83, 137, 164, *167*
Kanci Pitha, 83
Kandukuri Virasalingam, 21–22
Kane, P. V., 183, 293*n*68
Kannada language, 12
Kapilavayi Agnihotra Sarma (son of Kapilavayi Rama Sastri), *33*, 124, 127, 152, 226
Kapilavayi Agni Rama Kumar (son of Kapilavayi Venkatesvara), 121, *122*, 123

Kapilavayi Chinna Rama Sastri (brother of Kapilavayi Yajnesvara Agnihotra Sastri), 118, 119, 121
Kapilavayi Pedda Rama Sastri (brother of Kapilavayi Yajnesvara Agnihotra Sastri), 118, 119, 123, 191
Kapilavayi Rama Sastri (son of Kapilavayi Yajnesvara), 116–117, 123, 124–132, *126*, *132*, 140, 150, 151, 167, 178, 189–190, 191, 208, 225–226, 234–235, 257
Kapilavayi Rama Yajna Varaha Narasimha (son of Kapilavayi Venkatesvara), 121, *122*, 123
Kapilavayi Venkata Somayajulu (father of Kapilavayi Yajnesvara), 118
Kapilavayi Venkatesvara Sastri (son of Kapilavayi Yajnesvara), 45, 116–117, 120–123, *122*, 124, 125, 127–132, *132*, 151, 164, 167, 171–172, 178, 204, 217, 225, 257
Kapilavayi Yajnesvara Agnihotra Sastri, 99, 107, 116–120, 124, 150, 175, 191, 204
karma (act/work), 78, 105, 113, 183, 186, 202
Kashikar, C. G., 41, 220
Kausika River, *3*, 6
Keith, A. B., 29
Knipe, David M., *101*, 254
Kolhatkar, Madhavi, 280*n*7
Konasima, 6–8, 21. *See also specific agrahara* and villages
Konasima Brahmans. *See also specific profiles of individuals*
knowledge of Taittiriya, 46
modernity and power shifts, 251–253
krama-patha (step-by-step recitation), 35
krama-pathi (one certified in *krama-patha*), 282*n*4
kravyad (Agni in cremation ritual), 49, 238
Krishna River, 20–21
Krishna Yajur Veda, *37*, 83, 151, 188
Krishnayya, M. V., xvi–xvii, 98, 114, *116*, 117, 255
kriya (ritual act), 42, 48, 56, 65, 67–68, 99, 105, 141, 160, 165, 181, 219, 221, 229, 234, 240, 241
Ksetrapati (deity), 207
Kuhu (goddess), 201
Kulke, Hermann, 9
Kumari (wife of Samavedam Venkatarama Ghanapathi), 95, 97
Kumbha Mela (Prayag), 154–155
kurma (tortoise), 56, 58, 227
kusa. *See darbha* (grass)

ladles, *195*, 203
Laksmi (Nagalaksmi) (wife of Duvvuri Phani), 82, 137, 138, 253
Laksmi (wife of Prabhala Krishnamurti), 95
Laksmikanta (wife of Renducintala Yajulu), 86, 158, 159, 185, 220–221
Laksmi Narasakanta (wife of Bhamidipati Yajnesvara Prasad), 68, *69*, 158, 172
Laksmi Narasimha Murti (son of Pullela Laksminarayana), 110
Laksminarayana (Pullela Laksminayana Soma-yajulu), 107, 109–110, 117, 200
agrayana and *agni-hotra*, 198
death of, 180
marriage of, 164, 171
soma, 220
wife's funeral rites, 242
Lanka (Lanka Venkatarama Sastri), 97–106, *98*, *100–101*, 113, 117
abhi-cara, 128
adhana, 191
as *adhvaryu*, 61
advanced learning, 149, 151

Lanka (*Cont.*)
agni-hotra, 198, 200
agni-stoma, 65, 103
brahmacarin period, 99–100, 111
brahma-medha, 66
catur-masya, 89, 207
comments on rites, 203, 204, 209, 210, 214, 220, 226, 228
death rites in home, 185
on family planning, 172
funeral of, 246
as gentleman farmer, 100–101, 102–103, 177–178
and honoraria, 77, 156, 179, 248, 249
on importance of *patni*, 160
on learning the texts on *amavasya*, 144
lineage of, 91, 102, 106, 143, 170–171, 247, 249
marriage of, 163, 164
as "new" Apastamba, 99, 103–104
on old age, 180
performance of marriage ceremonies, 167–168
receives Padma Bhushan award, 105, 250
as *rtvij*, 52–53
on *sabha*, 154
sama-vartana, 147–148
soma ritual, 110
as Traditionalist, 252–253, 255
vaja-peya, 229–230
Lanka Annapurna Sastri (son of Lanka), 183
laukika (secular Brahman), 28, 41, 67, 247, 251. *See also specific individuals*
linga (phallic symbol of Siva), 8, 13, 25–27, 62, 106, 121, 124
loka (world). *See brahma-loka* (heaven of Brahma); Gauri-*loka* (heaven of Gauri); *pitr-loka* (heaven of ancestors); *svarga* (heaven)
loka-prna (space filler in *cayana*), 222
Lord of the Seven Hills temple complex, Tirupati, 25
losta-cayana or *losta-citi* (funerary replica of *agni-cayana*), 66, 67, 90, 185, 240, 241, 242

Madan, T. S., 185
Madhava, 15
madhu-kara (brahmacarin begging rite), 30, *31*, 226
Madhuri (great-granddaughter of Baballa), 68, *69*, 179
madi (ritual purity), 96, 159–160, 249
Mahabharata, 12
Maha-Sivaratri, 26
maha-vedi (great altar), 44, 47, 50
Maha-vira (great hero), in *pravargya* rite, 218–219, 238
maha-vrata (great vow), 47, 74, 188, 221, 230–232
maila (ritual defilement), 160, 197
Malamoud, Charles, 216, 227–228
Manava Dharma Sastra, 152
mancam (bed/throne for *soma*), 211, 213
mandala (circle), 149, 150, 213, 223
Mandal Commission, 253
mangala-sutra (bride's neck thread), 169
mantra, 29, 142, 147, 150, 162–163, 173–174, 257–258
Mantrapatha, 168
Manu, 254, 256
maps
Andhra Pradesh, *xxi*
river deltas of coastal Andhra, *xxii*
marriage. *See vivaha* (marriage)
Marriage Act (1955), 164–165
Maruti (wife of Kapilavayi Rama Sastri), 125, *126*, 158, 161, 171–172, 178, 208
Maruts (deities), 209, 229

masa (moon/month), 44, 64, 79, 136, 184, 199–204, 221
matha (meditation center), 11
mekhala (waistband), 45, 142
menarche, 34, 168–169, 172–173. *See also* puberty rites
menarika (cross-cousin marriage), 59, 137–138, 165–166, *167*
menses, 50, 160, 165, 282*n*18, 285*n*3
Mimamsa, 144, 151
Mitranarayana (Bhamidipati Mitranarayana Sarvatomukha Somayaji), 25, 110–116, *115–116*, 117
  catur-masya, 207–208
  comments on rites, 184, 204, 220, 230
  on cultural change, 250–251
  family of, 171
  and honoraria, 156, 179, 248
  marriage of, 102, 103
  on modern mobility, 249
  in old age, 180–181
  and recitations with Sathya Sai Baba, 183
  sarvato-mukha, 228
  soma, 190, 191, 210
  and TTD service, 182
modernity. *See* India and modernity
moksa (liberation from rebirth), 183, 186, 225
Mrtyu (deity), 208, 238, 246
mrtyu-cakra (astrological death chart), 105, 180
muhurta (auspicious time for rite), 68, 101, 167–168
murti (image of deity), 14
musi-vayanam (funeral for wife who dies first), 185–186, 242, 244, 287*n*26
  for Rama Suryakanta (wife of Cayanulu), 86, 186, 242
  for Surya (wife of Duvvuri Yajulu), 78–79, 186
mystical experiences, 30–31, 49, 51, 66

Naciketas (sage), 227
Nagarjuna (Buddhist philosopher), 9
naksatra (constellation), 203–204, 290*n*22
naksatresti (*isti* offering to twenty-eight constellations), 199
Nambudiri Vaidika Brahmans of Kerala, 46
naming of children, 76, 174
Nannaya (poet), 12, 27
Narasamamba (wife of Gullapalli Sita Ram Sastri), 134, 135, 138, 164, 171
Narasamamba, Lakshmi, xvii
Narasimha (deity), 121
National Highways Development Project, 249
Nedunuri Srirama Murti, 102–103, 177
nidana (correspondence), 142, 193, 226
nirudha pasu (animal sacrifice), 215, 217
nitya (obligatory rituals), 41–42, 44, 46
nomu (woman's vow), 90
nyasa (bodily purifying/touching), 143

Oil and Natural Gas Company (ONGC), 257–258
Olivelle, Patrick, 286*n*11, 287*n*17
Opportunists, 248, 251, 253

pada-patha (word-by-word recitation), 35, 148
paka-yajna (offering of cooked food), 221
Pali language, 8
Palkuri Somanatha, 12
panna (set of Vedic textual lessons), 29, 40, 48, 68, 86, 95, 121, 136, 137, 144–145
Paramesvara (deity), 244

parayana (scheduled public recitation), 40, 63. *See also* Tirumala Tirupati Devasthanam (TTD)
parayatta (dependent portion of Veda), 144
parisad (organization, e.g. of Vedic Brahmans), 284*n*16
Parjanya (deity), 207
Parpola, Asko, 41, 215, 220, 229, 231, 290*n*22, 292*n*56
Parsis, 50
pasu (animal), 170
pasu-bandha. *See* animal sacrifice
patha (recitation pattern), 35, 46, 148, 153, 154
patha-sala (Vedic school), 30, 112–113
pati (husband/lord), 8
patni (wife). *See also specific wives*
  ability to speak freely, 283*n*10
  as co-sacrificer, 160, 285*n*3
  in menses, 50
  pitr-medha (funeral rites for), 67–68, 239
  selection of, 31–32
patni-sala (secluded space for *patni*), 50
Pattabhi Sitaramayya, 22
Patton, Laurie, 196, 206
paundarika (forty-day fire-altar sacrifice), 36, 47, 50, 74, 88, 109, 112, 119, 126–127, 128, 131, 132, 152, 161, 170, 181, 220, 225–226, 231–232
pinda (cooked rice ball offering), 205, 209, 245
pinda-dana (rice ball offering), 243
pinda-pitr-yajna (offering to ancestors), 200
Pisapati Venkata Siddhanti, 133
pitr. *See* ancestors (*pitr*)
pitr-loka (heaven of ancestors), 209, 243
pitr-medha (funeral rites for *ahitagni*/*patni*), 67–68, 239
pitr-tarpana (offering to deceased), 243
Polo, Marco, 13–14
Prabhala Krishnamurti, 60, 95
pracina-vamsa (fire enclosure for *srauta* rites), 211
praghasa (second *catur-masya* rite), 211
Prajapati (deity), 43–44, 196, 199, 200, 201, 206, 221, 222, 228, 235
Prakrit language, 8
prakrti (paradigm), 199
prana (breath), 142, 143
Pranati (daughter of Duvvuri Sita Ram Sastry), 84
prasna. *See panna* (set of Vedic textual lessons)
pravara (ancestral lineage), 163–164
pravargya (hot milk offering), 188, 218–219
prayascitta (expiations), 78, 197
preta (disembodied spirit of deceased), 68, 174, 185–186, 218, 238, 245
puberty rites, 165, 286*n*9
Puhvel, Jaan, 234
puja (worship), 49, 93, 106, 134, 160, 177, 196, 198, 205, 250
pujari (temple priest), 39, 40
Pullela. *See* Laksminarayana (Pullela Laksminayana Soma-yajulu)
pumsavana (prenatal rite), 173
pumscali (prostitute), 74, 231
punar-adhana (rekindling fire), 194
punar-adheya (rekindling fire), 194
punar-dahana (second cremation fire), 66, 67, 90, 239–240, 241, 242
punya (auspicious), 146, 165
Puranas, 13
purnima (full moon), 110, 112, 198, 200
purodasa (loaf of rice-flour dough), 44
purohita (family priest), 30, 36, 69, 87, 143, 152
purusa (human), 85, 219
Purusa-Prajapati (deity), 46, 241

Pusan (deity), 208, 238
Pushkara, 155

Radhakrishnan, Sarvepalli, 22
railroads, 20
raja (king), 8, 14, 45, 234
raja-suya (consecration of king), 8–9, 232, 237
rajasvala-purva (pre-pubescent girl), 31, 86, 123, 128, 137, 138, 162, 164–165, 243
Raka (deity), 201
Ramam (Chirravuri Srirama Sarma), 60, 67, 70–71, 96, 103, 240
Ramana Murti (son of Bulusu Cayanulu), 86, 91
Ramanuja (reformer/ philosopher), 11, 13
Ramarao, N. T. "NIR" (film star/ politician), 252
Rama Suryakanta (wife of Bulusu Cayanulu), 86, 171, 186
Rani Hayagriva Avadhani, 92, 107
Rao, P. Raghunanda, 21
Rao, P. V. Narasimha, 89, 253
Rao, Velcheru Narayana, 285*n*3
rasi (astrological house), 40
ratha (chariot), 230
ratha-cakra citi (chariot-wheel altar), 223, 229
ratha-patha (chariot recitation), 35, 149
Ravi Cayanulu, 80
"Red Knight's Song" (Carroll), 97
Rekha (great-granddaughter of Baballa), 68, 69, 179
Religious and Charitable Endowments Acts (1951/1969/1979/1987/2006), 38
remarriage, 169–170
Remella Surya Prakasa Sastri Avadhani, 80, 113
Renducintala (Venkatacalu) Yajulu, 86–88, 91, 99, 107, 111, 119, 159, 196, 220–221, 224, 228, 231, 247
Renducintala Canandrasekhara Yajulu (son of Renducintala Yajulu), 228
Renducintala Krishna Cayanulu, 132, 225
Renducintala Satyanarayana Avadhani (son of Renducintala Yajulu), 248
Renducintala Yajulu Narayana (son of Renducintala Yajulu), 185
renunciation, 180–184, 287*n*17
retas (semen), 193, 202, 206, 214
Reynolds, Holly, 285*n*3
Rg Veda, 29, 35, 36, 37, 38, 45, 47, 49, 50, 99, 120, 121, 125, 145, 149–150, 169, 188, 193, 201, 203, 213, 214, 227, 234, 235, 237–238, 242, 244
rice, *1*, *2*, 7, 18, 21, 179
Ricoeur, Paul, 147
rna (debt), 29
Rothermund, Dietmar, 9
rsi (sage), 29, 31, 146–147. *See also specific individuals*
rtvij (priest in a sacrifice), 36, 44, 47, 51, 52–53, 65, 86, 110, 161
Rudra, Pratapa, 13–14

sabda (sacred sound), 146, 257
sabha (debate), 36, 99, 103, 153–156
Sacred Books of the East, The (Eggeling), 224
sacred thread, 29–30, 107, 142, 172
sadas (bamboo-screened sacrifice area), 52–53, 211, 212, 219
sadhu (ascetic), 30, 119, 146
sakha (branch/school of Veda), 35, 37, 39, 121, 149, 150–151, 153, 163–164, 201. *See also specific schools and texts*
sallekhana (fast to death), 11

saman (Sama Veda chant), 35, 48, 150, 193, 219, 236
sama-vartana (return of student from guru), 34, 147–148
Sama Veda, 35, 37, 45, 47, 48, 99, 120, 121, 145, 149, 150, 188, 193, 219, 236
Samavedam (Samavedam Suryanarayana Avadhani), 91–97, *92*, *95*, 117
  agni-hotra, 198
  on Baballa, 66
  brahmacarin period, 60–61, 149
  comments about Knipe, 254
  family of, 171, 247
  funeral of, 240, 241
  and honoraria, 168
  lineage of, 164, 243
  livelihood of, 176–177, 178
  sabha, 156
  and TTD service, 179, 182, 248, 249
Samavedam Bhaskara Ghanapati (son of Samavedam), 95, 97, 240, 255
Samavedam Venkatarama Ghanapathi (son of Samavedam), 95, 97, 240
Samavedam Venkata Ramana, 82
sambhavana (honoraria), 40, 80, 154, 156
samhita (collection of verses), 35, 46, 136, 148
samnyasin (renouncer-ascetic), 30, 58, 182, 183
samsara (worldly existence), 28, 70, 93, 143, 186
samskara (rite of passage), 80, 172–175
samstha (*soma* sacrifice), 46, 220, 221
Samudragupta, 9
sandhya-vandana (worship at sunset and dawn), 29, 43, 143
Sankara (reformer/philosopher), 11, 13
Sankaracarya of Kancipuram, 104
Sankara Veda Patha-sala, 133
Sanskrit, 12
sapindi-karana (twelfth-day funeral rite), 68, 245–246
sapta-santana (seven offerings), 24
Sarasvati (deity), 229, 233
Sarma, Pavan Kumar (son-in-law of Kapilavayi Rama Sastri), 127, 132
sarvato-mukha (*soma* sacrifice with four directional altars), 47, 228
sastra (Rg Veda verses), 45, 46, 48, 74, 134, 211, 228. *See also* Rg Veda
Sastri, Nilakanta, 10–11
Satapatha Brahmana, 46
Sathya Sai Baba, 94, 182–183
Sathya Sai Baba Trust, 183
satkara (cash honoraria), 94
sattra (year-long or longer sacrifice), 221, 230–231, 239
Satyam Computers, 84
Satyanarayana temple (Annavaram), 124
Satyavati (wife of Kamesvara), *43*, 74, 107, *108*, 158, 159–160, 161–162, 163, 170–171, 201
**sauma* (hypothetical Indo-Iranian name for *soma*), 50, 188, 213
sautramani (offering to Indra), 232–233, 292*n*59
Savai Jayasing (*raja* of Amber), 234
savitri (Rg Veda mantra, cf, *gayatri*), 29, 142
Savitri (wife of Bullebbayi), 158, 159
Sayana (Vedic commentator), 15
Sayers, Matthew, 290*n*27
Selecters, 247, 248, 251, 253
seventeen, significance of number, 46, 228–229, 281*n*13
Shende, Ganeshashastri, 280*n*7
Silpa Sastras, 40
simantonnayana (prenatal rite), 173, 174
Sinivali (goddess), 201
Sira (deity), 207

sisya (student), 70, 137, 150, 240. *See also brahmacarin/brahmacarya*
Sita (deity), 207
Sita Mahalaksmi (wife of Kapilavayi Yajnesvara), 120
Sita Naga Laksmi (daughter of Kapilavayi Rama Sastri), *126*, 127, 132, 158
Sita Rama Laksmi (wife of Kapilavayi Venkatesvara), 121, *122*, 123, 164
Siva (deity), 13, 76–77, 103
Siva Purana, 76–77
Siva-*ratri* (all night Siva worship), 113, 155, 182
sixteen, significance of number, 47–48, 134, 173, 175
smarta (domestic rites and texts), 56, 61, 69, 87, 109, 134, 188
smasana (cremation ground), 184, 239, 240, 241
Smith, Brian K., 184, 244
Smith, Frederick M., 281*n*10, 282*nn*19–20
snana (ritual bath), 34, 148
sodasin (*soma* sacrifice), 46, 221
Soma (deity), 45, 168, 200, 201, 205, 206, 214, 216
soma (sacred plant), 35, 44–45, 213–214, 215, 217–218, 235, 243
soma-bhaksana (drinking *soma*), 65
soma-pa (drinker of *soma*), 233
soma-pravaka (mediator), 47
Somayaji/Somayajulu (title), 45, 59, 158, 174
Somi-devamma (title), 45, 158, 160
sraddha (faith), 75, 106, 162
sraddha (funeral rite), 66, 101–102, 106, 155, 184, 185–186, 246
srauta (extended fire rites/texts), 30–31, 36–37, 41, 280*n*1
srauta-kaksa (ritual rivalry), 127–132
srautin (performer of *srauta* rites), 30–31, 36, 225
Srinatha (poet), 13
Sripada Laksmi Narasimha Soma-yaji, 109
Sripada Manikya Avadhani Ghanapathi, 60, 103, 107
Sriramapuram *Agrahara*, *4*, 54–97
  overview, 54–56
  establishment of, 24, 177
  profiles of *ahitagni* from. *See* Baballa (Bhamidipati Yajnesvara); Cayanulu (Bulusu Vyaghresvara Cayanulu); Duvvuri Yajnesvara Paundarika Yajulu; Samavedam (Samavedam Suryanarayana Avadhani)
Sri Venkatesvara University, 83
Staal, Frits, 41, 46, 142, 215, 225, 283*n*12
stages of life. *See asrama* (stages of life)
sthali-pakana (offering), 35, 169, 189, 280*n*7
stoma (arrangement of verses in *soma* sacrifice). *See agni-stoma* (initiatory *soma* offering)
Subbalaksmi (wife of Cayanulu), 85, 86, *87*, 88–89, 90–91, 158, 170, 171, 185, 196, 202, 242
Sukla Yajur Veda, *37*, 46, 47, 119, 145, 150–151, 237
su-mangali (auspicious married woman), 162
Suna (deity), 207
Sunasiriya (deity), 206
Sundari (wife of Baballa), *57*, 59, 62–63, 67, 68, 70, 159, 163, 171, 179, 205, 226, 227, 242
Sundari (wife of Samavedam Bhaskara), 95, 97
sura (ritual beverage), 46, 221, 226, 228–233

surpa (ritual winnowing fan), 200, 208, 238, 241
Surya (deity), 43, 196, 199, 206
Surya (wife of Duvvuri Yajulu), 72, 74, 75–76, 78–79, 110–111, 117, 163, 170–171, 181, 186, 201, 206, 242, 243
Surya Prakasa Pavankumar Sarma (son of Duvvuri Phani), 82–83
sutra (manual), 204, 233. *See also specific texts*
Svaha Devi (daughter of Kapilavayi Rama Sastri), 127
svarga (heaven), 184, 203, 232, 239, 244–246
svasti-vacana (Rg Veda mantras), 73, 155
svayam-atrnna (stones in *agni-cayana*), 222
svista-krt (offering for Agni), 236
Syama Sundara Srirama Sarma (son of Duvvuri Phani), 82–83
syena (eagle steals *soma*), 223
syena-citi (flying eagle altar), 46, *223*

Tachikawa, Musashi, 280*n*7
Taittiriya, *37*
Taittiriya Aranyaka, 144–145
Taittiriya Brahmana, 144–145, 188, 193, 202, 204, 214, 227, 232, 245
Taittiriya Samhita, 29, 32, 35, 46, 77, 96, 112–113, 120, 136, 144–145, 149, 155, 188, 202, 203–204, 208, 216, 226, 234, 242, 245
Taittiriya Upanisad, 144–145
Talbot, Cynthia, 10, 24, 278*n*15
Tamil language, 12, 22
Tangirala Balangangadhara Sastri, 120, 150, 254
Tangirala Rama Somayajulu, 134
Tangirala Subba Avadhanulu, 134
tapas (heat of ascetic practice), 218
tarpana (offerings to deceased), 243
Tata Nano, 249
Telegu language, 12
Thapar, Romila, 9
Thite, Ganesh, xx, 216
Thomas, Dylan, 232
Tikkana (poet), 12
tila (sesame seed), 245
tirthankara (Jaina saint), 11
Tirumala Tirupati Devasthanam (TTD)
  Bhamidipati Mitranarayana's service under, 111–112
  and cash economy, 176
  Cayanulu's service under, 89, 178
  disavowment of, 99
  Duvvuri Surya Prakasa's service under, 80
  explanation of, 38–40, 63
  honoraria for temple recitations, 40
  Laksminarayana's service under, 110
  opposition to, 39, 248
  retirement income, 181
Traditionalists, 247–249, 251
transcendence, 187
tretagni (three-hearth fire), 42–43, 50
TTD. *See* Tirumala Tirupati Devasthanam
Tvastr (deity), 201, 226
tyaga (abandonment of merit to gods), 244

ucchista (food/drink leavings), 76, 195–196, 214
udgatr (major priest), 47, *48*, 231, 235
United East India Company, 17
United Kingdom
  Hindu temples in, 40
United States
  Hindu temples in, 40–41
  Indian immigration to, 84, 254–258
  invitations to serve in urban Hindu temples, 83, 84, 97

University of Madras, 21
Upadhyayula Nagendram, 43, 190
upanayana. See sacred thread
Upanishads, 11, 37, 38, 189
Uppuluri Ganapati Sastri, 38, 40, 111–112
uttara-vedi (eastern altar), 211, 212, 219

vaisva-deva (offering), 37, 43, 196, 207–208
vaja-peya (drink of strength), 10, 46, 188, 228–230
Vajasaneya Samhita, 150–151
Value Labs, 84
vana-prastha (wilderness wanderer), 181
vana-prasthin (one who retires to forest), 181
vapa (omentum of sacrificed animal), 216, 236, 238–239
varna (class), 28
Varuna (deity), 208, 209, 226
Varuna-praghasa (second *catur-masya* rite), 207, 208, 209
vasanta (spring season), 206
Vayu (deity), 206, 213, 226
Veda. *See also vedamlo unnaru* (existing in Veda); *specific branches*
  textual tradition, 37
  as without human authorship, 37–38, 145
veda (brush), 201–203, 214
Veda, process of becoming, 141
  advanced degrees, 148–152
  bramacharin period, 141–144
  learning the texts, 144–147
  sabha (debates), 153–156
  sama-vartana (graduation day), 147–148
vedamlo unnaru (existing in Veda), 28–53
  bonding with Agni, 49–52
  and career options, 38–41
  stages of life and learning with Veda pandits, 28–38
  vocabulary of *ahitagni*, 41–49, 280*n*8
  voices of *ahitagni* and other Veda pandits, 52–53
Veda Pandits in Andhra (book), 40
veda-vikriya (selling of Veda), 39, 53, 63, 65, 104, 248
vedi (space between hearths), 42, 43, 44, 200
Venkatesvara (patron deity of Andhra), 25
vesya (prostitute), 231
vidhi (injunction), 151, 152
Vidyaranya (Advaita scholar), 63
vikrti (text modification for recitation), 35, 148, 151
Virabhadra, an *avatara* of Siva, 13
Virabhadra Somayaji (ancestor of Baballa), 58
Visalaksi (daughter of Samavedam), 96
Visnu (deity), 15, 214
Visnubhatla Laksminarayana, 82
Visvanatha Jagannatha Ghanapathi, 134
Visve Deva (All Gods), 43, 154, 196, 205, 209, 246
vivaha (marriage), 31, 162–170
vrata (vow), 13, 97, 120
vrddhi (retired), 40
Vyaghresvaram Village, 106–110
  establishment of, 24–25
  profiles of *ahitagni* from. *See* Kamesvara (Bulusu Kamesvara); Laksminarayana (Pullela Laksminayana Soma-yajulu)
vyasana (passion), 146

Weaver-caste families, 17
White Yajur Veda. *See* Sukla Yajur Veda
Widow Remarriage Association, 22

widows, 22, 56, 79, 123, 158, 169–170, 185–186, 283*n*10
wives. *See patni* (wife)

yajamana (sacrificer), 42, 47
yajna (sacrifice), 45
yajnopavita. *See* sacred thread
Yajulu (title), 45, 59, 158, 174
yajus (directive mantra), 151
Yama (deity), 204, 224
yoktra (*patni's* ritual belt), 45, 160, 201–202
yoni (female genitals), 51, 193
yupa (sacrificial pole/post), 46, 211, 212, 216, 228

Zoastrian tradition, 45, 50, 145